TRUDEAU*MANIA*

The Rise to Power of Pierre Elliott Trudeau

ALSO BY ROBERT WRIGHT

The Night Canada Stood Still

Our Man in Tehran

Three Nights in Havana

TRUDEAUMANIA

The Rise to Power of Pierre Elliott Trudeau

ROBERT WRIGHT

HarperCollins*PublishersLtd*

Trudeaumania

Published by HarperCollins Publishers Ltd

First edition

HarperCollins books may be purchased for educational, business, or sales promotional use through our Special Markets Department.

HarperCollins Publishers Ltd
2 Bloor Street East, 20th Floor
Toronto, Ontario, Canada
M4W 1A8

www.harpercollins.ca

Library and Archives Canada Cataloguing in Publication
information is available upon request

ISBN 978-1-44344-500-9

Printed and bound in the United States of America
RRD 9 8 7 6 5 4 3 2 1

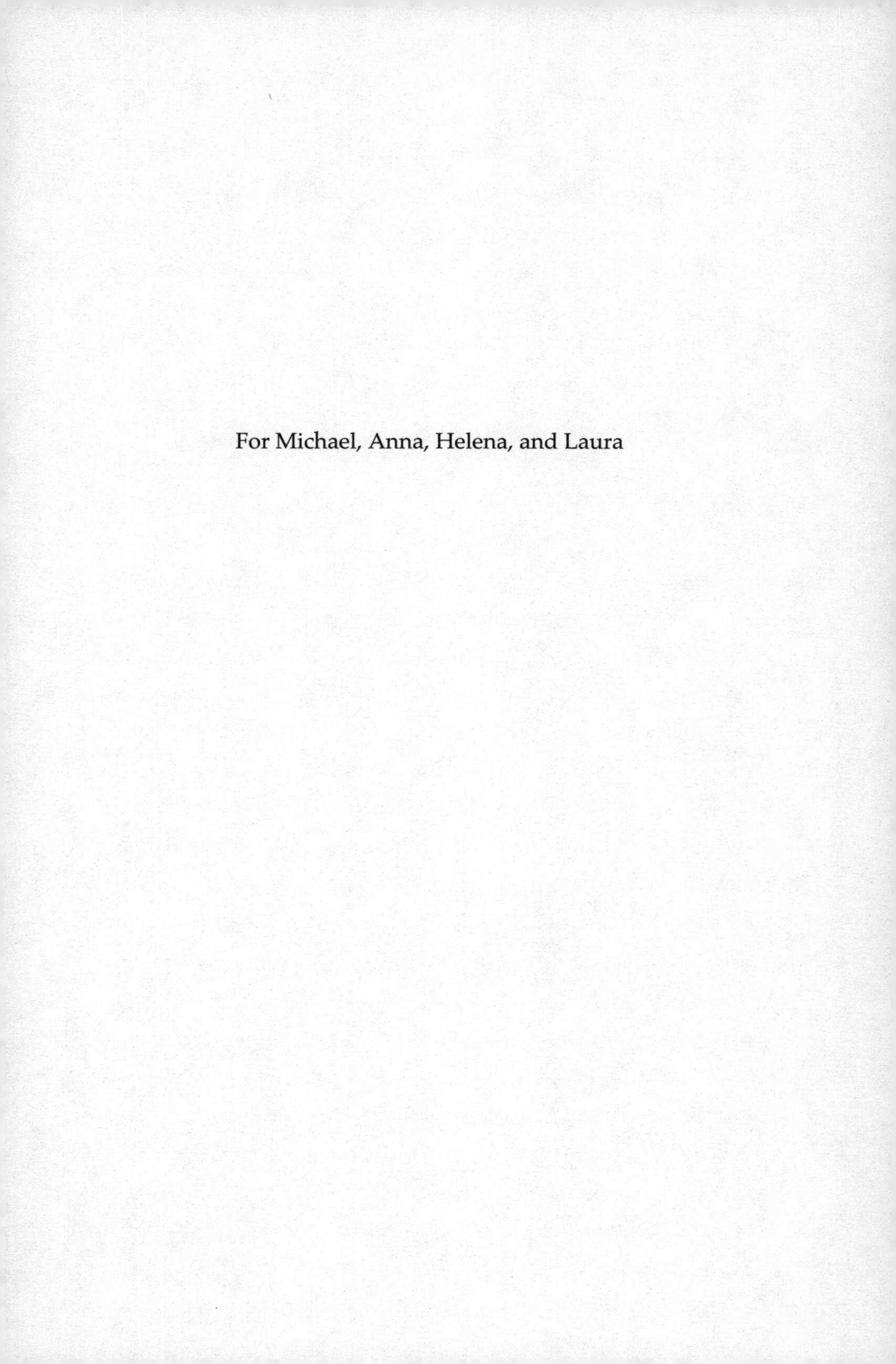

For Michael, Anna, Helena, and Laura

CONTENTS

Preface		xiii
Prologue	Trudeau to the Gallows!	1
Chapter One	The Stubborn Eccentric	29
Chapter Two	The Three Musketeers	53
Chapter Three	Forks in the Road	82
Chapter Four	From Celebration to Survival	114
Chapter Five	The Sacred and the Profane	150
Chapter Six	Now You're Stuck with Me	171
Chapter Seven	We Want Trudeau!	201
Chapter Eight	Telling It Like It Is	222
Chapter Nine	A Man for Tomorrow	249
Chapter Ten	The Calm after the Storm	272
Epilogue	Trudeaumania 2.0	287
Notes		301
Index		357

I consider nationalism to have been a sinister activity
in world history over the last 150 years. And that goes for
English-Canadian nationalism, French-Canadian nationalism,
or Gaullist nationalism, or whatever.

—Pierre Trudeau, 1968

PREFACE

He haunts us no longer. Nearly twenty years after his death and more than thirty since his retirement from active politics, Pierre Elliott Trudeau is at long last receding from the lived memory of Canadians. His son Justin is the current occupant of 24 Sussex Drive, but as he has demonstrated from the moment he entered politics in 2008, he is his own man. Pierre did not live to see Justin take even his first step into public life, and he never sought it. "Our family has done enough," he told his boys.

Trudeaumania is about Pierre Trudeau's rise to power in 1968. Like many Canadians, perhaps, I thought I knew this story—the epic saga of the hipster Montrealer who drove up to Ottawa in his Mercedes in 1965, wowed the country with his dictum that "there's no place for the state in the bedrooms of the nation," rocked the new medium of television like no one since JFK, and in scant months rode the crest of Canadians' centennial-era euphoria into power. This is Canadians' own Camelot myth. It embodies the quirkiness, the passion, and the youthful exuberance we ascribe to the 1960s even now. Many of us cherish it. I confess that, as a professional historian, I have been casually reproducing this mythology myself since I first started writing about the sixties over three decades ago.

Unfortunately, it is almost entirely wrong.

Pierre Trudeau's 1968 victory owed almost nothing to the heady vibes that had washed over North America during 1967's summer of love. By the frigid winter of 1968, the emotional highs of Canada's own Expo 67 were already a distant memory, eclipsed by the continuing violence of the Front de libération du Québec, the appalling atrocities of the Vietnam War, massive civil unrest on both sides of Europe's Iron Curtain, and, above all, the disintegration of American civil society after the murders of Martin Luther King, Jr., and Bobby Kennedy. Peruse virtually any newspaper from this period. What you will find there is the world aflame, figuratively and literally.

It is true that Pierre Trudeau's entry into federal politics came as a breath of fresh air after John Diefenbaker and Lester B. Pearson. Many young Canadians (the so-called teenyboppers) were enamoured of Trudeau's high cheekbones and ice-blue eyes, and he obliged them with smiles and kisses. Many older Canadians were impressed with the pedigree he carried to Ottawa—his fluent multilingualism, his high-flying record of academic and athletic achievement, his world travels, his straight talk, even his sartorial flair.

But Trudeau did not triumph in June 1968 through charisma and cunning, as his critics claim. He neither ingratiated himself with Canadians nor sought their affections. Indeed, throughout the period of Trudeaumania, he fretted that his campaign team was exciting expectations that he could never meet.

Trudeau vaulted to political stardom because he provided both a cogent diagnosis of the crises facing Canada and the world, and a uniquely Canadian set of solutions born of decades of study and debate. By the time he ventured to Ottawa in 1965, just weeks before his forty-sixth birthday, the essentials of Trudeau's vision for Canada were firmly in place: the separation of church and state; the need to distinguish between sin and crime; the rejection of nationalism in all of its forms; the primacy of individual rights, including language rights, in a Constitution that would bind not only citizens but also governments; and the establishment of a culture of bilingualism across Canada paired with the uncompromising rejection of biculturalism (what Quebecers called *deux nations*).

In 1968, Trudeau put forward this vision of Canada, without guile, without dissembling, and without a hard sell. *Take it or leave it,* he told Canadians. *If you do not like my ideas, vote for someone else.*

We took it.

Trudeaumania is the second of my books to foreground the life of Pierre Trudeau. It is also the second in which the perennial debate over Quebec's place in Canada provides the backdrop. Trudeau told a group of lawyers in 1967 that one should approach the latter only with "fear and trembling." I am not a lawyer, but I consider this sage advice.

In writing this book, I have been mindful of three considerations: to get the story right, to treat all of its principal characters fairly, and to allow them to speak for themselves wherever possible. For ease of reading, I have taken one minor liberty with the text. I have closed extended excerpts without ellipses and square brackets in instances where I judged continuity and context to be unaffected. In every other respect, the sources cited in the endnotes conform to established scholarly standards. There is no invented dialogue in this book. All translations from the original French are my own unless otherwise noted.

Trudeaumania could not have been written without the help of others. It gives me great pleasure to acknowledge them here. Research funding was provided by the Symons Trust Fund for Canadian Studies, to which I am indebted. For putting themselves at my disposal early on in my research, I am grateful to Professor Geneviève Dorais, Bev Slopen, and especially Rianna Genore. I owe a special debt of gratitude to my research assistants, Nicholas Ashmore, Damien Cardinal, and especially Anna Harrington. Thanks as well to John Wales and Ken Field of the Trent University Durham Library, and to Heather Gildner of the Toronto Public Library. For granting me access to the archival papers of the late Pierre Trudeau, I am indebted to Sacha Trudeau and Marc Lalonde. For making that access navigable and indeed enjoyable, I thank Michael MacDonald and Alix McEwen of Library and Archives Canada. Thanks as well to Dan Wright, Stacey Young, Patricia Taylor, Louis Balthazar, Barbara Nichol, Linda McQuaig, Rena Zimmerman, Leo Groarke, Marilyn Burns, Joe Muldoon, Kate Ingram, Amber Ashton, and Hailey Wright.

Trudeaumania is the fourth book I have written under the sharp eye of my friend and editor Jim Gifford. I extend to Jim, Iris Tupholme, Noelle Zitzer, Lisa Rundle, Rebecca Vogan, and the rest of the team at HarperCollins Canada my warmest gratitude.

Ken Taylor passed away in October 2015, while *Trudeaumania* was in progress. Ken was a confidant, a steady source of inspiration, and a great friend. He was also a voracious reader who did me the favour, among many others, of reading and commenting on my work in manuscript form. Although he did not get the chance to read this book, he discussed its contents with me often—and with all of the enthusiasm and affection for which he was justly renowned. For that, I feel most fortunate.

Professors David Sheinin and Yvon Grenier read a manuscript draft of this book in its entirety, as did John Nichol, former president of the Liberal Party of Canada, and Andrew Potter, current director of the McGill Institute for the Study of Canada. For their generosity and kindness, I am deeply indebted. I need hardly add the standard authorial caveat. I have tried to bring balance and objectivity to the story of Trudeaumania, but where I have failed, I have done so single-handedly.

As always, this book is for my family, with my warmest gratitude and affection.

PROLOGUE
TRUDEAU TO THE GALLOWS!

The morning of Monday, June 24, 1968, Pierre Elliott Trudeau awakened in his Oshawa hotel room, pulled on some sweats, and, accompanied by two officers from his RCMP security detail, headed out to the gym.

This was to be the last day of a gruelling sixty-one-day election campaign that had seen the prime minister touch down in almost every strip mall or soccer field that could accommodate a helicopter. Trudeau's Liberal Party was riding high in the polls and was almost certainly going to form the first majority government in a decade.

Trudeaumania—the Beatles-esque outpouring of adulation that greeted the prime minister everywhere he went, often in crowds numbering in the tens of thousands—had made this one of the most electrifying campaigns in Canadian history. But the cost to the man himself, famously protective of his personal freedom and his privacy, had been considerable. Trudeau had taken on the mantle of leadership in the wake of Lester Pearson's retirement only a couple of months earlier. Yet, like his opponents, Tory leader Robert Stanfield and NDP leader Tommy Douglas, he was now utterly bored with his own stale talk and feeling mind-numbingly overexposed. Surely, the prime minister had earned an hour or two of precious solitude before heading out for one last day of campaign bedlam.

No such luck. Trudeau's aides—a group of young "amateurs" who had clambered up Ottawa's greasy pole alongside their candidate—insisted that he squeeze every last opportunity out of the dying campaign. There would be time enough for solitude after he won. Trudeau conceded the point as he had done repeatedly in recent weeks, sometimes in resignation, usually under protest.

Reporters and photographers, road-weary and hyper-caffeinated, crowded into the gym, dutifully recording Trudeau's every move. They had the unenviable job of covering a politician who openly disparaged their profession. "I don't read the press," Trudeau had said at the beginning of the campaign. "So many bad things have been said about me that, now that they are saying good things, I try not to know about it. Because tomorrow they will start saying bad things again. That's the way journalists are."[1] Out on the hustings, he had harangued the press corps about their sloppy reportage. They had returned the favour by capturing him in his most iconic moments—kissing the girls, flipping off diving boards, waving from open limos Kennedy-style. Now more than ever, as the campaign reached its crescendo, the media machine was insatiable. A photo op at a suburban gym was a perfect opportunity. Here was the Canadian prime minister, the epitome of Zen-master cool, doing calisthenics, riding a stationary bicycle in his bare feet, ambling into the steam room. Nothing Trudeau did, no matter how quotidian or banal, seemed beneath the notice of Canadians. He was endlessly fascinating—to everyone but himself. His ennui merely enhanced his mystique.

Smiling, stretching, and pedalling away, as flashbulbs flashed and journalists scribbled, the prime minister chatted effortlessly, revealing nothing of himself, as usual. Today, he was soft-spoken, witty, supremely self-confident, and completely under control. If he was feeling anxious, he gave no hint of it.

As his nearby security detail knew, however, all was not well. The previous evening, the Montreal newspaper *Dimanche-Dernière Heure* had run a front-page story alleging that a cell of the Front de libération du Québec (FLQ) was planning to assassinate the prime minister. One

Felquiste was quoted as saying, "We shall kill Trudeau Monday"—that very day.[2] According to the report, the Mounties were aware of the threat, knew the person who had made it, and had him under "close surveillance." At several Montreal radio stations and at the city's Canadian Press bureau, similar threats on Trudeau's life had been made anonymously. With the assassinations of Martin Luther King, Jr., and Robert Kennedy agonizingly fresh in Canadians' minds—King had been murdered in early April, Kennedy in early June—such threats on the life of the Canadian prime minister were taken not merely seriously but with grim foreboding.

Certainly, there was no mystery about the timing of the threats. In late May, officials of the Société Saint-Jean-Baptiste of Montreal had invited Trudeau to watch the Saint-Jean-Baptiste parade, held annually on June 24, from the official reviewing platform. Trudeau's tough stand against Quebec nationalism had hardly endeared him to members of the Société.[3] Yet they felt a duty to extend the invitation, and he felt an obligation to accept it.

The moment it was announced that the prime minister would appear alongside Quebec VIPs, Pierre Bourgault, the outspoken leader of the Rassemblement pour l'indépendance nationale (RIN), issued a statement of his own. He and his separatist comrades would use "all possible force and all means necessary" to thwart Trudeau's appearance.[4] Trudeau's friend and booster, the historian Ramsay Cook, told him that it would be "a risky provocation" to confront separatists in the home stretch of a campaign he had already won. He would do well to invent a "prior engagement" as an excuse for not appearing.[5] Trudeau ignored his friend's advice. He had never cowered when threatened with violence, and he was hardly about to start now.

A journalist asked Trudeau whether his decision to attend the parade would be seen as an affront to Quebec sovereignists. "Some say that," he replied, "but don't you think the prime minister has a right to be at a popular event?"[6]

As for Ramsay Cook, he later admitted that his wise counsel had missed by a mile. "Obviously, I did not know Trudeau as well as I thought," he mused.[7]

The origins of Saint-Jean-Baptiste Day—or *la fête nationale* as it is known to French-speaking Quebecers—date back to the early seventeenth century, when the French presence in North America was in its infancy. Traditionally, the *fête* has been celebrated with bonhomie and revelry. In the mid-twentieth century, bonfires, speechmaking, feasting, and singalongs were standard fare, capped off by a family-friendly *défilé* (parade) along Montreal's rue Sherbrooke. During the Quiet Revolution of the 1960s, when Quebecers first demanded that they be *maîtres chez nous,* Saint-Jean-Baptiste Day acquired a political salience that has persisted to the present. Thus, although it remains primarily an occasion to celebrate Québécois culture, *la fête nationale* is also an opportunity for Quebec sovereignists to promote their dream of independence and for opponents of sovereignty to mount their own public protests. Violence has darkened Saint-Jean-Baptiste Day more often than Quebec officials would wish.

There was no mistaking the mounting tension in the streets of Montreal on June 24, 1968. City workers spent the day building a reviewing stand the full length of the great stone steps of the Bibliothèque de la Ville de Montréal. An imposing classical structure on the south side of Sherbrooke at Montcalm, the building served as Montreal's main public library until it was supplanted in 2005 by the Bibliothèque et Archives nationales du Québec on Berri. (In 2009, the original *bibliothèque,* now beautifully restored, was renamed Édifice Gaston-Miron after the Quebec poet.)

The placement of the VIP reviewing stand was a gift to Pierre Bourgault, who intended to hold a mass rally to protest Trudeau's presence on this most hallowed of holidays. The platform faced north, overlooking the deep sidewalks and broad boulevards that merge at Sherbrooke and Cherrier to form a single expansive tarmac. Beyond the pavement, roughly eighty metres from the steps of the library, lay Parc La Fontaine, a green space of stolid statues and rolling hills that is today the preserve of Sunday-morning dog walkers. The south-facing slopes of the park rise gently in a shallow-bowl configuration, providing several acres of open lawns perfectly suited to the sort of demonstration envisaged by Bourgault. He was hoping that as many as five thousand separatist protesters would answer the call. If they did, Parc La Fontaine could not only accommodate them but afford them the strategic advantage of easy manoeuvre on foot. Seen from the vantage of the prime minister's bodyguards, the site was a security nightmare.

The parade itself was scheduled to begin at 8 p.m. It was expected to attract at least 100,000 flag-waving spectators of all ages. Estimates of the number of Quebecers who actually lined the streets on that balmy June evening would later range as high as 400,000—roughly one-quarter of Montreal's population.

The promise of violent separatist demonstrations and now death threats against the prime minister preoccupied Mayor Jean Drapeau and the hundreds of civic and police officials charged with keeping public order. Yet Jean-Paul Gilbert, Montreal's forty-eight-year-old chief of police, was imperturbable. He had seen his fair share of heated demonstrations since taking on the job in 1965. Roughly a thousand uniformed police officers would line the parade route. Another 250 plainclothes officers were assigned to protect the VIPs, in addition to an RCMP security detail of sixty men assigned to Trudeau. By the dinner hour, police cruisers were patrolling the parade route. Motorcycle and mounted units were standing by. A press box, strategically located across the street from the reviewing stand, ensured that, whatever happened, it would be recorded in real time.

Beginning in the late afternoon, boisterous young Quebecers filed into Parc La Fontaine and staked out their positions across from the library facade. By 8 p.m., when the crowd was at its largest, the demonstrators numbered roughly one thousand—a far cry from Bourgault's promised five thousand but a formidable mob nonetheless. Most of the youths would be described condescendingly in the mainstream press as "scruffy." Their average age was estimated to be seventeen.

Waving separatist placards and banners, the crowd chanted "*Québec aux Québécois!*" and "*Vive le Québec libre!*" The reviewing stand remained mostly vacant, but the security cordon surrounding it was imposing. The inevitable storm gained energy as the protesters taunted the police and the police stared down the protesters. Suddenly, a *pop-pop-pop* sound rang out. A girl fell to the ground, injured by what turned out to be firecrackers and not gunfire. Uniformed police moved in on the crowd. One of the approaching officers suffered an eye injury when a firecracker was thrown directly into his face. Undercover officers planted among the demonstrators pointed out the provocateurs. White-helmeted police then converged on the youths, subduing some of them with nightsticks and hauling them off to waiting paddy wagons. Chants of "Gestapo, Gestapo!" filled the air.

Some of the demonstrators had come prepared for battle. They now hurled bottles, sticks, eggs, tomatoes, and more firecrackers at the police. Under this unexpected barrage, the line of uniformed officers pulled back momentarily, then charged into the crowd. At the same time, a second group of protesters, positioned curbside at the south end of the park, crashed through police barricades and charged the officers standing point on the parade route. Mounted officers and police on motorcycles confronted the mob, bloodying many of the protesters before delivering them to nearby ambulances. Officers dragged at least one demonstrator to a police van by his long hair. A girl with a bandaged head wound and blood running down her face was photographed entering an ambulance.

By now, a full-scale riot was under way. The crowd chanted, swung bludgeons made of metal and wood, and threw Molotov cocktails—pop bottles filled with gasoline, kerosene, and other flammable liquids. The air filled with the acrid scents of smoke, rotten eggs, and chemicals. Two police cruisers were flipped onto their roofs, and one of them was set ablaze. Ten other police cars were vandalized, as were civilian vehicles parked around the library. Six police horses were injured, one of them fatally. A man carrying an English-language placard that read "Separatists are people with narrow minds" was assaulted. Some of the young demonstrators, their clothes torn and their bodies bloodied, gave up the fight and made their own way to the ambulances.

Roughly an hour into the melee, just before 9 p.m., Pierre Bourgault was hoisted triumphantly onto the shoulders of some of his RIN supporters and then carried defiantly straight into the police line. Trapped in the ensuing crush of bodies, Bourgault could not break free. He was wrestled to the ground by a uniformed officer, hauled off to a paddy wagon, and booked.

Blocks away, another group of Quebec youth were falling into formation. They adjusted their costumes, tuned up their musical instruments, and climbed aboard their floats. Parc La Fontaine was in flames, and the *défilé de la Saint-Jean-Baptiste* had not yet even begun.

Outside Quebec, Pierre Bourgault was never as well known as Quiet Revolutionaries like Jean Lesage or René Lévesque—liberals who eschewed violence and rejected both ethnic nationalism and revolutionary socialism. Yet in the early 1960s, the RIN was at the cutting edge of the separatist movement in Quebec, and Bourgault was its unrivalled spokesperson.

Bourgault was born in 1934 in Quebec's Anglo-dominated Eastern Townships. Like Pierre Trudeau, he received a classical education at the Jesuit-run Collège Jean-de-Brébeuf in Montreal, and he was fluently bilingual. But unlike Trudeau, he had wanted nothing to do with English Canadians and had nothing but contempt for Canadian federalism. A devoted separatist and social radical, Bourgault emerged as one of the most determined Québécois *artistes* of his day to champion Quebecers' dream of nation. Until his death in 2003, he was seldom out of the spotlight in his home province—as an actor, broadcaster, university professor, and adviser to premiers up to and including Jacques Parizeau.

Bourgault was twenty-six when he joined the RIN in October 1960, just a month after its founding as a sovereignist organization. He was fifteen years younger than Pierre Trudeau and thus the product of a very different experience of Quebec politics. Trudeau had cut his teeth in the 1950s as a civil libertarian confronting Premier Maurice Duplessis. By the time Bourgault's star was on the rise, Duplessis was dead, the Quiet Revolution was transforming Quebec into a modern secular state, and Premier Jean Lesage was working overtime to protect his province from the nationalist genie he had himself let out of the bottle. In October 1960, Bourgault helped to write the RIN's separatist manifesto. Four years later, by which time the RIN had become a full-fledged political party, he was elected its president, appealing to Quebecers to throw off the yoke of Anglo domination and reclaim their birthright. His oratorical gifts were legendary. "There was an icy brilliance to his style," wrote one observer of the young Bourgault, "a theatrical, precise rhetoric that had none of the slang or *joual* that marked the speech of many Quebec politicians."[8] Ironically, perhaps, people would say exactly the same thing about Trudeau.

Bourgault's talent as a provocateur blossomed alongside his knack for speechmaking, but these gifts would turn out to be too much for the mainstream sovereignist movement in Quebec. As RIN leader, he organized non-violent protests and sit-ins demanding, among other things, that French be the sole working language of the province. Then, in 1964, during Queen Elizabeth's visit to Quebec, Bourgault gave an inflammatory separatist speech that caused an ugly riot, cementing his reputation as a militant. Moderate Quebec sovereignists including René Lévesque distanced themselves from him. (Lévesque thought Bourgault a demagogue and a troublemaker, and he was also reportedly uncomfortable with Bourgault's homosexuality.) Pierre Trudeau, by then an avowed enemy of Quebec separatism in any incarnation, congratulated the RIN leader for turning the peaceful people of Quebec against his own movement.[9] "The separatists despair of ever being able to convince the public of the rightness of their ideas," Trudeau wrote sneeringly in the journal *Cité libre* in 1964. "So they want to abolish freedom and impose a dictatorship of their minority. They are in sole possession of the truth, so others need only get into line. And when things don't go fast enough they take to illegality and violence. On top of everything, they claim to be persecuted. Imagine that, the poor little souls."[10] Journalist Peter C. Newman, then covering Quebec politics for the *Toronto Star*, reported that Bourgault was so loathed in rural Quebec that people refused to rent him a hall.

Undaunted, Bourgault announced that the RIN would run candidates in the provincial election of 1966. They would campaign on a platform combining separatism and socialism, infused with a hard-hitting critique—perfectly suited to Bourgault's own rhetorical skills—that blamed the Lesage Liberals for having delivered on neither. By all accounts, the RIN took the campaign extremely seriously, taking pains to overcome its hooligan image. On election day, RIN candidates won 5.6 per cent of the popular vote but no seats. Their share of the popular vote in Montreal was over 9 per cent, Bourgault himself coming second in the riding of Duplessis with 33 per cent. Author Graham Fraser later revealed that Union Nationale leader Daniel Johnson, the winner of the 1966 provincial election, had cut a secret deal with Bourgault at the start of the campaign. In an effort to prevent vote splitting, the UN and the RIN had agreed not to run strong candidates in ridings where the other had a chance of winning. Fraser rightly concluded that the deal did more for Johnson than for

Bourgault, drawing off votes from left-leaning Quebecers that would otherwise have gone to the Liberals.[11]

Bourgault continued to rabble-rouse in the cause of an independent Quebec over the course of 1967, a year in which the dream of nation seemed to many sovereignists to be within reach. By this time, Pierre Trudeau was making headlines across Canada as Lester Pearson's dashing young justice minister, making him, in Bourgault's books, the worst sort of *vendu* (sellout). In late June 1967, just days before Canada's July 1 centennial, Bourgault gave a fiery speech in Montreal. "We are just a little province, not a state or a country," he said of Quebec. "We, a poor little people, are basking in an illusion of riches." Liberal MPs who claimed to speak for Quebecers merely fuelled this illusion, Bourgault continued. Pierre Elliott Trudeau "is not a French Canadian so there's no problem." Trudeau's friend and ally Jean Marchand, then serving as Lester Pearson's immigration minister, was another federalist turncoat. "I say a man is a traitor," railed Bourgault, "when he literally vomits every day on the nation from which he emerged."[12]

When French president Charles de Gaulle famously cheered "*Vive le Québec libre!*" from the balcony of Montreal city hall in July 1967, Bourgault and his rowdy RIN comrades were present in the crowd, their separatist placards hoisted, ecstatic to hear the *général* mouthing one of their signature slogans. And when René Lévesque resigned from the provincial Liberal Party just weeks later to found the Mouvement souveraineté-association (MSA)—precursor to the Parti Québécois—Bourgault announced his support for a unified sovereignist push led by Lévesque, promising to bring in the eleven thousand card-carrying members of the RIN. More doubtful than ever about Bourgault, Lévesque refused a formal merger with the RIN.[13] He did, however, agree to join his MSA with Laurent Legault's Ralliement national and René Jutras's Regroupement national. In late 1968, Bourgault would dissolve the RIN to allow its members to join

Lévesque's MSA. The embittered leftist rump of the RIN would re-form as the Front de libération populaire.

Lurking on the radical fringe of the sovereignty movement in these years was *Parti pris,* an intellectual collective advocating the decolonization of Quebec through revolution, and the avowedly militant FLQ. Inspired by Algerian and Cuban guerrillas and promoting the violent overthrow of the Canadian state, FLQ members organized themselves into commando-style paramilitary cells and set out to bomb, kidnap, and ultimately murder their way towards a classless utopia. "Quebec is a colony!" shouted the FLQ manifesto in April 1963. "QUEBEC PATRIOTS, TO ARMS! THE HOUR OF NATIONAL REVOLUTION HAS STRUCK! INDEPENDENCE OR DEATH!"[14] The immediate targets of *Felquiste* attacks were nominally English-Canadian and federal institutions, most of them in Montreal. They included armed police and military units but also unarmed English-language media outlets and businesses believed to discriminate against francophones. FLQ sabotage began in earnest in the spring of 1963, with bombings at a federal armory, a section of the rail line running between Montreal and Quebec City, RCMP headquarters, and a Canadian Forces recruiting centre. *Felquistes* blew up mailboxes in the affluent Montreal suburb of Westmount using time bombs, one of which critically injured Canadian Forces bomb-disposal expert Walter Leja. Trudeau's close friend and ally Gérard Pelletier excoriated FLQ terrorism in *La Presse* in May 1963. "As I write, a man is lying in hospital, hovering between life and death," wrote Pelletier. "He is the second victim of the FLQ in less than a month, the second tragedy in the blind violence unleashed in Montreal by a group of madmen."[15]

The *Felquistes* were unmoved, even as their own young foot soldiers were rounded up and imprisoned. The carnage continued. Four civilian deaths and many more injuries were attributed to the FLQ in the first three years of its quixotic struggle. In September 1966, eight *Felquiste* youth were convicted of criminal responsibility in the death of sixty-four-year-old Thérèse Morin, a secretary killed during the bombing of the H.B. La Grenade shoe factory. One of those convicted was an underage "Mod" who, in full Pete Townshend regalia, had delivered the time bomb on his souped-up scooter. One of two men later incarcerated for the same attack was the writer Pierre Vallières, once a protégé of Gérard Pelletier and contributor to Pierre Trudeau's own *Cité libre*. While serving time, Vallières would pen the incendiary separatist tract *Nègres blancs d'Amérique* (*White Niggers of America*). As historian David A. Charters has concluded in a recent survey of terrorism in Canada, the fear generated by the *Felquistes* in the 1960s turned out to be disproportionate to their modest organizational size and capability. In other words, the FLQ succeeded as a terrorist group in spite of its amateurism and incompetence, right up to the moment in October 1970 when members of Paul Rose's Chénier cell murdered Quebec cabinet minister Pierre Laporte in cold blood.[16]

René Lévesque, for whom political violence was anathema, would later dismiss the FLQ as "a couple of dozen young terrorists, whose ideology was a hopeless hodgepodge of anarcho-nationalism and kindergarten Marxism."[17] Pierre Bourgault, too, understood that any perception that the RIN was connected with the FLQ would destroy his own credibility. At least once, in April 1964, Bourgault threatened the *Montreal Star* with a $1 million libel suit for implying that the mastermind of an FLQ bank robbery and armory raid, François Schirm, was a member of the RIN.[18] This legal threat did not change the fact that the three founders of the FLQ were RIN activists who had together created the Réseau de résistance (Resistance Network) as the forerunner of the FLQ.[19] Nor did it mitigate the public scorn heaped onto Bourgault when he or other members of the RIN threatened federal politicians like Pierre Trudeau with violence.

It is unlikely that Trudeau lost much sleep when Bourgault impugned him as a *vendu* or sneered that he had no right to call himself a French Canadian. As Trudeau would later say after hearing one of President Richard Nixon's more colourful slurs against him, "I've been called worse things by better people." Moreover, Trudeau was comfortable in the role of the separatists' *bête noire*. He knew better than most of his youthful adversaries that what he called the "rough and tumble" of politics affected everyone.[20] Several days after Trudeau had declared his candidacy for the Liberal leadership, in February 1968, Bourgault announced that the RIN would be supporting him—because he was the candidate most likely to "hasten Quebec's separation" from Canada.[21] "The RIN approves Trudeau," said Bourgault wryly. "He's the best candidate we could hope for. He has never been popular in Quebec. He has complete disrespect for the people."[22]

On the evening of June 20, 1968, just days before Trudeau was to appear at the *défilé de la Saint-Jean-Baptiste*, Bourgault pleaded with his supporters to come out to Parc La Fontaine and challenge the prime minister. Trudeau had to be resisted as "a traitor and a sell-out," he fumed. "It is intolerable to us that a man who does not believe in our nation and spits on it every day should hold the limelight at these celebrations. If an English-speaking prime minister came here and told us what he is telling us, we would kill him."[23]

At 9:40 p.m., Trudeau arrived at the Bibliothèque de la Ville de Montréal, entered inconspicuously by a side entrance, and made his way through the towering black doors out onto the reviewing stand.

By now, the riot on rue Sherbrooke was well into its second hour. The separatist demonstrators had been expecting Trudeau, of course, but so, too, had some of the other Quebecers in the crowd. When the prime minister made his entrance, he was greeted by a rousing round of cheers. Trudeau smiled and waved in response. Hurrahs and *Vive*s turned to hisses and boos, however, as the demonstrators responded en masse to Trudeau. *"Trudeau au poteau!"* (Trudeau to the gallows!) and *"Trudeau vendu!"* they shouted. The prime minister shrugged and took his seat in the front row of the platform. A bottle smashed on the sidewalk in front of him. Some of the demonstrators got close enough to Trudeau to leer directly at him. The two-dozen-strong police and RCMP officers standing point in front of the reviewing stand linked arms to form a protective chain, just in case anyone tried to leap up onto the platform. More bottles smashed onto the sidewalk and the street. More rioters were escorted into paddy wagons, passing noisily right in front of the prime minister and the other VIPs. An unconscious police officer was carried by one of his comrades in front of the reviewing stand just as Trudeau was taking his seat. Nothing in the prime minister's cool demeanour suggested that he was fazed by any of this turmoil.

The president of the Montreal Société Saint-Jean-Baptiste, Dollard Mathieu, was seated to Trudeau's right. Premier Daniel Johnson, Mayor Jean Drapeau, Drapeau's wife, Marie-Claire Boucher, and *Le Devoir* editor Claude Ryan were seated to the right of Mathieu. Montreal archbishop Paul Grégoire sat to Trudeau's immediate left—an arrangement that Trudeau later joked had afforded him divine protection. Among those standing on the sidewalk was Trudeau's young tour manager, Bill Lee, with whom the prime minister would lean over and chat from time to time. All told, there were perhaps as many as sixty people on the VIP platform, those in the front row seated, the rest standing three rows deep. The dignitaries included several women, most of them wearing the brightly coloured suits and pillbox hats that were the style of the day. Two police officers were posted to the roof of the library, their feet dangling in front of the building's massive facade.

Just minutes after 10 p.m., the parade arrived, with banners, bands, and majorettes in full regalia. Trudeau smiled broadly and applauded—even though the demonstrators drowned out the sound of the marchers almost entirely. Occasionally, a police van would interrupt the parade and pass in front of the stand. Knowing, perhaps, that they were being broadcast, most of the dignitaries, including Trudeau, did their best to ignore the demonstrators. (Archival footage of the action on the reviewing stand was shot from a stationary camera to the north, which captured almost nothing of the chaos unfolding on the street and sidewalk below.) At one point, Trudeau stood up to blow kisses to a float loaded with young women in bikinis.

At 10:50 p.m., with the parade stalled yet again, a young man darted from the pack of rioters to the front of the library and threw a Molotov cocktail into the reviewing stand. It was a pop bottle containing some kind of flammable liquid, possibly gasoline. Since the television lights set up to illuminate the reviewing stand blinded everyone on the platform, no one saw the projectile as it sailed between Trudeau and Dollard Mathieu, roughly six feet over their heads. But everyone heard it shatter on the library wall behind the prime minister. Most of the people, including Trudeau, instinctively ducked for cover. Moments later, many of them, including all the women, moved either on their own or with police escorts to safety behind the library doors. From the back row, RCMP officers moved purposefully, directing the exiting VIPs into the library and converging on those still in the front row. Premier Daniel Johnson left his seat to take shelter in the back. Mayor Drapeau escorted his wife into the library and returned immediately to the front of the platform.

As soon as they heard the bottle shatter on the wall behind them, three men—two Mounties and Trudeau's campaign aide Pierre Levasseur—leapt forward to shield the prime minister where he sat. They urged him to leave the stand as the others had done. Trudeau bent forward to pick up his coat, presumably with the intention of going. Then, in one of the most dramatic moments in Canadian political history, he threw his coat defiantly to the ground. Waving off his bodyguards, Trudeau alone took his seat—fully exposed to the projectiles of the demonstrators. Raw anger animated his normally inscrutable face. Moments later, just to accentuate his defiance, he sat *forward*, with his arms hanging over the rail of the platform, plainly visible to the crowd. A second bottle smashed into the wall below him. He did not flinch. Plainclothes police officers took seats beside him, one of them apparently trying to shield him from any additional projectiles with a large raincoat. On the sidewalk, officers in the street formed themselves into a barrier two men deep.

The crowd yelled out, "Bravo Trudeau!" In the press box across the street from the library, journalists including Peter C. Newman jumped to their feet to applaud the prime minister's courage. A pretty young woman on the stalled float blew Trudeau a kiss. The prime minister, now at his ease and smiling, shook hands and chatted warmly with Mayor Drapeau and Archbishop Grégoire. The parade resumed. Less than three minutes had passed since the bottle had crashed into the wall behind the prime minister. The scene was as unscripted as it was electrifying, and all of it was captured live on television.

A new round of clashes between the rioters and uniformed officers began, but after the bottle-throwing incident, security officials were taking no chances. They reinforced the police cordon around the reviewing stand and prevented anyone from passing for the remainder of the night.

At 11:15 p.m., the parade ended, but not the riot. It petered out an hour later. The police continued to drag demonstrators into paddy wagons or escort them to ambulances. Several officers, believed to have had acid or other chemicals thrown in their faces, were themselves taken by ambulance to hospital. Montreal officials would tally the butcher's bill the next day. Roughly 1,200 police officers had squared off against an almost equal number of protesters. Eighty demonstrators were injured, most of them with fractured skulls, broken limbs, and cuts and bruises. Another 290, including Pierre Bourgault, were in police custody. Forty-three police officers were hurt.

After the parade, Trudeau and most of the other VIPs made their exit through the library and into their waiting cars. Daniel Johnson,

Jean Drapeau, and Claude Ryan were among those who stuck around, trying to make sense of the events they had just witnessed. What they saw before them as they made their way out onto Sherbrooke was the smouldering detritus of the riot scene—fires burning, scorched patches of park lawn, smashed park benches and signs, broken glass strewn everywhere. The air stank of gasoline, burning rubber, and firecrackers. On the still-floodlit street, cameras captured a visibly frustrated police officer smashing his fist into the face of a young demonstrator. At that point, the lights were switched off, and so were the cameras. "Trudeau should not have come," said Claude Ryan gravely. "If he had any sense of timing, he would have stayed away. I can just see the papers in English Canada tomorrow. I have never seen anything like this before. Not here."[24]

Around midnight, Trudeau reunited with the other dignitaries at a reception hosted by the Société Saint-Jean-Baptiste. There he ran into Premier Johnson and Marcel Faribault, the high-profile federal Tory candidate from Quebec. Trudeau wished Faribault good luck in the election the next day. Faribault took the opportunity to reprimand the prime minister. "I don't agree with you," he lectured Trudeau. "I didn't go up on the parade reviewing stand because I didn't want that to be interpreted as a provocation to anyone."[25] Trudeau smiled. "This is not the first time we disagree," he said, "and it probably won't be the last."[26]

As the dust settled on Parc La Fontaine the next day, dismayed Canadians and Quebecers alike took stock. "Scenes of St. Jean Baptiste Day violence in Montreal might have shocked Canadians more had they not been conditioned by films of terrorism in the streets of New York, Paris and Belgrade," observed a *Globe and Mail* editorial. "It was chilling to hear the chants of 'Trudeau to the gallows.' And it was awful to know that there were, in that crowd, men who had threatened the Prime Minister's life."[27] Trudeau was fortunate, everyone agreed, that the rioters' weapons of choice had been bottles and not bullets. Montreal police chief Jean-Paul Gilbert told reporters that the mob had been well trained and well organized. "We are launching a full investigation to find out who trained them," he said. "Our investigation will bring those responsible in the open." Charges of police brutality were raised. Gilbert asserted that police had shown complete restraint until the violence had begun and the utmost professionalism after that. "If anyone has to complain about police brutality," he said, "let him write to me personally and his complaint will be investigated."[28]

The big story in the headlines the next day was Trudeau himself, the prime minister who had stood up to the worst civil unrest in Quebec since the conscription riots of World War II. "Trudeau Defies Separatists" and "Trudeau tient tête aux manifestants" ("Trudeau stands up to protesters"), declared the headlines.[29]

Already, the man himself was downplaying the incident, joking with the press that it was election day in Canada and he had more important things to think about. A journalist asked him why he had refused to take shelter from the mob. "I was curious," he replied. "I wanted to see what was happening."[30] Speaking on Montreal talk radio later that day, Trudeau was philosophical. "It is most regrettable that the people of Quebec can't have their St. Jean Baptiste Day in peace," he said. "I think the population will reject this resort to violence. The people who use it will be pushed out of society as time goes by."[31]

As Canadians headed to the polls, they, too, were philosophical. "It was the most remarkable ending to an election campaign in Canadian political history," the *Canadian Annual Review* observed. "The price was a savage one, but nothing would have better dramatized the issue of Canadian unity."[32]

Dalton Camp, the Tories' top campaign strategist and no stranger to controversy, had the last word. He believed that Trudeau was probably unbeatable the moment he won the Liberal nomination, but his performance in Montreal clinched it. "When you are lucky in politics," quipped Camp, "even your enemies oblige you."

The *Globe and Mail* editorial noted above was dead right. The Saint-Jean-Baptiste riot was indeed symptomatic of Canada's existential crisis in 1968. It was also part of a pattern of social upheaval that swept the North Atlantic world that year, one that has since given the era of the sixties some of its most potent myths. Today, almost fifty years later, the generation of student radicals and others who gave youthful voice to "the spirit of '68" are growing older. As they well know, the twenty-first-century world bears little resemblance to the countercultural utopia of "personal and collective liberation" they once dreamt of.[33] Nostalgia for sixties radicalism is today in its death throes. It barely survived the collapse of Soviet-style collectivism. It will not survive the threat of global terror. The city of Paris, venerated by radicals everywhere in May 1968 for its crippling strikes and massive student protests, is today terrorized by a far more vicious generation of young revolutionaries. Ordinary citizens everywhere react with unsentimental resolve. Aging sixties radicals are writing their last apologia.

To date, Pierre Trudeau's rise to power has been viewed almost entirely through the prism of this sixties nostalgia trip. In the spring of 1968, we are told, Canadians were still blissed out from Expo 67 and hungry for a charismatic, youthful leader in the mould of John F. Kennedy. Intelligent, irreverent, flirtatious, telegenic, a millionaire playboy in a two-seater Mercedes, Pierre Elliott Trudeau merely had to step into the breach.

Little wonder that Trudeau was, and remains, an enigma to so many of his critics. Canadian conservatives disparage Trudeau circa 1968 as the worst sort of socialist—the kind who imposed his collectivist fantasies on his own people by stealth.[34] Canadian left-nationalists dismiss Trudeau as a laissez-faire liberal who did nothing to counter the rapacious American takeover of Canada.[35] Quebec nationalists hold Trudeau almost single-handedly responsible for *la fin d'un rêve canadien* (the end of a Canadian dream).[36] It is not unusual to read, in even the most erudite Trudeau scholarship, the aspersion that Pierre Trudeau felt no genuine sense of belonging to either Quebec or Canada, and was thus all the more dangerous for having been a perennial "outsider."[37] Even Richard Gwyn, who in 1981 lionized Trudeau as a Canadian star in a world of mediocrities, claimed in 1997 that he "teases, taunts, inspires, and bugs the hell out of Canadians because they know he is utterly un-Canadian."[38] Gwyn meant this as a compliment.

Admittedly, it requires a huge suspension of disbelief to revisit Trudeaumania in 1968 without reference to everything that came later. But the project is timely, and the reward great. Why? Because to the extent that we now live in (and indeed contest) the Canada that Pierre built, Trudeaumania has become a Canadian creation myth in its own right. There is a good reason why Trudeau's political enemies continue to write breathless exposés of his nefarious deeds as if the man himself were still alive, and it has nothing to do with Justin. It is because they detest living in Trudeau's Canada.

This book challenges at least three common myths about Trudeaumania.

The first is that Trudeau captivated the imaginations of Canadians as the direct result of nationalist exuberance born of the 1967 centennial. "Canadians wanted more of that good old Centennial-Expo feeling," wrote journalist Larry Zolf in 1973. "They were ready for Oneness—One Canada, Justice, the Just Society and Love, Love, Love."[39] Nineteen sixty-seven was Canada's last good year, observed Pierre Berton, twenty years after the fact. "Canadians wanted the same excitement in their politics that they enjoyed in their hockey. Behind that fervour was the yearlong love affair with the country engendered by thousands of centennial projects and the giddy triumph of Expo. What was wanted was a kind of political version of ["Ca-na-da" composer] Bobby Gimby. And there, quietly waiting in the wings in his ascot scarf and sandals, was the man most likely to succeed to the throne."[40] Professional historians have since added their voices. Trudeau's "pent-up power exploded in the spring and summer of 1968," writes labour historian Bryan Palmer. "The fireworks were dubbed Trudeaumania. It was the pyrotechnics of a Canadian identity struggling to be born, shooting wildly out of the euphoria that had, for some, begun with the architectural imagination of Expo 67."[41]

In fact, the proposition that Trudeaumania flowed directly from the 1967 centennial and was the product of nationalist euphoria is counter-historical. It makes an easy (and, of course, appealing) connection where there is very little connective tissue. Take the case of Peter C. Newman, who, as this book will show, rightly took credit for discovering Trudeau.[42] When he was watching the Trudeaumania phenomenon unfold in 1968, Newman knew that there was nothing foreordained about it. "Pierre Elliott Trudeau's conquest of the Liberal Party appeared in retrospect like a royal procession predestined to glory," Newman wrote in *The Distemper of Our Times* that year. "But in the bleak chill of December [1967] just after Lester Pearson's resignation, Trudeau's victory seemed far from inevitable; in fact, it was scarcely credible."[43] Yet one year later, when *Distemper* was reprinted in the United States as *A Nation Divided: Canada and the Coming of Pierre Trudeau*, Newman added a preface that directly contradicted his own real-time observations. "For Americans," Newman now wrote, "Expo was a revelation; for Canadians it was even more; it changed our view of ourselves. It gave us a fresh appreciation of our own capabilities. It inspired new self-confidence and out of this transformed environment came a new man—Pierre Elliott Trudeau."[44]

For most Canadians, there was far more of the bleak chill to the winter of 1968 than there was of self-confidence. Lester Pearson would recall in retirement that Canada's centennial celebrations had offered a much-needed respite "because our country was going through a difficult time, especially in Quebec."[45] When British Columbia premier W.A.C. Bennett came out squarely against Trudeau in March 1968, he said Trudeau was not the right leader for Canada "in these times of emergency."[46] McGill University political scientist Michael Oliver noted in 1964 that Canada was "entering into a period of great stress." The "criminal lunacy" of the FLQ was merely the most visible symptom of a seismic shift in French Canadians' views of Confederation, warned Oliver. "If Canada is to survive in a recognizable form—and this is not putting the point too strongly—changes are indicated."[47] McGill dean of law Maxwell Cohen agreed. "It is clear that Canada is possibly facing the gravest threat to federal unity since Confederation," Cohen observed in October 1967. "The Centennial celebrations have shifted, ironically, from arts and games to survival."[48]

By the winter of 1968, the public mood in Canada was one of quiet desperation. Just weeks before election day, June 25, 1968, Martin Luther King, Jr., and Bobby Kennedy were murdered by gun-toting loners. President Lyndon Johnson announced that he would not seek re-election as the Vietnam War escalated and the Paris peace process stalled. So-called race riots consumed U.S. cities, giving every impression that American civil society was imploding. In Quebec, Pierre Bourgault, René Lévesque, and other separatists were not just dreaming of sundering Canada but planning for it. What was worse, the English-Canadian political establishment, personified by John Diefenbaker and Lester Pearson, appeared to have no clue how to respond. That the FLQ, Canada's own homegrown terrorist outfit, was bombing its way towards a Marxist utopia merely gave the crisis its visceral urgency. Pierre Trudeau did not appeal to Canadians because they were intoxicated with the "new nationalism" of the 1960s. He appealed to them because the public mood was one of deep disquiet, and he alone brought both toughness and clear-eyed solutions to the worst national-unity crisis in memory.

The second myth is that Pierre Trudeau rose to national prominence as the result of superficial media processes and particularly through his adroit handling of the new medium of television. "Trudeau was quick, cool, detached, articulate, shrewd, a man whose drifting past seemed romantic, whose lack of involvement suited a nation sick to death of the screams and whines of its politicians," wrote Walter Stewart in his 1971 book *Shrug*. "Above all, he looked superb; whatever quality it is that makes TV work for one man and not another, Trudeau had it."[49] In their award-winning 1990 book *Trudeau and Our Times*, Christina McCall and Stephen Clarkson took this idea even further, claiming that Trudeau used television to deceive Canadians. Citing Marshall McLuhan's famous remark that Trudeau's face was a "perfect mask" for the TV age, Clarkson and McCall asserted that "McLuhan was shrewder than anyone knew. *The real Trudeau was being falsified.* What the public saw was indeed a mask, a heroic image it wanted to believe in that sat uneasily on a man whose complexities were unknown to his euphoric admirers" (italics added).[50] The enduring implication of this assertion is that Trudeau was complicit in the fabrication of his own media persona. He was the political equivalent of the Monkees.

Pierre Trudeau despised television. "I can hardly stand it," he remarked during the Liberal leadership campaign.[51] He opposed Lester Pearson's introduction of TV cameras into the House of Commons in 1965 and thereafter appeared to have no sense of its utility to his own political ambitions. Trudeau performed so poorly during the televised leaders' debate in June 1968 that network executives wondered whether they would ever broadcast another one.

Many of his contemporaries thought Trudeau ill-suited for modern televisual politics because he was far from telegenic in the Kennedy style. "Visually, Trudeau is a poor parliamentarian," observed the *Toronto Star*'s Frank Jones. "His medium stature, casual stance and rather high-pitched voice make only a small impression."[52] Larry Zolf later recalled that Trudeau did not strike anyone as particularly sexy in 1964. "His pock-marked face gave him a tough street-kid look, accentuated by his cold blue eyes," wrote Zolf. "If anything, he seemed asexual."[53] Trudeau's cabinet colleague John Turner—a fluently bilingual Rhodes Scholar—was far more handsome and telegenic. Yet television did nothing for him in 1968.[54]

As this book will show, Pierre Trudeau was not a creature of the screen but of the text. Whatever effect his telegenic mask may have had on TV-watching teenyboppers—most of whom were too young to vote—it was the power of his ideas that impressed the 45.4 per cent of Canadians who voted for him in 1968. Equally important, it was the content of those ideas that turned off the majority of Canadians who did not vote for him. Decades of intense study, debate, and writing—in *Cité libre* and elsewhere—put Trudeau's oeuvre within reach of reading Canadians, in both French and English. It is commonly said that few people outside Canada's political elite actually read Trudeau. But the historical record suggests otherwise. Trudeau's ideas were circulated widely among Canadians via a pervasive print culture of books, newspapers, and journals, one that assumed ordinary citizens could grasp complicated political concepts and had the inclination to do so. All the major players in the national-unity debate wrote "popular" books in the mid-1960s. They included Daniel Johnson's *Égalité ou indépendance* (1965), Marcel Faribault's *Vers une nouvelle constitution* (1967), René Lévesque's *Option Québec* (1968), and Trudeau's own *Federalism and the French Canadians* (1967). All were national bestsellers, Trudeau's lingering in the top five throughout the spring campaign. Television helped Trudeau, but mostly in the sense that it helped to spread his ideas. In 1968, the message was still the message.

The third myth is related to the second, and it is the most damning. Pierre Trudeau, it is said, was an imposter who lied to Canadians to serve his own ambitions. "Both his Frenchness and his intellectualism were acceptable," wrote Christina McCall-Newman in her 1982 book *Grits*, "mostly because they came wrapped in a number of other attributes—physical prowess, a powerful sexuality which he enhanced with his calculated flirtatiousness, a talent for romanticizing his past, and a genius for sounding as though he knew how to solve Canada's bi-racial problems. *All these things masked his real nature*" (italics added).[55] According to McCall-Newman, Trudeau planned his ascent in federal politics brilliantly, from 1965 to his leadership victory, by claiming that he did not want it. "Trudeau won the leadership and the country by cunning and charisma," she concluded.[56]

Almost nothing in the public record or Trudeau's private papers supports this claim. There was no grand design behind Pierre Trudeau's rise to power, nor any method, covert or otherwise, for achieving it. Far from it. What emerges instead is a picture of a man painfully ambivalent about seeking the nation's top office.

At every stage, Trudeau expressed serious reservations about his lack of political experience and doubts about what he could actually accomplish if he ever did lead a government. He vacillated right up to the day he declared his candidacy, February 16, 1968, making endless excuses for his own lack of conviction. Worse, he spoke and acted like a man who believed he could not win. When Trudeau finally agreed to throw his hat into the ring, he did so not as an imposter but as a straight shooter. In the parlance of the day, he told it like it was. He laid out his ideas, asked Canadians to reflect on them, and told them blithely that if they did not vote for him, he would neither blame them nor be disappointed. He could just as easily find other things to do.[57] Out on the hustings, Trudeau campaigned without guile. He freely admitted when his own knowledge was too limited to give a sensible answer to a policy question—on aboriginal affairs, for example. He conceded when his own speeches were dull, sometimes while they were in progress. Almost unbelievably, he acknowledged publicly when he agreed with his opponents or when he had overstated his case against them.

It was a mystery, first to his Liberal leadership rivals and later to Robert Stanfield and Tommy Douglas, how Trudeau got away with this forthrightness. Whenever *they* committed such faux pas, they were pilloried as bumblers and rank amateurs. Were Canadians really so mesmerized by Trudeaumania, so much in need of a "messiah," as Claude Ryan put it, that they were willing to give this untried playboy a shot?

Trudeau got away with it because his ideas about Canada and the world preceded him. As a curious youth, as an Ivy League student, and as a lawyer and professor, he had spent decades honing his ideas about Canadian federalism. When he vaulted into federal politics in Canada in the mid-1960s, he did so carrying a fully formed theory of constitutional government, language rights, and what we now call Charter rights. As his friend Gérard Pelletier said of him in 1967, "It is rare to find persons in whom an entire lifetime of study and meditation has resulted in a genuine theory of politics—that is, a complete and coherent system of responses based on a clear conception of men and society."[58] Not only his comrades expressed this view. In mid-June 1968, at the height of the election campaign, Canada's most famous sociologist, John Porter, author of *The Vertical Mosaic*, pronounced on the corpus of Trudeau's constitutional writing in the years before he entered politics. "I do not think I have ever read a more coherent, consistent and articulate blueprint for contemporary Canada than in this collection of papers," Porter commented. "One is astounded at the clarity and the logic of it all."[59]

Trudeau's critics would later call his preoccupation with the Constitution his magnificent obsession. But what is striking about the evolution of his constitutional thinking in the 1960s is how measured and cautious it was. Although Trudeau had begun to formulate his idea of a "charter of human rights" as early as 1955, he spent the next decade telling Canadians, and particularly Quebecers, that such reforms were completely unnecessary.[60] Forget about separatism, he said. The powers laid out in the 1867 *British North America Act* were perfectly adequate for Quebec to take its place in a vibrant and internationally competitive modern Canada. When Trudeau did finally accept the need to rewrite the Constitution, it was not because he sought to change it himself. It was because the pressure from Quebec City and indeed from Ottawa had grown so intense that he could not, even as minister of justice, contain it. Repeatedly in the years 1965 to 1967, he told both his federalist allies and his nationalist adversaries to be careful what they wished for: tinkering with the Constitution could open up a can of worms. (How right he was.) Only in late 1967 did he finally relent and agree to spearhead constitutional reform on Prime Minister Pearson's behalf.

But there was more to his popular appeal than "Trudeau's charter," as the idea came to be known. In the spring of 1968, he put in motion a national policy—a fully developed set of ideas about Canada and the world that Canadians (including Quebecers) liked well enough to vote for in four elections out of five between 1968 and 1980, and that would come to define Canadian citizenship in the second century of Confederation. Some of its component parts were already visible when Trudeau was Pearson's justice minister. These included the separation of church and state, the easing of divorce, the decriminalization of homosexuality and abortion, and the eviction of the state from the bedrooms of the nation. The rest came into view over the course of the 1968 campaign: rejection of nationalism in all of its forms, including Quebec nationalism and economic nationalism in English Canada; the entrenching of individual rights, including language rights, in a charter binding not only citizens but governments; the establishment of a culture of bilingualism across Canada paired with the rejection of biculturalism (*deux nations*); the beginnings of official multiculturalism; a Canada-first foreign and defence policy; and a frugal approach to government finance that included balancing the budget, stimulating regional development, and implementing equitable social policies without turning the government into Santa Claus.

There was nothing superficial about this process. The first constituency to back Trudeau was not the teenybopper crowd. It was the English-Canadian intellectual set, foremost among them historians of Canada—teachers and scholars who presumably knew something about their country and perceived that Trudeau did, too. Some, like professors John Saywell of York University and Pauline Jewett of Carleton, were Liberal partisans. Others, including the University of Toronto's Ramsay Cook, were NDP stalwarts who in 1968 embraced Trudeau's vision for Canada and abandoned their own parties. Peter C. Newman, Pierre Berton, and Robert Fulford were early supporters of Trudeau. And from the moment Trudeau appeared on the national scene, he inspired students everywhere. Bob Rae, Michael Ignatieff, and Stephen Clarkson were among the many undergraduates who rode the Trudeau wave in 1968. Some of them are riding it still.

It would take Trudeau and his Liberal confreres a decade and a half after 1968 to bring this vision fully into being, legally and especially constitutionally. They would encounter no small degree of hostility from some highly vocal Canadian constituencies along the way, most notably in Quebec and in the West, and they would take their fair share of missteps. But when it was over, when Trudeau retired from active politics in 1984, he had bequeathed to Canadians a new idea of themselves, one based on Charter values. These values, more than any other national attribute—more than peacekeeping, more than health care, more than even hockey—became the proud hallmark of Canadian citizenship.

This is how it all started.

CHAPTER ONE
THE STUBBORN ECCENTRIC

The city of Montreal was Pierre Elliott Trudeau's lifelong home and the inspiration for nearly everything he accomplished over the course of his extraordinary life. With the exception of the two years he worked for the Privy Council Office, the nineteen he spent in federal politics, and another handful he spent travelling or studying abroad, he was an abiding fixture in the city of his birth. To a degree that is difficult to imagine today, when Canadians are always on the move and communities are ever changing, Trudeau was thoroughly, almost organically, integrated into the fabric and the rhythms of twentieth-century Montreal. He knew its streets, its social hierarchies, its traditions, its strictures. He spoke both its major languages and practised its predominant faith. He attended and later taught at some of its finest schools. He loved its history and its geography, its poets, its artists, and, of course, its women. Montreal cradled Pierre Trudeau as a child and again as an old man. He raised his boys there. He died there. And like generations of his forebears, he was laid to rest there.

What Trudeau knew above all—both of Montreal and of the province beyond it—was their politics.

Many aspects of Quebec's political culture at mid-century are enduringly fascinating. But the key to understanding Trudeau's unique place within it is the remarkable insularity of that culture. In the 1960s, the French-Canadian clerical, political, academic, and cultural elites were small, isolated (both by language and geography), and thoroughly intertwined. Everyone seemed to know everyone else. Moreover, Quebecers seemed to know everything *about* everyone else—people's family histories, where they had studied and with whom, where they had attended Mass, which organizations they had joined, which books and journals they had read, whose ideas and influences they had imbibed. Open almost any issue of *Le Devoir* in the Trudeaumania period, and you will discover an unmistakable subtext, a sense that the leading lights in Quebec society—even those who called themselves adversaries—were part of the same big extended family. They knew which names to drop. They knew how to ingratiate themselves with each other. They certainly knew how to push each other's buttons.

This insularity helps to explain the virtually linear trajectory of Pierre Trudeau's thinking about Quebec—from doctrinaire nationalist to uncompromising anti-nationalist. But more interestingly, and far more subtly, it helps to account for the decidedly non-linear and sometimes puzzling milieu in which those ideas took shape. To cite what is perhaps the best example of this insular world, Trudeau penned his most scathing critique of his nationalist adversaries, "La nouvelle trahison des clercs" ("The New Treason of the Intellectuals"), in the fall of 1961. One of the most ostensibly treacherous of those intellectuals was René Lévesque, then a provincial Liberal cabinet minister. Yet over the next two winters, Trudeau and Lévesque met fortnightly in Gérard Pelletier's living room as part of a small group of progressives dedicated to charting Quebec's future. (The other members were journalist André Laurendeau and labour leader Jean Marchand, both of whom were also nationalists.) In other words, the famously intense public debate between Lévesque and Trudeau that culminated in the 1980 referendum on sovereignty was but one layer of a long-running, even fraternal conversation between the two men.[1] The same familiarity was evident in Trudeau's relationship with premiers Jean Lesage and Daniel Johnson, with prominent academics like Léon Dion, and with influential editorialists including Pierre Laporte and Claude Ryan.

It was this culture of familiarity that made Trudeau the black sheep among Quebec's Quiet Revolutionaries and, ultimately, the nemesis of the separatists. But never did it make him, as his critics have claimed, *un inconnu très connu* (a famous outsider).

As political scientists Max and Monique Nemni have demonstrated so powerfully, Quebec's hothouse political culture in the 1930s and the early 1940s was the crucible of Trudeau's maturation as a thinker.[2]

If, in June 1968, Trudeau understood the separatist enthusiasms of Pierre Bourgault and his ilk, it is because the young Trudeau had himself embraced radical separatism and carried its slogans defiantly into the streets. In 1937, at the age of seventeen, he gave a speech to his Brébeuf classmates. "To maintain our French mentality," he asserted, "what we must do is to preserve our language and to shun American civilization."[3] In November 1942, in the midst of World War II, Trudeau gave an even more conventionally nationalist speech in support of Jean Drapeau, then a young law student contesting a federal seat in the riding of Outremont. Both Drapeau and Trudeau believed that Prime Minister Mackenzie King had defiled democracy by backtracking on his promise not to conscript Canadians in the war against Hitler. "If we are not in a democracy," Trudeau raged, "let the revolution begin without delay!"[4] As Trudeau would later admit, his youthful beliefs were almost entirely the product of his political isolation. Once he was outside the Quebec fishbowl, he abandoned them wholesale.

In 1944, just two years after his fiery anti-conscription speech, he set off for Harvard University to study political economy. There, at the age of twenty-five, Trudeau became, as he put it himself, a "citizen of the world." He read foreign newspapers for the first time, mingled with American GIs who had served in Europe, and discussed world issues from an international perspective. Until then, the fight against European fascism had been little more than an abstract concept for him. (Never would Trudeau's English-Canadian detractors let him forget the patent callousness of his horsing around in Prussian military regalia during the darkest days of the conflict.) The "historic importance" of World War II came as an epiphany to Trudeau. It changed everything, including his understanding of Quebec politics. "I realized that the Quebec of the time was away from the action, that it was living outside modern times," he would later write. "Quebec had stayed provincial in every sense of the word, that is to say marginal, isolated, out of step with the evolution of the world."[5]

Trudeau's classroom training at Harvard, meanwhile, cemented his belief in the sacred importance of the individual. Under the influence of exiled European professors like the German Heinrich Brüning, he came to reject all collectivist thinking as fundamentally tyrannical. The first thing to go was the theory of corporatism. This was a reactionary ideology popular in Catholic Quebec (and Catholic Europe) that envisaged a hierarchical conception of social organization based on the family.[6] Like practically all young French Canadians of his generation, Trudeau had been a devotee of corporatism. No longer. "French-Canadian thinkers, politicians, journalists, and editors advocated corporatism as a kind of extraordinary panacea," Trudeau would later say of his own formative years. "No one was far-sighted or courageous enough to say that it was all nonsense."[7] Although the adult Trudeau would occasionally write as a democratic socialist, after Harvard his deepest political convictions would remain resolutely those of a near-classic liberal. "The view that every human must be free to shape his own destiny," he said, "became for me a certainty."[8]

Harvard (and the smattering of graduate courses Trudeau subsequently took at the École des sciences politiques in Paris and the

London School of Economics) also confirmed his status as a self-styled "contrarian." He was always happiest "paddling against the current," he liked to say. In the context of mid-century Quebec, this stance meant challenging nationalist thinking in whatever form happened to be *au courant.* By definition, nationalism privileges one collectivity vis-à-vis others. It protects the in-group from the outsiders. Seen from the perspective of liberal individualism, nationalism is fundamentally unjust—irrespective of whether it is bundled with high-minded appeals to "imagined communities" or any other such fiction.[9] "A nationalistic government is by nature intolerant, discriminatory, and, when all is said and done, totalitarian," Trudeau would aver throughout his political career. "A truly democratic government cannot be 'nationalist,' because it must pursue the good of all its citizens, without prejudice to ethnic origin."[10]

Not surprisingly, Trudeau also cast off the popular nationalist version of Quebec history promulgated by the Université de Montréal historian Michel Brunet. Just as Trudeau was renouncing corporatism, Professor Brunet, just two years Trudeau's senior, was reimagining it as a defining moment in Quebec's national rebirth. "Many French Canadians began to ask themselves if it would not be more realistic to promote the economic and cultural progress of their community inside the borders of Quebec," Brunet would write of the 1930s, "instead of waging exhausting and fruitless fights to establish bilingualism throughout Canada."[11] The question was, of course, rhetorical. Well into the sixties, Brunet and other members of the so-called Montreal School would urge Quebecers to use the tools of modern democracy to reclaim Quebec as their "fatherland."[12] After the horrors of the Nazi period, the suggestion that Quebec should be the fatherland of the French Canadians repelled Trudeau. So, too, did Brunet's willingness to scapegoat English Canada for Quebec's economic underdevelopment. Blaming *"les Anglais"* for Quebec's problems was "ridiculous," Trudeau would say flatly.[13]

In 1948, Trudeau embarked on a year-long spiritual quest that took him to Asia via Eastern Europe and the Middle East. He intended the trip not as an intellectual exercise but as an immersion in the language, dress, and labour of local people. "This trip was basically a challenge I set myself," he later wrote, "as I had done with sports, with canoeing expeditions, and with intellectual explorations. I wanted to know, for instance, whether I could survive in a Chinese province without knowing a word of Chinese, or would be able to travel across a war-torn country without ever succumbing to panic."[14] He got his wish, experiencing jail in Jerusalem and Belgrade, an attack by the Viet Cong when he was on his way to Saigon, myriad death threats, and deportation from at least one Communist-bloc country. "It was incredible," he later wrote. "Everywhere I went seemed to be at war."[15] Israel, Pakistan, Indochina, China, Iraq—anywhere Trudeau found himself on the front lines, he was only too happy to rely on "the courage and kindness of ordinary people."[16] Such experiences made him more worldly and less intolerant, shaping the two precepts that would later govern his conduct even with his nominal Cold War enemies: that people of differing views could agree to disagree, and that one must always seek out the humanity of one's enemies.[17]

Canadians would come to know Trudeau as tough ("Just watch me"), irreverent ("Fuddle duddle"), and even crass ("*Mangez de la merde*"). He had a sharp mind, an even sharper pen, and a taste for the jugular when he was heckled or provoked. But once he had jettisoned his youthful fanaticism and embraced "reason over passion," he was almost never hateful—not even to those who would make death threats against him.

As Justin Trudeau has said often, most poignantly in his October 2000 eulogy for his father, Pierre's highest ideal in political debate was to critique his opponents' ideas without demeaning them personally—an ideal he would occasionally honour in the breach.[18] Yet well before he entered politics, tolerance and a genuine interest in people's differences were defining features of Trudeau's personal philosophy. He never wavered from this attitude or apologized for it. What is more, he seldom even bothered to explain it. As justice minister and as a Liberal leadership hopeful, for example, Trudeau would be accused of carrying "the stench of Sodom" into federal politics for having liberalized Canadian law on homosexuality, abortion, and divorce. Yet never did he strike back at his critics in kind, with ad hominem slurs. And never, even when the political dividends might have been considerable, did he attack any of the usual suspects—Jehovah's Witnesses, Jews, homosexuals, Americans, Cubans, Russians. He thus left himself wide open both to innuendo (that he was gay, or soft on crime, or irreligious) and to outright smears (that he was a Red or a fascist). And when his enemies manoeuvred to take full advantage, he gave every appearance that he could not have cared less.

As he observed at the height of Trudeaumania, such "garbage" was beneath Canadians. He had better things to worry about.

His world travels and his studies at an end, Trudeau returned to Montreal in the spring of 1949. He arrived just in time to witness the dramatic (and illegal) strike of five thousand miners at the town of Asbestos, Quebec. Trudeau drove out to the Eastern Townships with Gérard Pelletier, who was covering the strike for *Le Devoir*. Expecting to hang around for a day or two, Trudeau was instead drawn into the struggle on the strikers' behalf. He attended meetings, made speeches, and, alongside Pelletier, ended up in police custody. At Asbestos, he later wrote, "I found a Quebec I did not really know, that of workers exploited by management, denounced by government, clubbed by police, and yet burning with fervent militancy."[19] In his seminal 1956 book *La grève de l'amiante*, Trudeau would describe the strike as a turning point in the history of Quebec. It exposed Quebec nationalism as an ideology of "discouraging impotence," he observed, and moved Quebecers to confront their antiquated social and political institutions, however tentatively.[20]

Towards the end of that same summer, 1949, Trudeau surprised all of his friends and took a job in the Privy Council Office in Ottawa. He wanted to see how the political theories he had studied so closely applied to the day-to-day workings of Canadian federalism. His stay in Ottawa turned out to be little more than a sojourn—evidence, said his detractors, that he could not stick to anything. Less than two years into the Privy Council job, Trudeau resigned. His biographer, John English, has suggested recently that he did so because he disapproved of the Liberal government's decision to participate in the Korean War.[21] Trudeau himself recalled only that he wanted to get back to Montreal. "In Ottawa, everything is going pretty smoothly," he explained to his boss, Gordon Robertson, clerk of the Privy Council. "Right now Quebec is where the important battles are being fought. That's where I can be most useful, even if my influence is only marginal."[22] Although he coveted a university teaching job in those years, Trudeau declined an invitation to join the faculty of law at Queen's University in Kingston, Ontario. He wanted to stay where the action was.

In the summer of 1950, while Trudeau was still living in Ottawa, he and Gérard Pelletier founded the French-language journal *Cité libre*. The new publication intended not only to advocate for liberal reforms in Quebec but also to provide a rigorous, peer-reviewed forum in which to formulate and fine-tune those reforms. Despite its latter-day fame as a hub of anti-Duplessis activism, *Cité libre* was no broadsheet. Its articles were often long and pedantic. Its circulation never exceeded five hundred copies in the 1950s and frequently fell well short of that number. What mattered to the *citélibristes* was not market share but the reach of their ideas among Quebec's francophone elites. Anyone who was anyone in Quebec politics read *Cité libre* or at least knew its contents, even Duplessis. And despite the premier's efforts to control the Quebec press, the *citélibristes'* ideas also trickled out to the reading public via op-eds in Montreal's leading dailies.

At every stage, Trudeau was the moving force behind *Cité libre.* He underwrote it, edited it, and gave voice to its core liberal-humanist precepts. "He had such a natural superiority over all of us in the international field," Pelletier later recalled. "We also discovered how far he had gone in evolving political ideas for French Canada—and for the rest of Canada."[23] Trudeau himself was brash about what the journal might accomplish. "We want to bear witness to the Christian and French fact in America," he wrote in the first issue. "But we must also throw everything else overboard. The time has arrived for us to borrow from architecture the discipline called 'functional,' to cast aside the thousands of past prejudices which encumber the present, and to build for the new man. Overthrow all totems, transgress all taboos. Better still, consider them as dead ends. Without passion, let us be intelligent."[24] A full decade and a half before Trudeau first appeared on English Canadians' radar, *Cité libre* would establish his standing in Quebec as a bold and brilliant iconoclast. In the Trudeaumania period, when English Canadians were scrambling to figure out what made him tick, his ideas were as familiar to Quebecers as maple syrup.

Much could be said about the long, dark decade of the 1950s, when *citélibristes* and other Quebec progressives opposed Premier Maurice Duplessis's autocratic rule. (The premier's personal interventions to deny Trudeau a teaching job at the Université de Montréal are particularly noteworthy.) Whether Duplessis was the black-hearted villain his critics made him out to be remains the subject of considerable debate. But the salient point for understanding Trudeau's standing in Quebec politics was the relative unity of the opposition that Duplessis inspired. This was not merely a tactical alliance but a united front—one that persisted beyond the death of *le chef* in 1959 and gave the Quiet Revolution its air of fervent optimism. "The style adopted as the 1960s dawned was one of daring,"

Gretta Chambers, former chancellor of McGill University, has recalled recently. "Nothing was sacred, including continuity. Particularly for the young the self-assertion that grew out of this movement to break out of the existing social, political, and cultural constraints was both heady and contagious."[25]

Quebec reformers welcomed the 1960 electoral victory of the Lesage Liberals as the dawn of a new day. "For all of us who had fought for ten years for the modernization of Quebec," Trudeau later recalled, "it was no small satisfaction to be governed at last by a young, competent, dynamic team urgently determined to move the clock forward and put Quebec onto the same time as the rest of the Western world."[26] With almost dizzying speed, the agrarian, Catholic, and patronage-ridden Quebec of the Duplessis era was torn down and replaced by a modern secular state. Health, welfare, and education were declericalized, replaced by vast new provincial bureaucracies of professionally trained specialists. In the five years after Duplessis's death, the provincial budget quadrupled, from roughly $500 million to $2 billion.[27] *Rattrapage*—catching up to "the rest of the Western world" in social and especially economic development—became the new watchword in Quebec politics.[28]

In 1961, Trudeau was finally appointed associate professor of law at the Université de Montréal, his dream job. His future seemed secure, even happy. Duplessis was gone, Lesage was in power, and Quebec was at long last taking its place in the modern world. All that remained, it seemed, was for Professor Trudeau to decommission *Cité libre* and dedicate whatever remained of his working life to moulding the minds of his bright young students.

It did not happen this way, of course. "Why did this happiness have to be so short-lived?" Trudeau lamented. "All this movement had barely started when people began hurrying to revive the old slogans."[29]

Predictably, perhaps, the centre could not hold. As the modernization of Quebec gained momentum, the consensus that had fuelled the Quiet Revolution exploded into a kaleidoscope of competing visions. Nationalist and separatist groups emerged, of which L'Action Socialiste, L'Alliance Laurentienne, and Pierre Bourgault's RIN were merely the avant-garde. Dr. Marcel Chaput's influential *Pourquoi je suis séparatiste* (*Why I Am a Separatist*) was published in 1961, making waves across Quebec and beyond.[30] Trudeau's students—and indeed some of his colleagues—were increasingly sovereignist and contemptuous of the raw deal they believed French Canadians had been dealt within Confederation. They mocked *Cité libre* as the boneyard of federalist squares who could not see that the future of Quebec lay in full-blown political autonomy. The appetites of the new generation of nationalists became insatiable. Quebecers must become *maîtres chez nous*, they demanded. The separatists, always a small but noisy minority, took this idea to its logical end point. Once Quebecers had acquired the constitutional and financial powers necessary to fulfill their national destiny, the separatists asked, what practical use could they possibly have for Ottawa, or even Canada?

Pierre Trudeau spent much of 1961—without question the decisive year in his evolution as a political thinker—formulating a programmatic response to this question. *Programmatic* is the key word, for as much as Trudeau liked to imagine himself as a contrarian, he was never above acknowledging the legitimacy of certain elements in his adversaries' critique of Canadian federalism. The question for Trudeau was not whether French Canadians had suffered injustices in the past. They had. Writing in *Cité libre*, Trudeau offered a sharp defence of Quebecers' historic instinct for self-preservation. "We must accept the facts of history as they are," he wrote.

> However outworn and absurd it may be, it was the Nation-State image which spurred the political thinking of the British, and

> subsequently of Canadians of British descent in the "Dominion of Canada." Broadly speaking, this meant identifying Canada, the State, with themselves to the greatest possible degree.
>
> Since the French Canadians had the bad grace to decline assimilation, such an identification was beyond being completely realizable. So the Anglo-Canadians built themselves an illusion of it by fencing off the French Canadians in their Quebec ghetto and then nibbling at its constitutional powers and carrying them off bit by bit to Ottawa. Outside Quebec they fought, with staggering ferocity, against anything which might intrude upon that illusion: the use of French on stamps, money, cheques, in the civil service, the railroads, and the whole works. In the face of such aggressive nationalism, what choice lay before the French Canadians over, say, the last century?[31]

Seen in retrospect, this statement is one of the most incisive in the entire Trudeau oeuvre. It gives the lie to the accusation made against him, especially in the Trudeaumania period, that he somehow sought to ingratiate himself with English Canadians by "putting Quebec in its place."

No, the pressing issue for Trudeau was how Quebecers could best move forward. "Without backsliding to the ridiculous and reactionary idea of national sovereignty, how can we protect our French-Canadian national qualities?" he asked. The answer was obvious. "We must separate once and for all the concepts of State and of Nation, and make Canada a truly pluralistic and polyethnic society." Let the past be the past, Trudeau told Quebecers. "Whether or not the Conquest was the origin of all evils and whether or not the English have been the most perfidious occupiers in the memory of man, it remains none the less true that the French-Canadian community holds in its hands, *hic et nunc* [here and now], the essential instruments for its regeneration; by the Constitution of Canada the state of Quebec can exercise the most extensive powers over the souls of French Canadians and over the territory where they live—the most rich and most vast of all the Canadian provinces."[32]

Trudeau was at his most persuasive, arguably, in the area of his own juridical expertise, namely the division of constitutional powers afforded by the *British North America Act*. Let the feds continue to manage foreign affairs, trade, navigation, postal services, money, and banking, he insisted. But let the provinces fully exploit the provisions of the same Constitution to protect and advance their "ethnic peculiarities"—education, municipal affairs, the administration of justice, marriage, and property and civil rights. "French Canadians have all the powers they need to make Quebec a political society affording due respect for nationalist aspirations and at the same time giving unprecedented scope for human potential in the broadest sense," asserted Trudeau.[33] In comparison, talk of a separate Quebec state was not merely self-indulgent but "preposterous," he believed. "We are not well enough educated nor rich enough, nor, above all, are there enough of us to man and finance a government possessing all the necessary means for both war and peace. The fixed per-capita cost would ruin us." As he would for the rest of the 1960s, Trudeau demanded that Quebecers avert their inward gaze and embrace the wider world. "*Ouvrons les frontières*," he said famously. "*Ce peuple meurt d'asphyxie!*"[34] ("Open the frontiers. This people is dying of asphyxiation!")

If there was a term that encapsulated Trudeau's theory of federalism, then and later, it was *functional*. He entitled his first *Cité libre* essay "Politique fonctionnelle" in 1950 and referenced the idea well into his tenure as prime minister. To describe his approach to governing, Trudeau frequently used the English term *pragmatic*, which was entirely apt. But it was an imperfect synonym, for the French word *fonctionnelle* carried a double meaning. On the one hand, a functional politics was a practical politics. It demanded the application of reason and problem-solving techniques to policy. On the other hand, the term carried an ideological meaning, which had implications not only for politics but also for power. A functional politics, as Trudeau construed it, would rationally assign powers within Canada's federalist structure to whichever level of government they best suited. In other words, there would be no redistribution of powers based on vague and ultimately emotional claims about "nations." In this way, *politique fonctionnelle* worked directly against Quebec nationalism. It was a cipher, fully understood by Trudeau's Québécois friends and foes alike. It meant no special status for Quebec.

The good news was that Quebecers had no need for special status. In 1961, Pierre Trudeau laid down this remarkable scenario for the future of Quebec and Canada—remarkable because it so closely resembled the Canada over which he presided as prime minister:

> If Quebec became a shining example, if to live there were to partake of freedom and progress, if culture enjoyed a place of honour there, if the universities commanded respect and renown from afar, if the administration of public affairs were the best in the land—and none of this presupposes any declaration of independence!—French Canadians would no longer need to do battle for bilingualism; the ability to speak French would become a status symbol, even an open-sesame in business and public life. Even in Ottawa, superior competence on the part of our politicians and civil servants would bring spectacular changes.
>
> Such an undertaking is immensely difficult, but possible; it takes more guts than jaw. And therein, it would seem to me, is an "ideal" not a whit less "inspiring" than that other one [separatism] that's been in vogue for a couple of years in our little part of the world.[35]

Trudeau could still break bread with René Lévesque when he wrote those extraordinary lines. Only in 1962 did Trudeau begin to distance himself from nationalists like Lévesque, and only because their runaway political successes now appeared to him to pose an existential threat to Canada.

The Lesage Liberals, just two years into their first majority mandate, called a snap election for November 1962. They adopted the slogan *maîtres chez nous* and ran a one-issue campaign on their plan to nationalize all of the privately owned hydroelectric interests operating in the province. It was Lévesque himself, then serving as Lesage's popular minister of natural resources, who laid the groundwork for nationalization, soothing North American capitalists with assurances that he was no Fidel Castro. Hydro-Québec thus emerged as one of the most potent symbols of the Quiet Revolution, one on which Lévesque and Lesage were prepared to stake their political careers. Their instincts proved impeccable. When the ballots were counted, the Liberals swept the province, taking 56.4 per cent of the popular vote and sixty-three seats out of ninety-five—a dozen more than they had won in 1960. They wasted no time implementing their nationalization promise. In December 1962, the government of Quebec bought out all of the remaining private hydro interests with a massive provincial bond issue.

Pierre Trudeau had little enthusiasm for Lévesque's Hydro-Québec deal, but his main objection to this neo-nationalist triumph remained one of principle. Like any good liberal, Trudeau adhered strongly to the principle of checks and balances, or what he himself called "counterweights." Democratic states worked best, he believed, when power was balanced among various levels of government.[36] Even before the Liberal landslide, Trudeau perceived that the new nationalism in Quebec had achieved critical mass. It now threatened to overwhelm Canadian federalism. "By 1962," he later recalled, "the Lesage government and public opinion in Quebec had magnified provincial autonomy into an absolute, and were attempting to reduce federal power to nothing."[37] Worse, Liberal sloganeering had reified the most retrograde elements of the old Quebec nationalism. "Instead of remaining committed to politics based on realism and common sense, we were plunged into the 'politics of grandeur' whose main preoccupation all too often was rolling out red carpets," Trudeau later fumed. "A province is not a nation but a mix of diverse people, differentiated by religion, culture, and mother tongue. Was it necessary to grind down all these differences and impose a dominating and intolerant ideology on all minorities? I found this change of direction aberrant. I knew that it led directly to doctrinaire separatism."[38]

Trudeau was fed up. His opposition to Quebec nationalism hardened. Polite debate gave way to hard-edged critique. He attacked his opponents with the polemic "La nouvelle trahison des clercs" ("The New Treason of the Intellectuals"), published in *Cité libre* in April 1962. Sympathetic Trudeau biographers have treated this essay as his Ninth Symphony, his critics as his most "murderous" tirade.[39] Both appraisals are correct. "It is not the concept of *nation* that is retrograde," Trudeau famously began. "It is the idea that the nation must necessarily be sovereign."

Trudeau's first target in "La nouvelle trahison des clercs" was RIN leader Marcel Chaput, who, in *Pourquoi je suis séparatiste,* had likened the plight of French Canada to that of the thirty or so former colonies in Africa and elsewhere that had declared themselves sovereign. "It is the turn of the French-Canadian people to arise and claim their rightful place among free nations," Chaput had written.[40] Nonsense, said Trudeau. "Putting the independence of Quebec into this historical context is pure sophistry." India was a sovereign republic of eight principal religions and even more languages. Ceylon consisted of three ethnic groups and four religions. "In Africa the polyethnic nature of the new states is even more striking," Trudeau insisted. "As for Algeria, which our *Indépendantistes* are always holding up as an example, there is no doubt what kind of state she is seeking to become. Besides inhabitants of French, Spanish, Italian, Jewish, Greek, and Levantine origin, in this particular country we must count Berbers, Kabyles, Arabs, Moors, Negroes, Tuaregs, Mazabites, and a number of Cheshire cats." The worst of the separatists' "cock-and-bull" analogies was that of Cuba, a country Trudeau had visited and knew well. Cuba was "sovereign under Batista and is sovereign under Castro," he railed. "Democratic self-government was non-existent there yesterday and is still non-existent there today. So what does that prove?"[41]

The nation is not a "biological reality," Trudeau continued, nor any hallowed feat of historical progress. "The tiny portion of history marked by the emergence of the nation-states is also the scene of the most devastating wars, the worst atrocities, and the most degrading collective hatred the world has ever seen," he affirmed. French-Canadian nationalism was nothing but an overreaction to Anglo-Canadian nationalism, which, despite its longevity, "never had much of an edge." "Constitutionalist" visionaries from French Canada had always understood this. "The multi-national state was dreamed about by Lafontaine, realized under Cartier, perfected by Laurier, and humanized with Bourassa," wrote Trudeau. "If Canada as a state has had so little room for French Canadians it is above all because we have failed to make ourselves indispensable to its future."[42]

Trudeau concluded "La nouvelle trahison des clercs" with a bold challenge to the new generation of Quebec nationalists.

> We have expended a great deal of time and energy proclaiming the rights due our nationality, invoking our divine mission, trumpeting our virtues, bewailing our misfortunes, denouncing our enemies, and avowing our independence; and for all that not one of our workmen is the more skilled, nor a civil servant the more efficient, a financier the richer, a doctor the more advanced, a bishop the more learned, nor a single

> solitary politician the less ignorant. Now, except for a few stubborn eccentrics, there is probably not one French-Canadian intellectual who has not spent at least four hours a week over the last year discussing separatism. That makes how many thousand times two hundred hours spent just flapping our arms? And can any one of them honestly say he has heard a single argument not already expounded ad nauseam twenty, forty, and even sixty years ago?
>
> The Separatists of 1962 that I have met really are, in general, genuinely earnest and nice people; but the few times I have had the opportunity of talking with them at any length, I have almost always been astounded by the totalitarian outlook of some, the anti-Semitism of others and the complete ignorance of basic economics of all of them.
>
> This is what I call *la nouvelle trahison des clercs*: this self-deluding passion of a large segment of our thinking population for throwing themselves headlong—intellectually and spiritually—into purely escapist pursuits.[43]

Undoubtedly, Trudeau had himself in mind when he referenced "stubborn eccentrics" in "La nouvelle trahison des clercs." But there were others. Most of his old comrades from *Cité libre* saw Quebec politics as he did. Many of the smart young intellectuals connected with Montreal's Centre des Recherches Sociales (CRS) were also liberal and federalist, including Albert Breton, Raymond Breton, Maurice Pinard, and Marc Lalonde, the thirty-three-year-old Montreal lawyer whose political fortunes would thereafter be umbilically tied to Trudeau's.

In early 1964—by which time Pierre Bourgault had taken his place as a leading sovereignist provocateur and the FLQ was one year into its inaugural campaign of separatist mayhem—Trudeau, Lalonde, and five other CRS members issued a short tract entitled "An Appeal for Reason in Canadian Politics." The document was published simultaneously in *Cité libre* and the English-language *Canadian Forum*, attracting the notice of editorialists across Canada, all of whom correctly identified it as an "anti-separatism blueprint."[44] Both the text and the voice of the manifesto were pure, undiluted Trudeau. "Canada today is a country in search of a purpose," the document announced. The impotence of the central government in the face of rising regionalism risked "the utter disintegration of the federal state." Quebec separatism was a "waste of time," as was the misguided economic nationalism rising in English Canada. "We must be more precise in our analysis of situations, more intellectually honest in debate and more realistic in decision," the tract concluded. "We must descend from the euphoria of all-embracing ideologies and come to grips with actual problems. If this country is to work, federalism must be preserved and refined at all cost."[45]

Trudeau knew which way the wind was blowing in Quebec, of course. By the time he and the other stubborn eccentrics were appealing for reason in Canadian politics, virtually all Quebec elites—the politicians, the artists and writers, the editorialists, and the intellectuals—were espousing a new constitutional deal for Quebec, one that acknowledged the existence in Canada of *deux nations*. René Lévesque gave popular voice to the idea. "All our action, in the immediate future, must take two fundamental facts into account," Lévesque told *Le Devoir* editor Jean-Marc Léger in 1963. "The first is that French Canada is a true nation. The second is that politically we are not a sovereign people." Obviously, Lévesque's private debates with Trudeau had sharpened his nationalist vision. "We must have a Canada which, to begin with, takes into account the existence of two nations and the specific position, the particular needs, of Quebec. It is infinitely more important to make Quebec progressive, free, and strong, than to devote the best of our energies to propagating the doubtful advantages of biculturalism."[46]

In the Quebec legislature, the consensus on *deux nations* was bipartisan and unassailable. Premier Jean Lesage envisaged amendments to the Canadian Constitution guaranteeing *statut particulier* (special status) for Quebec. The leader of the Opposition, Daniel Johnson, believed that an entirely new deal for Quebec was necessary. "The constitution should be conceived so that Canada is not only a federation of ten provinces but a federation in which two nations are equal in law and in fact," Johnson wrote in his book *Égalité ou indépendance*.[47] As premier, Johnson would carry this thinly veiled ultimatum—equality or independence—to Ottawa and lay it directly at the feet of Prime Minister Lester Pearson.

In public, Trudeau continued to state as bluntly as ever his aversion to the *deux nations* conception of Canada. Party leaders who demand special status, he quipped, "cannot admit that they are separatists. We have lost the habit of asking our politicians what they think."[48] But behind closed doors, Trudeau continued his work as a legal scholar to promote Canadian federalism, painstakingly and dispassionately, for the benefit of Quebecers. Over the winter of 1965, he composed a long essay on "Quebec and the Constitutional Problem." The piece was commissioned as a brief for several Quebec groups appearing before the Constitution Committee of the Quebec legislature, which had been struck in May 1963 to study Quebec's constitutional options. Trudeau's essay was widely circulated among Quebec's political elite and came to be seen as the defining statement of his doctrine of federalism before he joined the federal Liberals.

"I recognize the right of nations to self-determination," wrote Trudeau.

> But to claim this right without taking into account the price that will have to be paid, and without clearly demonstrating that it is to the advantage of the whole nation, is nothing short of a reckless gamble. Men do not exist for states: states are

> created to make it easier for men to attain some of their common objectives.
>
> In my opinion, the "two nation" concept is dangerous in theory and groundless in fact. It would be disastrous if—at the very moment when French Canadians are at last awakening to the modern world and making their presence count in the country—their politicians were to be won over to anti-federalist policies. On the other hand, if Quebec were part of a Canadian federation grouping two *linguistic* communities as I am advocating, French Canadians would be supported by a country of more than eighteen million inhabitants, with the second or third highest standard of living in the world, and with a degree of industrial maturity that promises to give it the most brilliant of futures.
>
> Consequently, there is no need to evoke the notion of a national state to turn Quebec into a province "different from the others." In a great number of vital areas, and notably those that concern the development of particular cultural values, Quebec has full and complete sovereignty under the Canadian constitution.[49]

Such eloquence was all for naught. By 1965, no one in Quebec appeared to be listening to federalist voices like Trudeau's, and, what was worse, no one in Ottawa seemed to know how to respond to the *deux nations* idea of Confederation that was now *de rigueur* in Quebec. Just months after Trudeau submitted his brief to the Quebec legislature, he and other like-minded Quebec federalists led by Jean Marchand and Gérard Pelletier pulled up stakes in Montreal and joined the Pearson Liberals in Ottawa. They loved Quebec as much as ever, but the country they wanted to save was Canada. As Trudeau told CBC correspondent Norman DePoe, "Our main objective was to join what we thought to be the only party which could find, now, a solution to the problems of Canada breaking up or not breaking up."[50]

Pierre Trudeau spent the period 1950 to 1965 not merely formulating his ideas about Canadian federalism but testing and retesting them—in *Cité libre,* in academic journals, at conferences, in seminars and think tanks, and especially in endless private conversations with other Quebecers. For the last four years of this period, he laboured as a professor of constitutional law. He listened carefully to the arguments of his allies and his opponents, continued to read voraciously in the field, and endeavoured whenever possible to invoke reason against passion.

Almost nothing of what Trudeau said or wrote in the years before he went to Ottawa, even including "La nouvelle trahison des clercs," suggests that he was harbouring ulterior motives. "People have often asked me whether, in the 1950s, I already had political ambitions," Trudeau later reflected. "I have always answered in the negative, which was the truth. Leaving Quebec was out of the question, as far as I was concerned; it was here that I wanted to be active."[51] On the contrary, had anyone else laid out a federalist program that Trudeau believed would be good for French Canadians, there is every reason to imagine that he would have supported it. But no one did. "After two years in Parliament," Gérard Pelletier observed in January 1968, "I have met very few people, English or French speaking, Liberal, Conservative or NDP, who possess as clear a view of the kind of country they want to build and the brand of federalism they wish to promote. Trudeau's views are certainly not popular with either the separatists or the outright centralizers. However, they are seldom challenged with serious arguments."[52]

Trudeau's critics would say, then and later, that he was out of step with Quebec's elites. But what they really meant was that he had failed to understand what was at stake in Quebec. This presumed failure is what put the sting in the accusation that Trudeau was "*un inconnu très connu.*" At best, he was a prisoner of his own ideological rigidity, his opponents stated. At worst, he was a *vendu* who would sell out the birthright of his own people.

Most of the time, Trudeau could not be bothered to answer such charges. But once in a while, he did. In March 1968, for example, when he was campaigning for the Liberal leadership, Trudeau gave a speech to the Liberal Reform Club in Quebec City. Some separatist students showed up to heckle him, and in true professorial style, Trudeau engaged them directly and without condescension. "Don't you feel a bit isolated in Canadian politics due to the fact that all Quebec parties and all Canadian parties have accepted the concept of two nations?" asked one student. "I don't feel isolated at all," Trudeau replied. "The fact that I'm the only person who thinks something isn't enough to make me think I'm wrong. When I believe something, I explain it and if I can't convince people, I say well okay maybe they're wrong and maybe they're right. I'll have another look at it."[53]

Trudeau knew Quebec politics root and branch. He knew the difference between Quebec nationalists like Jean Lesage and outright separatists like Pierre Bourgault. He knew that the violence of the FLQ was repulsive to most of the francophone Quebecers in whose name it was perpetrated. He also knew—as did everyone else—that support for outright separatism among Quebec voters was never more than a paltry 13 per cent, even in the headiest period of the Quiet Revolution.[54]

But Trudeau also had two key insights about the nationalist ferment exploding around him. The first was that even though nationalists like René Lévesque, Jean Lesage, and Daniel Johnson claimed they did not want to destroy Canada, they advocated constitutional reforms that would either tear the country apart or Balkanize it irrevocably. Well into the Trudeaumania period, Trudeau would ask his opponents to explain how a *deux nations* Canada would work and, in particular, whether it could win the support of Canadians outside Quebec. If there was a formula by which the other provinces would accept special status for Quebec in a strong and united Canada,

Trudeau asked, what was it? The answers he got—from Quebec politicians, from his Liberal leadership rivals, and ultimately from his opponents in the 1968 election campaign—were uniformly vague and unconvincing.

Trudeau's second insight can be stated even more concisely. He believed that the nationalist elites in Quebec did not speak for Quebecers—and not merely because he believed that their ideas "led directly to doctrinaire separatism."

In contrast with many Quebec politicians who, like René Lévesque, patently loved Quebec but thought very little of the country beyond it, Trudeau genuinely believed that Canada belonged as much to Quebecers as to other Canadians.[55] This is what he meant when, in the early 1960s, he fulminated against the "ghettoization" of French Canadians. Ironically, Trudeau was often accused of defending the constitutional status quo in Canada. Absolutely not, he replied. He was "fighting for the only thing that can make Canada united—to take the fuse out of explosive Quebec nationalism—by making sure that Quebec is not a ghetto for French Canadians, that all of Canada is theirs. It's obvious that [I am] saying to French Canadians: No, not only the Quebec government can speak for you. On the contrary, only the Ottawa government can give the French Canadians their due across the country."[56]

During the 1968 election campaign, Trudeau would be asked where "love of country" fit into his political thinking. "What you're really asking me is whether I have a gut feeling for Canada or not," Trudeau replied. "Obviously I do. Otherwise I wouldn't have spent so much of my life and energies fighting for the kind of society I think is right. I wouldn't have spent so much of my working life and my studying life learning about Canada and doing something about it if I weren't at least concerned with patriotism or with Canadian identity as I want to see it developed."[57]

CHAPTER TWO
THE THREE MUSKETEERS

It would be an exaggeration to say that Pierre Trudeau was unknown to English Canadians when he arrived in Ottawa in 1965, but only a slight one. In bilingual university circles, Trudeau's reputation as a *citélibriste* preceded him. His essay "Some Obstacles to Democracy in Quebec" appeared in 1958 in the *Canadian Journal of Economics and Political Science* and was reprinted two years later in an academic tome on "French-English relations."[1] But in general, Quebec politics in the Duplessis era did not interest Canadians elsewhere in the country, and they noticed nothing even remotely resembling a national-unity crisis until the Quiet Revolution was well under way.

Not until the early 1960s did "Pierre-Elliot" Trudeau—his name invariably misspelled—begin to attract notice in the English-Canadian media, and even then the attention was fleeting. His first mention in the *Toronto Star*—the mass-circulation daily that would later do so much to promote Trudeau's vision of Canada—appeared in Robert Fulford's review of Marcel Chaput's *Pourquoi je suis séparatiste* in January 1962.[2] Fulford positioned Trudeau as a "left-liberal" opponent of nationalist ideology in Quebec and surmised, wrongly, that he represented the predominant intellectual position on that question. Even so, Fulford's early identification of Trudeau as "one of the civilized men of Canada" (as well as the writer's characterization of René Lévesque as "the brightest of all the important politicians") helped to set a high-minded tone across the country for the constitutional debate then brewing in Quebec.[3]

The same effect was achieved during Trudeau's first appearance on CBC's English-language television network. It came in the winter of 1963, when Trudeau joined moderator Gérard Pelletier, historians Peter Waite and Michel Brunet, McGill law professor Frank Scott, Hautes Études Commerciales professor Jacques Parizeau, and a number of other intellectuals to discuss the future of Confederation.[4] The four-evening series took the form of dour (but bilingual) scholarly exchanges, complete with the presentation of position papers and simultaneous translation. It was just the sort of high-brow affair for which CBC was famous before the tabloid-style *This Hour Has Seven Days* revolutionized the network's current-affairs programming the following year. If Pierre Trudeau appeared telegenic or sexy debating the distribution of taxation powers with future premier Parizeau, no one mentioned it.

It is probably fair to say that until 1965 Trudeau was better known to English Canadians as an anti-nuclear activist and a civil libertarian than as any kind of political philosopher. In March 1962, for example, it was announced that the "Montreal lawyer and economist" Trudeau was to sit on the board of the Canadian Peace Research Institute, an initiative of the acclaimed Canadian nuclear scientist Norman Alcock.[5] The following year, in an ironic twist that did not escape the notice of Trudeau's critics in Quebec, English-Canadian editorialists lauded "Professor Trudeau" for defending the civil liberties of FLQ detainees held by Montreal police without charge or access to legal counsel.[6] In January 1965, the *Globe and Mail* reported that Trudeau would sit on a five-person commission established by federal justice minister Guy Favreau to study "the problem of hate literature."[7] (On that commission, Trudeau would meet thirty-three-year-old University of Toronto professor Mark MacGuigan, setting in motion a long and close political association that would later see MacGuigan serve as Trudeau's foreign minister.)

Not until January 1965 did English Canadians get their first real introduction to Trudeau, when Peter C. Newman ventured to Montreal to interview him for the *Toronto Star*. At that time, the thirty-six-year-old Newman was a far bigger star in the Canadian cultural firmament than Trudeau and, in truth, a more influential presence in the national political conversation than many elected officials. He was still riding the crest of his massive success with *Renegade in Power* (1963), a groundbreaking political portrait of Prime Minister John Diefenbaker that had sold thirty thousand copies in its first ten weeks in print and vaulted Newman into the publishing stratosphere.[8] If a single English Canadian can take credit for inventing Trudeau and sparking Trudeaumania, it is Newman. As the *Star*'s man in Ottawa in the 1960s and as the country's leading popularizer of Canadian political history, Newman and his florid prose would become the narrative voice of Trudeau's ascent in Canadian politics.

Newman likely knew in January 1965 that Trudeau was sequestered away, grinding out his signature brief "Quebec and the Constitutional Problem." He certainly recognized Trudeau as a formidable intellectual and iconoclast. "Trudeau, who works in a bare cubicle at the University of Montreal's Institute of Public Law, is the founder of *Cité libre*, the journal which provided the Lesage reform movement with its original ideological thrust," Newman wrote. "Now 45, he wears outrageously ill-matched clothes and maintains the detached view of his environment which has often got him into difficulties." Even then a lively raconteur, Newman indulged his readers with the tale of how Trudeau had caused a "minor riot" in Moscow's Red Square in 1952 by throwing snowballs at a statue of Stalin. For his part, Trudeau was only too happy to report to Newman that separatism was already a spent force in Quebec politics and, moreover, that ordinary Quebecers were more interested in bread-and-butter economic issues than in lofty appeals to nationalism.

Newman concluded astutely that Trudeau may have spoken too soon. "Despite Trudeau's optimism," he warned, "the Quebec revolution could be reignited through unforeseen violence or a breakdown in the already strained relations between the Lesage and Pearson governments."[9]

Trudeau knew by 1962 that he and his small band of federalist allies in Quebec were powerless to stop the tsunami of *maîtres chez nous* nationalism. The key question, then, is not why they opted to join the Pearson Liberals in 1965 but why they did not do so sooner. The answer is a simple one. They were not welcome in the federal Liberal Party until the national-unity crisis had become truly desperate.

Pierre Trudeau, Jean Marchand, and Gérard Pelletier—the "three wise men" or "*les trois colombes*"—began discussing the idea of entering federal politics together as early as 1961. Had it not been for Lester Pearson's *volte-face* on the question of acquiring nuclear warheads for Canada's Bomarc missiles, Trudeau and Marchand would likely have sought Liberal nominations in the 1963 federal election. But they were furious about Pearson's nuclear flip-flop, Trudeau especially, judging it to be nothing but a crude political gamble designed to confound the Diefenbaker Tories. By agreeing to place nuclear warheads on Canadian soil, the Liberals had acted with "brutal cynicism" and "selfish docility," Trudeau fumed in *Cité libre.* "What idiots they all are!"[10] (He was not alone in his anger. The election took place a mere six months after the Cuban Missile Crisis, when superpower brinksmanship had very nearly brought the world to nuclear war.)[11] In the 1963 campaign, Trudeau threw his support behind the NDP candidate in the riding of Mount Royal, Charles Taylor, rather than the Liberal incumbent, Alan Macnaughton. He did so in spite of his objection to the NDP's *deux nations* policy on Quebec, so strong was his aversion to nuclear weapons.[12]

On the Bomarc issue, the thick-skinned Pearson was not fazed by being called an idiot—by Pierre Trudeau or anyone else. "I was right and they were wrong," he wrote bluntly of his critics.[13] Moreover, as Pearson well knew, this was not Trudeau's first shot across the federal Liberals' bow. In his 1958 article "Some Obstacles to Democracy in Quebec," Trudeau had blasted the party for cynically maintaining its "machine" approach to Quebec politics well after it had abandoned the practice elsewhere in Canada. "The shameful incompetence of the average Liberal M.P. from Quebec was a welcome asset to the government," Trudeau had asserted. "The party strategists had but to find an acceptable stable master—Laurier, Lapointe, St. Laurent—and the trained donkeys sitting in the back benches could be trusted to behave."[14] Trudeau knew, of course, that such comments did nothing to endear him to the Quebec caucus of the Liberal Party.[15] More surprising, perhaps, was that some Liberal stalwarts from outside Quebec never forgave him for this drubbing. Toronto-area MP Ralph Cowan, for example, would wage a one-man vendetta against Trudeau well into the Trudeaumania period, circulating copies of his old speeches among party members with terms like "idiots" and "trained donkeys" duly highlighted.[16]

"You can well imagine," Trudeau wrote in a private letter to historian Ramsay Cook, who was then a member of the NDP, "that my decision to enter politics on the Liberal side was a difficult one."[17] The decision was just as difficult for the Liberals. Even if they ignored his earlier diatribes, they knew that Trudeau was a complete neophyte in electoral politics. His friends acknowledged as much. "There was no great pressure in the Liberal Party to get Trudeau to run," Marc Lalonde later recalled. "Nobody in 1965 said, 'Here goes the next PM.' He still had this image of a semi-dilettante, and therefore that he would be a kind of patrician in politics—you know, do it for a while, and then go on to something else."[18]

The truth is that Pierre Trudeau was invited into federal politics in 1965 not as a messiah but as an adjunct. The real prize—the man Pearson had been courting for years—was the charismatic, bilingual Quebec labour leader Jean Marchand. "He was one of the most attractive personalities I had met in a long, long time," Pearson said of Marchand, "quick in every respect: physically, mentally, emotionally."[19] The only problem was that Marchand flatly refused to enter federal politics without his friends Trudeau and Pelletier. "We are of the same generation," said Marchand of the trio. "In going alone to Ottawa there would be the risk of being overwhelmed. By being three, without necessarily always having the same views and the same ideas about things, we can enrich one another and protect one another."[20]

Pearson did not hesitate. Like any smart head coach, he agreed to take the second-stringers Trudeau and Pelletier in order to get the star Marchand. He just had to finesse the deal a little to satisfy his recalcitrant party colleagues, particularly when it came to the former *Le Devoir* editor, Pelletier. "It was more difficult to get enthusiastic acceptance in the organization for Pelletier than it was for the other two," Pearson said later, "because, while Pierre Trudeau had made some pretty tough speeches about nuclear arms and about myself in that context, Pelletier had been writing editorials day after day about the iniquity of the Liberal regime. He had made it very hard for some of our men to get elected in 1963, and it was not easy for them to welcome him with open arms or, for one or two of them, to welcome Pierre Trudeau with any enthusiasm."[21]

As it happened, the prime minister's plan to bring the three Montrealers into the Liberal caucus could not have been better timed. Over the course of 1964 and well into the 1965 federal election campaign, the party's old guard from Quebec was hobbled by a series of low-grade scandals from which it would never recover. Two of

Pearson's ministers, Maurice Lamontagne and René Tremblay, were implicated in the so-called furniture scandal for having allegedly taken gifts in kind from a bankrupt Montreal furniture dealer. Yvon Dupuis, Pearson's minister of state, was charged with conspiracy and influence-peddling for allegedly taking a bribe in the course of licensing a racetrack in his riding (he was later acquitted). Most damning of all, Guy Favreau, Pearson's justice minister and the head of the Quebec caucus, was forced to resign following the "Rivard affair," in which government officials were alleged to have taken bribes to abet the prison escape of a Quebec drug dealer.

The tarnishing of so many leading Quebec Liberals was a gift to Marchand, Pelletier, and Trudeau, and they knew it.[22] The party had sanctioned members of the old guard, Trudeau reiterated smugly in 1964, "not so much for their ability to serve democracy as for their ability to make democracy serve their party, their main qualification being familiarity with machine politicians and schemers."[23] If he and his friends had anything to say about it, Trudeau was signalling, the days when Quebecers would sit quietly in the backbenches and let English Canadians run the country were over.

Lester B. Pearson is today a far more venerated Canadian prime minister than he was in his own time. As his biographer Andrew Cohen has observed, Pearson's long list of policy firsts—the Canada Pension Plan, the *Medical Care Act*, the Order of Canada, the Canadian flag—have taken their place as some of the most important identity markers for modern Canadians.[24]

Where the Pearson Liberals foundered was on the national-unity file, though not for want of trying. The arch-Tory John Diefenbaker was prime minister when the Quiet Revolution transformed Quebec in the early 1960s. He dismissed French-Canadian nationalism and openly stonewalled Quebecers' *deux nations* conception of Canada with the blunt assertion that as long as he was in charge, there could be but "one Canada." Pearson, on the other hand, who spent the years 1958 to 1963 as leader of the Opposition, was sympathetic to Quebec nationalism and temperamentally inclined to accommodate it. "While Quebec is a province in this national confederation," he observed in a 1963 speech, "it is more than a province because it is the heartland of a people. In a very real sense it is a nation within a nation."[25] After winning the April 1963 federal election—albeit with only a minority government—Pearson actively sought out new opportunities to reform Canadian federalism. He believed that if the central government ceded certain powers to the provinces, particularly in matters of social and cultural policy, it could meet Quebecers' demand that they be *maîtres chez nous* without undermining national unity.

One vehicle through which the new prime minister hoped to achieve these reforms was the Royal Commission on Bilingualism and Biculturalism (the Bi and Bi Commission), which he launched in 1963 under the leadership of Davidson Dunton, president of Carleton University, and André Laurendeau, editor of *Le Devoir*. For months, the ten-member commission held informal hearings across Canada. Its official mandate was to report on the status of Canadian francophones in government bureaucracies, private businesses, and public education, but it ended up taking the pulse of the entire country. On February 1, 1965, the Bi and Bi Commission released its highly anticipated interim report (the so-called *Blue Pages*). "Canada, without being fully conscious of the fact, is passing through the gravest crisis in its history," it announced ominously. "What is at stake is the very fact of Canada: what kind of country will it be? Will it continue to exist?"[26] Although the commissioners' own opinions varied as greatly as those expressed in the mountain of briefs and transcripts they had amassed, they unanimously recommended a national policy of two official languages for Canada.[27] But the big story was the public "uproar" the commission itself had caused, as Pearson put it.[28] On its first day in print, the *Blue Pages* sold an incredible five thousand copies, becoming an instant bestseller and demonstrating that national unity was a growing national obsession.

In July 1964, when Laurendeau, Dunton, and their co-commissioners were still out on the road talking to Canadians, Prime Minister Pearson and the premiers convened a federal-provincial meeting in Charlottetown, P.E.I. The idea was to pay homage to the Confederation conference that had been held in that city one hundred years earlier and to use the anniversary to sign off on the "Fulton-Favreau formula" for amending the Canadian Constitution. Named after Diefenbaker's and Pearson's justice ministers, this complex amending procedure had been negotiated by the feds and the provinces over several years. It envisaged different thresholds of consensus for different sorts of constitutional change. But on the key question of language, it demanded full-blown federal-provincial unanimity. Bora Laskin, then a University of Toronto law professor and later chief justice of the Supreme Court of Canada, observed at the time that the Fulton-Favreau formula was far too "rigid" and thus "too high a price to pay for what would be a rather empty trapping of independence."[29] Like most of Canada's constitutional scholars, including Pierre Trudeau, Laskin was wary of both decentralization and constitutional tinkering. In the end, though, the debate over Fulton-Favreau mattered little. To Pearson's everlasting disappointment, the formula foundered in 1965 when the Lesage government withdrew its support.

Like so many of his successors, Prime Minister Pearson was far more successful in accommodating Quebec's demands through practical negotiations on specific problems than through sweeping constitutional change. He consulted often with Premier Jean Lesage, whom he knew well but thought "highly strung, brilliant and rather temperamental."[30] Pearson's government institutionalized new channels of federal-provincial coordination, even helping to facilitate the international outreach of Quebec's cultural agencies.[31] Before establishing the Canada Pension Plan, for example, the feds met secretly with the Lesage government not only to negotiate the conditions under which Quebec could opt out but to make the idea palatable to the rest of the provinces.[32] So great and so genuine was Pearson's eagerness to accommodate Quebec that by 1965 his efforts began to look, even to impartial observers, like appeasement.[33] "The dynamism of the new Quebec and the confused and undiscriminating responses of the rest of the country to its demands have resulted in a situation where Canadians as such are not agreed on pursuing a common set of important purposes together," wrote UBC political scientist Donald Smiley, echoing the Bi and Bi report. "Some such consensus must be created in the foreseeable future if Confederation is to survive in recognizable form."[34]

Pierre Trudeau shared Smiley's views entirely. If the Canadian prime minister himself held a *deux nations* notion of the country, there would be no satiating the nationalist appetites of Quebec (or even Canadian) politicians. Trudeau did not attend Pearson's Charlottetown conference in July 1964, but he did submit a thirty-one-page brief (in English) entitled "Concepts of Federalism." It contained all of the defining elements of the political program he had formulated in "La nouvelle trahison des clercs" and "Quebec and the Constitutional Problem," but it came bundled with prescriptive advice for the English-Canadian politicians he presumed would now be reading him. Only federalism, wrote Trudeau, could find "a rational compromise between the divergent interest-groups which history has thrown together." And only a functional politics could dissolve "the glue of nationalism," Trudeau wrote. "I am not predicting which way Canada will turn. But because it seems obvious to me that nationalism—and of course I mean the Canadian as well as the Quebec variety—has put her on a collision course, I am suggesting that cold, unemotional rationality can still save the ship."[35]

Trudeau concluded his 1964 Charlottetown brief with an appeal for a "constitutional bill of rights binding on all governments in Canada," an idea he had been kicking around since 1955. If Canada were to entrench a bill of rights, he observed, "problems such as centralism, regionalism and provincial autonomy would be drained of much of their emotional content, and would become amenable to rational solution."[36] In public, Trudeau continued to state categorically that the *British North America Act* contained all the tools necessary for Canada and Quebec to boldly reimagine Canadian federalism. But when he had the opportunity to place his ideas directly into the hands of Canada's power brokers, as at Charlottetown, he made it clear that he had conceptualized his own Plan B for Canada. It was a bold and brazen vision. If federal and provincial politicians could not act rationally in the interests of all Canadian citizens, he was suggesting, then power must be vested in the citizens themselves.

What Prime Minister Pearson thought of Trudeau's proposed bill of rights in the summer of 1964 is difficult to discern. Not until the fall of 1967 would Pearson adopt Trudeau's ideas as the federal government's position, and only because the pressure from Quebec for constitutional change was by then implacable. In any case, when Trudeau, Marchand, and Pelletier were making their way to Ottawa in 1965, Pearson kept to his own conciliatory script—undoubtedly in the belief that the addition of such strong Quebec voices would bolster his bargaining power.

Some of Trudeau's friends, Ramsay Cook among them, had their doubts. "Pearson seemed to believe, perhaps drawing on his experience as a diplomat, that every problem could be solved by compromise," Cook later observed. "By 1965 I had concluded that while the Lesage Liberals were as unclear as anyone else about exactly what Quebec wanted, they nevertheless would continue to expand their demands indefinitely. Someone had to call Quebec's bluff, and Pierre Trudeau seemed to be the person."[37]

On September 7, 1965, Lester Pearson announced that a general federal election would be held on November 8. His two-and-a-half-year-old minority government had lasted longer than anyone expected, he told the House of Commons, and it had passed some important legislation. But Opposition MPs had returned to the fall session of Parliament determined to defeat the Liberals, so it was in the national interest that he seek a new mandate. "My decision had to be made in the knowledge that we are now facing, in Canada, issues and problems of great importance to our country's future," Pearson explained. The most pressing of these problems was the need to "reduce tensions in our country so that we can all go forward as Canadians, in unity and strength."[38]

For weeks, the prime minister's election plans had been the subject of mostly indolent speculation. Few Canadians believed that an election was warranted if, as they suspected, Pearson's main reason for calling one was simply to win himself a Liberal majority. There had been four elections since 1957, all but one had returned a minority government, and neither of the two major parties had had a change in leadership since 1958. Canadians rightly asked whether the spectacle of a fourth Pearson-Diefenbaker contest in seven years was worth either the effort or the expense. Peter C. Newman captured the public mood perfectly with the title of the book he was then writing, *The Distemper of Our Times.*

Given the alarmist tone of the Bi and Bi report and Quebec City's increasingly strident demands for a new deal within Confederation, it was in Pearson's power to make national unity the defining issue of the 1965 election. But he opted not to do so. He would run instead on a stay-the-course platform of economic and social-welfare reforms—important issues, without question, but too little differentiated from his 1963 platform to appease disgruntled voters. Pearson would live to regret this strategic blunder. From the beginning of the campaign to the day they voted, Canadians gave every impression that they neither knew nor cared what the election was really about. And not surprisingly, their ballots would reflect that caustic sentiment.

In this sense, Pierre Trudeau's entry into federal politics was anticlimactic. He, Marchand, and Pelletier had given up high-flying careers in Montreal to prevent the breakup of Canada. Yet outside Quebec, almost without exception, the stand-pat choreography of the 1965 election campaign made the three candidates little more than curiosities to ordinary Canadian voters. This fact alone explains why Trudeau appeared to come out of nowhere to take the country by storm three years later.

Inside Quebec, it was a different story. On September 2, five days before Pearson's election call, *Le Devoir* leaked the story that Jean Marchand (always first-mentioned), Gérard Pelletier, and Pierre Elliott Trudeau were in secret negotiations with the prime minister to run as Liberal candidates. Speaking freely to the Quebec press over the next few days, Marchand acknowledged that there had been agreement "in principle," essentially confirming that he would indeed be heading up the Liberal Party's "New Wave."[39] The official announcement came on September 10, when Marchand, Pelletier, and Trudeau held a standing-room-only press conference at a Montreal hotel.[40] Three members of the party's old guard—Guy Favreau, Maurice Lamontagne, and Maurice Sauvé—dutifully accompanied the new men, wearing "great big plaster smiles," as the *Toronto Star*'s Dominique Clift put it.[41] With the scandalous "Rivard affair" still in the headlines, the old guard understood that they must make way for the heirs apparent. (Indeed, Lamontagne, ever loyal to Pearson, had orchestrated the Liberals' "new look.") It fell to Trudeau to explain to intrigued reporters why he and his friends were now in cahoots with the Liberals. "Quebec's role will be fulfilled not by withdrawing and turning inward, but by accepting the challenge of living in a pluralistic society," he said. "The Liberal Party is the instrument most likely to help Quebec assume a role within Confederation and not outside it."[42]

If Marchand, Pelletier, and Trudeau thought their entry into federal politics would be smooth, they were mistaken. Quebecers had good memories and so, too, did other Canadians. Maurice Lamontagne's best efforts notwithstanding, the three newcomers were so unpopular within the Quebec wing of the party that the Liberals had difficulty finding safe ridings for them. "Their leftward-leaning opinions as well as their attacks on the Liberal 'slush fund' and the party's undemocratic structure in Quebec have earned them plenty of ill-will," noted one observer.[43] The *Globe and Mail* ran an editorial dredging up Trudeau's invective against the party just two years earlier. "The philosophy of the Liberal Party is very simple," Trudeau had said in 1963. "Say anything, think anything, or what is better, do not think at all but put us in power because it is us who govern you best." Trudeau's sudden conversion merely confirmed the wisdom of his own critique, admonished the *Globe*. Canadians should reject the Liberals' blatant hypocrisy and opportunism. "It would be a reckless country indeed that gave them the power they demand."[44]

More unexpectedly, perhaps, Marchand, Pelletier, and Trudeau were also popularly seen as having burned bridges with New Democrats. Quebec NDP leader Robert Cliche, who had himself defected from the Liberal Party in 1960, believed that if the trio had shown the least bit of grit, they would have joined the New Democrats. On September 8, Cliche published an open letter in *Le Devoir* stating that Marchand and his friends had cynically abandoned their social-democratic principles in favour of the "progressive pragmatism" of the Liberal Party.[45] Stealing the three Quebecers from the NDP was "the cleverest intellectual holdup ever organized" by the federal Liberals in Quebec, railed Cliche.[46] A week later, he gave a tough speech in Quebec City in which he predicted that the three Liberal newcomers would be "gobbled up" by the business class that owned the party.[47]

Tory leader John Diefenbaker was delighted with Pearson's election call, of course. Hoping that voters would punish the scandal-plagued Liberals at the polls, he was only too happy to fuel Canadians' disenchantment. Diefenbaker reminded voters that he was the only party leader with the fortitude to stand firm against Premier Jean Lesage's escalating demands. Now that the three wise men, and Pierre Trudeau in particular, had arrived in Ottawa to fight for a united Canada, Diefenbaker went on the offensive. Speaking in Brownsburg, Quebec, he reminded a partisan crowd that Trudeau had once said of the Liberals, "There doesn't seem to be an individual in the party to whom principles mean more than power." Now, however, Trudeau and his friends were hoping that Canadians would forget their past. "These are the men who now say they saw a new light!" hooted Diefenbaker.[48] Quebec Progressive Conservative Association president Jacques Bouchard also disparaged the trio. "They've entered the arena at last and will be watched with interest," Bouchard told an Amos, Quebec, crowd, "but I don't think they'll be the Maurice Richards of the Liberals."[49]

The heat on at least two of the wise men—Trudeau and Pelletier—was so intense that they felt compelled to defend their decision to join the Liberals in a jointly written article in *Cité libre.* "For Quebeckers in search of a dynamic federalism and of a progressive social policy, the Liberal option at this time is the most realistic and the most constructive," they wrote. "For us, there has been no break and we renounce none of our convictions. We have resolved only to lead in another setting and through different means the intellectual and social struggles we have always led."[50]

The English-Canadian press corps was mostly unimpressed with Pearson's early election call, calling it cynical and wasteful. (In this estimation, they were joined by much of the world press, from the

New York Times to *Pravda.*) Yet many of the country's leading news outlets had by this time adopted the language of crisis to describe Quebec's demand for a new constitutional deal within Confederation. In early September 1965, to cite but one example among many, the Canadian Press posted an alarmist report, quoting Oxford professor Max Beloff to the effect that separatism or even associate statehood for Quebec could be "fatal" for Canada.[51] Dailies across Canada duly reprinted such stories, invoking the doom-laden tone of the Bi and Bi report.

In this unsettled atmosphere, many Canadian editorialists were plainly relieved by the appearance in federal politics of such distinguished Quebecers as Marchand, Pelletier, and Trudeau—but not unreservedly. "Trudeau, after fifteen years of sniping from the sidelines, finally decided to join the Liberals," wrote Keith Cronshaw of the *Montreal Gazette*, the English-language daily with the largest stake in the constitutional debate.[52] The *Globe and Mail* called Pearson's recruitment of the three Montrealers a "truly exciting occurrence" but insisted that they more properly belonged in the NDP.[53] Before the *Globe* was willing to give the trio its endorsement, Canadians would have to know "how far left of centre are their views on such non-racial subjects as the welfare state and the nation's economy."[54] A *Toronto Star* editorial gushed about what a "prize catch" the three Quebecers were. "In effect, three of the best minds and hearts in French Canada have decided to join in the main task of nation-building," said the *Star*.[55] Peter C. Newman called Trudeau, Pelletier, and Marchand "the Three Musketeers" in his *Star* column. "These gallant, middle-aged ex-revolutionaries have taken a risky stand," Newman wrote, "which clearly identifies them as Quebeckers who believe in the Canadian future."[56]

Even those not entirely enamoured of Trudeau and his friends agreed that they had shown courage in entering federal politics, not least because they had been cast as "traitors" to Quebec by the likes of the RIN's Pierre Bourgault.[57] "Unlike many other aspiring politicians," the *Globe and Mail* noted wryly, "Mr. Gerard Pelletier, Mr. Jean Marchand and Mr. Pierre-Elliott Trudeau were not motivated by dreams of fame and influence—and $18,000 a year—which attract most members of Parliament."[58]

On September 26, 1965, Trudeau announced that he would seek the Liberal nomination in Mount Royal, a seat the party had held since 1940 and considered safe. "It is a riding which as far as I can see has a democratic organization, a fairly active association and a very honest one," he told reporters. "It has a mixed population, English-speaking and French-speaking, with several ethnic groups within each language group. It is the kind of riding I'd like to work in and a convention where I'd stand a good chance."[59] Alan Macnaughton—the Liberal incumbent against whom New Democrat Charles Taylor had run in 1963 with Trudeau's support—graciously announced his retirement to make way for Trudeau. A minor controversy erupted because Mount Royal was considered by some constituents to be a "Jewish riding" in need of a Jewish MP. But Trudeau paid scant attention to it. He was far more anxious about the prospect of running against Charles Taylor, with whom he disagreed fundamentally on the concept of *deux nations* but maintained a close professional relationship.[60]

In contrast with Marchand and Pelletier, whose nominations went unchallenged in the ridings of Quebec West and Montreal Hochelaga, respectively, Trudeau had a fight on his hands. Competing for the Mount Royal nomination were Monty Berger, a public-relations executive, Sophie Cresthol, the widow of long-time Liberal MP Leon Cresthol, and Victor Goldbloom, a Montreal pediatrician. Vote-carrying delegates in the riding association numbered 265, but nearly a thousand people turned out on the evening of October 7 to hear the "law professor and millionaire bachelor" Trudeau debate his challengers.[61]

By all accounts, there was not the slightest hint of Trudeaumania in evidence on that auspicious night. Whereas the charismatic Jean Marchand was already out on the campaign trail tearing strips off the Tories—"A federal government which crushes the provinces and imposes one language from coast to coast—you may achieve this, Diefenbaker, but over our dead bodies!"—Trudeau's political skills were described as "fledgling," his personality as "coldly logical."[62] Yet pedantic though it was, Trudeau's first political speech contained all the key elements of the program he had been developing since the 1950s. He was opposed to Quebec separatism, he told the Mount Royal crowd, but also to Canada's becoming "a loose confederation of provinces." He was not in favour of "tinkering" with the Constitution, since he believed that the *British North America Act* contained the right balance of powers. "I pledge to maintain Confederation intact," Trudeau concluded, "and to help this country achieve the great future which I believe is in store for it."[63]

Always better in print than at the podium, Trudeau distributed a one-page "Open Letter to the Delegates to the Mount Royal Nominating Committee" to shore up his candidacy. Again, he highlighted the key elements of his program, including his commitment to Canadian federalism and his worry that Quebec was drifting towards "extreme provincialism." The letter began, "After many years as a critic of the political scene, I decided to take an active part in politics and for the first time joined a political party. The Liberal party provides me with the best means of fulfilling my political ideals."[64] The prose was not his most exhilarating, but the Mount Royal delegates must have liked what they heard and read. On October 8, Trudeau won the nomination on the first ballot (the vote count was not made public). The scene was thus set in Mount Royal for the battle of the academics, as one observer put it, Trudeau versus Taylor.

As it turned out, there was not much of a battle—in Mount Royal or anywhere else. Across Canada, turnouts at all-candidates meetings were abysmally low, confirming voters' indifference. Most Canadians perceived that the Liberals had concluded the campaign just as they had started it—by appealing to voters for a majority mandate but saying little about what they hoped to accomplish with it. On election night, November 8, Canadians voted almost exactly as they had in 1963, their distemper now fully fused. The Liberals were returned with a second minority government, winning 131 seats of 265—a meagre four-seat increase. Only 74.8 per cent of eligible voters cast a ballot, compared with 79.2 per cent in 1963. The prime minister was said to be "bitterly disappointed" by the election results, but he rejected any suggestion that he would make common cause with the NDP.[65] British Columbia premier W.A.C. Bennett spoke for many exasperated Canadian voters. "I'm very pleased that the people of Canada did not give a majority to the Pearson government because as I said in the election campaign, they had not earned the right to it," Bennett said. "And now the prime minister has no alternative but to resign."[66]

Pearson did not resign, of course, but instead suffered through one of the most merciless media onslaughts ever to greet a victorious Canadian prime minister. "The Liberal Party subjected the electorate to the most sophisticated, the most premeditated, the most cold-blooded blackmail this country has ever seen in an election," complained a *Globe and Mail* editorial. "Give us a majority, they threatened, or you will face another election within weeks. As it should always be with blackmail, the people declined to submit."[67] British Columbians congratulated themselves for "refusing to go along with Liberal pleas for majority government" and voting for the status quo (the exception being the addition of a new B.C. seat for Social Credit).[68] Only in Quebec did Liberals make notable gains. Their share of the popular vote, at just over 45 per cent, was the same as it had been in 1963. But they acquired eight additional seats for a total of fifty-five (of seventy-four). Even so, Quebec's pundits were unimpressed. "Les

Canadiens ont voté exactement pour rien" (Canadians voted exactly for nothing), observed the *Journal de Montréal*.[69] "Du pareil au même" (Just more of the same), added *Le Soleil*.[70]

All three of the wise men were elected—Trudeau and Pelletier easily, Marchand only with a last-minute surge to defeat Créditiste Lucien Plourde.[71] There was never any doubt that the Liberals would hold on to Mount Royal. Trudeau won handily, with 27,877 votes to Charles Taylor's 14,911. It was a decisive victory, but Taylor could take credit for reducing the Liberal vote since 1963, when Alan Macnaughton had won with 28,793 votes to Taylor's 8,911.[72] At 9 p.m., Charles Taylor called Trudeau at his headquarters on chemin de la Côte-des-Neiges to concede defeat.

"I'll be back again, Pierre," said Taylor.

"You'll be welcome," replied Trudeau.[73]

Taylor was gracious in defeat but not uncritical. "It is always sad to see a man of the left in a right-wing party," he told the Quebec press. "Canada has demonstrated a new polarization of its politics between two parties. My friend Pierre Elliott Trudeau has been elected through the votes of conservatives."[74] (Taylor would take one last shot at elected office, in 1968. After that, as his sister Gretta Chambers has recalled recently, "he decided to settle down and become a philosopher.")[75]

Trudeau gave a short but ponderous victory address. "This vote is a clear indication of ethnic and cultural maturity in a riding with a small minority of French-Canadians," he told his constituents. "The fact that I am the first French-Canadian chosen to represent you is, to me, an indication that Canada can, if it wishes, hold fast to that ideology deeming all men equal."[76] Ambushed by a CBC journalist before he knew that the Liberals had failed to win a majority, Trudeau made far more assertive off-the-cuff remarks. "I still think that the Liberal government can do a darn good job in Ottawa," he said, "and I think the onus will be on the opposition now to try and defeat any laws which we think are urgent for the future of the country."[77] Asked (in English) whether the strengthened Quebec contingent in the Liberal caucus would mean an inordinate focus on that province, Trudeau rejected the idea. "It will not be biased toward Quebec," he said of the new Liberal government. "It will be governing for Canada as a whole."[78] Later in the evening, Trudeau joined Pelletier and Marchand for a victory celebration at the Club de réforme in Montreal.[79] His friends joked that it was now too late for him to back out of federal politics.

Canadians took note of the changing of the Liberal guard in Quebec. The election had "purged the taint of scandal," wrote the *Vancouver Sun*'s man in Montreal, Stan McDowell. "With its new and highly respected recruits, the party can now begin to rebuild its prestige."[80] Frank Howard at the *Globe and Mail* warned that a second Liberal minority government might "make it easier than ever for Quebec to slip quietly and almost painlessly out of Confederation."[81] Howard's *Globe* colleague Robert Rice, on the other hand, speculated that the progressive views of Trudeau, Pelletier, and Marchand "would dovetail with the demands of the NDP, and help to keep the Government in power despite its lack of a majority."[82]

The big story coming out of Quebec on election night, however, had nothing to do with ballots. A bomb threat was received at a polling station in the Montreal riding of Cartier, prompting officials to evacuate the building and call in the bomb squad. "I received the word from Ottawa to clear the polls," said returning officer Jean Bouchard. "I've been pretty rattled by the whole thing."[83] Other irregularities reported from Montreal included the break-and-enter theft of Liberal voting lists from party offices and vandalism at Guy Favreau's riding headquarters. Police cruisers had had to patrol all of the city's polling stations.

The final edition of the *Vancouver Sun* ran the sensational front-page headline, in forty-eight-point type, "'Bomb' Slows Montreal

Voting."[84] Minority governments had become a Canadian commonplace. Separatist violence had not.

Prime Minister Pearson had missed one enormous opportunity when he chose not to put national unity at the centre of the 1965 campaign. He missed another when he selected his new ministers.

Jean Marchand entered the cabinet directly, as everyone knew he would. But he was named minister of citizenship and immigration, a second-tier appointment that highlighted Pearson's continuing reluctance to put a Quebecer in charge of a financially significant portfolio (finance, trade and commerce, external affairs, defence, health and welfare, transport).[85] Some Canadians' hopes were dashed. The Quebec caucus was once again "padded" with mediocrity, lamented Peter C. Newman. "Not only did [Pearson] by-pass the luminous talents of Pierre-Elliott Trudeau and Gérard Pelletier, but he also failed to promote Jean Chrétien, a young but solid New Guarder."[86] Only in January 1967—over a year later—would Pearson promote Marchand to the position of Quebec leader. This was an important symbolic gesture, but it failed to mitigate the perception in some quarters that English Canadians were still running the country.

One person who was not disappointed by Pearson's cautious cabinet manoeuvres was Pierre Trudeau. The newly elected member from Mount Royal wanted to ease into his new job. This meant mastering his brief as a novice MP but also, apparently, striking the right work-life balance. On January 3, 1966, the Liberal caucus met for the first time since the election to confer upon Pearson the traditional unanimous vote of confidence. Trudeau was one of only six MPs missing from the meeting. He was "on holiday."[87] When the prime minister informed Jean Marchand that he was considering naming Trudeau as his own parliamentary secretary, Marchand had to strong-arm his friend into accepting the opportunity.

"Give me time to get settled, to do my homework. You know I don't like to go into anything unprepared," Trudeau pleaded.

"We didn't come here to refuse to work, Pierre," Marchand replied. "What brought us here is that there's a job to be done, and we have to grab every opportunity to do it."[88]

Trudeau agreed to take the position, which essentially meant serving as the prime minister's mouthpiece in the House of Commons. Once again, the country's pundits mined out Trudeau's earlier jabs at Pearson and the Liberals, drawing Canadians' attention to the "amusing irony" that he would now serve as Pearson's underling.[89]

Where the prime minister actually stood on the Quebec question at this critical juncture remains the subject of debate. Historian Kenneth McRoberts believes that Pearson never gave up on the idea that Quebec was "a nation within a nation." He therefore sought to groom Jean Marchand rather than Pierre Trudeau as his successor, in part because Marchand "did not have the same objections as Trudeau to special arrangements for Quebec, nor did he share Trudeau's visceral antagonism to Quebec nationalism."[90]

But Pearson's position on Marchand and Trudeau may have been more nuanced, even in early 1966. In his diary, André Laurendeau related a fascinating conversation on January 25 of that year, after bumping into his old friend Jean Marchand. (The two had worked together most recently on the Bi and Bi Commission.) "Pierre T." was astounding English Canadians, Marchand told Laurendeau. "I'm willing to bet my shirt that within a year Pierre will be their big man in French Canada, eclipsing all the others." At this news, Laurendeau "made a face." He told Marchand that the anti-nationalist Trudeau was "a poor informer when it comes to present-day Quebec." Marchand responded sympathetically. "I wanted him in Finance," he told Laurendeau. "But when I learned the Prime Minister wanted him close by, what could I do?" Laurendeau concluded this diary entry by noting that Marchand had taken the extraordinary step of warning Pearson "in writing" about Trudeau's being out of step with Quebecers.[91]

Wherever Pearson might have stood, no one had trouble decoding the optics of Trudeau's promotion to parliamentary secretary. Opposition leader John Diefenbaker observed haughtily that the Liberals finally appeared to be "running away" from special status.[92] "In the national field I say deliberately that this is a government which has whittled away the basic principles of Confederation," Diefenbaker told the House of Commons on January 20, 1966.

> It has bent to demands. It has virtually brought about a position in this country whereby provinces may become, if not sovereign states, associated states. I am glad to see that there are now some in the Liberal party who are standing against that. I think of the hon. member for Mount Royal (Mr. Trudeau), already honoured as Parliamentary Secretary to the Prime Minister. Read what he has to say about this idea of special status for any one province or associate states. He takes the strongest possible objection. It is of interest that when we took that stand we were pictured as being anti-Quebec. What was heresy when we stood for it is now approaching orthodoxy within the Liberal party.[93]

Other Canadians agreed that Trudeau had moved a considerable distance up Ottawa's greasy pole. "This New Wave Liberal, with his vast knowledge of political and economic affairs, will likely be playing a key role in the establishment of federal policies toward Quebec," observed the *Toronto Star*'s Dominique Clift. "As parliamentary assistant to Prime Minister Lester Pearson and as one of his trusted advisers, Trudeau will be in a strategic position to make his influence felt."[94]

Clift was correct. Trudeau was now in a strategic position, and it was not an opportunity he intended to squander. Over the winter of 1966, Trudeau began to hit his stride, both as a stump speaker and as a parliamentarian. With ever-increasing rhetorical precision and power, he offered his Liberal colleagues, Parliament, and Canadians in general his views on how best to move federalism forward. On the evening of February 23, 1966, for instance, Pierre Berton interviewed Trudeau on his CTV television show. Berton asked Trudeau directly what he thought about Quebec's demand for special status. "You can't have an operative system of government," Trudeau replied, "if one part of it, province or state, has a very different set of relationships to the central government than the other provinces."[95] Trudeau also suggested that the federal government stop crafting policies that allowed Quebec to opt out—the modus operandi of the Pearson Liberals, though he did not say so expressly. Pressed by Berton as to whether he would "go against" Quebecers on special status, Trudeau replied with the bravado for which he was becoming well known. "That's their tough luck, Mr. Berton."[96]

Other opportunities followed. In May 1966, Trudeau told a Montreal meeting of the American Society of Newspaper Editors that bilingualism could be legislated, but biculturalism could not. "There is no way in which two ethnic groups can be made equal before the law in one country," he said. "To talk of two nations is to introduce something corrosive."[97] To the Canadian Club of Montreal, Trudeau argued that the effect of special status would be to reduce recognition of Quebec in the rest of Canada. "If Quebec is to be the nation-state of the French Canadians, then the rest of the country will be the nation-state of the English-speaking," he observed. "Under this type of set-up, French-speaking persons would have no reason to be in Ottawa."[98] Speaking in Vancouver, Trudeau warned English Canadians not to underestimate the sovereignist threat to Canada. "Once a section of a nation finds that the values it holds precious would be better protected by withdrawing from that nation, then there is nothing you can do to prevent the withdrawal."[99]

In Parliament, where Trudeau now had one of the best seats in the house (compared to Pelletier, who was stranded on the remotest backbench), he was not only becoming "more vocal" but impressing the gallery with his "facetious interjections during Opposition speeches."[100] In June 1966, Independent Progressive Conservative MP Maurice Allard asked Trudeau to set up a joint parliamentary committee on the Constitution, followed by a national constitutional conference. Trudeau rejected the proposal outright, calling it "absolutely useless."[101] Not only would such a committee do nothing to advance the constitutional debate, Trudeau told Allard, but it would become "a place of discord or mutual sterilization."[102] A week later, the Opposition raised the matter again, suggesting that an all-party constitutional committee could take advantage of "the spirit of our centenary" and reaffirm national unity. Trudeau was again dismissive. "Members of the opposition who are asking for this committee remind me of men walking in the dark who do not know where they are going and who want to hold hands with other people because they are afraid of getting lost alone," he replied. "I think this is the precise time when we should not throw the constitution open to this kind of debate."[103]

At this early stage of his political career, Trudeau was still extraordinarily patient in his verbal responses to Opposition parliamentarians—knowing, of course, that he spoke for the prime minister. (*Hansard* for these years is filled with page upon page of Trudeau's painstaking expositions.) But every once in a while, he demonstrated his dry wit. Créditiste MP (and sovereignist) Gilles Grégoire, for example, asked the following question of Trudeau during a tedious 1966 debate on agricultural production. "If the minister wants to quote statistics in this house, he should also be ready to give the source of such statistics. Otherwise, how can we know what they are worth? He did not quote the source of his statistics. What is the source of his statistics, that is what we want to know from the minister." Trudeau's answer: "Statisticians."[104]

In the spring of 1966, when Trudeau was only three months into his tenure as parliamentary secretary, a watershed event occurred—for him and for Canada. Over the weekend of March 25, the founding convention of the Quebec section of the National Liberal Federation of Canada was held in Quebec City. The convention was attended by roughly 1,200 Quebec Liberals, representing nearly every federal riding in the province. Sixty wide-ranging policy resolutions were tabled, many of them openly nationalist, others designed to promote biculturalism in Canada, one even demanding the abolition of the monarchy.

Into this cacophony of competing voices strode Trudeau, who over three days dominated the meeting and imprinted the Quebec wing of the party with his own ideas. At a workshop on "constitutional realism," Trudeau stood firmly against "provincial autonomists" like Michel Robert and argued that there was no need to open the Constitution.[105] He ridiculed Quebecers who wanted to spend "undetermined sums of money in a constitutional adventure which they have not defined, but which would consist more or less of undermining Canadian federalism and substituting a still vague form of sovereignty which would give birth to something like an independent Quebec, or associate states, or a special status, or a loose alliance of ten states, or something to be invented after political, economic and social chaos had been achieved."[106] Trudeau sponsored several key resolutions, all of which the convention ultimately approved. These included transferring social security to the provinces along with the tax resources to support this responsibility, and institutionalizing permanent federal-provincial consultation on economic policies.[107] "Quebec should not isolate itself in any way," Trudeau lectured his Liberal colleagues, "but rather integrate itself in a larger complex where it will not only find markets, but also competition."[108]

This performance was a tour de force. Trudeau was subsequently heralded as the most influential policy-maker at the convention and the main reason why the nationalist "extremists" present—many of them young Liberals—"took a beating."[109] The *Globe and Mail* devoted an editorial to the event, congratulating the three wise men for speaking "in a straightforward fashion for which their party had not recently been noted. They were strong, but they were reasonable; and they were able to take, and persuade the convention to take, a more Canadian—as opposed to Quebec—position than has yet come out of Quebec."[110] Trudeau was widely praised for saying that the only constitutional changes he would approve were those that granted all provinces equal autonomy and those that treated anglophones and francophones equally. Peter C. Newman, who attended the convention, recognized that Trudeau's ideas had the power to transform Pearson's national-unity policy. "By officially committing themselves to keeping Quebec not only within confederation, but within the existing constitution, the federal Liberals have, for the first time, achieved a coherent point of view to defend."[111]

Newman interviewed Trudeau in the aftermath of the convention. Trudeau knew that he had set Quebec Liberals on a new trajectory, of course, but he also appreciated that this was no time for self-congratulation. "The main thing is that we rejected any kind of special status for Quebec," he told Newman. "In essence the meeting was an affirmation that federalism can't work unless all the provinces are in basically the same relations toward the central government, and that the federal system as it was conceived by the fathers of confederation is still sound."[112] Far from taking credit himself for the outcome of the conference, Trudeau mused about the lift it had given his boss. "When you think of the next big hurdles," Trudeau told Newman, "bilingualism and constitutional rights, Pearson is the best man to achieve results. If these battles are won, Pearson will probably emerge very strong."[113]

Newman and every other close observer of the Quebec scene could not miss the irony that Trudeau should credit the prime minister for steering the Canadian ship of state on its new course—Lester Pearson, the man whose directionless leadership was the very reason Trudeau had entered politics. English-language media that reported on the Liberal convention featured photographs of Trudeau for the first time, most of them unremarkable head shots. No one was yet enamoured of Trudeau's sparkling blue eyes and boyish good looks. It was his ideas they were falling for.

CHAPTER THREE
FORKS IN THE ROAD

On April 4, 1967, Pierre Trudeau bounded up the stairs of Parliament wearing a tailored blue pinstriped suit, vest, and dark tie. He was tanned and fit from a week of skiing. He would turn forty-seven the following October, but with his hair combed forward "in the style now in favor with younger ad men," as one observer put it, he looked as if he were in his thirties.[1] The parliamentary press corps was by now used to Trudeau's beatnik wardrobe—corduroy trousers, turtlenecks, bulky sweaters. But today, he was all spit and polish. Something important had to be in the offing.

It was. During the afternoon session of Parliament, Prime Minister Lester Pearson announced dramatic changes to the Liberal cabinet. Two old-guard Quebecers, Lucien Cardin and Guy Favreau, retired from the cabinet and federal politics altogether. Jean Chrétien, then thirty-three, became parliamentary secretary to the finance minister, Mitchell Sharp. Thirty-eight-year-old John Turner was named registrar general. And Pierre Trudeau, now just a year and a half into his political career, was sworn in as justice minister, the top legal job in Canada. Introducing his new lineup to the press, Pearson joked that everyone knew Trudeau was up for a promotion because he had shown up in the House of Commons wearing a tie.[2] Trudeau, Turner, and Chrétien posed for photographs with the prime minister. "The four of us are a pretty good young quartet," said the sixty-nine-year-old Pearson. "But take a picture of them six months from now and see what they look like."[3]

The new justice minister was plainly delighted with his promotion. In contrast with his indifference at being named Pearson's parliamentary secretary, Trudeau knew that he had now made the big time. "It's a wonderful position, a powerful ministry whose decisions have considerable effect on the lives of the citizenry," he later recalled. "And I had carte blanche."[4] A reporter asked him how he felt after his swearing-in as justice minister. Trudeau replied that it was a good job, but he was "not sure about the prospects." Everyone present got the joke. Liberal ministers of justice were famous for their high rate of turnover. Asked what he would bring to the justice department, Trudeau replied that he was reluctant to comment on specifics. He mentioned that a review of the Canadian *Criminal Code* was already under way, which was timely because he held liberal views on divorce, homosexuality, and abortion. (It would take the Canadian Conference of Catholic Bishops less than two days to produce a formal letter cautioning the government against liberalizing Canada's abortion law.)[5] Trudeau added that he thought there was also room for reform of administrative tribunals, contempt-of-court cases, and other legal mechanisms.

In English Canada, Pearson's cabinet shuffle was widely seen as a much-needed infusion of youth into the Liberal ranks. The *Toronto Star* called the newcomers "men of ideas and vigor."[6] The *Calgary Herald* agreed, expressing the hope that they would "help to shift the political outlook in Quebec from its narrow, separatist bent."[7] Peter C. Newman observed that the "big winner" was Canadian federalism. "By promoting Pierre-Elliott Trudeau and Jean Chrétien, the Liberal party's most articulate and impassioned French advocates of federalism," wrote Newman, "Lester Pearson appears to be abandoning his longtime policy of non-confrontation with Quebec."[8] The *Montreal Gazette* praised the prime minister for putting Trudeau's "rigorous intellect to good use."[9] *Globe and Mail* columnist Dennis Braithwaite caught an early glimpse of the emerging Trudeau mystique, noting that the new justice minister was "the closest thing to a Kennedy image in Canadian politics. Trudeau is handsome, he has the well-known Gallic voltage, he is cool, intelligent, amused, articulate; and he speaks English with scarcely a trace of accent."[10]

Opposition leader John Diefenbaker congratulated Trudeau on his promotion. "I like to see young men finding their way on Parliament Hill," he said.[11] The day after the swearing in, Diefenbaker took Trudeau to task in Question Period, as everyone knew he would.

Would the new minister "give early consideration to the convening of a national constitutional conference?" asked the Tory leader.

"I want to thank the Leader of the Opposition particularly for starting off gently by asking me a difficult question," Trudeau replied. "On the issue itself, I must say that I have not been in Cabinet long enough yet to change my mind." This riposte provoked a round of laughter in the House. Assuming a more serious tone, Trudeau asserted that because there was no consensus in Canada on how best to approach the Constitution, he thought the country was not yet ready for such a conference. "I feel that precisely because we have avoided such confrontations," said Trudeau, "we are permitting responsible politicians everywhere to arrive at the conclusion which we on this side of the house have reached, namely that time is on our side."[12]

In Quebec's French-language press, the headline story following the cabinet shuffle was not Trudeau's move to justice but Pearson's inspired decision to name Roland Michener Canada's governor general. Editorial commentary on Trudeau was perfunctory. *Le Droit* and *L'Action* ran headlines quoting John Diefenbaker's quip that Trudeau was his "*âme soeur*" (soulmate) because he opposed the theory of *deux nations*.[13] An unusually combative Claude Ryan, whose worries about Trudeau's influence on the prime minister had been mounting since the Liberal convention the previous spring, accused the English-language press of grossly misunderstanding Quebec and thus of always looking for a "messiah." "The latest candidates," Ryan complained in *Le Devoir*, "are naturally Mr. Jean Marchand and Mr. Pierre Elliott Trudeau."[14] The *Globe and Mail* responded immediately to Ryan's rancour. "It's depressing that English-Canadian pleasure over the emergence of these men on the national stage should draw dour lectures from Quebec. Please allow us to be pleased, Mr. Ryan. There's little enough to cheer about in Quebec-Ottawa relations these days."[15]

Such faint appeals from English Canada did little to influence elite opinion in Quebec, of course. This was because—as *Globe and Mail* columnist George Bain put it so poignantly—"Mr. Trudeau is endlessly on record as rejecting separatism or special status."[16] Before the end of his first month as justice minister, Trudeau was widely credited with having united his nationalist adversaries in Quebec. They included party leaders Jean Lesage and Daniel Johnson, and also press luminaries like Ryan, Jean-Marc Léger of *Le Devoir*, and Marcel Gingras of *Le Droit*. Trudeau's intellectual opposition to *deux nations* had for years made him the *bête noire* of Quebec nationalists. But now that he was federal justice minister, the stakes were incomparably higher. If Quebec's national character was not accommodated in some new constitutional arrangement, the nationalists were signalling, Canada would not survive. "Mr. Marchand, Mr. Trudeau and Mr. Chretien, our great hopes of yesterday, will certainly have to readjust their aim and take the aspirations of the Quebec people into account," asserted Sylvio St.-Amant of *Le Nouvelliste*. "Otherwise they will be contributing to the completion of separatism in Quebec."[17]

The irony was not lost on Trudeau. Indeed, he had anticipated it. The closer he came to power, the more he was accused of instigating the precise catastrophe he had gone to Ottawa to prevent.

Despite Trudeau's dogged aversion to tinkering with the Constitution, events over the course of Canada's ebullient Centennial Year overtook him.

The Liberal government of Jean Lesage was defeated in the Quebec election of June 1966. The new premier, Union Nationale leader Daniel Johnson, assumed power promising to make Quebec "a true national state" within Canada. Johnson believed that if Quebec's particular needs could not be accommodated by a reformed Confederation deal, a new Canadian Constitution should be drafted from scratch. He thus announced that his government would continue the work of Lesage's two constitutional committees—one a bipartisan legislative committee and the other a group of academics. By January 1967, the academic committee was rumoured to have produced a five-thousand-page report for the government of Quebec.[18]

Not wanting to be caught flat-footed, Lester Pearson followed Johnson's lead. In January 1967, he quietly created what McGill law professor Edward McWhinney called a "task force on Confederation."[19] The new group was headed by Pierre Trudeau, still serving as Pearson's parliamentary secretary, and managed by Jean Beetz, head of the provincial-relations secretariat in the Privy Council Office. On May 10, 1967, one month after Trudeau was appointed justice minister, Pearson announced in the House that this task force would now be enlarged and run by the justice department. It was rechristened the Steering Committee on Constitutional Questions. Trudeau and Beetz remained in charge.

One person who understood immediately what it meant to place Pierre Trudeau in charge of constitutional reform was federal NDP leader Tommy Douglas. The day after Pearson announced the creation of the new steering committee, Douglas tabled a non-confidence motion in Parliament criticizing the Liberal government for failing to provide special status for Quebec.[20] The motion was defeated easily.

Diefenbaker's Tories wanted nothing to do with the NDP's *deux nations* approach to Quebec and voted with the Liberals. Undaunted, Douglas chastised Trudeau for refusing to adapt. "The Government no longer talks about patriating the constitution or bringing it up to date," said Douglas. "The Minister of Justice now wants to embalm the constitution, to put a little rouge on it and dress it up. But it will still be dead."[21]

In one respect, Douglas was correct—and it bears underscoring. Between January and September 1967, the prime minister tasked Trudeau with coordinating revisions to the Canadian Constitution—revisions that Trudeau believed were both unnecessary and dangerous. As a legal scholar, he had maintained this position since the mid-1950s, and it demonstrated his remarkable capacity for compartmentalization. In cautioning Canadians against precipitous action on the Constitution, Trudeau was not being coy. "My students are always yelling for an immediate rewriting of the Constitution," Trudeau had said during the 1965 election campaign. "But they are yelling against a dragon after his fire has gone out. It is not necessary to grab for more powers. What is necessary is to tell the politicians, 'You already have enough—do a job with them.'"[22] Two years later, he spoke philosophically about the fragility of Canadian federalism. "I feel there are a number of people who are being reckless with the constitution," he said. "I don't think people realize what a delicate mechanism the federal system is. It's not difficult at all to break up the country. Not only Quebec can do it but at least three or four provinces can."[23]

Yet Trudeau remained pugnacious when it came to his adversaries in Quebec. In late May 1967, Trudeau announced the appointment of two English-Canadian jurists—lawyer and labour mediator H. Carl Goldenberg and Professor Ivan L. Head—as his top advisers on the Canadian Constitution.[24] Asked by the press how he would respond to protests from Quebec that he had not appointed a Quebecer, Trudeau replied with a "terse obscenity" in French. Asked in the

House whether the appointments would be followed by a white paper, Trudeau dismissed the idea out of hand. "I do not think it would be necessary or proper to debate the subject in question," he said.[25]

One of the reasons Canadians seemed willing to reimagine Confederation was that they were by the summer of 1967 intoxicated by the country's centennial celebrations. As Pierre Berton recalled in his book *1967: The Last Good Year*, Canadians young and old were dreaming of limitless possibility and—uniquely in Canadian history—displaying exuberant national pride.

Never before, in peacetime at least, had patriotism been so visible, so pervasive, and so thoroughly conjoined with the Canadian state. Centennial stamps were issued, coins minted, parks and pools built or renamed, songs commissioned and sung unabashedly, histories written, films produced, and countless parades and festivals attended. Ironically, perhaps, given the simultaneous surge of French-Canadian nationalism, the crowning achievement of this outburst of national euphoria was Expo 67, the world's fair held in Montreal between April and October. When Tommy Douglas, normally an unsentimental political scrapper, tried to force the Pearson Liberals into amending the Constitution, he did so invoking the spirit of Canada's centennial. And when Pierre Trudeau's supporters defended his constitutional views against such initiatives, they did the same thing. "Let's confess: it's great to be Canadians," cheered the *Toronto Star* on July 1, 1967. "As Justice Minister Pierre-Elliot Trudeau noted the other day, we Canadians under a century-old constitution still enjoy domestic peace and liberty equaled by few other nations."[26]

It was no coincidence that the first bona fide instance of Trudeaumania took place in early July 1967 under the influence of this giddy centennial euphoria.

Lester Pearson had known by January 1967 at the latest that he could not postpone indefinitely the thankless job of reforming the Constitution. That was the month Ontario premier John Robarts announced that he would host a premiers' constitutional conference within the year. Pearson knew that he would have to get out in front of the premiers on the constitutional issue, and on July 5 an opportunity presented itself. Queen Elizabeth was visiting Ottawa as part of the city's centennial celebration, and nine of the premiers were in attendance (the only absentee being Premier Robert Stanfield of Nova Scotia, who could not attend due to the death of his brother). Pearson took full advantage. He met privately with the premiers that afternoon and invited them to a federal-provincial constitutional conference to be hosted by the feds in early 1968. In a convoluted three-paragraph communiqué issued after the meeting, the prime minister specified that a discussion of a bill of rights, "while in no way preventing a review of other constitutional matters as might later be required, would provide the opportunity to begin an examination of the constitution in relation to the fundamental rights and freedoms that should form the basis of Canadian federalism."[27]

At long last, after years of foot-dragging, the prime minister had agreed to host the constitutional conference that Quebec had been demanding since 1962. Moreover, he had paired his invitation to the premiers with a powerful assertion of Pierre Trudeau's signature idea, namely that the language rights of French Canadians should be protected everywhere in Canada by a constitutionally guaranteed bill of rights.

This announcement should have rocked the country. But almost no one noticed.

Instead, what dominated Canadian headlines that balmy July day was a brouhaha over the wardrobe of the justice minister. Pierre Elliott Trudeau had had the impudence—in this era when all men dressed in identical dark suits, white shirts, and plain ties—to wear a yellow-and-red-dotted ascot into the House of Commons!

During question period, in the midst of a tedious exchange over Trudeau's intention to pension out a disgraced judge, the straight-laced, grey-flannel Diefenbaker simply could not help himself. "The honourable gentleman," Diefenbaker admonished Trudeau, "should be more considerate of the House, dressed most improperly as he is."[28] With Pearson tucked away among the premiers, it fell to acting prime minister Paul Martin to respond. "I am sure you will agree with me," Martin told the Speaker, "that it is not within the rules of the House for one member to comment on the dress of another member."[29] Diefenbaker would not be silenced. "The proprieties of parliament are to be upheld even by the Minister of Justice," he snorted.[30]

The entire exchange took less than a minute. Yet it vaulted images of the ascot-wearing minister of justice onto the nation's front pages, inflated the question of parliamentary decorum into a national debate, and became a defining moment in the evolution of Trudeau's public persona as a sartorial renegade. True to form, Trudeau was nonchalant about the matter. "People are more interested in ideas than dress," he said afterwards.[31] When a journalist needled him about the incident, Trudeau took the bait. "If you have the address of a good tailor will you please send it to me?" Trudeau asked. "I don't think I'd like your tailor," the reporter sniffed back.[32]

George Bain at the *Globe and Mail* noted sardonically that an important milestone had been passed in Canadian democracy—and he was not referring to Pearson's proposed constitutional conference. "July 5, 1967, is a day worth remembering. July 5 is the day that Pierre Elliott Trudeau, the Minister of Justice, broke the haberdashery barrier (as we shall always remember the occurrence). So off with the collar and tie. Down with blue and grey. Never more the feet encased in restrictive oxfords. Away convention. Freedom—that's the cry."[33] The *Toronto Star* noted that Trudeau stood in good company with the likes of Victorian British prime minister Benjamin Disraeli, a dandy who once showed up in the Commons with lavender trousers, a green coat, and a purple cravat.[34] Questions were raised as to whether Trudeau's fashions had been purchased for him by a woman. "No" was Trudeau's response to this suggestion. "I'm afraid I'm responsible for all my clothes. I can't recall any woman ever giving me anything to wear."[35]

The day after the ascot incident, Trudeau arrived at the House in a traditional suit and tie, but this time with open-toed sandals. Reporters asked the prime minister whether his justice minister was under orders to wear the tie. "I don't give Mr. Trudeau orders about what to wear," replied Pearson. "Mr. Trudeau always looks in order."[36] The press dutifully sought out the opinions of stylish female MPs. "Very fetching," said Margaret Rideout, Liberal MP for Westmorland. "Mr. Trudeau would lose something that is refreshingly individual if he couldn't be himself and dress as he pleases."[37] Grace MacInnis, NDP member for Vancouver–Kingsway, added her view. "There should be as much leeway in men's fashions as in women's. Mr. Trudeau has always dressed informally. He wore his Ascot tie when he was just a member of the House and no one raised any objection."[38] Jean Casselman Wadds, Conservative member for Grenville–Dundas, played the contrarian. "I personally don't like a holiday sort of garb in the House," she said. "It wouldn't be allowed in many public dining rooms. If a man wears informal clothes to work, what does he wear to relax in?"[39]

By 1967's summer of love, of course, clothing had emerged as a key marker of generational difference in North America—along with music, hairstyle, slang, and inebriants. The public record is silent as to whether John Diefenbaker thought Pierre Trudeau was on the slippery slope towards hippiedom, but he had certainly got his point across. Later that year, as if to affirm that the times were indeed a-changin', the *Globe and Mail* awarded Pierre Trudeau the Maharishi Mahesh Yogi Award for the best-dressed man in the House of Commons, as selected by John Diefenbaker.

The morning of July 23, 1967, French president Charles de Gaulle, then seventy-six years old, stepped off the French cruiser *Colbert* and onto the federal docks at Quebec City. There, to the cheers of hundreds of ordinary Quebecers and a noisy contingent of RIN supporters, the *général* commenced an official five-day visit to Canada that had been on the books for months.

The Canadian prime minister was apprehensive about the visit, and for good reason. No one knew better than the ex-diplomat Pearson that the optics of state visits mattered more than the substantive talks. Yet even before de Gaulle had set foot on Canadian soil, Pearson knew that the feds had lost control of the choreography. The Quebec government had boldly usurped Ottawa's prerogative to plan de Gaulle's itinerary, and Pearson, rather than making a scene about it, acquiesced. This meant that de Gaulle would visit Quebec City and Montreal before Ottawa—a true diplomatic coup for a provincial government more insistent than ever that Quebec was "a nation within a nation."

Seen from the perspective of Canadian federalism, de Gaulle's visit was literally a wreck on a wreck. It started with the *général*'s official speech at a banquet at the Château Frontenac hotel on the evening of July 23. Federal ministers (and Montrealers) Paul Martin and Jean Marchand attended the banquet, but neither was seated at the head table. "What we are witnessing here," de Gaulle said solemnly of Quebecers, "is the advent of a people which wishes, in every field, to determine its own future and take its destiny in its own hands. France salutes this accession with all her soul."[40] Quebec nationalists were delighted with such a vote of confidence, of course, but as the *Toronto Star* noted tersely, de Gaulle's "brinksmanship" had put Canadians "on edge."[41]

De Gaulle, it turned out, was just getting started. The next night, speaking to a boisterous crowd from the balcony of Montreal city hall, the *général* gave the six-minute speech that famously shook Canada to its foundations. "I am going to tell you a secret which you must not repeat," he told the crowd, his body straight, his hands gripping twin microphones like handlebars, his voice throaty and hoarse. "This evening, here, and along the length of the route, I felt an excitement to match that of the Liberation!" Again, de Gaulle praised Quebec's exemplary progress and spoke of France's bonds of intimacy with French Canadians. His speech gained momentum. With every comment, he grew more animated, his voice more forceful. "*Vive le Montréal, Vive le Québec*," he said, pausing in mid-sentence to let the crowd cheer. Then, a moment later, in full voice, like a schoolmaster driving home the day's most important lesson, he said, "*Vive le Québec libre!*" (Long live a free Quebec!)

As soon as the words left his lips, the crowd roared its appreciation. The atmosphere was electric. *Fleur-de-lis* flags were hoisted and people embraced, some of them overcome with raw emotion. There was no mistaking either the context or the meaning of de Gaulle's careful phrasing. Ecstatic separatists watching him from below the balcony had been chanting "*Vive le Québec libre!*" during his speech, some of them in sweatshirts that bore the same slogan, others waving huge RIN placards.[42] "It's unbelievable!" said one elated sovereignist in the Montreal crowd.[43] And he was right.

Lester Pearson was alone at 24 Sussex that evening, watching de Gaulle's performance on television. "I could hardly believe my ears when I heard the words he uttered: '*Vive le Québec libre*,'" he later recalled. "This was the slogan of separatists dedicated to the dismemberment of Canada."[44] Pearson immediately ordered a transcript of the speech and called a special cabinet meeting for the next day. The prime minister who had done so much to accommodate Quebec nationalism—indeed, the most affable prime minister Canada had ever had—was plainly furious. "That his entry into Montreal should be compared in any way, shape, or form with his entry into Paris following the Nazi occupation was entirely unacceptable," Pearson seethed.[45]

Pierre Trudeau was in Ottawa during de Gaulle's tour, but perceiving that this was the prime minister's fight, he remained in the shadows. When Trudeau and his cabinet colleagues met with Pearson the next morning, they found their boss still angry, more determined than ever to reproach de Gaulle for his outrageous speech. Some, including the external affairs minister, Paul Martin, urged Pearson to refrain from scolding de Gaulle publicly. Trudeau, Marc Lalonde (then serving as a policy adviser to the prime minister), and some other Quebecers, on the other hand, advised Pearson to retaliate forcefully. Pearson took this hawkish advice. He went on national television and read aloud a letter he had presented to the French ambassador in Ottawa. "Certain statements by the President tend to encourage the small minority of our population whose aim is to destroy Canada," said Pearson, "and, as such, they are unacceptable to the Canadian people and its Government. The people of Canada are free. Every province of Canada is free. Canadians do not need to be liberated. Canada will remain united and will reject any effort to destroy her unity."[46]

An incensed John Diefenbaker called Pearson's letter "a mild reproof which would hardly have frightened a fly."[47] The old Tory had caught the public mood. Canadians were beside themselves. The prime minister's office was deluged with angry phone calls and telegrams advising him to cancel the remainder of de Gaulle's visit—something Pearson actually considered doing. There were protests at the French consulate on Bay Street in Toronto, where Toronto students hoisted placards that read "Go Home de Gaulle!" Editorial commentary was scathing. The *Toronto Star* published an editorial bearing the title "This Meddlesome Old Man Abuses Our Courtesy."[48] The *Edmonton Journal* characterized de Gaulle's conduct as "monstrous," the *Montreal Gazette* called it "deplorable," the *Calgary Herald,* "boorish."[49] "If ever during the Algerian war a foreign head of state had taken advantage of France's hospitality to utter publicly opinions on the solution to the Algerian problem," observed a *Le Soleil* editorial, "President de Gaulle would not have been slow in notifying him that his presence was no longer wanted and welcome."[50] Only Claude Ryan at *Le Devoir* was prepared to give the *général* the benefit of the doubt. "One hesitates to believe that a statesman as prestigious as General de Gaulle would take advantage of a foreign country's hospitality to intrude into its internal affairs," he wrote.[51]

The day after his controversial Montreal speech, de Gaulle seemed intent on tempering his apparent support for Quebec separatists. Speaking before seven thousand people at Place des Nations at Expo, he cheered "*Vive le Canada et vive le Québec!*" Daniel Johnson attended a formal dinner that evening as a guest of the French, thanking de Gaulle for opening "a new era" in Quebec's relations with France but insisting that the province would "be careful to keep open to Canada and the world the ways of fraternity and cooperation."[52] If Canadians believed de Gaulle would respond with contrition to their reproaches, they were mistaken. De Gaulle refused to apologize, saying instead, "If I am unacceptable, too bad."[53] He cancelled his scheduled meeting with Lester Pearson and announced that he would cut short his visit to Canada. "Good riddance" was the overwhelming response from Canadians.[54] The *général* flew home to Paris directly from Montreal on July 27, having never left the province of Quebec. Pearson responded with a prepared statement. "General de Gaulle's decision to cut short his visit to Canada is understandable in the circumstances," he said. "But those circumstances, which are not of the Government's making, are greatly to be regretted."[55]

In Quebec, a poll revealed that two-thirds of francophones thought de Gaulle's words meant "Quebec is free in fact but that it must try to become more so, in its own way, while remaining part of Canada." Only 17 per cent thought that de Gaulle had endorsed Quebec separatism.[56] In English Canada, the *général* had made the opposite impression. A majority of English Canadians thought that de Gaulle had indeed sanctioned separatism and that Pearson's response was not nearly strong enough.[57] RIN leader Pierre Bourgault lashed out at what he called the "extreme hypocrisy" of English Canadians. "If the Queen Mother of England can, as she has just done in New Brunswick, interfere in our internal affairs by praising the benefits of Confederation, I don't see under what pretext Gen. de Gaulle can be prevented from encouraging with all his prestige, his passion, his strength and intelligence, the poor little people of Quebec in their fight for life and liberty."[58] Interestingly, 57 per cent of Parisians polled in the aftermath of de Gaulle's "*Vive*" cheer did not approve of it.[59]

On Monday, July 31, de Gaulle escalated his public quarrel with Pearson. At a packed Paris press conference, French information minister Georges Gorse read a government statement to a standing-room-only crowd of reporters. French Canadians, said the communiqué, were not assured of "liberty, equality and fraternity" in Canada, and thus France would assist them in the "liberationist aims they have set for themselves."[60] The next day, after consulting once more with his top ministers, including Pierre Trudeau, Pearson coolly reiterated his objection to de Gaulle's meddling. "The Government of Canada has noted the statement by the President of the French Republic regarding his recent visit to Canada," he said. "It has already made its position clear on the unacceptability of any outside interference in Canadian affairs and has nothing to add in present circumstances."[61]

Not surprisingly, de Gaulle's gall was entirely too much for Pearson's justice minister, who could countenance neither Quebec separatism nor foreign interference in Canadian affairs. Now that Pearson had closed the file, Trudeau emerged from the shadows to condemn the French president outright. De Gaulle's claim that Quebecers were not guaranteed liberty, equality, and fraternity was "absurd," he said. "It is as though the Canadian Government allowed itself to say the present French constitution does not provide justice for the Basques, for Brittany, and for the islands of St. Pierre and Miquelon."[62]

On Wednesday, September 4, 1967, the Canadian Bar Association (CBA) met in Quebec City for its forty-ninth annual meeting. Pierre Trudeau was invited to give the keynote address. It was to be his first high-profile public appearance since becoming justice minister, and it was intended to establish his authority as Prime Minister Pearson's point man on national unity. More significantly, it would demonstrate that the feds' position on constitutional negotiations with the provinces—which the prime minister had promised for early 1968—was derived almost entirely from the program Trudeau himself had been developing since the 1950s. When the federal justice minister took to the stage to win over the Canadian legal establishment, he believed that he had the backing of the prime minister.

Trudeau's CBA address was succinct and powerful, couched not in arcane legalese but in the language of national unity. In other words, it was as much a political speech as a juridical one. Trudeau began by observing that one should "undermine" the existing Constitution of a democratic country only "with fear and trembling." Everyone present knew that he had taken a tough stand against tinkering with the Constitution and paid a high price for it in Quebec. Now, however, the time had come to act. The task for the federal government, said Trudeau, was to determine the best foundation on which to begin a dialogue with the provinces. "We have reached the conclusion that the basis most likely to find a wide degree of acceptance, and one that is in itself a matter calling for urgent attention, is a constitutional Bill of Rights," he said. "Essentially, we will be testing—and, hopefully, establishing—the unity of Canada. If we reach agreement on the fundamental rights of the citizen, on their definition and protection in all parts of Canada, we shall have taken a major first step toward basic constitutional reform."

Trudeau made explicit reference to the 1960 *Canadian Bill of Rights*—a federal statute in which many Canadians, John Diefenbaker foremost among them, took immense pride.[63] As every lawyer in the room knew, that bill was "statutory in character," which meant that it applied only in areas of federal jurisdiction and could be superseded by new laws. Undoubtedly for the benefit of Canadians who would before long be drawn into the debate, Trudeau took pains to explain in simple terms why the feds intended to put citizens' rights beyond the reach of the legislatures. "We all agree on the familiar basic rights—freedom of belief and expression, freedom of association, the right to a fair trial and to fair legal procedures generally," said Trudeau.

> We would also expect a guarantee against discrimination on the basis of race, religion, sex, ethnic or national origin. These are the rights commonly protected by bills of rights. But there are rights of special importance to Canada arising from the fact that this country is founded on two distinct linguistic groups. The right to learn and to use either of the two official languages should be recognized. Without this, we cannot assure every Canadian of an equal opportunity to participate in the political, cultural, economic, and social life of this country. A constitutional change recognizing broader rights with respect to the two official languages would add a new dimension to Confederation.[64]

Members of Trudeau's CBA audience had the evening hours of September 4 to digest his ideas and discuss them informally among themselves. And discuss them they did. Over the course of the next day's proceedings, it became clear not only that many of the country's top legal minds opposed Trudeau's idea of a bill of rights but that Trudeau had no interest whatsoever in hearing their views.

Several deans of Canadian law schools weighed in on Trudeau's proposals at a plenary session the morning of September 5. William Lederman of Queen's University sounded much like the Trudeau of old. He suggested that Canada would be better off without invoking constitutional change. "Remember," said Lederman, "when you specially entrench a particular matter, you take the disposition of it out of the hands of the regular legislative bodies and give the courts the last word about the limitations involved."[65] Professors Wilbur Bowker of the University of Alberta and Walter Tarnopolsky of the University of Toronto expressed similar reservations about making the courts "the ultimate guardians of political freedoms." But it was Université de Montréal law professor Jacques-Yvan Morin who challenged Trudeau's claim that enshrining individual rights could do the work of protecting collective rights. "Canada consists of two nations and if Canada wishes to endure she must guarantee the existence of two nations," Morin insisted. "Anyone who tries to use human rights as a precondition of constitutional reform is playing with fire."[66]

No one who knew Pierre Trudeau had any doubt about how he would respond to such a spirited defence of *deux nations*. Against the advice of his closest advisers, including Marc Lalonde, Trudeau insisted on participating in the afternoon's press conference. At first, Trudeau was assertive but controlled. "I think particular status for Quebec is the biggest intellectual hoax ever foisted on the people of Quebec and the people of Canada," he remarked. "Quebec is going to discover there is a lot of opposition to its demands, that they are simply not going to be met, and Quebec is going to have to back down."[67] When asked to comment on Professor Morin's commentary, Trudeau called the idea of *deux nations* a hoax as well. "If the rest of Canada is generous enough—or fool enough—to give Quebec the powers these people demand and then let Quebec impose its will on the whole country, then that is fine," he said. "You should always spoil your minorities a little bit, but this is a different thing. Behind these demands from

Quebec are people who want to have their cake and eat it, too."[68] Trudeau reiterated his central point about the political advantages of entrenching language rights. "If English Canada would take steps to guarantee and safeguard the language of their French minorities, then French Canada would lose 95 percent of its gripes," he said.[69]

If the press conference had ended at that point, Trudeau might have emerged the victor. As it was, journalists from Quebec continued to challenge his ideas, and his frustration mounted. Finally, to the astonishment of everyone present, Trudeau used the profane term *une connerie* to dismiss the notion that Quebec was the French-Canadian homeland. (Loosely translated, the word means "bullshit.") Coming from the federal justice minister, the remark was a showstopper. Even Canadians sympathetic to Trudeau's views on Quebec were jarred by it. "Mr. Trudeau has probably added to his own difficulties by allowing an element of professional intellectual arrogance to have crept into his speeches and his off-the-cuff answers to questions," McGill law professor Edward McWhinney observed. "His description of the case for a particular constitutional status or associate state status for Quebec as *connerie* was at best inelegant."[70]

Because the CBA press conference had taken place entirely in French, some English-Canadian pundits missed the significance of Trudeau's recourse to profanity. Others judged his momentary lapse of propriety as evidence of his passion for national unity. Two days after Trudeau's keynote address, the *Toronto Star* endorsed Trudeau's bill of rights categorically. "Mr. Trudeau has now put his full weight behind the bicultural solution by proposing that the right of a Canadian 'to learn and to use' either English or French be put in a bill of rights and entrenched in the constitution," said the *Star*. "We support this objective, believing that this country will not achieve unity unless French Canadians are convinced that all Canada, not just Quebec, is their homeland."[71] The *Globe and Mail* concurred. "It is good, while we ponder the privileges of collectivities, that a voice should be raised to remind us that all groups can claim dignity and worth only because they are composed of individuals," said the *Globe*. "That is the meaning of citizenship without which Canada has no meaning."[72]

In Quebec, on the other hand, Trudeau's frontal attack on special status and his warning that Quebec would have to "back down" stoked the constitutional debate as nothing had since Charles de Gaulle's "*Vive*" salute. Premier Daniel Johnson remarked that Trudeau's attitude towards Quebec was now as "paternalistic" as John Diefenbaker's. John Robarts's forthcoming constitutional conference, Johnson warned, was now "the only hope that Canada will not blow up."[73] Johnson's cultural affairs minister, outspoken Quebec nationalist Jean-Noël Tremblay, disparaged Trudeau's views as "incomprehensible and illogical."[74] Several days later, Tremblay jolted Canadians by calling for a form of sovereignty-association. Quebec now had no choice but to write its own Constitution "consecrating the French-Canadian nation" and "building our national state," he asserted. After that, a "new form of association" with the other Canadian provinces could be negotiated.[75] Rumours swirled that separatists within Daniel Johnson's government had prepared a secret document setting out a plan for Quebec's secession from Canada.[76] English Canadians rightly wondered how influential sovereignist ideas were in Daniel Johnson's cabinet.[77]

Quebec Liberal leader Jean Lesage also reacted strongly to Trudeau's CBA speech. Speaking to the Quebec Federation of Liberal Women, Lesage accused the minister of justice of being more out of step with Quebecers than ever. "By these declarations," said Lesage, "Mr. Trudeau has proven that he does not accept the soundness of certain great principles to which the great majority of our compatriots adhere."[78] Lesage then took the surprising step of asking Premier Daniel Johnson for a rapprochement. "For the love of the French-Canadian, for the love of Quebec, I ask the leader of the Union Nationale for a truce between us on partisan politics on the constitutional question," said Lesage. "We French Canadians must stop fighting among ourselves. We have got to show everyone the greatest possible unanimity on the constitutional question."[79] Lesage added that his party would never agree to Trudeau's bill of rights, since "most of citizens' rights fall under provincial jurisdiction."[80] Daniel Johnson was already on record as taking the same position.

This last point was by no means insignificant. Lesage was correct about Quebec's—or any other province's—prerogative to safeguard citizens' rights. Pierre Trudeau knew this better than anyone and, indeed, had been known in his *Cité libre* days to defend even the Duplessis government against Ottawa's meddling. What Trudeau was now saying, however, was that both levels of government, federal and provincial, would have to cede sovereignty to Canadian citizens under the terms of his proposed bill of rights. Just at the moment when Quebec's political leaders were speaking with a single voice on their demands for *more*, in other words, Trudeau was explicitly offering *less.* And he was doing so in the belief that Quebecers had a clearer sense of their own destiny than the politicians who presumed to speak for them. In the aftermath of his CBA speech, Trudeau expressly rejected Jean Lesage's claim that only nationalists could speak for Quebecers. "Those who believe in federalism do so for the same reasons that Mr. Lesage apparently does not believe in federalism," said Trudeau. "They want to promote the progress of the French-Canadian people."[81]

Trudeau's tough talk at the Canadian Bar Association turned out to be too much even for members of his own caucus. Meeting behind closed doors at the Maison Montmorency in Courville, Quebec, in mid-September 1967, federal Liberals quarrelled over how best to "crawl out of the political dead-end" in which Trudeau's "constitutional rigidity" had trapped them.[82] Some Quebec MPs, led by Maurice Lamontagne, urged Prime Minister Pearson to seek his own rapprochement with Daniel Johnson. (In response to Lamontagne's vague support for a policy of special status, Trudeau quipped, "Your particular status is the status quo, so I guess that makes me for it.")[83] The same MPs also criticized Jean Marchand, leader of the Quebec Liberal caucus, for siding with Trudeau and thus polarizing the debate. There was so much heat on Marchand, in fact, that he tried to occupy a middle ground. "Since Quebec already has an unusual constitutional status," he told the press after the first evening's deliberations, "one cannot say in advance that all notions of particular status are unacceptable. But some of these notions are not put forward very seriously, for they would lead to the disintegration of the country."[84]

Lester Pearson was unsettled by the intensity of the reaction to Trudeau's constitutional proposals, both in his own caucus and in Quebec. (It is also highly likely that the prime minister was unimpressed by Trudeau's lapse into profanity before members of the Canadian Bar Association.) Pearson's resolve weakened. He was, according to some of his own MPs, now "deeply worried by lack of unanimity in the party as to how to deal with the Quebec question."[85] In late September, the prime minister took the extraordinary step of stating publicly that as yet Trudeau spoke for neither the Liberal Party nor the government. All members of the Liberal caucus took the debate over Quebec "very, very seriously," Pearson told the press. "We'll be discussing this in Cabinet and caucus a lot. Then I think it will be up to me to make a statement."[86]

If Pierre Trudeau was disappointed or, worse, if he thought Pearson had thrown him to the wolves, he did not show it. Regret was a wasted emotion, he liked to say. He cut his losses, accepted that caution was again the watchword on the Constitution, and plunged into his work on the Canadian *Criminal Code*.

Pearson's de-escalation of the constitutional standoff impressed his Liberal colleagues, at least for a time. He had been musing aloud about retiring before the next federal election, which everyone expected to come within a year. But a leadership contest held in the current climate might take the form of a very public row over Quebec, which everyone agreed would be disastrous for the party. At a caucus dinner held on September 25, 1967, the prime minister was pleasantly surprised when two of his backbenchers, G.R. McWilliam and T.H. Lefebvre, rose to table a warmly worded "draft Pearson" resolution. In light of persistent divisions within the caucus, they stated, only Pearson could lead the party into constitutional negotiations with Quebec and, if necessary, into the next election. Every MP present voted in favour of the resolution and rose to give the teary-eyed prime minister a standing ovation.

Pearson was not the only political leader endeavouring to tiptoe through the constitutional minefield. Far from it. By the fall of 1967, it was evident that the feds and the provincial governments could postpone their date with destiny no longer. Premier John Robarts had not intended to trigger a national-unity crisis, of course, but that was the inevitable consequence of his fixing a date—November 27, 1967—for his premiers' meeting. Every party with a stake in the constitutional debate was now forced to scramble towards some kind of unified position. "The Centennial celebrations have shifted, ironically, from arts and games to survival," fretted the dean of law at McGill University, Maxwell Cohen.[87] And he was not alone in fretting.

While Lester Pearson was quietly trying to heal the breach in his own caucus, members of the Progressive Conservative Party were feuding openly over the related questions of special status for Quebec and John Diefenbaker's fitness to lead. In August 1967, the Tories had held their own "Thinkers' Conference" at the Maison Montmorency. The keynote speaker was Marcel Faribault, the prominent Quebec businessman and federalist whose personal commitment to *deux nations* would decisively affect the course of the 1968 federal election.

At Montmorency, Faribault pressed hard to persuade the Tories that special status for Quebec was the only means of saving Confederation. "The question of the two nations is no longer debatable in the province of Quebec," he insisted. "You must put, in the preamble of a new constitution, something which recognizes that there are in this country two founding peoples."[88] Faribault faced considerable opposition, but he managed in the end to persuade the convention's resolution committee to adopt the following precepts: "That Canada is and should be a federal state. That Canada is composed of two founding peoples (*deux nations*), with historical rights who have been joined by people from many lands. That the Constitution should be such as to permit and encourage their full and harmonious growth and development in equality throughout Canada."[89]

Then and later, Tory strategists agonized over the exact meaning of the parenthetical insertion of the phrase *deux nations*. This question would come to haunt them throughout the 1968 campaign against Pierre Trudeau. Some PCs read the French term *nation* as more or less synonymous with the English word, an interpretation that evoked the idea of a "sovereign state." Others, including Nova Scotia premier and federal leadership hopeful Robert Stanfield, understood the term *nation* to carry a more nuanced meaning. They believed that it considered Quebecers as a "people" or a "society"—or what Faribault himself would later call "a nation in the sociological sense."[90] On September 6, at the national convention of the Progressive Conservative Party, the policy committee voted to approve Faribault's *deux nations* concept by a vote of 150 to 12. The members also voted to extend protections for French-language education across Canada.

Both ideas were extremely contentious. Party leader John Diefenbaker gave a rousing speech to convention delegates the evening of September 7, urging them to vote against the policy committee and support instead a "one Canada" policy.[91] To Diefenbaker, *deux nations* remained anathema. "The theory that Canada is two nations can only lead to division and dissension and finally to de-confederation," he told convention delegates, sounding very much like Pierre Trudeau. "I don't believe that the true heart of French Canada wants the two nation idea. I hope that the convention will repudiate it before we leave here."[92] Although Diefenbaker's struggle to retain the party leadership had more to do with internal party politics than with national unity, he nonetheless put delegates on notice: a vote for *deux nations* would be a vote against him personally. He was delighted when the convention agreed to table the *deux nations* resolution but not vote on it. He could not, however, salvage his leadership bid. Diefenbaker went on to lose the Progressive Conservative leadership to Stanfield, and lose badly.

Even the federal Tories' headaches paled in comparison with the emergency now facing the Quebec Liberal Party. The day after leader Jean Lesage appealed to Premier Daniel Johnson for a truce on the Constitution, his star MLA, René Lévesque, appeared before his Montréal-Laurier riding association and asked delegates point-blank to support *souveraineté-association*. "Quebec should become a sovereign state," said the plain-speaking Lévesque. "To English Canada we must then propose to maintain an association not only of neighbours but also of partners. We would have a regime within which two nations, one whose homeland would be Quebec, the other arranging the rest of the country to suit itself, would associate themselves in a new adaptation of the current formula of the common markets to form a new entity which could, for example, call itself the 'Canadian Union.'"[93] There was never any doubt what the Liberal delegates of Montréal-Laurier would decide. They voted to approve Lévesque's proposal and also to table it at the convention of the Quebec Liberal Federation scheduled for October 13, 1967.

Lévesque's *souveraineté-association* speech was published in full in *Le Devoir* and excerpted extensively across Canada. Editorialists everywhere recognized immediately that Lévesque's words had escalated the constitutional crisis. "The tension in the dialogue between French and English Canada increases," said a *Globe* editorial. "The prospects for derailment of a united Canada seem to grow greater."[94] In Ottawa, the Liberals were reportedly "jolted" by Lévesque's speech, prompting Prime Minister Pearson to accelerate planning for his 1968 federal-provincial conference.[95] Lévesque's proposal also had the effect of bringing Pierre Trudeau and Maurice Lamontagne into agreement on both the need for a timetable for constitutional reform and "the necessity of making a more articulate strategy."[96] Some of Trudeau's allies credited him anew for his incisive critique of nationalist politics in Quebec, since it now appeared that bipartisan demands for special status in the province had indeed emboldened the separatists. Ironically, René Lévesque's speech also appeared to strengthen Canadian federalism, at least superficially, since it forced advocates of *deux nations* in Quebec to distance themselves explicitly from his sovereignty option.

Chief among these advocates was Quebec Liberal leader Jean Lesage, who announced immediately that he would fight Lévesque's separatist vision. Quebec should seek "the maximum degree of autonomy compatible with the existence of Canada," Lesage asserted.[97] Eric Kierans, president of the Quebec Liberal Federation, also rejected Lévesque's proposal out of hand. "This party is not a separatist party," he said. "It is an anti-separatist party and it will remain so."[98] Later the same week, Kierans told CBC-TV that he would resign from the Liberal Party if it endorsed Lévesque's separatist program. In truth, this was not much of a threat. Even before Lévesque had pitched *souveraineté-association* to his own constituents, a poll of Liberal MLAs revealed that 88 per cent supported special status for Quebec but not sovereignty.[99] By the time the provincial Liberals held their party convention as planned over the weekend of October 13, the major players had already staked out their positions. The defeat of *souveraineté-association* was a foregone conclusion. Lévesque did not wait around for the inevitable. He withdrew his resolution and announced his resignation from the Liberal Party.[100] Hundreds of Quebec Liberals left with him.

For Pierre Bourgault, his young RIN comrades, and thousands of other sovereignists, René Lévesque's break with the Liberal Party was the fork in the road they had long been waiting and hoping for. Thereafter, events moved at lightspeed. Two weeks after he left the Liberal caucus, Lévesque held a press conference to proclaim that a broad-based sovereignist party could win power in Quebec within four years. (He was off by five.) Two weeks after that, on November 19, 1967, he hosted a meeting of sovereignist groups from across Quebec that resulted in the founding of the Mouvement souveraineté-association.[101] Less than a year later, the MSA would be recast as the Parti Québécois. It would unite all but the FLQ extremists and their ilk under a single sovereignist banner with the genial social democrat Lévesque at the helm.

All of a sudden, the separatist threat to Canada was no longer hypothetical.

In early October 1967, before René Lévesque's formal break with the Liberals, Premier Daniel Johnson offered the feds an olive branch. It could not have come at a better time.

Johnson happened to be in Hawaii, where he was taking a rest cure for a bout of phlebitis. *La Presse* reporter Martin Pronovost flew to Hawaii to track down the premier and query him on the recent surge of separatist activity in Quebec. For his efforts, Pronovost had to settle for a statement from Johnson, which *La Presse* published on October 3. "The Union Nationale did not receive a mandate to build a Great Wall of China around Quebec," read the communiqué. "We promised the people to exercise the rights recognized in the *British North America*

Act and to put them to work to obtain a new Canadian constitution, made in Canada, by Canadians and for Canadians, by virtue of which every citizen, French-speaking or English-speaking, regardless of ethnic origin, would feel at home everywhere in Canada." The statement concluded with a gentle prod at federalists who refused to see that Canada could be the homeland of two nations. "It is a disservice to the country to label as separatists all those who are looking for democratic and peaceful ways to achieve the emergence of the French Canadian nation," it stated.[102]

"Made in Canada" was certainly a far cry from "égalité ou indépendance," Daniel Johnson's earlier appeal. The relief felt in Ottawa at the premier's new spirit of co-operation was almost palpable. It fell to the federal justice minister to respond on the government's behalf. "We are in perfect agreement with Premier Johnson," Pierre Trudeau told the House of Commons on October 5. "We are happy that he is finally coming around to our point of view."[103] In a press scrum later the same day, Trudeau affirmed that government ministers were truly delighted. "This is the position we have taken for a devil of a long time," he said. "I think it takes some of the heat off, in the sense that the statement is a very reasonable position." As for Johnson's point that all nationalists were not separatists, Trudeau responded with an equally light touch. "I think this is perfectly true, but I hope the converse is also true, that one doesn't become a traitor simply because one wants to defend Quebec's rights at the federal level and works for continuance of a stronger Canada."[104]

When the interprovincial Confederation of Tomorrow conference convened in Toronto in late November 1967, Premier Johnson carried with him a twenty-two-page brief that set out the position of his government. It began with a fallacy that has bedevilled negotiations between Quebec and the rest of Canada up to the present. "In Canada there exists a French-Canadian nation of which the mainstay is Quebec," stated the brief. "It can likewise be said that there exists an

English-speaking nation, although its cohesion and self-awareness may, for understandable reasons, be less apparent than they are among French Canadians." The document was half-correct. Quebec may well be imagined as the national homeland of French Canadians, but as constitutional experts have been reminding Canadians for decades, *there is no Canada without Quebec.* "The Rest-of-Canada enjoys only a shadowy existence," Professor Alan C. Cairns wrote poignantly in 1997. "It is the empty chair at the bargaining table. It is headless and therefore officially voiceless."[105]

Under the subheading "An Impotent Constitution," the Quebec brief went on to state that the *British North America Act* was "no longer capable of providing the guarantees that should properly be expected from it." It must, therefore, be scrapped. A new Constitution must be written to "acknowledge the existence in Canada of two nations, bound together by history, each enjoying equal collective rights." It must clearly designate English and French as the country's official languages, and it must include a "charter of human rights" governing areas of federal jurisdiction. In order to placate the other provinces, such a constitutional makeover would have to be accompanied by massive decentralization. "All provinces would, at the outset, be granted identical constitutional powers," asserted the brief. Once the provinces had acquired all of the powers that Quebecers needed to achieve their dream of nation—in "international relations, culture, manpower and the administration of justice"—the other provinces could cede them back to Ottawa if they wished.[106]

Unsurprisingly, Johnson's proposal did not appeal to his fellow premiers. Even before Alberta premier Ernest Manning showed up in Toronto, he stated that he would oppose any plan to extend French-language rights across Canada. (When Trudeau learned of this reaction, he responded drily, "I am sure Mr. Manning's point of view will be listened to with great respect and I am suggesting that it won't change our plans.")[107] Other provincial delegations proved more accommodating. Ontario and New Brunswick offered to provide French-language educational opportunities province-wide, while Newfoundland, Saskatchewan, and B.C. agreed to offer French-language instruction in areas where student numbers warranted it. These initiatives derived mainly from the *Blue Pages* of the Bi and Bi Commission, which had recommended almost two years earlier that English and French become the official languages of any province where francophones made up 10 per cent or more of the population. Seen from the perspective of Quebec nationalists like Daniel Johnson, these accommodations did little to "acknowledge the existence in Canada of two nations." Tellingly, Johnson could find no takers among the premiers for his proposal to junk the Canadian Constitution.

Pierre Trudeau kept a wary eye on the premiers' meeting. Months earlier, he had stated publicly that he hoped it would not be "a demolition job" on the federal government, setting off a minor row with Premier John Robarts.[108] Several days before the start of the conference, NDP MP Andrew Brewin pressed Trudeau in the House of Commons to attend the meeting himself and make clear his government's position on a bill of rights. Trudeau skewered this suggestion and along with it the New Democrats' *deux nations* policy. "Mr. Speaker," said Trudeau, "the member should know that the federal government is not invited to that conference; it is an interprovincial and not a federal-provincial conference. Nevertheless, I hope that members of his party will attend the conference to get better information on special status. It seems that his own party shilly-shallies on that matter."[109]

After being confronted by reporters at the Canadian Bar Association conference, Trudeau knew a political trap when he saw one. He remained in Ottawa and dispatched his top advisers Jean Beetz, Carl Goldenberg, and Marc Lalonde to serve as his eyes and ears on the ground in Toronto.

In public, Lester Pearson continued to put the best face he could on national unity. In a year when the world had beaten a path to Expo 67, the prime minister had no desire to sound alarmist. He met with Premier John Robarts on December 1, 1967, and enjoyed an amicable debriefing on the Confederation of Tomorrow conference. Robarts reported that premiers Daniel Johnson and Ernest Manning had departed Toronto in a more conciliatory frame of mind than when they had arrived, and thus the future of constitutional negotiations looked promising. The genial Pearson played into Robarts's optimism, telling the premier that "we should capitalize on the momentum and good will of Toronto, and transfer progress to the federal-provincial front."[110]

Among his top ministers, however, the prime minister was far less sanguine. In a "secret" cabinet memorandum entitled "Preparations for Constitutional Discussions," Pearson recounted, in detail, his steadily deepening anxiety about national unity over Canada's Centennial Year. "A full constitutional confrontation in the course of 1968 and after is probably unavoidable," he concluded ominously.[111]

Trudeau pored over the prime minister's twelve-page memo and made copious marginal notes.[112] With only one or two caveats, he was pleased with what he read, and for good reason. Pearson had finally cast off his own doubts and moved decisively towards Trudeau's tough-minded position on Quebec. (It is even possible that the prime minister had by then decided to retire and leave the next round in the constitutional debate to his successor, whom he hoped would be a French Canadian.) "Time is running against National Unity and the Federal Government," Pearson warned. No longer content to "avoid being drawn into any federal-provincial negotiations," the prime minister now perceived that the feds had to act decisively "before provincial positions become crystallized." In particular, "there is a serious risk that Quebec [could] endorse some new principles without any regard for whether they are negotiable." What was needed, Pearson asserted, was a "Constitutional Bill of Rights" that would frame the entire constitutional debate and "put the provinces in the position of having to react."[113]

The words were Pearson's, but the ideas were mainly Trudeau's. There would be no more hedging, no further concessions to accommodationist voices in the federal Quebec caucus. The prime minister knew that his minister of justice had a few items to clear off his desk over the last few weeks of Canada's eventful Centennial Year. But the scene was now set for a showdown with the government of Quebec, with Pierre Trudeau cast in the role of gunslinger.

CHAPTER FOUR

FROM CELEBRATION TO SURVIVAL

One of the items cluttering up Pierre Trudeau's desk in December 1967 was a major revision to Canada's divorce laws.

According to a central tenet of the Trudeau myth, it took a determined forty-eight-year-old bachelor to drag Canada's divorce law kicking and screaming into the modern era after nearly a century of nervous neglect. But what is striking in retrospect is the extraordinary prudence with which Trudeau steered an unremarkable bill into law. Striking as well in this context, and therefore worth repeating, was his capacity for compartmentalization. An enduring element of the Trudeau enigma today—although a fact little known to his contemporaries, apparently—is that Lester Pearson's liberal justice minister was a devout Catholic who could not personally countenance divorce. (When Trudeau's own marriage broke down in the 1970s, his departing wife, Margaret, had to petition for divorce in a manner prescribed by the law that Pierre himself had written. The irony could not have escaped her.)[1]

The question before Canadians in 1967 was whether the existing legal grounds for divorce—what Trudeau himself called the "traditional marital offences" of adultery, sodomy, bestiality, rape, homosexuality, and physical or mental cruelty—remained sufficient. Trudeau's view, and the view of the vast majority of Canadians who had appeared before the House of Commons / Senate joint committee on divorce, was that they did not. The time had long since passed, almost everyone agreed, when a bad marriage should be granted dissolution only when one spouse could prove the guilt of the other. What was needed was language acknowledging that couples themselves knew best when their differences were irreconcilable and their marriages unsalvageable. Trudeau thus proposed that "marital breakdown" be added to the list of grounds on which a divorce petition could be sought. Whether this addition was a radical departure from the existing law, or merely a minor modification of it, would turn out to be open to debate.

Trudeau tabled his *Divorce Act*, Bill C-187, for first reading in the House of Commons on December 4, 1967. Knowing that MPs had not yet had the opportunity to read the twenty-seven-clause bill, he had the advantage of describing it in broad strokes and extolling its virtues. The challenge in drafting the new legislation, Trudeau began, was to codify what, exactly, the concept of marital breakdown meant. Since the courts obviously could not be left to themselves to decide when a marriage could not be salvaged, the bill contemplated five criteria: the long-term imprisonment of one spouse, gross addiction to alcohol or narcotics, the disappearance of a spouse for more than three years, the refusal (or inability) of one partner to consummate the marriage within a year, and desertion.

Anticipating that his liberalized divorce law might get a rough ride from Canadian conservatives, Trudeau adopted the obvious strategy. He positioned himself as a conservative. He was not ten minutes into his introductory remarks before he had paid sentimental homage to the sanctity of the Canadian family and twice boasted that his bill had earned the approval of "many of the Christian churches."[2] Indeed, as Trudeau would point out repeatedly over the course of the debate, his bill did not go nearly as far in the direction of liberalizing the law as many of Canada's religious leaders would have liked! In their briefs to the joint committee, the United Church of Canada, the Anglican Church of Canada, and the Canadian Jewish Congress had advocated discarding the old grounds for divorce wholesale and replacing them with the single, all-encompassing ground of marital breakdown. "While recognizing that this viewpoint has much to commend it," Trudeau told the House, "the bill has not been prepared on this basis, but retains the traditional marital offences as grounds for divorce."[3]

Trudeau's cautious, pedantic, and at times obsequious defence of the bill was masterful. Tory leader Robert Stanfield told the House that his party fully supported reform of the divorce law and looked forward to reading the bill. New Democrat Andrew Brewin, who sat on the joint committee, congratulated the minister of justice for having the courage to modernize an antiquated law but then rebuked him for playing it safe. Trudeau, said Brewin, had had a "clear-cut choice between two basic theories in respect of the dissolution of marriage." He could have affirmed "divorce by consent" but instead saddled Canadians with the same old "divorce by judicial decision."[4] Trudeau asked Brewin, a lawyer, whether he thought there was any "legal propriety" in asking the courts to assess marital breakdown. "I think not," Brewin responded. "Once the marriage has broken down, then I suggest the marriage is dead and it is the duty of the court to dissolve it."[5]

The next evening, December 5, Bill C-187 progressed to second reading. Trudeau spoke from a prepared text for roughly an hour, discussing the history of Canadian divorce law, jurisdictional issues (including provincial jurisdiction over legal separation), and what he believed his new bill could accomplish. He spoke most eloquently on one principle, however, which had implications well beyond the divorce law: that "theological or sacred" concepts could no longer be legislated in multi-ethnic societies like Canada. "I think one of the fundamental tasks we must achieve in this parliament is to avoid mixing the sacred and the profane," said Trudeau. "We must realize we are living in a pluralistic society, and even though some laws may be repugnant to the morals of individual members they must realize that we are all here to legislate not our own personal morals upon the country but to seek solutions to evils which arise in a civil society."[6] He reiterated that the reform of Canada's divorce code had been undertaken with the greatest respect for Canadians' religious convictions. "This is merely a permissive law," said Trudeau. "It is not dealing with moral beliefs. Indeed I think it is theologically acceptable, even to the most stringent of Christians."[7]

In response to the criticism that retaining the traditional marital offences left a needless burden on Canadian couples, Trudeau made three points. First, if marital breakdown were the sole criterion for granting a divorce, Canada would require a new system of courts, which would take years for Ottawa and the provinces to negotiate. Second, he affirmed, under the new law, the courts would enjoy a good deal of leeway. "If honourable members read the law very carefully," said Trudeau, "they will see that some of the sections are quite wide."[8] His third argument was the cleverest. What if conservative judges used a vague law to obstruct the granting of divorce altogether? "We did not want a situation to develop where some courts would not be granting divorces in any and all cases," Trudeau assured the House. "We wanted to put in our law a direction to the courts that they must grant a divorce when certain evidence of breakdown or of offences exist."[9]

All in all, it was a compelling defence. The bill received unanimous approval in principle on second reading, which Trudeau correctly read as evidence that he now had the upper hand.

Final debate on Bill C-187 began on December 14. For four days, MPs weighed in, and Trudeau simply listened (or at least appeared to do so). Not until the late afternoon of December 18 did he re-enter the debate, thanking MPs for their input and responding methodically to their concerns. With passage of the bill now assured, an emboldened Trudeau emphasized how innovative and progressive it was. "The bill itself speaks of breakdown and this is more than lip service," he bragged. "This is a completely new approach in our law, of course."[10]

The final day of the debate, December 19, was the longest and by far the most tedious. Clause by clause, hour after hour, Trudeau stood in the House fielding questions and deflecting proposed amendments. Even as the conversation went back and forth and around in circles, he evinced a degree of forbearance entirely at odds with his later reputation as a haughty and sometimes hot-headed parliamentarian. There was no trace of the *connerie* brawler here. When the debate ended, at 9:47 p.m., Bill C-187 passed unanimously and without substantive revision. All members of the House pounded their desks in approval and rose to give Trudeau a standing ovation. Bill C-187 would receive royal assent on February 1, 1968, and become law three months later.

For the minister of justice, the entire performance was a triumph. "Mr. Trudeau handled himself coolly throughout the debate," observed *Globe and Mail* correspondent Geoffrey Stevens, no doubt relieved to finally exit the spectators' gallery.[11] On editorial pages across Canada, Trudeau's pithy phrasing—we must "avoid mixing the sacred and the profane"—was commended almost without reservation. Some pundits, following Andrew Brewin's lead, took Trudeau to task for not pushing his reforms far enough. But Trudeau was quick to respond that the government had accomplished as much as it could, given the constraints of Canadian federalism. "I think we have gone as far as we can under this law," he told the press. "That is to say, we have gone as far as we can without embarking on a prolonged and involved process of federal-provincial consultation."[12] (He was correct about this. When asked to comment on Trudeau's new law,

Quebec premier Daniel Johnson stated that he thought divorce should become an area of provincial jurisdiction.)[13]

Marc Lalonde had cautioned Trudeau early in December 1967 that he was taking a huge gamble in reforming Canada's divorce law. But he noted as well that the potential upside was enormous. If he got his bill passed, the justice minister would be credited with taking the lead on what could have been an ugly, divisive, and career-ending national debate.[14] Lalonde was proven right. Trudeau got credit not only for defending his own convictions but for demonstrating statesmanship. He had correctly gauged Canadians' evolving views of the private and public spheres, he had steered the divorce debate with consummate professionalism, and, above all, he had won the day. "Justice Minister Pierre Trudeau grappled with a huge and hoary issue," observed the *Globe and Mail*. "By urging members of Parliament not to impose on the country their own religious, moral and ethical convictions, Mr. Trudeau expressed a growing—and healthy—conviction that the state has no business legislating individual morality."[15]

Trudeau gained momentum. Two days after his triumph on the *Divorce Act*, he tabled Bill C-195, an omnibus bill designed to update some of the most controversial aspects of the Canadian *Criminal Code* (alongside less contentious changes to Canadian penitentiary, parole, and customs law).

Work on the seventy-two-page bill had begun before Trudeau was named justice minister, but by the time it entered public debate, Canadians saw it as his legislation (and do still). By agreement with Opposition parties, he introduced the bill for first reading in the House of Commons on December 21, thus allowing MPs the Christmas recess to familiarize themselves with its contents.[16] What this timing meant in practical terms was that the contents of Bill C-195 would be debated not in Parliament but in the media. Perhaps not surprisingly, two aspects of the omnibus bill—the legalization of therapeutic abortions and the decriminalization of homosexuality—drew the most coverage. In any other context, several other elements in the bill—the abolition of capital punishment, the tightening of gun control laws, the creation of government-run lotteries, and the mandating of roadside Breathalyzer tests—would probably have received far more public scrutiny.

Lester Pearson first raised the matter of reforming Canada's abortion law in February 1967, stating that he hoped it could be achieved within a year.[17] The existing abortion statute dated from 1869 and was draconian. Anyone procuring an abortion could face life imprisonment, a punishment that had inevitably driven the practice underground.[18] The law was also ambiguous. As Trudeau himself noted, section 209 of the *Criminal Code* allowed abortion in cases where the life of the mother was at risk, while sections 237 and 238 forbade abortion altogether. (Journalist Michael Gillan discovered in December 1967 that of the roughly one hundred therapeutic abortions performed in Toronto hospitals over the previous year, the great majority were performed on women whose lives were not at risk.)[19] Under pressure from members of the medical profession and various women's groups—and in the face of mounting evidence that tens of thousands of illegal abortions were being performed every year with sometimes lethal consequences for Canadian women—the public debate had shifted over the course of the 1960s. The health of pregnant women, broadly defined to include mental as well as physical health, became the pre-eminent concern. Medically sanctioned "therapeutic" abortions thus represented a cautious first step towards women's reproductive freedom.

Pierre Trudeau knew, of course, that revising the abortion law would be a political minefield—worse even than reforming the divorce code. At a June 1967 press scrum, when the Breathalyzer reforms were making headlines, a journalist had asked him about his intentions regarding abortion. Caught off guard, Trudeau replied candidly that he was not yet even certain that he could proceed. "It is a very complex problem, abortion," he mused. "A lot of the suggestions made about abortion are well-meaning, but not very operational."[20] Limiting abortion to cases of rape or incest looked good in theory, Trudeau noted, but what if such constraints led women to trump up charges? The normally loyal *Toronto Star* eviscerated Trudeau for this suggestion. "This is legalism run mad," fumed the *Star*. "The *Criminal Code* should be amended to permit a doctor to perform an abortion on a woman at her request, if he is satisfied, on reasonable grounds, that her pregnancy is the result of rape or incest. It is utterly repugnant that a girl should be forced to bear a child conceived under such circumstances. These victims should not be denied relief by the kind of legal technicalities dreamed up by Mr. Trudeau."[21] Pro-choice groups, meanwhile, demanded that the minister of justice grant women complete reproductive freedom.

Trudeau got the message. When he rolled out his omnibus bill, he announced that abortion would now be lawful in instances where a hospital abortion committee deemed it essential to the health of the mother. "I don't think lawyers are as competent as doctors to judge in these matters," said Trudeau, adding that the key word "health" could be interpreted by doctors to include a woman's mental state.[22] This middle-of-the-road reform was bolstered by the interim recommendations of the Commons standing committee on health and welfare, which had been published just two days earlier. But as the chair of that committee, Dr. Harry Harley, was forced to concede, debate had been so fractious (and the in-camera vote so close) that no consensus could be reached. Like the views of the many Canadians who had appeared before the committee or submitted briefs, MPs' opinions ranged from wanting to ban abortion outright to granting women abortion on demand. Trudeau shared Harley's belief that permitting therapeutic abortions under medical supervision was the best compromise that could be achieved in the current climate. "We've gone about as far as we dared," said Trudeau.[23]

A second and equally controversial reform contemplated by Trudeau's omnibus bill concerned homosexuality—in 1967 still classified as a pathological disease by the American Psychiatric Association and still punishable in Canada by life in prison. Seeking once again to separate the sacred from the profane, Trudeau proposed to decriminalize homosexual acts between consenting adults, knowing, of course, that many Canadians (including members of his own caucus) believed that such acts were unnatural.

Trudeau's task was eased by Alfred Kinsey's studies in the United States and the 1957 *Wolfenden Report* in the United Kingdom, both of which rejected the traditional idea of homosexuality as pathological.[24] But what clinched Trudeau's case for decriminalization above all was the timely story of Everett George Klippert. Klippert, a thirty-eight-year-old gay man living in Pine Point, N.W.T., had been charged with "gross indecency" in 1965 for the crime of having sex with other gay men. He pleaded guilty. Two psychiatrists testified during Klippert's trial that his liaisons had been consensual, non-violent, and limited strictly to adults. He was nonetheless convicted and sentenced to "detention for an indeterminate period" as a "dangerous criminal offender" under section 659(b) of the *Criminal Code.*[25] On November 7, 1967, the Supreme Court of Canada dismissed Klippert's appeal in a three-to-two split decision, affirming that he was indeed a dangerous offender. Chief Justice John R. Cartwright and Justice Emmett Hall dissented. They argued that "however loathsome" Klippert's behaviour might have been, he was patently not in the class of offenders "whose failure to control their sexual impulses renders them a source of danger." Cartwright added for good measure that he thought it was "improbable" that Parliament meant to imprison all homosexuals for life.[26]

Many straight Canadians were troubled by the Supreme Court ruling, their ambivalence about homosexuality notwithstanding. In an editorial entitled "A Return to the Middle Ages," the *Toronto Star* attacked the proposition that a gay man who had never committed a violent offence should be imprisoned for life. "Homosexuality is a practice intensely repulsive to normal people," said the *Star*. "But there is a growing doubt whether it is wise to treat homosexual acts between consenting adults as a crime."[27] The *Globe and Mail* observed that it was "strange to the point of being unbelievable that conduct in Britain which would not even bring a criminal charge can, in Canada, send a man to prison for life."[28] Toronto psychologist Stephen Neiger reported that "homosexuals are already a frightened group. This will make things even worse for them."[29] To his enduring credit, NDP leader Tommy Douglas protested the injustice of the Supreme Court ruling in the House of Commons. Since homosexuality was now understood to be "a social and psychiatric problem rather than a criminal one," said Douglas, the prime minister should move quickly to remedy the injustice.[30]

Pierre Trudeau did not have to be convinced. Two days after the Supreme Court ruling on the Klippert case, he stated that he favoured something "along the same lines" as recent British reforms that had decriminalized homosexual acts.[31] Rejecting suggestions that he strike some sort of commission to study the question, Trudeau instead acted decisively. When he tabled his revisions to the *Criminal Code*, they included an amendment permitting "acts done in private between husband and wife or any two persons, each of whom is 21 years or more of age, both of whom consent to the commission of the act."

Trudeau was also decisive in his defence of such reforms. "We decided to go for broke on this one," he told a press scrum after tabling his omnibus bill. "I feel that it has knocked down a lot of totems and overridden a lot of taboos. Take this thing on homosexuality. I think that the view we take here is that there's no place for the state in the bedrooms of the nation. And I think that what's done in private between adults doesn't concern the *Criminal Code*."[32] Pressed to defend his nonchalance about homosexuality, Trudeau was brash, then and later. "There are people saying queers will be able to pick up little boys on the street if the bill is passed," said Trudeau. "The people who say that are pretty stupid."[33] A reporter asked him slyly, "Do you expect to run into any personal roadblocks in the House over the homosexuality provisions?" Trudeau broke into howls of laughter. "I have had many homosexual friends in my life in both the artistic and intellectual communities," he liked to say. "But I was never one myself."[34]

Gay Canadians and their professional advocates were delighted with Trudeau's proposed amendment. "It will take a great deal of pressure, fear and anxiety from homosexuals," observed Dr. R.E. Turner, director of the forensic clinic at the Clarke Institute of Psychiatry. "I think this is a considerable step, with more to go."[35] An unnamed thirty-year-old lesbian spoke candidly to the press. "I think it's good to know that it's finally legal," she said. "I mean, everybody's been doing it. It would be very nice to be able to hold hands in public if you wanted to. It would be nice to be able to get married legally (homosexually) if you wanted to. But I don't think we'll ever make the grade there. You can't win them all."[36] A thirty-five-year-old gay man gave his view. "I want the right to live and be accepted as a homosexual," he asserted. "I want to be judged by my worth as an individual. If I'm dishonest, immoral or indecent, then reject me for these reasons—not because of my homosexuality. We homosexuals are here to stay."[37]

The public impact of Trudeau's omnibus bill was immense. Detailed analyses of his proposed changes to the *Criminal Code* dominated the nation's newspapers for days as Canadians tried to determine just how much of the imperious and prudish Canada of old might be jettisoned. "The Criminal Code amendments proposed by Justice Minister Pierre Trudeau amount to a radical redefinition of the state's attitude toward private conduct," gushed the *Toronto Star*. "Trudeau is the boldest reformer of them all."[38] The *Montreal Star* agreed. "The whole tenor of the amendments reflects the civilized humanity which has, since the appointment of Mr. Trudeau, characterized the government's overall attitude to the law," it affirmed.[39] Trudeau was singled out yet again for his sharp intellect, his "gutsiness," and his high-minded aversion to hypocrisy. "Anyone who saw it at first hand or on television could hardly fail to be impressed with the lucidity of the minister's explanations and the obvious quality of the thinking that went into them," wrote *Globe and Mail* columnist George Bain.[40]

Trudeau's legislative triumphs enhanced his reputation in more subtle ways as well. As a rookie MP, he had been dogged by speculation that he was a dilettante or just plain lazy, but now Trudeau's work ethic was above reproach. He had spent most of Canada's Centennial Year working fourteen hours a day on the divorce bill, the omnibus bill, and the Constitution, and everyone in Ottawa knew it. A related revelation was that Trudeau turned out to be both a good listener and a valued collaborator. "When the omnibus bill was being prepared he held a series of study groups with the members over many weeks," Liberal MP Robert Stanbury later explained. "Once a week we'd go over parts of the amending bill in the areas where there was a lot of controversy, such as firearms, abortion, lotteries, and gross indecency. When he evolves an opinion he states it vigorously and defends it vigorously. But I found him open to change if you can convince him. Once he's developed an opinion he challenges you to convince him."[41] This willingness to listen had always been Trudeau's modus operandi, wrote his friend Gérard Pelletier. "Trudeau can display enormous patience with those who discuss in good faith and he is not oblivious of the concrete consequences, whenever he puts forward a new idea."[42] Such testimonials served to humanize Trudeau, leavening his reputation as a cold and aloof intellectual.

Trudeau's original plan for his *Criminal Code* amendments was to pilot them through the House of Commons after the Christmas recess and into law by February 1968. It did not happen. The omnibus bill would die on the Order Paper, only to be resurrected as Bill C-150 and passed in the spring of 1969, after Trudeau had become prime minister.

What did happen was as unscripted as it was unprecedented. Pierre Trudeau's fortitude, inspired leadership, and straight talk on matters that touched the private lives of all citizens vaulted him into the political stratosphere. His simple, quotable aphorisms—*We must avoid mixing the sacred and the profane, The state has no business in the bedrooms of the nation*—spoke directly to those Canadians, likely the majority, for whom the sixties ethos of personal and political liberation was apposite, but never as an invitation to radicalism.[43] Then as now, Canadians understood that yoking the tools of democracy to the cause of social change took more grit than chanting revolutionary slogans or turning on, tuning in, and dropping out.

In an era when the formal political process was hobbled by incessant partisan squabbling and dithering obfuscation, Canada's clear-eyed justice minister had pushed the envelope—not nearly as far as some Canadians might have liked but "as far as we dared," as he put it himself. In doing so, he acquired a powerful new aura, captured in the slogan that would thereafter characterize his rise to power. *Pierre Trudeau is a man for tomorrow.*

At 10 a.m. on December 14, 1967—the first day of the formal parliamentary debate on Trudeau's divorce bill—Prime Minister Pearson told his caucus colleagues that he had decided to retire. "It was a dramatic moment, followed by gasps of surprise and attempts to begin a discussion," Pearson himself later recalled. "I cut this short by telling the Cabinet that this was settled, and that there was no point in anyone saying anything at all. I was going out to meet the press immediately."[44]

Verdun MP Bryce Mackasey exited the caucus meeting with tears streaming down his face, but no one else seemed particularly surprised. Pearson had turned seventy the previous April. Over the course of four general elections, he had failed to restore his "natural-governing" Liberal Party to majority status, despite Canada's enviable track record of economic growth and low unemployment.[45] As Pearson well knew, whispers about his possible successors had turned into feverish speculation after the lacklustre campaign of 1965. Since then, perspicacious journalists had been tracking the clandestine organization-building and stealthy infighting of Liberal leadership hopefuls—Mitchell Sharp, Paul Hellyer, and Paul Martin foremost among them.[46] The prime minister had won a reprieve in September 1967 when the Liberal caucus supported a "draft Pearson" motion to deal with the mounting national-unity crisis. Yet now, with René Lévesque's Mouvement souveraineté-association rallying the separatist cause in Quebec, the constitutional emergency appeared to be escalating. As veteran *Globe and Mail* correspondent Anthony Westell fretted, Pearson was exiting politics just as "Canada passes through the severest crisis of 100 years."[47]

Pearson was taken aback. He tried to reassure Canadians that he would not be a "lame duck" leader as the country headed into negotiations with Quebec but rather "an elder statesman, above the political fray." Opposition leaders Robert Stanfield and Tommy Douglas expressed doubts, wondering whether Pearson would not now end up in the role of mere "mediator" of talks with the provinces. Quebec premier Daniel Johnson had reservations of his own. "I wonder if, with the Prime Minister going, the federal government will be ready to commit itself to something specific," he said.[48] Pierre Trudeau, now routinely identified in the press as the "architect of the Bill of Rights plan," stated wryly that he was as optimistic as ever about the forthcoming constitutional conference.

The prime minister also seemed to underestimate the impact his decision would have on the day-to-day priorities of some of his top ministers. With a leadership convention looming from April 4 to April 6, 1968, and 2,475 delegates to court, the frontrunners knew they had very little time to waste. "Once I had announced my decision to resign," Pearson later recalled, "the campaigns for the leadership, which had been going on surreptitiously, came out into the open. I was aware of the great change in the devotion of these ministers to their jobs. They could not be out in the country campaigning and at the same time carry on the work they had been appointed to do in their departments." Pearson also found himself besieged by ministers seeking his advice. "One or two of them almost begged me to tell them what they should do," he recalled. "I found this rather trying, and it went on for three or four weeks as the various candidates entered the ring."[49]

Pearson was canny, of course. He wanted to give the appearance of neutrality on Liberal succession, but he also held strong views about how his party—and Canada—might move forward in light of mounting pressures on national unity. On the day he announced his retirement, he spent most of the time on the phone with party officials, family members, and at least one of his top ministers, Paul Martin, who was then in Brussels attending NATO meetings. He ate his lunch (oysters and whisky) alone and later enjoyed a quiet dinner with his wife.[50] Only two of his cabinet colleagues were summoned to 24 Sussex Drive on that historic day for an in-person chat. They were Jean Marchand and Pierre Trudeau.

It was no secret that the prime minister subscribed to the unwritten rule in the Liberal Party that its leadership should alternate between English and French Canadians. In recent months, he had gone even further, telling party members that a French-speaking leader would greatly enhance the federal government's negotiations with Quebec City—and greatly impede the Tories' electoral prospects, since they were now led by the unilingual Nova Scotian Robert Stanfield.

Among Liberals, and among Canadians more generally, it was widely believed that Jean Marchand was Pearson's odds-on favourite. Pierre Trudeau, for example, later recalled being entirely blasé about Pearson's retirement announcement because he thought Marchand the heir apparent. "In my view, the obvious successor, if he was to be a Quebecer, was Jean Marchand," Trudeau said. "It was he who had dealt with all partisan party matters, it was he who had strong public support in Quebec and the rest of Canada, and it was his candidacy that prominent Liberals were promoting in Toronto and Montreal."[51]

Yet Trudeau knew better than anyone that Marchand did not want the job. The two friends had for months been quietly discussing the Liberal leadership with Gérard Pelletier and like-minded ministers, including Edgar Benson, Larry Pennell, and Walter Gordon. "My name was being put forward," Marchand said later of these conversations, "and I always disagreed."[52] He was not in the best of health, Marchand had to remind his comrades. He also believed that he was too little known to Canadians outside Quebec and not nearly fluent enough in English.

What, exactly, Pearson, Marchand, and Trudeau discussed the evening of December 14, 1967, was therefore significant for the future of the party and the country. (Lester Pearson's memoir is light on specifics, affirming only that the prime minister hoped at least one of the wise men would allow his name to stand.) Jean Marchand later recalled that date—the first day of the divorce bill debate—as the point he realized that Trudeau was the party's best hope. "From that moment on," Marchand later recalled, "I said, 'Pierre, I think you will have to change your mind.'"[53] By all accounts, Trudeau was genuinely stunned. He had laboured in Marchand's shadow for so long that even his closest friends had not given a Trudeau candidacy the slightest consideration. Trudeau began immediately to stonewall Marchand. "I don't know this party," he told his friend, "and they don't know me. I just entered in '65. Let me work with it another five or ten years, and then I will have built my power bases, and I'll have learned something about politics and the House of Commons and the party and everything else. And then I'll do it."[54]

And that is how the situation was left when Marchand and Trudeau departed 24 Sussex Drive together. Both men agreed with Pearson that there should be a strong Quebec presence in the Liberal leadership race, but each thought the other better suited to the job. The only certainty was that they would not run against each other.

Ramsay Cook was another friend who believed that Trudeau could lead the Liberal Party to victory.

Starting in the summer of 1967, the young historian took it upon himself to boost Trudeau's profile in English Canada and also to popularize his ideas about Canadian federalism. On August 3, Cook wrote a feature op-ed for the *Globe and Mail* endorsing Trudeau's position on the Constitution. "The trouble with Trudeau," wrote Cook sardonically, "is that he states his mind clearly. He believes, in effect, that if the federal government treats Quebec as a distinct nation within Canada, Quebec will ultimately become a distinct nation outside of Canada. Consequently Mr. Trudeau favors a federalism that provides equal status for French Canadians and equal status for all provinces."[55] Several weeks later, Cook persuaded his neighbour, John Gray, president of the publisher Macmillan Canada, to bring out an English-language edition of *Le Fédéralisme et la société canadienne-française*, a collection of Trudeau's *Cité libre* essays. Prominent York University historian John T. Saywell was enlisted to write an introduction to the book in the hope that it would enhance Trudeau's name recognition in English Canada. But by the time *Federalism and the French Canadians* appeared in bookstores early in 1968, the justice minister's fame far exceeded both Saywell's and Cook's. The book became an instant bestseller.

Significantly, the French-language edition had already made waves in English Canada. All of the major dailies had received review copies of the book in October 1967. Some, including the *Globe and Mail,* ran front-page stories setting out Trudeau's federalist ideas and reacquainting readers with his *Cité libre* past.[56] Others, including the *Toronto Star,* ran editorials congratulating the justice minister on the "impeccable logic" of his case against special status for Quebec.[57] Trudeau held a press conference in Montreal on October 16 to launch his book, where he spoke openly about his vision for a bilingual Canada. "What I am thinking of is a bill of rights which will guarantee French rights across the country," he told the crowd. "If you say the government of Quebec alone represents French-Canadian aspirations, if you say that to start with, it is clear that my formula won't work. My formula tries to preserve Canadian unity."[58] For Canadians who might have found Trudeau's dense academic prose challenging to read, there was an elegant simplicity to this three-sentence précis of his federalist "formula."

In November 1967, Ramsay Cook met privately with Marc Lalonde in Toronto. Lalonde asked Cook what he thought about a Trudeau leadership bid. Cook loved the idea. He had long since abandoned the NDP and its *deux nations* policy in favour of Trudeau's federalist program. Cook agreed to discreetly promote the idea of a Trudeau candidacy among his academic friends.

With Lester Pearson's retirement announcement in mid-December, this nascent "draft Trudeau" movement went public. Just as Trudeau was riding the crest of his popularity as the author of the omnibus bill, Cook and his friends Mashel and Ethel Teitelbaum published an open letter to the justice minister. "A group of friends involved with the universities, the media, the arts and politics (in that order) would like to see you stand for the nomination this spring," the letter read. "We feel that you are the most talented candidate the Liberal Party can offer. As well, we feel that you personally may offer the best chance of a French-English rapprochement. In fact, yours is a Liberal candidacy that we could actively, enthusiastically support in the coming election. Therefore, we would like, with this letter, to extend our active support should you consider taking up the challenge."[59] Within days, the "Toronto Committee for Trudeau," as Cook's small band of artists and intellectuals became known, had also published a petition containing the signatures of six hundred Trudeau supporters.

Peter C. Newman would later suggest that academics rallied to Trudeau because they knew his work in *Cité libre* and thought of him as "one of their own."[60] Yet as Newman well knew, professors seldom agree on anything, least of all anything political. Significantly, these young university faculty members mobilized early behind Trudeau because they appreciated his ideas about Canadian federalism, which derived not from short-term political expediency but from decades of study and analysis. Trudeau's *politique fonctionnelle* and especially his reasoned anti-nationalism seemed to strike exactly the right chord in the turbulent sixties. As veteran University of Toronto historian Michael Bliss has recalled in his recent memoir, both Canada and Quebec seemed at that time to be awash in "ethnic nationalism, a kind of neo-tribalism that had ugly overtones." Bliss, who spent much of 1967 at Harvard University watching "the gathering crisis in American life," returned to Toronto as a new hire in the University of Toronto history department. He was ecstatic to find that a smart French-Canadian federalist had a concrete plan for averting a national-unity crisis. "It was astonishing to hear of the rise of the dark-horse minister of justice, the urbane intellectual, Pierre Trudeau, and also to hear of the role that Ramsay Cook had in furthering Trudeau's campaign among intellectuals in English Canada," Bliss writes. "Here was the historian engaging in the best kind of political activism on behalf of the best kind of candidate."[61]

Outside the hallowed halls of academe, the idea that a few Canadian eggheads might elevate one of their own into the prime minister's office seemed ludicrous. Frank Jones at the *Toronto Star* called Ramsay Cook and his friends "the most ineffective bunch of political rooters a candidate ever had. To start with, most of its members vote for another party—the NDP. Secondly, none of its members so far as is known are delegates to the leadership convention. And if that isn't enough, committee members admit their endorsement may be the kiss of death to a Trudeau who has to convince delegates he is a practical politician and not just a woolly academic."[62] Ramsay Cook certainly understood the optics. "The delegates may feel they can't trust the judgment of a bunch of ivory tower professors," he told Jones. But Trudeau had come up with an eminently practical plan for Canadian federalism, and Canadians would do well to consider it for themselves. "He is an extremely intelligent man with a sense of the central Canadian problems, the French and English question and the relationship between the federal and provincial governments," Cook affirmed.[63]

Veteran *Globe and Mail* correspondent George Bain pondered the virtues of the historians' candidate in twin columns published on December 27 and 28, 1967. "At the moment, old and skilled hands in the Liberal Party are inclined to hoot at the idea that Mr. Trudeau could be elected leader," Bain conceded in the first piece. But the fact that Canadian intellectuals were flocking to the justice minister might suggest to the party's "pros" that he had "the style to capture popular imagination."[64] By the end of his second column, Bain appeared to have convinced himself that Trudeau really was the Liberal heir apparent. "The one man who seems capable of catching on between now and April 4 in a way to break the race open is Mr. Trudeau," Bain concluded. "He has impressive qualifications—teacher of constitutional law, political economist, polemical journalist, late-come but fast-rising politician. Old enough at 47 not to alarm the senior element in the party, and young enough, in appearance and thought, to satisfy the youth movement."[65]

Reporting from the trenches of the draft-Trudeau movement, Peter C. Newman noted astutely that most of the presumed successors to Lester Pearson—Martin, Sharp, Hellyer, Robert Winters—came from within the party machine, where original ideas counted for very little. Far more important to establishment Liberals was nurturing the alliance between the country's political and business elites.[66] This fact alone made Trudeau a different sort of candidate. "During his brief but exciting tenure in the justice portfolio Trudeau has established himself as a child of his times," wrote Newman. "His candor, his intellectual curiosity, his astute use of the media, his championing of social reforms have suddenly thrust him into inevitable contention."[67] Pierre Berton, the popular broadcaster and author, agreed. "Trudeau is the guy who really excites me," he told Newman. "What we need is a guy with ideas so fresh and so different, that he is going to be able to view the country from a different point of view."[68]

Twenty-nine-year-old *Toronto Star* reporter Alastair Dow agreed that Trudeau's reputation as a bohemian made him the obvious anti-establishment candidate. "There's a sophomore MP who tools around Ottawa in an expensive Mercedes sports model, who is said to date some of Canada's most beautiful women, who is a French-Canadian graduate of Harvard and the London School of Economics, and who this week proposed to rip layers of Victorian prudery off Canada's *Criminal Code*," wrote Dow. "And what's more, people are saying this swinging bachelor who wears zippy (for the Commons) attire and who affects what can best be described as a receding, early-Beatles haircut should be the prime minister of Canada."[69]

Much of this feverish speculation took place during the "Christmas party season," as Ramsay Cook later put it, and was wasted on Trudeau himself. With Parliament in recess, Canada's swinging justice minister had quietly flown off to Tahiti to skin-dive and—as fate would have it—to flirt with a beautiful young woman named Margaret Sinclair.

While the tweed-jacket set was mobilizing on behalf of the absent and still-very-much-undecided Pierre Trudeau, a group of his friends in the Liberal Party began plotting in secret to build him a campaign organization. Again Marc Lalonde played the leading role, working alongside Toronto Liberal MPs James Walker, Robert Stanbury, and Donald Macdonald to broaden Trudeau's appeal to party insiders. Lalonde hosted a meeting of Trudeau loyalists on December 15, 1967—the day after Pearson announced his retirement. The group included Michael Pitfield, Pierre Levasseur, Jean-Pierre Goyer, and André Ouellet. Two other young and enthusiastic Trudeau acolytes, Gordon Gibson and Eddie Rubin, acting on their own initiative and using their own money, had by then acquired office space in Ottawa to anchor the still-undeclared Trudeau campaign. Jim Davey, a trained physicist and market researcher, agreed to manage the shop.[70]

Marc Lalonde knew his friend only too well. If Trudeau got wind of these clandestine operations to mount a candidacy to which he had not yet agreed, he might well say forget it. "I remember him going to Tahiti over Christmas, 1967," Lalonde later admitted. "He left us with no indication that he was interested at all. If anything, the indication was no, he was not interested. He really felt that Marchand was the guy who should run, that he owed it to Marchand to rule himself out."[71] With the draft-Trudeau movement gaining momentum and a campaign organization up and running, Lalonde knew he had to act. He cabled Trudeau in Tahiti and asked him not to talk to the press. It was a ruse, designed as much to keep Trudeau in the dark as to plug leaks in Ottawa. As usual, Trudeau's aides and friends had dissembled about his whereabouts to protect his privacy. The media knew only that he was "somewhere in the South Pacific."[72]

On Sunday, January 14, Trudeau returned from Tahiti to Montreal. Tanned and fit, he caught up with Jean Marchand and Gérard Pelletier over lunch at Café Martin on boulevard Saint-Laurent.

Much had happened while he had been away, they told him. Quebec Liberal Federation president Eric Kierans had become the first declared leadership candidate on January 10, followed the next day by federal defence minister Paul Hellyer. The Nova Scotia Liberal Association was holding its policy conference in Halifax that very weekend. There the federal minister of labour (and native Nova Scotian) Allan MacEachen had announced his candidacy. Several other leadership hopefuls, including Mitchell Sharp and Paul Martin, had given campaign-style speeches. When the conversation rolled around to the critical question of placing a Quebecer in the leadership race, Trudeau discovered that little had changed since he and Marchand had met at 24 Sussex Drive exactly one month earlier.

"Pierre, you have to run," said Marchand.

"My God, Jean, are you serious?" Trudeau replied.

The good-humoured Marchand would later remark that Trudeau was so shocked by this turn in the conversation that he never did finish his lunch. Trudeau listened dutifully to Marchand's remonstrations against allowing his own name to stand, which he had heard many times before. He pondered his own options. "If you won't run," Trudeau finally told Marchand, "then I'll consider it at least. But in Quebec wouldn't I be a catastrophe?"[73]

It was the right question. And as Pelletier and Marchand knew, the news from Quebec was good. Trudeau's star had been rising in Quebec Liberal circles since the Canadian Bar Association debacle the previous September. With Lester Pearson's decisive move in cabinet to support Trudeau's bill of rights, the minister of justice now spoke for the government whenever he discussed constitutional reform with party officials. The more Quebec Liberals got to know Trudeau, the more impressed they were with both the clarity of his ideas and his willingness to work within the party organization.[74] Like many other Canadians, they had also come to appreciate his parliamentary skills, never more on display than in December 1967. Following Trudeau's success with the divorce and omnibus bills, even the Quebec press had begun to give the justice minister favourable coverage.[75] It was common knowledge that Jean Marchand would enjoy enormous support in Quebec if he contested the Liberal leadership race. But as word spread that he felt he was not up to the job, Trudeau got the benefit of his long association with the popular labour leader. The Liberal tradition of alternating French and English leaders, coupled with Marchand's ability to rally the Quebec caucus behind Trudeau, presented formidable advantages should he enter the leadership race.

Just how formidable came to light mere hours after Trudeau's lunch with Pelletier and Marchand. Trudeau agreed to meet with John Turner, the federal consumer and corporate affairs minister and another as-yet-undeclared leadership hopeful. Though Turner was a bilingual Montrealer and a member of the Quebec caucus, he was not a French Canadian. He thus had an insider's appreciation of the fact that most Quebec Liberals were waiting for Marchand and Trudeau to figure out what they were doing.[76] Trudeau told Turner that he had not yet decided whether he would run. Marchand told Turner the same thing at a private meeting the next day.

On January 16, citing unnamed "informants," the *Globe and Mail* announced that Marchand and Trudeau had struck an agreement not to back any of the English-Canadian candidates in the Liberal race.[77] The news came as a shock to John Turner, who knew that time was not on his side. With the Western Liberal Policy Conference scheduled for Winnipeg over the following weekend, Turner announced on January 17 that he would join the Liberal leadership race. He thus became the fifth declared candidate. Turner acknowledged that his discussions with Marchand and Trudeau had reached a dead end. "I have made arrangements with no one," Turner told the press. "I'm my own man. I'm running my own campaign."[78]

Media coverage of Turner's declaration illuminated something critically important about the public perception of the Liberal leadership candidates. The "experienced" establishment men—Kierans, Martin, Sharp—were understood to represent the party's past and thus to be competing mainly against each other. The "young" hipsters Turner and Trudeau, on the other hand, were perceived to be in a two-man fight for the party's future. In the youth-obsessed 1960s, there was never any question about where the strategic advantage lay. "Mr. Turner is the closest thing to a young swinger in the leadership race," observed the *Globe*'s Geoffrey Stevens. "He possesses youth, glamour, access to money, a solid academic background (including a Rhodes Scholarship), and is fluently bilingual. But he could lose this advantage if Mr. Trudeau, 46, the acknowledged swinger on Parliament Hill, enters the contest."[79] When Mitchell Sharp announced his candidacy on January 18, the collective yawn from Canadians was practically audible. "We would be in for a period of good gray Canadian government with all the style and flair of an endless civil service seminar," commented former Tory MP Frank McGee.[80] And when Paul Martin entered the race the next day, even the most generous editorialists acknowledged that he had been in politics "a long, long time."[81]

John Turner was not the only person frustrated with the early jockeying of the leadership contenders. On January 16, five senior cabinet ministers—Martin, Sharp, Hellyer, MacEachen, and Marchand—were summoned to 24 Sussex Drive for dinner with the prime minister. After the meal, as the ministers were enjoying drinks, Pearson launched into a stern lecture about the continuing need for cabinet solidarity. The prime minister's tone was later reported to have ranged from "firm to furious."[82] This dressing-down had an immediate pretext. At the Halifax convention the previous weekend, Liberal ministers had publicly debated the implementation of medicare, which was still under consideration by cabinet. (The debate centred on whether implementation of this shared-cost program, which was supposed to have begun on July 1, 1968, would be delayed as a courtesy to the provinces.) Neither Jean Marchand nor Pierre Trudeau had attended the Halifax conference or made any public pronouncement on the implementation of medicare. Indeed, the two were reportedly "dodging all questioners" and refusing to "lay their cards on the table."[83] As far as the prime minister was concerned, they alone were above suspicion.

By January 19, 1967, all of the Liberal Party heavyweights had declared themselves leadership contenders. The only exception was trade minister Robert Winters, who, like Marchand and Trudeau, was hedging. (Winters was telling insiders that he intended to quit politics and return to the private sector early in 1968.[84] This rumour had the predictable result of producing a draft-Winters movement, led by Toronto-area Liberal Barry Monaghan.) A group of "second-tier" candidates would also trickle into the race, of whom the most likeable was Pearson's lively and fluently bilingual agricultural minister, Joe Greene. The least comprehensible was Ernst Zündel, then a crusader for immigrants' rights in Canada and later one of the world's most notorious Holocaust deniers.[85]

The morning after Lester Pearson harangued his senior ministers for breaching parliamentary protocol, the Liberal cabinet endorsed Trudeau's position on the Constitution as the one the government would carry to the February 5 federal-provincial conference. From that point on, there would be no ambiguity. Pierre Trudeau would speak for the prime minister and the government any time he discussed Canadian federalism.

Marc Lalonde knew an opportunity when he saw one. He suggested to Lester Pearson that he dispatch the justice minister to the provincial capitals to personally lay the groundwork for a successful constitutional conference. While Trudeau was out selling his plan for Canadian federalism to the premiers, Lalonde reasoned, he could also be selling himself to Liberal convention delegates and to Canadian voters more generally. Pearson liked the idea. National unity was the overriding issue facing Canada, he believed. The upcoming federal-provincial conference would therefore mark "the beginning of the making of a new Confederation."[86] When the prime minister announced that Trudeau would be meeting with the premiers, Pearson stated explicitly that these visits had nothing to do with the leadership contest.[87] Predictably, that affirmation had exactly the opposite effect. The pundits immediately began to write about the enormous advantage a tour of the provincial capitals would bring the non-candidate Trudeau. It was a "highly unusual mission," noted the *Globe and Mail*.[88] "Unless he resolutely bars his hotel room door wherever he goes," added columnist George Bain, "the Justice Minister is likely to be sought out both by the news media and by Liberals anxious to see and assess even just-possibly-maybe candidates."[89]

Wherever Lalonde's and Pearson's ulterior motives lay, Trudeau resolved to play it absolutely straight. He was not a leadership candidate, he insisted, and he would be giving no interviews. His only concern was to forestall "useless clashes" at the upcoming federal-provincial meeting.[90]

Trudeau's first stop was Edmonton, where he met with Alberta premier Ernest Manning the morning of Friday, January 19. He was accompanied by his top constitutional expert, Carl Goldenberg, who would sit in on all of his meetings with the premiers and later write a tight nine-page précis of their views for the feds' use at the constitutional conference.[91] Later the same day, Trudeau flew to Victoria, where he had a friendly tête-à-tête with B.C. premier W.A.C. Bennett. In both Western capitals, journalists found themselves shut out. "I'm not here publicly," Trudeau told them. "I'm not seeing the press. I'm not granting any interviews."[92] Premier Bennett was less publicity-shy, however. "I've just had a very frank discussion with the minister," he told reporters. "We reached complete agreement. If he ever decides to move to British Columbia, there's a place for him in my cabinet. He's a great Canadian."[93] Some indication of what Trudeau and Bennett discussed came to light a few days later when Bennett stated that British Columbia intended to "stand pat" on the Constitution at the upcoming conference. "That's where we have stood for the past 100 years," he said. "It is a solid thing, working well. We are prepared to discuss details only."[94] (Quebec premier Daniel Johnson responded immediately to Bennett's statement, telling the press that Quebec's position was unchanged. The province would continue to press for an entirely new Constitution.)[95]

On Saturday, January 20, Trudeau met with Saskatchewan premier Ross Thatcher in Regina. The following day, he met with Ontario premier John Robarts at Queen's Park. The Toronto meeting was conducted under heavy police security and described by local media as "hush-hush." (Trudeau and his aides had to present their credentials to breach the cordon around the premier's office.) When Trudeau and Robarts emerged from their meeting, the poker-faced Trudeau again refused any comment. "I'm sorry," he told the press. "You can see how it is."[96] But there was no mistaking Robarts's happy demeanour. "We are working towards what we hope will be a successful conference and we're all pleased with the outcome of this meeting," he said with an exuberant smile.[97] Jean Marchand, who had sat in on the Toronto meeting, was cornered by reporters while he was waiting for an elevator. He could not conceal his delight at the positive press Trudeau was attracting. "What leadership race?" he asked with a broad grin. "Is there a leadership race on?"[98] To Torontonians, all of this warm camaraderie indicated something significant. The next day, the front-page headline in the *Toronto Star* speculated, "Ontario, Ottawa Reach Accord on Confederation Meeting."[99]

Trudeau met with Manitoba premier Walter Weir in Winnipeg on Monday, January 22. The next evening, he appeared on the CBC-TV show *Newsmagazine,* where he broke his silence and chatted casually for half an hour about the state of Canadian federalism. Well-briefed and lucid, Trudeau made it clear that his long-standing reservations about opening constitutional negotiations prematurely had not abated. Perhaps the provinces were correct, and the time was right for a "showdown" on the division of powers, he said. But Premier Robarts's Confederation of Tomorrow conference had demonstrated that "no province had any clear idea of what the new constitution should be." The federal government would agree to "rewrite the *British North America Act* if people want to," he said, but it would not participate in a Canadian version of "Munich" (a reference to Neville Chamberlain's 1938 appeasement of Adolf Hitler). If the provinces and the feds could address the language issue in a bill of rights, he concluded, then negotiating the "mechanics" of constitutional reform might follow relatively easily.[100] Otherwise, nothing was certain.

Trudeau's articulation of his federalist ideas on *Newsmagazine* was widely interpreted as a watershed moment in his televisual appeal to Canadians. Analogies were made to JFK. "A new and totally unforeseen thing has happened in the past month that has turned Canadian eyes—at last—away from the U.S. political scene," gushed media critic Roy Shields. "Overnight, Pierre Elliott Trudeau has arrived. There has been nothing like him since the beginning of television in this country. The justice minister's few television appearances, such as last week's interview on *Newsmagazine*, have stirred Canadians from coast-to-coast. Viewers (and I have tested a lot of them on this) are strangely reminded of John Kennedy." Yet even for Shields, Trudeau's appeal was not primarily about style but about substance. "The basic issue that turns all Canadians to their television sets," he asserted, was "Will we get a leader who can hold the nation together?"[101] Elsewhere, Canadian editorialists lavished praise on Trudeau for not "visiting Munich." "Canadians who want their federal government to draw a line somewhere against the ballooning pretensions and demands of Quebec will be heartened by the statements of Justice Minister Pierre Elliott Trudeau in his appearance on CBC *Newsmagazine* last night," said the *Toronto Star*. "He is right in opposing a racial division of political power."[102]

On Thursday, January 25, Trudeau resumed his tour of the provincial capitals, meeting with Newfoundland premier Joey Smallwood and Nova Scotia premier G.I. Smith. Echoing W.A.C. Bennett and John Robarts, the gregarious Smallwood refused to reveal specifics but gave every indication that he was smitten with Trudeau. "We have come to complete and unanimous agreement on what Canada's future should be," he said. Trudeau was "the perfect Canadian" and a "brilliant" MP.[103] The not-so-subtle message was that Smallwood would be only too happy to deliver Newfoundland's convention delegates to Trudeau whenever the justice minister decided to enter the Liberal leadership contest. After his three-hour evening meeting with Premier Smith, Trudeau was asked if he could think of anything that might make him run for the Liberal leadership. "No, not right now I can't," he answered.[104] He met with New Brunswick premier Louis Robichaud and P.E.I. premier Alexander Campbell the next day.

Back at Trudeau headquarters, Marc Lalonde and his inner circle could not have been more delighted. If the twin goals of Trudeau's tour had been to assert his dominance on the constitutional debate and raise his profile in English Canada, the strategy had exceeded everyone's expectations. In the premiers' offices, on the country's editorial pages, and on Canada's television screens, Trudeau was a hit. Peter C. Newman, never one for understatement, caught the public mood. "Because it contains so many mysterious elements, the Pierre Trudeau candidacy for the Liberal leadership is more interesting than all the others put together," he wrote. "While the other candidates talk themselves hoarse, most of the whispers about the race concern the enigmatic swinger who is currently Canada's minister of justice, and who could become the most exciting prime minister this country has ever had."[105]

In this heady atmosphere, with the non-candidate Pierre Trudeau riding a wave of popularity, Quebec Liberals gathered in Montreal for their own policy convention. The timing could not have been more propitious. It would be the delegates' first opportunity to hear from the party's leadership hopefuls and their last opportunity to hammer out a unified position on the Constitution before the February 5 federal-provincial conference.

The convention took place over the weekend of January 26 at Place Bonaventure and drew roughly 1,500 delegates. From the outset, the media called it the "Trudeau show." "It was a little too chilly for sandals, such as he wears on summer afternoons in the House of Commons," said one report. "But otherwise, cool cat Pierre Elliott Trudeau took his 'different' world of style with him to the Quebec Liberal convention this weekend, turning up in a skinny knit tie, bright sport coat, green leather overcoat and a leather fedora."[106] All of the top-tier leadership hopefuls were also in attendance—Sharp, Kierans, Turner, Martin, and Hellyer. But as *Globe* correspondent Lewis Seale observed, they knew even before they got there that they would likely spend the weekend "running like mad in order to keep from being knocked right out of Quebec by the Trudeau boomlet."[107]

Members of Trudeau's entourage knew that they were indeed holding all the cards. The feds' "showdown" with Premier Daniel Johnson was just days away, and the shock waves of René Lévesque's *souveraineté-association* proposal were still reverberating around the province. In the electric atmosphere created by these events, Trudeau's cerebral calm thrived. More important, Trudeau's supporters had deftly manoeuvred themselves into positions from which they could stage-manage the event. Jean Marchand gave the opening address on Friday night. Sounding very much like Trudeau, he blasted Quebec politicians who claimed that only they could represent the interests of Quebecers. "In certain cases we are in the presence of a shameless exploitation of French Canadian nationalism," he told the crowd. "And it is a sure thing that the people will ultimately foot the bill for this embryonic and virulent racism."[108] There had been considerable speculation that Marchand might use his speech to announce that he would not run for the Liberal leadership—which, of course, would all but guarantee that Trudeau would run.[109] It did not happen. Instead, Marchand told delegates not to be distracted from the main issue—the Constitution. "During the next two months you will have all the time you need to worry about the leadership convention," he said. "This is why we have asked the leadership candidates to abstain from using this convention for electoral purposes."[110]

Even more important than Marchand's role in setting the scene for Trudeau were the preparations that had been laid by Jean-Pierre Goyer, MP for Dollard and chair of the Liberal policy committee. Goyer scheduled policy workshops on culture, regional development, and foreign affairs for Saturday, leaving Sunday free for the climactic debate on the Constitution. Well before delegates began filing into Montreal, they knew that Goyer would sponsor an "omnibus resolution" on the Constitution and that Trudeau would take to the convention stage to present it. The resolution, distributed to party members in advance, contained three general provisions. The first was to require that the Bi and Bi recommendations on official bilingualism be implemented. The second was to affirm the right of the federal government to legislate for all Canadians in the fields of social and tax policy. The third and most important was to press for a constitutional bill of rights to protect the linguistic rights of French- and English-speaking minorities across Canada.[111]

Of the many topics debated on Saturday, January 27, the most newsworthy was the monarchy. After a heated debate that ran well into the evening hours, delegates voted 135 to 33 to abolish the monarchy and establish Canada as a republic.[112] This dramatic gesture was widely seen as a move by young Liberals to undercut the sovereignists' exploitation of the issue, since, as Pierre Bourgault had been telling Quebecers for years, the monarchy was a demeaning symbol of their colonial status. As always, Pierre Trudeau was indifferent to this debate. He had no interest in "flapping his arms" in sterile squabbles over symbols. "I want the good of the French Canadians," he commented after the vote. "I don't want them just to be emotionally satisfied. I want them to become a great people and doing away with the monarchy won't change them a little bit. It would make a few people happier, that's all. Let them keep the monarchy and let them have something to attack if they want, but they should spend their time on more important things."[113] Oddly enough, Quebec premier Daniel Johnson felt exactly the same way, and for the same reasons.

The debate on the Constitution got under way as scheduled the morning of Sunday, January 28. Trudeau addressed an animated crowd of roughly a thousand delegates, speaking for fifty minutes. Using a slide show illustrating the various political options that lay before Quebecers, Trudeau critiqued René Lévesque's *souveraineté-association* as well as the *deux nations* concept favoured by Jean Lesage and Daniel Johnson. "Personally," Trudeau told the delegates, "I believe that it is not a particular status in Confederation for the government of Quebec but an equal status for all French-speaking Canadians in all of Canada that will bring enduring unity to our country. But we must not confuse the rights of French-Canadians with the legitimate or illegitimate desire of a provincial government to build itself a little empire. I ask you to keep your minds clear and sharp. Don't confuse the rights of French-Canadians with provincial powers."[114] Trudeau promised to forge "*une alliance*" with Daniel Johnson to entrench French-language rights across Canada—a proposal that would later play extremely well in Quebec.[115] To add some levity to the proceedings, he also joked about the fondness of certain Union Nationale politicians for the "Peugeot cars and bureaucratic empires" of Charles de Gaulle's France. "France has adopted 17 constitutions in the last 180 years," Trudeau quipped. "When a constitution lasts a few years, the French become bored and try to give new constitutions to other countries!"[116] His partisan audience roared with laughter.

When Trudeau concluded his speech, the crowd burst into a standing ovation and sang "Il a gagné ses épaulettes." Everywhere he went for the remainder of the day, he was besieged by reporters and cameras. Before the conference broke up Sunday evening, convention delegates voted unanimously to approve the Goyer/Trudeau resolution on the Constitution. The justice minister returned to Ottawa knowing that his bill of rights now had the solid support of Quebec Liberals.

The Montreal conference was hailed as a triumph for Trudeau, particularly in English Canada. Veteran *Toronto Star* reporter Dominique Clift called his performance "dazzling" and speculated that "all Trudeau has to say now is 'I'm running' and he'll get almost solid backing from the Quebec delegates to the leadership convention."[117] Lewis Seale at the *Globe* correctly gauged the impact of Trudeau's constitutional ideas on party members. "His offer of the closest co-operation with Quebec Premier Daniel Johnson in seeking the equality of French-Canadians and English-Canadians—but not for helping Quebec City build its own little empire—made the federal Liberals feel for the first time in years that they are in the van of the struggle."[118] The *Edmonton Journal* congratulated Trudeau for challenging "the myth that Quebec, as opposed to Canada as a whole, is the homeland of the French-Canadian."[119] The *Toronto Star* praised him for "going to the heart of the Canadian crisis with a boldness which we hope other federal Liberals will emulate in dealing with Quebec."[120] It was all too much for Claude Ryan, who again accused the English-Canadian press of "*un messianisme*."[121]

Premier Daniel Johnson was listening closely to Trudeau, of course. Commenting the day after the convention ended, Johnson protested that he was no separatist and thus Trudeau had no reason to call him an empire builder. "If I felt that separatism was the solution, well, what better time could we hope for than now?" Johnson demanded. "He for one has no excuse for using a word like 'empire,' intimating that Quebec might want to represent not only its population but also all the French. There's nothing imperialistic in our minds."[122]

To many Canadians, Trudeau's performance at the Liberal policy convention had been yet another tour de force—from the perfect choreography of Marc Lalonde, Jean Marchand, and Jean-Pierre Goyer to Trudeau's own flawless execution. The minister of justice, still touted as a man for tomorrow, emerged as the man of the hour, his name on everyone's lips, his face on the nation's front pages.

Yet doubts remained. Trudeau's closest friends knew that he was far too savvy to be beguiled by his own press. Furthermore, they knew that one of his non-negotiable conditions for entering the leadership race was to have the solid backing of Quebec Liberals. Alas, while the convention had proven a triumph on the constitutional front, questions remained about Trudeau's appeal to Quebecers. Forestry minister Maurice Sauvé had been stating publicly for months that Quebec Liberals should vote en masse for an English-Canadian candidate, preferably Paul Martin.[123] Claude Ryan, still one of the most influential public voices in the province, remained tentative on Trudeau. "We will have to wait until the delegates get back to their constituencies," said Ryan. "I'm not sure that Pierre is prepared to go far enough in satisfying the demands of Quebec. I haven't made up my mind."[124] Peter C. Newman, whose personal attachment to Trudeau was now beyond question, nonetheless continued to report that Mitchell Sharp was the most highly favoured leadership contender among Quebec Liberal ministers, including Jean Chrétien and Jean-Luc Pépin.[125] Even among rank-and-file Quebec Liberals, there were persistent whispers that Marchand's "dictatorial" leadership style had skewed the pitch in Trudeau's favour.[126]

There was no guarantee, in short, that a Trudeau candidacy could win the support of Quebec's 626 delegates to the leadership convention or, indeed, anything close to that number. The justice minister thus remained as uncertain as ever about running. As an exasperated aide of one of the declared leadership candidates said, "We don't know what the hell Trudeau is going to do!"[127]

CHAPTER FIVE
THE SACRED AND THE PROFANE

To a degree that is almost impossible to imagine today, Canadians in the era of the five-channel universe were enthralled by the prospect of a nationally televised federal-provincial conference. In February 1968, the phrase "constitutional fatigue" lay decades in the future, the product of a history Canadians today know only too well (two Quebec referenda on sovereignty, the 1981 *nuit des longs couteaux*, the 1982 repatriation, René Lévesque's *beau risque*, the Meech and Charlottetown accords, the *Clarity Act*). Over the winter of 1968, when Canada was widely understood to be facing the worst national-unity crisis in memory, Canadians anticipated the Canada of Tomorrow conference on February 5 with a degree of anticipation they normally reserved for the NHL playoffs.

For the first time in history, television crews would broadcast the faces, voices, and ideas of Canada's political leaders as they debated the Constitution in real time. This fact alone made the conference a milestone in participatory democracy. In the weeks leading up to the event, the two national networks, CBC and CTV, fought a "battle for prestige" over broadcast rights that Canadians had until then identified exclusively with American politics.[1] To no one's surprise, CBC/Radio-Canada was the eventual winner. The national broadcaster set up four cameras around the horseshoe-shaped table in the Confederation Room of Parliament's West Block, where the main sessions would be held. Two more cameras were placed in an anteroom designed to function as an interview studio. A crew of 125 technicians, journalists, and commentators was mobilized.[2] Newspapers ran frothy columns pressing Canadians to do their civic duty and tune in to the proceedings. "All Canada belongs at this conference," said the *Globe and Mail*. "Nothing could more surely bring home to all Canadians the vastness of Canada, the variety of Canada, the pressures that beat upon and the hopes that gleam ahead of Canada than to take the whole nation to the talks."[3] The *Toronto Star* ran the unambiguous headline "At Stake Next Monday Morning: National Survival."[4]

Lester Pearson adopted the same urgent tone, invoking the spectre of Quebec separatism to emphasize the gravity of the conference. "I pray to God we may succeed because it could be our last chance," he said. "There are now powerful forces, powerfully aided from outside, that would divide us as a people and destroy us as a state. Let us not be deceived by the slogans of those who demand a freedom that will be no greater than we have."[5] The prime minister reiterated that he was no lame duck. He would speak for all Canada at the conference, and he would use his considerable skills as a diplomat to forge a bold new consensus on Canadian federalism. Most of the ideas Pearson would bring to the table, however, were those of the man who would sit Sphinx-like by his side throughout the proceedings, Pierre Trudeau.[6]

The feds' objectives were laid out in *Federalism for the Future*, a forty-nine-page white paper written specifically for the conference and tabled in the House of Commons on February 1, 1968.

This document—the product of months of painstaking work by the minister of justice and his constitutional steering committee—was bound in a black-and-red cover adorned with a maple leaf and the signature of Pierre Trudeau. Its conceptual centrepiece was a "Canadian Charter of Human Rights" designed to enshrine political, legal, and egalitarian rights, as well as linguistic rights, for French- and English-speaking Canadians. The proposed charter was entirely Trudeau's, of course, and so was its raison d'être. "The division of powers between orders of government should be guided by the principles of functionalism, and not by ethnic considerations," the document affirmed.[7] When Lester Pearson introduced the white paper in the House of Commons, he threw the full weight of his government behind it. "I recommend to all Canadians the acceptance of a Canadian Charter of Human Rights," he said.[8] The English-Canadian media adopted the phrase "Trudeau's charter" to describe the proposal.

As Pearson and Trudeau knew—and as Canadians have since come to appreciate—the invocation of constitutionally entrenched rights marked a significant departure from British parliamentary tradition. Some Canadians regarded the phrase "supremacy of Parliament" as sacrosanct, and some premiers would cite it, in fact, to stonewall Trudeau's charter, then and later. As noted above, the *Canadian Bill of Rights* that was John Diefenbaker's pride had been passed in August 1960. But as an act of Parliament it applied only to the federal jurisdiction and could be changed or superseded at any time by new legislation. Trudeau's charter, in contrast, would apply everywhere in Canada and to all Canadians. Since it had constitutional weight, no government could override it without amending the Constitution itself.

As a scholar of federalism, Trudeau believed that national unity would be strengthened (and separatism undermined) if the federal and provincial governments agreed to cede some of their powers to the Canadian people.[9] But he also knew, as did his critics, that constitutionally guaranteed rights would move Canada much closer to the American model, in which the Supreme Court serves as the arbiter of citizens' rights. Such a redistribution of power was entirely appropriate, Trudeau believed, particularly where language rights are concerned.

"The U.S. bill of rights is contained in the first ten amendments of the constitution," he acknowledged. "It's just written in there that Congress can make no law abridging the basic freedoms. If Parliament or the provinces passed a law abridging, shall we say, equality of the two languages, they just wouldn't have the power to do so."[10]

In the months leading up to the conference, when Trudeau was working to entrench individual rights in his draft charter, he was also intervening forcefully in the work of his steering committee to thwart any *deux nations* concept of Canada. A remarkable document from his private papers, for example, shows his handwritten annotations on a late-1967 draft "Bill of Rights for Canadians." The draft, marked "Confidential," was one of many working documents prepared by Jean Beetz and other constitutional experts in advance of the federal-provincial conference. With several strokes of his pen, Trudeau gutted the preamble's allusion to a bicultural Canada. The original text read:

> THE PEOPLE OF CANADA
> Recognize that Canada is composed of two linguistic communities sharing a common tradition of democratic practice and fundamental individual rights, and seeking to ensure an equal partnership in confederation;
>
> that all persons in Canada of whichever community possess by right the opportunity of pursuing their individual social and economic advancement free from unwarranted interference . . . .

Trudeau's handwritten revisions altered the text fundamentally:

> THE PEOPLE OF CANADA
> Recognize that ~~Canada is composed of two linguistic communities sharing~~ all Canadians share a common tradition of

> democratic practice and fundamental individual rights, and ~~seeking to ensure an equal partnership in confederation;~~
>
> ~~that all persons in Canada of whichever community~~ possess by right the opportunity of pursuing their individual cultural, social and economic advancement free from unwarranted interference . . . .

With an additional stroke of his pen, Trudeau renamed the same draft document from a "Bill" to the now-familiar "Charter."[11]

On February 1, 1968, with the federal-provincial conference just days away, Peter C. Newman asked Trudeau whether his position on the Constitution amounted to a defence of the status quo. "It is not," Trudeau replied. "It amounts to fighting for the only thing that can make Canada united—to take the fuse out of explosive Quebec nationalism—by making sure that Quebec is not a ghetto for French Canadians, that all of Canada is theirs." Trudeau also gave Newman a glimpse of the aloof, take-it-or-leave-it leadership style that had already begun to colour public perceptions of him. "We may not succeed," said Trudeau, "but I would rather try than let the country break up because the rest of Canada says to Quebec: No, you must stay in your French ghetto. Then I will pack my bags and I will go and live in the ghetto myself."[12]

Ivan Head, then a young legal adviser to Trudeau, was asked what his boss really wanted out of the conference. "We are suggesting to the provinces that every person in this country has a right to a high standard of dignity," said Head. "It's Trudeau's view that for the past hundred years the provinces and the federal government have been too concerned with squabbling over taxes. They haven't been concerned enough about trying to decide what the purposes of Canada are and how can we make it a swell place for everybody to live in."[13]

Making Canada a swell place was a tall order, as the justice minister and his advisers well knew. Under the terms of the *British North*

America Act, Trudeau's charter would require the unanimous consent of the federal government and the provinces to become law—unless, that is, a different amending formula could itself be negotiated. Premier Daniel Johnson was already on record as saying that his government would not support Trudeau's plan to make a federal charter the precondition of constitutional reform. On January 19, Quebec's brief to the constitutional conference was leaked, revealing that the premier's agenda had not changed since the interprovincial meeting in November. Johnson would again propose a massively decentralized Confederation arrangement in which each province would be offered the powers Quebec demanded for itself. "In order to be valid, a new Canadian constitution must be the product of an agreement between our two nations," stated the brief. "Indeed, this is the price of equality. For how could two cultural communities be equal if one has to depend on the goodwill of the other for its survival and its growth?"[14] When the feds' white paper was published, Johnson accused Trudeau of bludgeoning the provinces with his charter before doing the hard work of revising the constitutional allocation of powers. "Mr. Trudeau is putting the cart before the horse," he said. "Property and civil rights come under the jurisdiction of the provinces and we are not ready to give that up."[15]

Pierre Trudeau anticipated this sort of response from Johnson, of course, and stood ready to challenge his *deux nations* vision of Canada. But to his credit, Trudeau also understood the enormous political pressures operating on the Quebec premier. On February 1, 1968, for example, just as the white paper was being tabled in the federal Parliament, the Société Saint-Jean-Baptiste presented a brief to the Quebec government recommending that French become the "sole official language" in that province.[16] When Johnson remarked to a journalist that Trudeau held a grudge against him because the justice minister could not distinguish between the present Union Nationale government and that of Maurice Duplessis, Trudeau corrected the record immediately. "No, there is no personal barrier and it has nothing to do with Premier Johnson being in the same party as Maurice Duplessis, nothing at all," he said. "Duplessis, to me, he's dead and gone. I look at Johnson's ideas, I look at his speeches, I see what he says on such things as equality and independence. I see the pressures that he is submitted to, which are completely different from those facing Duplessis. Johnson is under pressure from the separatists and from the René Lévesques, which Duplessis never was."[17]

Lester Pearson agreed. He thought Johnson a cool and courteous adversary, which was tantamount to admitting that of all the Quebec politicians then making demands of Ottawa, Johnson was the most reasonable. "It was not easy, even had it been desirable," Pearson later wrote, "to provoke a real confrontation with him."[18] Other English Canadians concurred, noting that Johnson's soft-spoken and stately manner worked against any accusation that he was a radical. "He simply doesn't look or behave like a man who would break up Canada," wrote Peter C. Newman. "The image he projects is that of a thoughtful politician, anxious to please, troubled that he is always being misunderstood."[19]

As for the other premiers, those whom Trudeau had taken the trouble to meet and impress, they were almost to a man noncommittal on his proposed charter. Only British Columbia premier W.A.C. Bennett issued a statement in advance of the conference, and it took the form of a warning that he was not prepared to cede power to the feds or anyone else. Ironically, this reaction put him in the same boat as Daniel Johnson and against Trudeau, the man Bennett had called a "great Canadian" just two weeks earlier. If the justice minister was disappointed that the premiers' warm private reception to his proposals had not translated into public goodwill, he did not let on. As an editorial in the *Globe and Mail* noted perceptively, none of the premiers could risk the appearance of being against the extension of Canadians' rights or of ceding power unilaterally. "Mr. Trudeau knows he will run into opposition," said the *Globe.* "Little of the opposition will be directed against the rights themselves. It will be argued instead that it is for the provinces to legislate in certain areas, which will turn out to be as many areas as they can keep their hands on."[20]

The federal-provincial conference opened as scheduled the morning of Monday, February 5. Prime Minister Pearson sat at the head of the horseshoe table, flanked by Pierre Trudeau. Marc Lalonde, Carl Goldenberg, and Gordon Robertson, clerk of the Privy Council, sat behind him. The premiers and their advisers sat in facing rows on either side of Pearson. For three days, Canada's leading politicians would sweat under the glare of television lights and the gaze of Canadians watching dutifully from their living rooms.

The prime minister opened the proceedings with a national-unity speech that was heartfelt but deliberately vague. "In this day it is folly to think that a country, let alone a province, can be an island unto itself," he said. "And it is that overlapping tissue of loyalties involving our hearts more than our minds, which more than anything else constitutes this country. To tear apart these loyalties would be to destroy the country and leave us all diminished. It lies within our power to prevent this, to remove the cause of discontent, to lay the groundwork for a great new act of accommodation which will ensure the hopes and aspirations of all Canadians. It is to nothing less than this to which we must commit ourselves at the conference."[21]

By general agreement, the first day was taken up with the presentation of the provinces' position papers. Ontario's John Robarts, arguably the English-Canadian premier with the most sympathy for Quebec, spoke immediately after Pearson. He announced that his government intended to adopt the recommendations of the Bi and Bi Commission and introduce French-language rights in Ontario. He stated as well that he was not keen to see such rights entrenched in a charter without extensive study, and proposed that a federal-provincial committee be struck to consider the question. Sounding very much like Pierre Trudeau, Robarts expressed his personal concern about the growing appeal of "narrow nationalism" in Canada and Quebec. "Some Canadians are so indifferent to the future of their country that they appear prepared to sanction its division into two politically separate parts," he fretted, "one chiefly English-speaking, the other predominantly French-speaking."[22]

Western premiers Ross Thatcher and Walter Weir agreed. Like Robarts, they advocated further study of Trudeau's charter proposal. The premiers from Atlantic Canada—Joey Smallwood, Alex Campbell, G.I. Smith, and Louis Robichaud—were the most in tune with Trudeau's thinking, all of them keen to extend bilingualism and to consider some sort of constitutional language guarantee. Robichaud, in fact, pledged to make New Brunswick officially bilingual. Not surprisingly, for the premiers of have-not provinces, safeguarding the prerogative of the federal government to tax and redistribute wealth in some new regional equalization scheme was itself a matter of national survival. Quebec's insistence that the provinces be handed massive new taxation powers worked against this prerogative—a point made repeatedly by Nova Scotia premier G.I. Smith. But it was the pugnacious patriot Joey Smallwood who challenged Daniel Johnson directly. "How anyone who loves Canada can advocate anything that would make Parliament impotent in order to make his own province strong baffles me," he told his Quebec counterpart. "I don't think any Canadian wants that. I don't believe ten percent of the people in Quebec would want to take away any power from Ottawa."[23]

Johnson smiled politely as he listened to the other premiers. When he took the floor himself, he offered them a genuinely moving description of Quebec's unique minority status in North America. If their provinces had found themselves isolated on an otherwise

French-speaking continent, he suggested, only then would they have a true sense of how Quebecers felt. "We want to survive, to be dynamic, but there's no intention of fragmenting the Canadian federation," Johnson reassured them.[24] He then tabled his proposal that a new Constitution be written to acknowledge the *deux nations* character of Canada. Cultural equality, he said, "depends not only on extending bilingualism territorially but even more on extending the jurisdictions of Quebec, the homeland of the French-Canadian nation." Time, Johnson concluded ominously, referencing both the Rassemblement pour l'indépendance nationale and René Lévesque's *souveraineté-association*, "is no longer on the side of today's Canada."[25] Johnson's statement clearly irritated some of the Western premiers. "I don't see how any English-speaking premier could be happy after hearing that speech," Ross Thatcher later commented.[26]

By day's end, it was evident that at most seven (and possibly only five) provinces might be willing to adopt Trudeau's charter and from there amend the Constitution. Premiers Johnson, Manning, and Bennett were the dissenters. Manning emerged as the most obstructionist, asserting that Alberta would extend opportunities for individuals who wished to learn French but not at the cost of a "constitutional Munich."[27] "Before approval is given to fundamental constitutional amendments relating to what is commonly called 'the French fact,'" said Manning, "it is imperative that there be a firm and definite understanding as to what, if any, further demands will be made."[28] For his part, W.A.C. Bennett distinguished himself by downplaying the national-unity crisis altogether, defending the supremacy of Parliament, and cracking jokes throughout his presentation. Lester Pearson, meanwhile, did his best to manage expectations. "Remember, it is the first scene of the first act," he reminded his peers. "You don't look for agreement on fundamental issues on the first day."[29]

Trudeau was stone-faced throughout. As he left the Confederation

Room at the end of the day, he was asked how he thought the discussions had gone. "It was a very good morning," he replied, "and a very good afternoon."[30] That was it.

Because there had been no debate during Monday's proceedings, the Tuesday morning session opened fairly amicably. "I have the impression things are moving," Daniel Johnson told the press before the session opened. "Where there is action, there is hope."[31] Journalists covering the session said Pierre Trudeau looked tired, undoubtedly because he had spent the previous evening revising the speech he was scheduled to give that afternoon. The minister of justice distinguished himself by wearing a grey suit and a "soft green" shirt—a stark contrast with all other participants, who appeared in conventional white shirts and dark ties.

The relative equanimity of the previous day did not last. By mutual agreement, the morning session took the form of an unstructured conversation about how to proceed with constitutional reform, and, inevitably, it revealed significant differences of opinion. Daniel Johnson was the first to speak. Following some introductory pleasantries, he expressed regret that the constitutional debate had been straitjacketed by the "spokesman for the federal government," by whom he meant Trudeau.[32] Lester Pearson interjected immediately. He reminded Johnson of the importance of cabinet solidarity and assured him that Trudeau spoke for the federal government. Trudeau himself then plunged into the conversation, taking direct aim at the Quebec premier and setting in motion a ninety-minute scrap that would become legendary.

"The moment one pretends that one province speaks in the name of a nation, or that certain powers are required to protect the interests of this nation," Trudeau lectured Johnson, "then the members of this nation cease participating in a federal form of government." What was needed to protect Quebecers was a guarantee of linguistic rights, said Trudeau. "This is what we mean by the equality of two communities. When this equality is reached and guaranteed in a constitutional document, then I believe the question of special powers becomes an affront to French-Canadians." Trudeau rejected Johnson's *deux nations* view of Canada out of hand. "I think the theory of the two nations is not a theory that the French Canadians support," he said. "It is not applicable from either a constitutional or a political point of view. This kind of confusion which has existed for some time in this country should not be perpetuated."[33]

Unaccustomed to such effrontery, a visibly irritated Johnson dismissed what he called Trudeau's "sophisms." "What would Quebec MPs do in Ottawa in such a case?" he asked. "Why not hand over everything to the same MPs—education, health, social security and so on? Why not close down the Quebec legislature and set up a unitary state?"[34]

"I'm a French-Canadian," Trudeau responded. "But your difficulties are not with the federal government but with federalism itself. If Canada wishes to give a very special status to Quebec and still grant everything that the French Canadians ask for, in terms of language and in terms of representation in Ottawa, this is fine. If we can have our cake and eat it too, I am very happy—and the frosting and the candles too!"[35]

Johnson then accused Trudeau of showboating with an eye to his undeclared leadership bid. If Trudeau were to succeed Pearson as prime minister, he said, "this would be enough to blow up Canada."[36]

"If Mr. Johnson's policies are followed, they will destroy federalism," Trudeau replied. "When you are the leader of the Union Nationale, you have to say that kind of stuff. You have to try to destroy French Canadians in Ottawa and that's the kind of tactics you use."[37]

Johnson reiterated his view that Trudeau's guaranteed language rights were hardly going to quench Quebecers' desire for greater autonomy. "It's not an aspirin that's going to regulate the problem," he asserted. "The problem goes deeper than that."[38]

Tensions escalated. At one point, Johnson referred condescendingly to Trudeau as "the member for Mount Royal," which everyone understood to mean that he represented a predominantly English-speaking constituency and could not therefore speak for French Quebecers. Trudeau responded by calling Johnson "the deputy for Bagot," presumably because Johnson had served as Premier Duplessis's deputy in the 1950s.

When the melee threatened to derail the proceedings, Pearson, ever the diplomat, called an unscheduled coffee break. The feud continued outside the room, as each man took questions from journalists. Johnson repeated his earlier charge that Trudeau's views did not represent those of federal MPs from Quebec. "To be leader of a federal party, it is necessary to show the rest of Canada that he can't be pushed around by Quebec," he asserted.[39]

An angry Trudeau responded. "Just because Mr. Johnson has separatists and federalists in his Cabinet who cannot agree," he observed, "he thinks that is the way all Cabinets operate. We hammered out all our positions over a long period."[40]

The prime minister had maintained a smiling facade throughout the standoff, but he was plainly unsettled by Trudeau's belligerence. It was redolent of the "terse obscenities" Trudeau had occasionally hurled at his nationalist adversaries in Quebec, which Pearson thought beneath a government minister. Premier Smith of Nova Scotia concurred with the prime minister, later remarking that "Trudeau should not have started by antagonizing his colleagues."[41] The other premiers, however, seemed to agree with Ross Thatcher, who remarked that it was "a good thing" that the minister of justice had injected some passion into the discussion. "I can only hope Mr. Trudeau's statements will give Mr. Johnson pause to stop and think about Quebec's demands," Thatcher commented.[42]

After the coffee break, all of the delegates reassembled in a closed-door session to consider whether or not to shutter the conference permanently to outsiders. The decision not to do so took only twenty minutes, after which the press was invited back in. For the rest of the morning, Lester Pearson stage-managed the proceedings carefully, avoiding any repeat of the earlier fireworks. He made sure the premiers kept to the relatively benign question of implementing Bi and Bi recommendations, deflecting allusions to Trudeau's charter whenever they arose.

On his way out to lunch, Trudeau was asked by a Quebec journalist to comment on his argument with Johnson. "There was no argument," Trudeau replied coolly. "There were explanations, which were begun yesterday by Mr. Smallwood, about the nature of federalism."[43]

Trudeau, having returned to his usual imperturbable state, took the floor Tuesday afternoon to present the premiers with his prepared statement on behalf of the federal government. "Ordinarily," he began, "one of the most embarrassing things that can happen to a speaker is for him to find that those who have spoken before him have anticipated his text and scooped his material. But on this occasion I know you will understand me when I say that I was very pleased yesterday to hear some of the speakers choose words which I would have been proud to use in describing the importance of a Canadian Charter of Human Rights."

From there, Trudeau offered the premiers—and Canadians watching via television—the most forceful defence of his constitutional vision for Canada that he had made to date. In simple language, it laid out the terms and logic of his charter of human rights. "What better place to start on constitutional reform than by asserting the human freedoms to which we believe people in this country are entitled as of right?" asked Trudeau.

> The Charter of Human Rights attempts to do that. It reflects the government's proposal that we take steps to recognize and protect the most fundamental of our social values. I wish to make it clear that in proposing this measure there is no suggestion that the federal government is seeking any power at the expense of the provinces. We are stating that we are willing to *surrender* some of our power to the people of Canada, and we are suggesting that the provincial governments surrender some of *their* power to the people in the respective provinces. It is because we are a federal state, with competence to legislate divided between provincial governments and the federal government, that we must *all* act in order effectively to protect *all* of the rights of all of the people. Knowing, whether they be Manitobans, Quebeckers or Prince Edward Islanders, that they have common values; that they are united in these respects as *Canadians*—not divided provincially by differences. This is the strength of Canada.[44]

It was a powerful speech, the more so because it came from the man who personified the ideas it communicated. But as Trudeau well knew—a day and a half into the conference and mere hours after his clash with Daniel Johnson—even the most rigorous defence of his charter was unlikely to secure its victory. Several of the premiers expressed their gratitude for his exemplary dedication and hard work but reiterated their misgivings about adopting his charter before they had studied it thoroughly. Daniel Johnson was gracious in his response to Trudeau's proposal but, to no one's surprise, held firmly to his position that Quebec would before long enshrine its own bill of rights, which it was well within its powers to do. Ernest Manning asserted that Trudeau's charter could not be embedded in the Constitution without the unanimous consent of the provinces—which some experts later identified as its true "death knell."[45] The minister of justice had taken his proposal as far as he could, on this day at least. His presentation concluded, the discussion shifted to issues of economic development.

Trudeau could take consolation in the knowledge that it was not his formal statement that made headlines across Canada the next day but his willingness to stand up to the Quebec premier. "Premier Daniel Johnson of Quebec and Justice Minister Pierre Trudeau squared off yesterday over the division of powers between Ottawa and Quebec in a discussion that shed more light on the root issues involved in the conference than all of the prepared speeches heard the day before," said a *Globe and Mail* editorial. "The exchange exposed nerve ends, personal attitudes and political ambitions. Far from breaking the conference up, the debate gave it new meaning and momentum."[46] *Globe* columnist Anthony Westell asserted that Trudeau's besting of Johnson had been an intellectual victory. Johnson, wrote Westell, "is not used to having his demands disputed in detail, to having contrary views put directly to Quebec over his head, and by a French Canadian. Trudeau is among the few men in Ottawa intellectually capable of debating with Mr. Johnson on his own ground, and the last thing the Premier wants is to have this opponent become Prime Minister."[47]

Oddly, the sarcasm in Trudeau's retort about "having our cake and eating it too" was lost on the *Toronto Star*, which roasted him for surrendering his prerogative to defend federalism. "The two were eyeball-to-eyeball and suddenly one blinked," said the *Star*. "Alas, not Daniel Johnson, the guerrilla raider from Quebec, but Pierre Elliott Trudeau, the champion of federal power and the new hero to Canadian intellectuals (English-speaking division). Why did Mr. Trudeau flinch?"[48]

The prevailing sentiment in French-speaking Quebec was disappointment. The spectacle of two Quebecers quarrelling on national television edified no one, Claude Ryan lamented in *Le Devoir*. That the feud appeared to have "delighted" some English Canadians, including Premier Bennett, simply exacerbated Quebecers' sense of isolation.[49]

On one thing almost everyone could agree. Only Trudeau and Johnson had shown panache. The other premiers were "depressingly drab."[50]

On the final day of the conference, Wednesday, February 7, delegates returned to their deliberations in a more conciliatory mood. The prime minister had hosted a dinner at 24 Sussex Drive for the premiers the previous evening, and a forthright private discussion of language rights had run into the early hours of the next morning. The makings of a face-saving consensus on language rights were within Pearson's grasp as he opened the final day's first session. An obliging Daniel Johnson took pains to reassure the others that he had not come to Ottawa to make trouble. "If we did not think it possible to live within federalism, we would not be here," he said. "We need a federal Government."[51]

Lester Pearson tried and failed in the morning to get the premiers to commit to a process for entrenching language rights. Hoping to salvage something concrete from the conference, he and his advisers spent their lunch break preparing a draft communiqué affirming the principle of language equality and the need for continuing constitutional discussions. The terms of the communiqué were accepted by all of the premiers with only minor modifications, and the document was later celebrated as a triumph for the indefatigable Pearson. "As a matter of equity, French-speaking Canadians outside of Quebec should have the same rights as English-speaking Canadians in Quebec," the statement affirmed.[52] As for next steps, seven subcommittees would be struck to study the issues raised at the conference and to meet regularly over the next several years. One of these would be "a special committee" mandated to examine "language rights and their effective provision in practice."[53] This was as close as the conference would get to affirming the principles set out in Trudeau's draft charter.

Most Canadians agreed that the gathering had achieved more than anyone had any right to expect but far less than they had hoped. Given the high stakes, observed Anthony Westell at the *Globe and Mail,* it was perhaps sufficient that three days of meetings had ended "in goodwill, a shower of mutual congratulations and an agreement on the practical machinery for reshaping Confederation."[54] Given the hype that had preceded the conference, though, and the attention accorded Trudeau's nation-saving charter proposal, some Canadians were bitterly disappointed. "A Constitutional Design Lies in Pieces" announced the editorial page of the *Toronto Star.* Trudeau's "high-minded and unifying" idea of a charter of rights had failed, the paper noted bluntly. It had been hived off to a committee of experts, but, in truth, "it is for practical purposes already dead, killed by the opposition of Ontario and others."[55]

Almost everyone in Canada agreed that Lester Pearson's performance at the conference had been "dazzling."[56] He had deployed every trick he had learned as a diplomat to prevent the conference from self-destructing—including reining in his combative justice minister. As Daniel Johnson noted wryly of the prime minister, "He knows when to call a coffee break."[57] If Pearson was disappointed not to have got more out of the premiers, he did not show it. "I think it was a most successful conference and all we could reasonably expect to do at this first meeting," he said—knowing that it would, in fact, be his last.[58]

Daniel Johnson was eminently gracious as the proceedings wound down. "I want the conference to have no doubt at all on what is in the back of my mind," he said. "I have not given up the idea of finding a new federal formula where the provinces will be happier, where French Canadians will feel at home all across Canada."[59] Johnson would later tell reporters that he thought the greatest achievement of the conference was to have undermined the appeal of Quebec separatism. "Without this breakthrough we would have had to drop all talk of a French-Canadian nation and everyone would have fallen back on the idea of a Quebec nation," he said. "Don't be misled by words. I am not looking for a special status."[60]

René Lévesque, on the other hand—the invisible twelfth man at the table, as Peter C. Newman memorably put it—told the Quebec press that the province's true interests had not been represented at the conference by anyone.[61] Since Lévesque had launched his Mouvement souveraineté-association the previous fall, his star had been rising along with Trudeau's—oddly enough, even in English Canada. On the evening of February 6, just hours after Trudeau's televised spat with Johnson, CTV broadcast a ninety-minute English-language documentary positioning Trudeau and Lévesque as larger-than-life titans battling for the hearts and minds of Quebecers. One critic called it "the finest program the network has ever produced," affirming that Trudeau and Lévesque had come to personify the debate about Quebec's future within, or outside, Canada.[62]

As for the quotidian question of whether the conference had strengthened national unity, it seemed to many Canadians that little had been accomplished beyond what the Bi and Bi report had recommended. It cannot have escaped Trudeau's notice that the voluntary implementation of bilingualism by some of the provinces actually worked against his charter. Although Daniel Johnson could not take credit for this outcome of the conference, he acknowledged that it had strengthened his own hand. "The French language in other provinces is in less danger now that several premiers have shown themselves ready to legislate in its favor," he observed. "I don't see any urgency in applying federal proposals since the French language will be given a proper place in several provinces. I wouldn't like to see something imposed by this conference, and far less by the federal government. We don't want federal authorities intervening in provincial matters, even for the sake of the Bi and Bi report."[63] Trudeau himself took the matter in stride. Asked after the conference about his "cherished" charter of human rights, he said, "We'll keep hammering away with it."[64]

The verdict on Trudeau's performance was mixed. *Globe and Mail* columnist Bruce West thought that the justice minister had come across as "a reasonable and persuasive voice which soothes the smarting feelings of the long-frustrated WASPs and yet, at the same time, says nothing which should bring a sense of outrage to his fellow French-Canadians."[65] Others thought the conference had dealt Trudeau a hard blow. "As the dust settles on this week's great constitutional debate in Ottawa," wrote Paul Fox in the *Toronto Star*, "one fact sticks out like a sore thumb. Justice Minister Pierre Elliott Trudeau was dead wrong in making a bill of rights the first requirement of any constitutional revision. It ignored the basic element in the present constitutional wrangle—the simple fact that Quebec is on fire with French-Canadian nationalism, and the blaze won't be extinguished by smothering it under a blanket of civil liberties."[66]

Writing in *Canadian Forum*, Abraham Rotstein, a University of Toronto economist and a leading Canadian nationalist, went even further. Like many Quebec nationalists, then and later, he identified Trudeau's own rigidity as a threat to Canadian national unity. "If the Constitutional Conference has bought us some time," wrote Rotstein, "and a new climate for an accommodation with Quebec, it would be a national disaster to have these dissipated by the forthright and intemperate exercise of Trudeau's ideological convictions on the evils of nationalism."[67]

And that is the salient point.

By February 8, 1968, Canadians could have no doubt whatsoever where Trudeau stood on Canada, Quebec, and the Constitution. As he had done during the parliamentary debates on his divorce and omnibus bills, Trudeau had mastered his brief, laid whatever groundwork he could for a successful outcome, stated his views clearly and simply, defended them in open debate with his adversaries, and accomplished it all with Canadians watching. "Mr. Trudeau has left no room for misunderstanding of his position," York University historians J.L. Granatstein and Peter Oliver affirmed in the *Globe and Mail*. "No one can doubt that he is against special status for Quebec; no one can doubt that he is a convinced federalist. As Mr. Trudeau himself is at pains to point out, for 15 years he has been saying the same thing."[68]

Of the many quotable comments Pierre Trudeau made during the constitutional conference, one stood out: "Ambiguity makes the problem insoluble."[69] Several days later, in a feature interview on CBC-TV, he elaborated. "I'm not quite sure what the Quebec delegation wants. I'm not quite sure that they know what they want either. We've been talking about a new constitution in this country for half-a-dozen years and still we're not quite sure what people want to put into it."[70]

"Ambiguity makes the problem insoluble" is not as famous a Trudeauism as "Just watch me," "Viva Fidel!" or "Fuddle duddle." But it should be. For it encapsulated a trenchant political style that would within weeks best Trudeau's rivals for the Liberal leadership and, ultimately, for power.

CHAPTER SIX
NOW YOU'RE STUCK WITH ME

"Marchand isn't going to be a candidate for the leadership," Lester Pearson remarked at the end of the constitutional conference.[1] For Canadian political watchers, this statement could mean only one thing: Pierre Elliott Trudeau would allow his name to stand.

Or would he?

In the wake of the recent Western, Atlantic, and Quebec policy conferences, Ontario Liberals would meet for their own convention at Toronto's Royal York Hotel over the weekend that began on February 9, 1968. Aides for the non-candidate Trudeau let it be known that their man would be flying into Toronto for the event. He would appear unofficially, and he would make no formal speech. Trudeau would, however, open a hospitality suite at the Royal York in order to mingle with delegates. His total commitment of time to the convention would be three hours, maximum. "He's coming because of pressure from us," said a forthright Donald S. Macdonald, Liberal MP for Rosedale and a leader in the draft-Trudeau movement. "We want him to get an idea of the strength and enthusiasm for his candidacy here."[2]

Trudeau made no secret of the fact that he did not appreciate being pressed into a public appearance in Toronto. His advisers had initially encouraged him to visit the city to meet a few friends, without fanfare, in order to discuss a leadership bid. But once he had agreed to go, they booked the Royal York's massive Ontario Room, issued invitations to conference delegates to meet Trudeau at a "coffee party," and set up a head table from which Trudeau could hold a press conference. "I should have known, of course," he later chided his supporters. "I want to tell you all that if I don't run I hope I won't be letting you down."[3] They had intuited what the justice minister himself did not yet appreciate. He was now the hottest ticket in the Liberal leadership race.

Even in his home province, where René Lévesque, Pierre Bourgault, and Daniel Johnson were now eviscerating Trudeau at every opportunity, new and influential sources of support continued to emerge. On February 15, a draft-Trudeau petition appeared in Quebec media, stating that Trudeau "possesses all the necessary qualities" to lead. It bore the signatures of two hundred prominent Quebecers, including actor Jean-Louis Roux, writer Gilles Marcotte, and Canada Council chair Jean Martineau, among other intellectuals and professionals. Even Claude Ryan conceded that this affirmation of Trudeau's popularity was an important development. "It must be admitted that the signatories are people with influence and definite authority in their respective milieux," he wrote in *Le Devoir*.[4]

In English Canada, it was the same story. To almost everyone's astonishment, Ramsay Cook's draft-Trudeau campaign had evolved from a modest local initiative into a national movement. "Academics," wrote the young *Toronto Star* journalist Andrew Szende, "are almost unanimously speaking out in favor of the former University of Montréal law professor."[5] One of the brightest lights in this movement was Pauline Jewett, a Harvard-trained political scientist who had served as an Ontario MP in the first Pearson minority government. Like Trudeau, Jewett was a dedicated federalist and civil libertarian. (During the October Crisis of 1970, she would break with the Liberal Party over Trudeau's invocation of the *War Measures Act*.) She was drawn to Trudeau in 1968 because she believed that only a French-speaking Quebecer could head off the separatist challenge.[6] But what she liked above all was his conviction. "If he decides certain things must be pursued, he pursues them with clarity and passion, as he has done with the French-English problem," said Jewett. "He has moved shrouds of prejudice and parochialism away from the divorce question, abortion, homosexuality. Why should not this same clarity of perception and passion be brought to bear on some of the other great problems?"[7]

Ramsay Cook and Pauline Jewett were among the roughly two thousand people to attend the policy convention at the Royal York. Of these, 727 would serve as Ontario delegates to the Liberal leadership convention in April.

Like the Quebec policy convention two weeks earlier, the Toronto event proved to be yet another Trudeau show, on the first evening at least. An estimated 1,400 people crammed into the Ontario Room to meet the minister of justice. The atmosphere was electric. As a portent of things to come, receptions being held simultaneously for declared candidates Paul Hellyer and Eric Kierans were practically empty. Between 5 and 7 p.m., Trudeau worked the packed room. Ramsay Cook, who had helped to engineer the spectacle, later wrote that "Pierre seemed surprised and even a little confused by the extraordinary reception he had received in Toronto."[8] Some of the young women in attendance, identified as university students, were plainly smitten—by the man but also by his message. "Pierre can excite people like no one else can," said one of them. "The thing has mushroomed. He's like a savior. And a lot of it has to do with his stand on the federal problem."[9]

After meeting delegates for two hours, Trudeau agreed to talk to the press. Dressed in a light tweed jacket and dark blue tie, he took a seat between Donald Macdonald and Russell Honey, MP for Durham and chair of the Ontario Liberal caucus. Archival footage of the press conference shows Trudeau at his Zen-master best, exuding an air of serene introspection completely at odds with the chaotic energy swirling around him. He was asked about his timetable for a decision on whether to run. "At the outside, ten days," he replied. "If I'm lucky, sooner. I don't know whether the answer will be yes or no. There are two kinds of contacts I have to make before I decide. This kind, when I meet people I haven't met before and try to find out what they want to do with the party and the country and why they think I should be the man to do it. Then, I will have to sift the information with close friends." Had he been pushed by his supporters to come to Toronto? "Not pushed—induced," he said with a smile. Did he think there should be a Quebecer in the leadership race? "Other things being equal, Quebec should be able to put forward a good candidate. But can you find him? Will he be good enough? If the answer is *No,* forget it! I hope there is no one in this room who is going to support me because I'm from Quebec. I have no magic solutions."[10]

After the press conference, Trudeau retired to Donald Macdonald's suite to discuss a possible leadership bid with members of his inner circle, including Ramsay Cook, Jean-Pierre Goyer, Jim Davey, and Gordon Gibson. The small group chatted for ninety minutes. Cook sensed that the meeting was historic and took notes, which he later published.

"What do you make of this whole thing, Ramsay?" Trudeau asked Cook. "Will they call me *un roi nègre,* will I fall under the same criticisms as Laurier and will I get the Uncle Louis image?"

Cook replied that Trudeau would inevitably be called a *vendu* by Quebec nationalists, just like Laurier and St. Laurent. "But did that really represent the thinking of Quebecers?" he asked. "After all, they'd voted for Laurier and Uncle Louis regardless of what the nationalist intellectuals had said."

The conversation then turned to Trudeau's résumé. Trudeau knew that he had the aptitude and the drive to be prime minister, but he was worried about his lack of experience. "He was afraid that he could not meet his own standards of excellence," Cook observed. Trudeau also wanted reassurance that, if he were to become prime minister, he could count on party members and senior bureaucrats in Ottawa to stand behind him. He did not want to end up another Diefenbaker.

Overwhelmed by the intensity of his reception in Toronto, Trudeau told his supporters that he needed solitude and the counsel of close friends to come to a final decision. "My general impression from as disinterested a view as I can take, was that I was talking to a genuinely undecided man," Cook concluded.[11] Trudeau was only too happy to escape Toronto and leave Ontario Liberals to their policy deliberations. He flew off to Montreal later the same evening.

Across Canada, there was a palpable sense the next day that something extraordinary had taken place in the Ontario Room of the Royal York. And it had. Trudeaumania was born.

Canadians had caught earlier glimpses of Pierre Trudeau's nascent sex appeal, his hip sartorial style, and, of course, his commanding intellect. But in Toronto, the mass adulation of Trudeau's supporters combined for the first time with the mainstream media's willingness to cover it positively. The day after this Royal York appearance, photographs of Trudeau being warmly attentive to pretty women made the front pages of the Canadian dailies, alongside headlines like the *Toronto Star*'s "Liberals Make It a 'Love-in' for Pierre Trudeau."[12] Press stories of the justice minister obliging autograph-seekers were filed. Analogies to JFK and the Beatles were made. Almost immediately, anxious journalists and broadcasters began asking themselves whether they were covering Trudeau or inventing him.

There were other, less obvious processes already at work in the burgeoning Trudeaumania phenomenon. Of these, the most influential (and enduring) were the calculated efforts of Trudeau's opponents to position him as a media-generated flash in the pan. In Quebec, his nationalist critics had fashioned a "messiah" myth to explain his apparently effortless ascent in federal politics. This fiction critiqued English Canadians' ignorance of Quebec as much as it disparaged Trudeau. But it was a powerful narrative nonetheless, the more so for having been repeated so often—and by moderates like Claude Ryan as well as separatists like René Lévesque. Naturally, many English Canadians thought this critique condescending. On February 9, the day Trudeau appeared at the Royal York, the *Globe and Mail* ran an editorial entitled "Not Sudden, Not a Messiah," condemning Claude Ryan personally. "It is wrong to hold that English Canadians are incapable of judging Mr. Trudeau on any grounds but his potential as a safe or 'messianic' French Canadian," stated the *Globe*.[13] The next day, Ryan conceded in *Le Devoir* that there was more to the Trudeau phenomenon than the search for "*un messie canadien-français*."[14] But the messiah narrative stuck, and it resonates still.

Members of the English-Canadian governing elites—many of whom saw Trudeau as a dilettante and interloper—also saw his sudden popularity as a potential Achilles' heel. "How long can Trudeau's non-campaign continue?" demanded one frustrated senior Liberal after the justice minister's Royal York appearance.[15] "Okay, okay," said another, identified as an aide to one of the declared leadership hopefuls. "Let's just cool off. He's not the new Messiah. I'm fed up to the teeth with all this charisma."[16] Again, it fell to Canada's seasoned political commentators to challenge the aspersion that Trudeau's popularity was manufactured. Trudeau's charisma was genuine, Anthony Westell wrote after the Toronto appearance. "In a sense, he is the man we would all like to be: charming, rich, talented, successful." But Trudeaumania was not an invention of backroom Svengalis or ravenous reporters, Westell insisted. "While it is always hard to decide when reporting a bandwagon becomes pushing it, it does seem clear that the press and TV began to hear about Mr. Trudeau from the grassroots before they took him seriously as a possible candidate and began to promote him by publicizing him."[17]

In short, the persistent claim that Trudeaumania was the product of superficial media processes did not arise in isolation. It was deployed actively as a strategy to undermine Trudeau even before he announced his intention to run for the Liberal leadership. That the strategy failed—in the sense that Trudeau won power in spite of this narrative—does not diminish its importance.

Trudeau knew exactly what he was up against, having spent so much of his adult life paddling against the current. Asked in mid-February about whispering campaigns from his Liberal leadership rivals, he replied with characteristic bravado. "They want a fight?" he said. "It makes me feel like running."[18]

In truth, Trudeau could no more be swayed by his own brawler's instinct than by the pleas of his supporters. He continued to ponder and procrastinate. Again, it fell to his closest friends to try to cajole him into running. Meeting with Jean Marchand in Montreal just days after the Ontario convention, Trudeau reiterated all of his reservations.

"I would prefer to wait," he told Marchand.

"If you don't go in, Hellyer or Winters will be the next leader, and how long will he stay there?" Marchand countered.[19]

Marc Lalonde encountered the same indecision. Trudeau acknowledged that he had succeeded in Toronto but continued to fret that he had not been in politics long enough to build up his own power base. He did not want to be one of the hapless candidates abandoned by his own people when the deals were struck at the leadership convention. "When we were arguing with him," Lalonde later recalled, "he brought a couple of us in and said 'If I go in, I want a commitment that you'll be around. I want to be sure you're not sending me out to war alone.'"[20]

Meanwhile, in public, instead of adopting the cautious, equivocating style of a campaigning politician, Trudeau continued to act like a man who had nothing to lose. On February 13, he appeared on the Ottawa television program *Under Attack*, which pitted him against a group of francophone students in open and unscripted conversation. For any other prime ministerial hopeful, it would have been a minefield. But speaking extemporaneously to thoughtful and idealistic young Canadians, Trudeau was entirely in his element. Asked why he rejected a *deux nations* view of Canada, he told them, "I think French Canadians have been betrayed by their elite for one hundred years." Asked how he felt about being called a *vendu* in Quebec, he replied that such insults evinced "the masochistic tendencies of just about all French Canadian nationalists."[21] At one point, the conversation turned unexpectedly to the quality of the French spoken in Quebec. Again Trudeau refused to dissemble. The government of Quebec had enjoyed full control over education for generations, he said, yet "a lot of the French spoken in Quebec is lousy (*pouilleux*). I don't think Ottawa should give one single whit of power to the province of Quebec until it has shown the rest of Canada it can teach better language in its schools."[22]

Trudeau's linguistic snobbery was by then well known to Quebecers—how he had gravitated to classical French literature in his teens and adopted correct French instead of the street slang of his local neighbourhood. "I remember being rather penalized for it," Trudeau would later recall, "because when you're fifteen and you suddenly begin to say '*le gateau*' rather than '*le gaaaateau*,' people begin poking fun at you. Not only in school, but in the neighbourhood, and even some of my relatives: 'Oh, look, he's putting on airs.'"[23]

In Quebec, the nationalist response to Trudeau's "lousy French" remark was predictably swift and merciless. "You are dying of hunger, you miserable little uneducated people," René Lévesque said mockingly. "But before you get the food which is yours you must learn to beg for it with the elegance which is customary in the circles I frequent."[24] Daniel Johnson trod lightly on the matter, accusing Trudeau of indulging a "passing political expediency" and pandering to English Canada.[25] In contrast, Jean-Noël Tremblay, Johnson's outspoken cultural affairs minister, fumed that there were "few better examples of opportunism so degrading." As journalists at the Canadian Press discovered, however, Tremblay had made the same criticism of Quebecers' French just months earlier. "The language of the Government is bad, the language of teachers is bad, the language of business is bad, the language of information media is far from being above reproach, and the language of the elite, infected by English, isn't much better," Tremblay had complained. Asked about this apparent double standard, Tremblay offered the sort of nationalist response that played to Trudeau's characterization of Quebecers as insular. "That was a family affair," Tremblay said. "One washed one's dirty linen in the family, if I may be permitted the expression. But it is absolutely indecent to display one's own weaknesses outside in a foreign land (*à l'étranger*)."[26]

On February 15, 1968, Trudeau had breakfast in Ottawa with Jean Marchand and Gérard Pelletier. He had made up his mind, he told his friends. He would run for the Liberal leadership.

Then, just hours later, he changed his mind.

Delighted that Trudeau had finally tipped off the fence, Jean Marchand hastily organized a noon-hour press conference ostensibly to announce that he would not seek the nomination himself. He then called a meeting of the Quebec Liberal caucus, the sole purpose of which was to rally party members behind a Trudeau leadership bid. Of the fifty-three MPs and twenty-one senators who made up the federal Liberal caucus, however, only twenty people showed up. Those not in attendance offered excuses about prior commitments. Trudeau's aides were reportedly stunned by the poor showing. So was the candidate himself. "If there are only twenty members from Quebec who support me then I'm not a candidate," Trudeau informed the press on his way out of the meeting. "I'm the Justice Minister."[27]

Marchand was dismayed. For the rest of the day, it was unclear where Trudeau stood. The press speculated that his advisers had likely prevailed upon him, quoting Jean-Pierre Goyer to the effect that more than 80 per cent of the Liberal caucus had said that they would fall in behind Trudeau. (Where Goyer got this number was itself an open question, since half of the Quebec caucus would back candidates other than Trudeau throughout the leadership race.)[28]

Not until ten o'clock the next morning did Canadians know for certain that the justice minister had decided to run. He arrived at his own press conference at the National Press Building wearing a dark grey suit and a brown fur hat, obviously at ease with his decision and exuding confidence. For an hour, Trudeau conversed casually with the hundred or so journalists who had shown up. The CBC carried the press conference live, something it had done for no other candidate.

The first question was the most obvious. Why had he declared himself? "If I try to assess what happened in the past two months," he replied,

> I have a suspicion you people had a lot to do with it. If anybody's to blame I suppose it's you collectively. To be quite frank, if I try to analyze it, well, I think in the subconscious mind of the press, it started out like a huge practical joke on the Liberal party. And what happened, I think, is that the joke blew up in your face and in mine. People took it seriously. And when members of Parliament formed committees to draft me, and when I got responsible Liberals in responsible positions in different parts of the country telling me seriously that I should run—I didn't think the Liberal party would take me, and suddenly they did. So I was stuck with it. Well, now you're stuck with me.

Trudeau was then asked about whether he thought he had the right kind of experience. "I think I have less experience than all the other, or most of the other, candidates, in terms of departments or belonging to a political party. But I have to reflect on other aspects of this question, and I must say to myself in honesty that there are some fields in which experience isn't much of a help, and the help is mainly through the approach you have to the problems." He was asked about his late entry into the race and his much-publicized hesitation. "I feel that it's going to be a very interesting campaign," he replied. "Now that I'm in it, I'm absolutely delighted."[29]

Decades later, when he was writing his memoirs, Trudeau cited only one exchange from this historic February 1968 press conference. A journalist asked him if it was true that he wanted to put Quebec in its place. "Yes, absolutely," Trudeau replied. "And its place is within Canada, with all the advantages and all the influence to which our province is entitled."[30]

The press response to Trudeau's announcement was mixed, in part because it seemed anticlimactic after all the feverish speculation. Claude Ryan lamented in *Le Devoir* that Trudeau's intractability on the Constitution threatened Canadian federalism when it was at its most fragile. Liberal delegates might elect Trudeau leader out of a "desire for novelty" or an "obsession with electoral victory," wrote Ryan, but this choice would surely demonstrate that "they do not understand what has happened in Quebec since 1960." The party would be far better off in the short term with an English-Canadian leader who was willing to negotiate a new division of powers with Quebec, even if he was less intelligent than Trudeau.[31]

Echoing *Le Devoir*, the *Toronto Star* editorial asked, "Is Canada ready for Pierre Trudeau?" It would be "exciting to have a brilliant, uninhibited intellectual in the prime minister's office," said the *Star*. "It would also be risky. Mr. Trudeau is constitutionally incapable of trying to be all things to all men."[32] The *Globe and Mail* welcomed

Trudeau into the race not merely as a Quebecer but as a principled minister who had earned respect across the country. The job now before him, however, was to tell Canadians how he would govern. "We know he would reverse the trend of governments to put reins on the liberties of individuals," said the *Globe*. "We know he doesn't think our problems can be resolved by switching to a republican form of government. But we don't know how he would tackle the housing crisis, development of resources, immigration, poverty, international relations; and we will want to know."[33]

How ordinary Canadians felt about the Trudeau candidacy also concerned the press. Patricia Jolivet, the wife of B.C. Liberal Federation president Larry Jolivet, was asked why she supported Trudeau. "We desperately need a new image and we need a strong federalist," she replied. "It's about time we took a gamble instead of sticking with the same stodgy old people. And anyway I think he's sexy."[34] Montreal lawyer G.J. Szablowski chastised Trudeau's Quebec adversaries for deliberately misrepresenting him. "It is clear, for those who have read or listened to the ideas of Mr. Trudeau, that rigidity and intransigence have no place either in ideas or in his manner of expression," wrote Szablowski in *Le Devoir*.[35] In Manitoba, where polls showed Paul Hellyer leading, party elites appeared to be more sceptical about Trudeau's résumé. "What does Trudeau know about hog prices?" asked one of them.[36]

Coincidentally, just as Trudeau was entering the leadership race, the *Watkins Report* on foreign investment in Canada exploded onto the nation's front pages. Mel Watkins was a University of Toronto economist heading up a task force on U.S. investment in Canada—an issue that had been on the national agenda since Walter Gordon's Royal Commission on Canada's Economic Prospects in the mid-1950s. Foreign direct investment in Canada would remain a red-hot topic in English-Canadian intellectual circles well into the 1970s, where it became a *cause célèbre* for left-nationalists who believed that nothing less than Canadian sovereignty was at stake.[37] Not surprisingly, the anti-nationalist Trudeau thought little of the sort of economic protectionism championed by Gordon and Watkins, and had been saying so since his *Cité libre* days. The day he announced his candidacy, he was asked his position on the *Watkins Report*. "I'm against nationalism and economic nationalism as defined by the economists, which is an excessive doctrine that could work against the country," he replied.[38] This was a message Trudeau would repeat, without guile or obfuscation, throughout the Trudeaumania period, alienating some of the intellectuals who might have otherwise gravitated towards him.

One Liberal who appreciated Trudeau's candour, oddly enough, was Walter Gordon. "If anyone wants to know who I think is the best man for the job of Prime Minister, I think it's Mr. Trudeau," Gordon would announce in mid-March. "I'm going to vote for him."[39] Trudeau was grateful to have Gordon's backing but took pains to reiterate his opposition to economic protectionism. "My approach to economics is the same as my approach to politics," he said. "It's a very great disgust of this thing called nationalism. And so far as Mr. Gordon's ideas are rightly or wrongly identified with high degrees of protectionism or of nationalism, I'm against them." Trudeau was asked his opinion of Gordon. "He is a man with a critical mind, an intellectual man, and I like a man who asks questions, asks what are you doing this for, and doesn't let the rest of us get away with things," he replied. "Having seen Mr. Gordon in action I must say he is not as much of a Gordonite as his disciples."[40] The closest Trudeau would get to "Gordonite" policies during the leadership campaign was to state his openness to the idea of a federal agency to foster Canadian competitiveness in transportation and communication technology (that is, a Canada Development Corporation). Otherwise, his position was unambiguous. "Neither hothouse cultures nor hothouse economics will survive in the rugged world of tomorrow," he said.[41]

Now that Trudeau was finally a declared candidate, his clandestine organization moved out of the shadows. Marc Lalonde and Gérard

Pelletier took charge of the campaign, ably assisted by speech writers Tim Porteous, Don Peacock, and Ramsay Cook. (Jean Marchand would resign as leader of the Quebec caucus on March 7 in order to join the Trudeau team. One of his first public statements was to warn Quebec premier Daniel Johnson not to meddle in the leadership race.) Money was managed by the capable but virtually invisible Robert Brouillard. Jim Davey ran the campaign on the ground up to the convention weekend, when Jean-Pierre Goyer took over. Pierre Levasseur anchored Trudeau's Ottawa headquarters. Gordon Gibson became Trudeau's executive assistant, accompanying the candidate out on the hustings. (After Gibson was injured in a motorcycle accident, Bill Lee would replace him in mid-campaign.) Other long-time loyalists and recent converts would also join Trudeau's youthful team, including legions of volunteers—many of them female and, in the parlance of the day, groovy.[42]

February 16, 1968—the day Trudeau announced his candidacy—was a cold and snowy Friday. The leadership campaign had already passed its halfway mark. The eight declared candidates had logged thousands of miles and shaken almost as many hands to win the support of Liberals across Canada. Polls showed that Trudeau was highly popular, particularly in Ontario and Quebec, but trailing Paul Martin nationally.

If the newest Liberal contender felt any pressure to catch up to his rivals, he did not show it. At the close of his press conference, he bid the press and his advisers *adieu* and promptly flew off to the Laurentians for a weekend of skiing.

Monday, February 19, appeared to be an unexceptional day in the House of Commons, except that the government benches were noticeably thin. Prime Minister Lester Pearson was on vacation in Jamaica. Another 47 of the Liberals' 130 MPs were away, including leadership hopefuls Paul Martin, Joe Greene, and John Turner. Of the government's top ministers, only Justice Minister Pierre Trudeau and Finance Minister Mitchell Sharp were present in the House.

Sharp was nominally in charge when Deputy Speaker Herman Batten unexpectedly called for a vote on Bill C-193, a Liberal measure to impose an income surtax. For seventy-eight minutes, the parliamentary bells rang out. The Opposition Tories managed to scramble some of their MPs into the House for the vote, but the governing Liberals were caught flat-footed. The Liberals lost the vote 84 to 82, when the NDP, Créditistes, Socreds, and one independent MP voted with the Tories.

Because C-193 was a money bill, the Opposition immediately launched into a chorus of "Resign!" Lester Pearson got a phone call at 10:30 p.m. from his executive assistant, Torrance Wylie, telling him breathlessly that the government had been defeated on a tax bill. "I was flabbergasted," Pearson later recalled. "When he indicated the circumstances of our defeat, I was not only flabbergasted, I was furious."[43] Pearson roused himself at 5:30 the next morning to catch an early flight to Ottawa. He met his cabinet over lunch, conveyed his anger in no uncertain terms, and began to navigate the tricky process of retaining power. "I was not too worried about the situation politically, when I learned that it had been a snap vote," Pearson later wrote. "It was a trap, of course, a legitimate parliamentary trick. When I heard all about this, I was concerned only with what to do. We had to refuse the demand that we resign on this vote."[44]

Pearson asked Tory leader Robert Stanfield for a twenty-four-hour adjournment of the House of Commons to allow the government some breathing room. Stanfield, to his everlasting credit as a parliamentarian and a gentleman, obliged the prime minister. Pearson took to the airwaves to tell Canadians that the vote had been merely "a hazard of minority government" and did not constitute a true defeat. He also met with his top advisers, including Pierre Trudeau, and drafted the following confidence motion: "That this House does not regard its vote in connection with third reading of Bill C-193, which had carried in all previous stages, as a vote of non-confidence in the government." The motion was tabled in the Commons on Wednesday, February 21. A week-long brouhaha followed, Stanfield arguing that the government must resign, Pearson countering that it need not. When the dust finally settled, on February 28, the minority Liberals were sustained in power by a vote of 138 to 119—in no small measure because the Créditistes, who feared the outcome of a snap election, voted with the government.[45]

Pierre Trudeau did not fare particularly well over the course of this non-confidence episode. Far from breaking party discipline or playing the renegade, the justice minister dutifully defended the prime minister's rationale for clinging to power and voted with the government. The *Globe and Mail* dedicated an entire editorial to Trudeau's apparent transformation into a party hack, calling him an "*erstwhile* man of principle" and accusing him of joining "the spineless Liberal herd" he had only a few years earlier excoriated.[46] Other pundits noted, however, that the justice minister may have benefited both from his spirited defence of the government's position and from the optics of taking a leadership role during the crisis. As Peter C. Newman observed, Trudeau along with John Turner and Eric Kierans had managed to project "a new style that dissociates them from the blunders of the Pearson administration."[47] Trudeau may also have benefited from having been in the House the evening the tax bill was defeated. That his rivals seemed more interested in campaigning than in governing—a perception for which Pearson had rebuked them more than once—could not have hurt him.[48]

The episode appeared not to have affected Trudeau's polling numbers. A national survey published on February 28 showed Paul Martin to be the first choice of 26 per cent of Canadians and Trudeau still lagging at 12 per cent. The same poll revealed that 16 per cent of

French Canadians favoured Trudeau, in comparison with only 11 per cent of English-speaking Canadians—a dramatic revelation given the hostility of Quebec's nationalists towards him.[49] A *Toronto Star* survey of 164 Ontario Liberals, on the other hand, showed Trudeau with a massive lead. He was the first choice of 74 respondents, followed by the non-candidate Robert Winters at 44. Paul Martin ranked fifth with only 9 votes.[50]

Winters drew the obvious conclusion. In addition to being the best-connected Liberal within the Canadian corporate elite, he now appeared to have sufficient grassroots support to take a serious run at the leadership. He would formally announce his candidacy on March 29, becoming the last of the cabinet heavyweights to join the race.

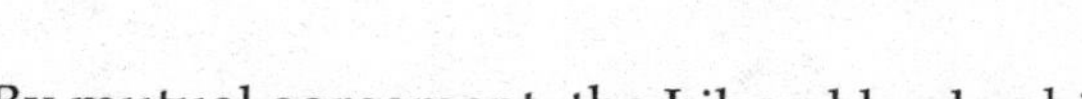

By mutual agreement, the Liberal leadership contest had been suspended during the non-confidence imbroglio. When it became clear that the Pearson government would survive the crisis, all of the candidates revved up their campaign machines and headed onto the campaign trail for what they knew would be five weeks of hard-scrabble politicking.

The novice Pierre Trudeau had two advantages from the outset. The first was that, at Trudeau's own insistence, his campaign would focus entirely on his own ideas and ignore what his adversaries were saying—the only exception being Quebec premier Daniel Johnson, whom Trudeau was increasingly happy to use as a foil. "The fact that he attacks me so much may prove I have a great deal of support in Quebec," Trudeau would say of Johnson on the hustings. "It may be that he would prefer to have someone in Ottawa who cannot support the federal position as well as I can."[51] Trudeau's second advantage was that the other candidates, with the exception of Eric Kierans and John Turner, opted to play it safe and steer clear of policy specifics in their appeals to Liberal delegates.[52] The result was a Trudeau-versus-the-rest campaign, in which Trudeau spoke frankly, even amateurishly, about his policy priorities and most of the others kept to carefully scripted performances emphasizing their long experience in government and their party connections. (There were important exceptions, including John Turner's principled efforts to put poverty on the campaign agenda.) Moreover, even as the April convention loomed, Trudeau's rivals could not agree on the need for a common front against him.

Whether Trudeau was advantaged by being the only French Canadian in the race is an open question. Two of his English-Canadian competitors, Kierans and Turner, were bilingual Montrealers offering special status and decentralization as the solution to Canada's national-unity woes—precisely the formula endorsed by Daniel Johnson, Claude Ryan, and other moderate Quebec nationalists. "The prime role of the provinces must be the distribution of wealth," Kierans would argue over the course of the campaign, "and I include authority over health, education and welfare. Some provinces may not wish to occupy all the field of social welfare. In such instances the provinces that do occupy these fields would enjoy a special status."[53] Turner would not go as far as Kierans on specifics, preferring to keep to high-minded appeals to Quebec federalists. "Quebec does, in a sense, represent the homeland of a people," Turner would say. "You can't treat Quebec as a province like the others. This doesn't mean that you sell Canada down the river."[54] Hellyer, Winters, Sharp, and the fluently bilingual Martin also commanded loyalty among moderate Quebec nationalists and for exactly the same reasons. But they, too, kept mainly to platitudes rather than policy prescriptions.

The wintry evening of February 28, Trudeau appeared before a standing-room-only crowd in Kingston, Ontario, to give the first public speech of his campaign. Kingstonians had turned out in the hundreds to get a taste of Trudeaumania, but by all accounts the candidate's rambling talk on participatory democracy struck them as uninspired. As a stump speaker, Trudeau had not yet reconciled the two sides of his public persona—the intellectual Trudeau who had made the mastery of politics his life's work versus the diffident Trudeau who claimed that he had no quick fixes or magic solutions. On this evening at least, it was the latter who took to the podium. "Basically, what we try to do in government is to sit down with the people and discuss the facts of the situation and hammer out the solutions together," he lectured his Kingston audience. "We don't have the answers to the problems that are asked of the Canadian people today. We are trying to find them." At a certain point, Trudeau realized that his seminar-style navel-gazing had lost the crowd. "I just better cut off here because, you know, university towns and all," he mumbled. "I usually speak for an hour and a half."[55]

Trudeau hit his stride three days later, however, when he spoke to a packed house at Toronto's four-hundred-seat St. Lawrence Hall. Again, the crowd was standing-room-only, "scores" of disappointed Torontonians having been turned away. "Grown men scrambled for his autograph," said one breathless report. "Girls tugged at his stylish check suit, only to dissolve in embarrassment when he turned his smile on them."[56] Leaving little to chance, Trudeau played entirely to his own strengths, speaking mainly about Quebec's place in Canada. During the Q & A session, he coolly took the fight directly to Premier Daniel Johnson. "He's trying to destroy me now," said Trudeau of the Quebec premier. "Last year, it was Marchand. Next year, it may be somebody else. Mr. Johnson claims to speak for French Canadians when he is really trying to make sure that French Canadians in Ottawa are nincompoops."[57] Asked about "special status" or "particular status," Trudeau dismissed such ideas as "gimmicks."[58] Once more, he cautioned Canadians against imagining, however, that he intended to put Quebecers in their place. "If people think I would be a good choice for PM because I would be hard on

Quebec, they had better not vote for me," he warned.[59] His warmest applause came when he answered the question, "How badly do you want to be Prime Minister?" Trudeau replied with a quotation from Plato: "A man who wants very badly to be head of the country should not be trusted."[60]

At this early stage in the leadership campaign, notwithstanding the unexpected deluge of public and media curiosity, Trudeau played it straight—touring the country, meeting Liberal convention delegates, and laying out his policy ideas. What is striking about his proposals, seen in retrospect, is how true they were to the now-familiar Trudeau vision of Canada. Speaking to a crowd of six hundred in Port Hope, Ontario, on March 2, for example, Trudeau pitched pragmatism and openness to the world as the touchstones of a government led by him. "Once we have protected the basic rights of all Canadians—and I include in that linguistic rights—then we should decide the other matters on the question of efficiency—not on an ethnic basis, or the morals of one church. In a decade where we will soon be able to dial in any country in the world on TV, it is futile to try and cut off any sector, or country of our world. We have to accept the challenge of changing times and not try to protect ourselves behind artificial walls."[61] On March 3, speaking in Vineland in the Niagara region of Ontario, Trudeau told the crowd that a government headed by him would move immediately to recognize the People's Republic of China (with the caveat, however, that Canada would continue to recognize Taiwan). He stated as well that he was prepared to appear in person at the United Nations to call for a halt to the American bombing of North Vietnam.

The U.S. war in Vietnam had by this time helped to inspire the student protest movement in North America and throughout the West. For many Canadian activists, restricting Canadian arms sales to the United States had become, like the trade and investment policies advocated by Walter Gordon and Mel Watkins, a matter of national sovereignty. Trudeau thus faced questions on Vietnam every time he stepped onto a university campus. His stated policy on the war was that the United States could not withdraw unilaterally from the conflict, but that bombing North Vietnam as a prelude to peace talks was wrong-headed. On the question of Canadian arms exports, however, Trudeau disagreed with the protesters, and he was blunt in saying so. Canadians had a huge economic stake in bilateral trade with the United States, Trudeau told a London, Ontario, crowd on March 8, and he was not prepared to undermine it. "We're not doing it to help the United States war effort," he said of this commerce, "but doing it to help ourselves."[62] When, during a campaign speech in Sudbury, Ontario, a Laurentian University student raised the matter of arms shipments to the United States, Trudeau asked the student whether he would risk the ruin of the Canadian economy by cutting off all exports that abetted the U.S. war effort. "Would you want to close down the nickel mines?" he demanded. [63]

Trudeau was also unafraid to test the limits of domestic policies that many Canadians regarded as sacrosanct. On a March 3 French-language television broadcast, for example, he announced that under his leadership welfare measures would be directed to the neediest Canadians and cease to be universal. Ten days later, he told a Moncton, New Brunswick, crowd that he thought Canada should not only reduce its NATO commitments but also withdraw its armed forces from Europe entirely and focus on the defence of North America.[64] Against the advice of his closest advisers, who appreciated that the division of powers within Canadian federalism might not be the stuff of great stump speeches, Trudeau continued to appeal to his old *Cité libre* idea of *politique fonctionnelle*. "We must view our constitution from the perspective of functionalism," Trudeau told the Newfoundland House of Assembly on March 25. "What level of government will be best able to do the job of making Canada, and all its parts, a better place in which to live?"[65]

Canadians were listening—and reading. On March 9, Liberal senator and celebrated social reformer David Croll announced his support for Trudeau's candidacy. "Pierre Elliott Trudeau is a new young face, a professional, who brings to the problems of today a trained mind, a clear grasp of principle, and a freedom from preconceived ideas," said Croll. "He speaks with clarity, boldness and realism. Moreover, he tells it 'like it is.' With him as leader, it is not going to be more of the same."[66] The same day that Croll was extolling Trudeau's potential as a reformer, Paul Fox of the *Toronto Star* announced after reading Trudeau's *Federalism and the French Canadians* that Trudeau was not radical in the least. "The truth is that beneath his dashing image, Pierre Trudeau is conservative," wrote Fox. "His attitude on many matters is cautious and conventional—on the constitution, for instance, as his book shows, and on medicare, the sale of war material to the United States, on NATO and other matters, as his public statements during the current campaign are now beginning to make clear."[67]

Virtually all Canadians, in Quebec and elsewhere, agreed that the main issue in the Liberal leadership contest was national unity, and that Trudeau's "rigidity" on the question made him both the *bête noire* of Quebec nationalists and the foil of his Liberal leadership rivals.[68]

As Lewis Seale noted perceptively in the *Globe and Mail,* every leadership hopeful other than Trudeau used the terms *flexibility* and *negotiation* to describe his approach to Quebec.[69] What these words appeared to mean in principle was openness to special status, but even this attitude was not always clear. Paul Hellyer's position was typical. "I recognize that Quebec, because of its ethnic identity, is the home of French culture in America and in Canada," he said on the campaign trail. "Thus it is obvious that the Province of Quebec is not a province like the others and it should be considered in this light. I submit to you my determination to discuss, negotiate and adopt a formula of continued research in constitutional matters in order to reach practical conclusions acceptable to the governments of the provinces and the federal Government."[70] Other candidates were similarly vague. "This Quebec society to which all French-speaking minorities in Canada turn imposes on its government responsibilities which are not necessarily imposed on other provinces and, in this sense, one is correct in proclaiming that Quebec is not a province like the others," said Paul Martin.[71] "I believe that without a strong Quebec there would be very little hope for the survival of the French fact in Canada," added Mitchell Sharp. "I will never refuse discussion and I will try to influence federal policies so that they take into account local circumstances. The rest is negotiation and good will."[72]

Given that Trudeau had for years been proposing a concrete program of constitutional reform based on a charter of human rights, his opponents' promises of *flexibility* and *negotiation* appeared to many Canadians to be confused, if not evasive. The *Globe and Mail*, for example, praised Trudeau in the middle of the leadership campaign for having the "guts" to defend his federalist stance—and castigated his leadership rivals, John Turner especially, for their opportunistic and faint-hearted statements on Quebec.[73] (Turner's rejoinder: "We are not going to solve any of our problems by trying to put any province in its place.")[74] Liberal delegates had before them, in other words, a choice between Trudeau's statement "This is what I will do" and his rivals' promise "This is how I intend to proceed."

Over the course of both the leadership contest and especially the subsequent election campaign, Trudeau's emphasis on policy over process gave him at least four tactical advantages out on the campaign trail. First, it allowed him to represent his own ideas as the only blueprint for Canadian federalism that would prevent Quebec nationalists from taking advantage of accommodationist sentiment elsewhere in the country. Second, it reinforced his claim that Quebec nationalists did not speak for all Quebecers. Third, it allowed him to paint his opponents as vague, opportunistic, and sometimes even cowardly. Last, it enhanced Trudeau's appeal among Canadian voters who preferred straight shooters. "This is my policy, take it or leave it," he said repeatedly. "If someone has a better policy, do not vote for me."

Canadians noticed something else. Trudeau said precisely the same things in Quebec as he said elsewhere in the country. On March 26, for example, he sparred with a group of nationalist students who had shown up to heckle his speech to the Liberal Reform Club in Quebec City. "Don't you feel a bit isolated in Canadian politics due to the fact that all Quebec parties and all Canadian parties have accepted the concept of two nations?" asked one of the students. "No, I'm not isolated," Trudeau replied. "I have support everywhere. I went West. I have just returned from Newfoundland." Said another student, "Only Mr. Diefenbaker would admit a position like yours." Trudeau hit back. "It's just a small number of intellectuals who are locked up in their two-nation concept," he said. "The population doesn't believe in it. You can speak of equality of two nations such as Guatemala or France, or Germany and Italy. But you couldn't speak of equality within France, for example, between the Bretons and the people of the Île de France or the Basques—that would be three nations in France—or four with the Alsatians or five with the Savoyards or six with the Provinciaux."[75] (Trudeau's statement was bolstered by a national poll showing that most Quebecers wanted a French Canadian in the job of prime minister.)[76]

Daniel Johnson agreed with the hecklers. Ignoring Jean Marchand's advice to stay out of the fray, he asserted that anyone espousing Trudeau's "retrograde" ideas about Quebec was completely out of touch. Speaking at a Union Nationale dinner in late March, the Quebec premier compared Trudeau with Lord Durham, whose famous 1839 *Durham Report* recommended that British North Americans assimilate the French Canadians because they were "a people with no literature and no history."[77] Trudeau saw an opportunity. Instead of lashing out at Johnson, he played the statesman. "It's obviously in Mr. Johnson's interest to dissociate any Quebec MP from the Quebec scene," said Trudeau. "And his comparison of me to Lord Durham shows how little he knows about history. Durham, while he was, I think, a brilliant political analyst, certainly didn't reach the same conclusions we did about linguistic rights. We're saying French Canadians should have them right across Canada. I think that he is playing a desperate game, which I have every reason to believe will backfire."

A week later, on April 2, Trudeau delivered one of the most elegant speeches of his campaign—in Montreal, in French, using the pronoun *nous* to self-identify as a Quebecer. "You will not be astonished if I affirm my faith in a form of government called federalism," he told the crowd.

> I would like to state precisely that, as far as I am concerned, federalism is not an expedient, nor is it a compromise. On the contrary, it is an avant-garde political formula, to which I would subscribe even outside the Canadian context. Why? The great advantage of federalism is that it brings the state and the citizen closer, it allows for local legislation for local needs, regional for regional needs, and federal for confronting global problems. As French Canadians, we have not yet given the quarter of our true capacities. Some people assert that Quebec's progress is incompatible with Canada's. I propose that we start with a contrary hypothesis, namely that the safest token of progress for Canada is a strong and dynamic French Canada, sure of itself, freed from fear, and thoroughly involved in all aspects of Canadian life. Masters in our own house? I agree. But our own house is the whole of Canada, from Newfoundland to Victoria, with its immense resources which belong to all of us and of which we should not give up even a patch.[78]

Needless to say, for some Quebec nationalists and their English-Canadian sympathizers, such talk remained anathema, the more so with the anti-nationalist Trudeau edging closer to power. One Quebecer who had for years counted himself a supporter of Trudeau but abandoned him in 1968 was Laurier LaPierre, then best known as co-host with Patrick Watson of the CBC's landmark public affairs show *This Hour Has Seven Days*. In an open letter postdated to the second day of the Liberal leadership convention, LaPierre lamented that he was "sadly disillusioned" by Trudeau's policy on Vietnam, his conservative indifference to Canada's domination by foreign capital, and especially his anti-nationalism. "The new nationalism is an instrument to propel change, to formulate it and to confront the stagnating forces within a society," wrote LaPierre. "Mr. Trudeau has completely refused to grasp the profound need we have for a new constitution; one which entrenches our collective rights and states clearly our *raison d'être*, which frees us forever from the platitudes of the professional *bon-ententistes*, and which redistributes legislative and executive powers in such a way as to take into account the simple fact that Quebec is and will remain for quite some time the major instrument of the on-going life of the Canadian who speaks French."[79]

LaPierre was not the only Canadian who had followed Trudeau closely and formed a contrary opinion of him. Over the weekend of March 23, for example, Trudeau spoke to large crowds in northern Ontario. After a Saturday night speech in Sudbury, several Liberal delegates who had originally intended to support Trudeau told his aides that they were no longer committed to him. One of these was Liberal MPP Elmer Sopha, who objected both to Trudeau's protests against the U.S. bombing of North Vietnam and to his willingness to recognize communist China. "I was going to support him earlier," said Sopha at the conclusion of Trudeau's Sudbury talk, "but I've changed my mind. He's shallow."[80] Sopha announced that he would support Joe Greene on the first ballot instead. A week later, Sopha announced that he would be launching his own one-man "stop Trudeau" movement. "At one time I, like many others, was rather favorably impressed with Mr. Trudeau," Sopha said at a March 28 press conference, "but since he became a serious contender and has been stating his position on some of the problems facing Canada, I have become completely disenchanted. On the vital question of national unity Mr. Trudeau has, to put it mildly, been grossly irresponsible."[81]

Such withering criticisms did not seem to slow Trudeau's momentum. By late March, polls showed that Trudeau had the "overwhelming" backing of Liberal MPs and that he had opened up a significant lead in first-ballot support, with Paul Martin trailing in second, and Turner, Hellyer, and Winters tied for third.[82] Premier Alex Campbell and Walter Gordon remained strong supporters. Premier Joey Smallwood "stunned" his old friend Robert Winters by throwing his support behind Trudeau as well.[83] Whispers of a "stop-Trudeau" coalition could be heard among some of the trailing candidates, but the party veterans remained confident. "The big threats are External Affairs Minister Paul Martin and Justice Minister Pierre Elliott Trudeau," mused Clyde Batten, Allan MacEachen's top Ontario organizer. "Martin's tough. He has pictures taken of him swimming. Looks like a frog. He has people's IOUs all over the country. Trudeau will fade. He's getting bored by it all now."[84]

Batten could not have been more wrong. Although Trudeau found campaigning mentally exhausting, he was obviously enjoying himself—far more than he ever thought he would. The evening of March 28, he held a reception in his Mount Royal riding. Instead of a formal Q & A, Trudeau agreed to answer questions rap-session-style, leaning casually on a table and firing off some of the witticisms for which he is best remembered today. Asked about his still-controversial intention to decriminalize homosexuality, Trudeau quipped, "The law permits fornication between two consenting adults—but not more than two. It is the law. And there must be at least two."[85] How did this viewpoint square with the Catholic conception of sin? "Different provinces and different religions have different notions of sin. It is not the purpose of the *Criminal Code* to forbid sin but to preserve peace and order. If you commit a sin you should have a conscience about it and ask the forgiveness of God, not the minister of justice."[86]

At least one person in the riding of Mount Royal was unimpressed with Trudeau's impish one-liners. She was Huguette Marleau, the riding's Progressive Conservative candidate. "The women of Canada are not marionettes," said Marleau. "We are far from the day when men said to women 'Beautiful but be still.' We accept to be beautiful but we will not be still."[87]

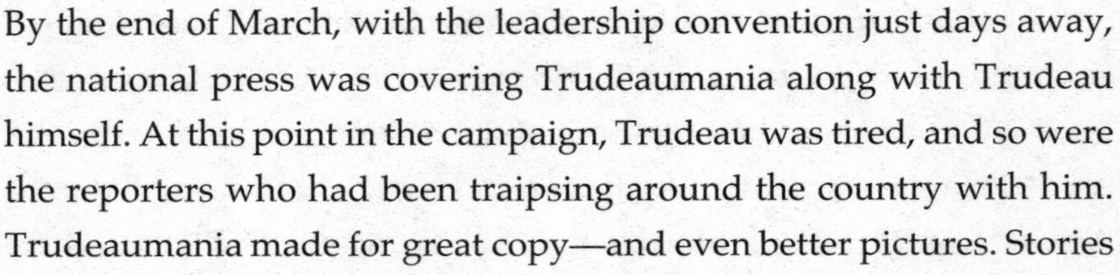

By the end of March, with the leadership convention just days away, the national press was covering Trudeaumania along with Trudeau himself. At this point in the campaign, Trudeau was tired, and so were the reporters who had been traipsing around the country with him. Trudeaumania made for great copy—and even better pictures. Stories about fainting teenyboppers, transfixed housewives, and awestruck businessmen multiplied. ("'I met him, I met him,' screamed Freda Chayka, a delegate to the Ottawa convention from Parkdale riding. 'I don't think I'll ever wash that hand again.'")[88]

A Laval University study revealed that Trudeau was attracting one-quarter of the nation's newspaper coverage of the Liberal race even though there were nine candidates.[89] Among even seasoned correspondents, the apparently mysterious sources of Trudeau's appeal to Canadians inspired fevered speculation. "Such is the charm of Pierre Elliott Trudeau that he might well be able to enthrall an audience by reading the local telephone directory," said a typical report. "This gift is all the more remarkable because he speaks quietly, unemotionally and without any evident appeal to the prejudices of his hearers."[90] Even Peter C. Newman filed columns bearing titles like

"What IS It about Trudeau?" and "The Trudeau Magic."[91] In a mid-March swing through Vancouver and Victoria, reporters seemed baffled as to how Trudeau had managed to appeal to everyone from hippies to seniors with a talk about Canadian federalism. Yet the answer was obvious to those listening. "I came not to be impressed and I was most impressed," said a Victoria woman identified as middle-aged. "He speaks his mind and he speaks it so clearly."[92]

On the nation's editorial pages, where politics was still a serious business, the tone just days before the Liberal convention remained one of sober-minded rectitude. On April 3, the editorial board at the *Globe and Mail* singled out Eric Kierans, Paul Hellyer, and Paul Martin as men of "special human and professional achievement," without actually endorsing any of them.[93] It did not even mention Trudeau. *Le Devoir* announced on the same day that it would be supporting Hellyer, even though Trudeau was his "superior" intellectually.[94] Trudeau was named "the best of a strong field" by the *Toronto Star*, which praised his position on Canadian federalism and his ability to inspire young people's interest in politics. But even the *Star*—a traditionally Liberal broadsheet that had done more than its fair share to fuel Trudeau's ascent in Canadian politics—would not endorse him.[95] Liberal delegates would have to decide for themselves.

As the leadership contest entered the home stretch, Tory leader Robert Stanfield and national party president Dalton Camp had already drawn their own conclusions. If Trudeau won, he could not be defeated in a general election. "It is going to be Trudeau and it is going to be bad for us," Camp told Stanfield. "It was because of you people in the media, making him into a god," Camp later chided a CBC News crew. "He was so beautiful, he was so lovely, he was so gorgeous, he was so intellectual, and he could quote from Descartes and Socrates. And everybody was having orgasms every time he opened his mouth."[96]

Yet if, as popular mythology would have it, Canadians had lost their minds and Trudeaumania was sweeping the land in the days before the Liberal leadership convention, the phenomenon was invisible to pollsters. A late March CBC poll, for example, put Trudeau in first place for delegate support but with only 606 votes out of 2,475.[97] Two other polls followed in short order and showed the same results. One of Trudeau's main supporters, Bryce Mackasey, stated confidently that Trudeau was well past the "sound barrier" of 700 votes on the first ballot, but this number put him nowhere near certain victory.

Meanwhile, a Canadian Institute of Public Opinion poll published on March 20, 1968, showed that most Canadians wanted a cautious English Canadian with a business background to be prime minister. And they did not care whether he was telegenic.[98]

CHAPTER SEVEN
WE WANT TRUDEAU!

The morning of Tuesday, April 2, 1968, Finance Minister Mitchell Sharp held a news conference in Ottawa to announce that he was pulling out of the Liberal leadership race and backing Pierre Trudeau. "I'm not supporting Mr. Trudeau because I think he's going to win," Sharp told the roughly 150 journalists who had shown up, "but because I want him to win. I would have preferred to beat Mr. Trudeau. But I preferred Mr. Trudeau to the rest of the candidates."[1] Sharp added that although he had consulted with the prime minister before withdrawing, the decision was entirely his own. No one in the Trudeau camp knew this announcement was coming. They read about it in the *Toronto Star*.

At 2:20 p.m. the next day, April 3, Pierre Trudeau arrived in Ottawa from Montreal by train. News of Sharp's support gave Trudeau a huge lift heading into the convention, scheduled to begin the next day. "Trudeau paraît maintenant invincible" ("Trudeau Now Seems Invincible") declared a front-page headline in *Le Devoir*.[2] As he descended from the train, Trudeau was greeted by a gaggle of reporters and an estimated two hundred Liberal party boosters—most of them orange-clad teenagers hoisting placards and shouting pro-Trudeau slogans. (Supporters of all of the candidates dressed in distinctive costumes and colours. Trudeau's happened to be orange.)

Trudeau was driven in an open motorcade to Parliament Hill, with reporters and camera operators trailing in their own cars. He headed directly to his own West Block office, where he met in private with Mitchell Sharp. From there, the two men walked together to the National Press Building for a news conference that had been choreographed the day before by Trudeau's organization. Four members of the Pearson cabinet were on hand to show their support: Jean Marchand, Jean Chrétien, Edgar Benson, and Bryce Mackasey. Chrétien had committed to Sharp before Trudeau had entered the race. At the press conference, he had the look of a man who was relieved at having a second chance to back the only French Canadian in the contest.[3] Seeing such Liberal firepower lined up behind Trudeau, a journalist asked him, "Is this your first Cabinet meeting?"[4]

Trudeau was clearly delighted to have Sharp in his camp. "Mr. Sharp's support means more than just more delegate votes," he said. "It means I have the confidence of a man of great ability and great integrity whom I have known and admired for many years."[5] Both men stated categorically that there had been no backroom deals. Trudeau had made it a precondition of his candidacy that he would never be beholden to anyone. "I have not made any promises," he insisted. "I have not said to anyone, 'If you run, you will be a minister.' It is not that important to me to be prime minister. It is very important to be prime minister in order to get my ideas across, but in order to get them through I have to feel free and I do not want to be saddled with 100 promises or 200 that I cannot fulfill."[6] In the hotel suites of Trudeau supporters who had crowded into Ottawa for the convention, there were toasts of "Sharp is dead, long live Trudeau!"[7] For the duration of the convention, Sharp, wearing a big "Pierre" button and a placid smile, would work to rally support for Trudeau. As Peter C. Newman noted, Sharp's endorsement was gold to Trudeau since it conferred on him the blessing of the Liberal "establishment."[8]

Newman's observation proved prescient. On April 4, the day after the paper had singled out Kierans, Martin, and Hellyer as the three most desirable leadership candidates, the *Globe and Mail* endorsed Trudeau with an editorial entitled "A Man Who Can Lead." Trudeau had stated his position on national unity, individual rights, economic nationalism, social welfare, NATO, and a host of other concrete matters of concern to Canadians, said the editorial. He had proven himself "flexible, inventive, imaginative," and he had shown "the courage to act where others have been content to sit." More significantly, he had excited Canadians "into arguments over issues and values and goals" and "made them feel their opinions are important."

Delegates could either sit in "the old Canadian cabana with some other delegate," concluded the *Globe,* or "move out to make tracks with Pierre Trudeau."[9]

A reception was organized for Trudeau at the Chaudière Club in Hull (now Gatineau), Quebec, the evening of April 3. The club could hold a thousand people, but more than two thousand showed up. It was a mob scene—and the first nationally televised instance of Trudeaumania. Trudeau took his time getting to the party. When he did finally arrive, he said a few words, danced for the cameras with a beautiful young woman, chatted briefly with a couple of delegates including Premier Joey Smallwood, then slipped away through a back exit. That was it.

Late the next morning, the candidates, their entourages, and 2,475 registered Liberal delegates straggled out to Ottawa's ten-thousand-seat Civic Centre (now TD Place Arena) on the bank of the Rideau Canal, where they would spend the next three days deciding the future of their party.

The first day was taken up with policy workshops. If anyone thought Trudeau would hold his tongue and quietly ride his newfound celebrity to victory, they were mistaken. At a morning session on social policy, Trudeau spoke at length against the freewheeling expansion of an unaffordable and undiscriminating welfare state. "It is my belief that we have enough of this free stuff," he told delegates. "We have to put a damper on this revolution of rising expectations. We must not be afraid of this bogeyman—the means test. We have to be more selective, to help those who live on uneconomic land or in city slums."[10] The speech, Trudeau's first at the convention, vaulted instantly onto the nation's front pages. Jack McArthur, financial editor of the *Toronto Star*, asserted that this "means test" remark was "possibly the single most important thing" Trudeau had said during the campaign. "Trudeau may be a man for the 20th century, but he has come up with a heckuva good 19th century idea," wrote McArthur.[11] Just for good measure, Trudeau also told a group of Western Canadian delegates that he was against farm subsidies.

As he moved between the policy sessions, Trudeau was followed by throngs of delegates and packs of journalists, so much so that other candidates complained about his hogging all the publicity.

At an afternoon workshop on the Constitution, Trudeau alone stood against rising Quebec nationalism, which had the effect, once again, of homogenizing the views of his rivals. "I believe you will never solve the problem of Canada by logic, by the mind or by the intellect alone," said an impassioned John Turner. "You'll solve it by the heart and you'll solve it by the gut because that's what Canada is all about. I believe the solution lies in negotiation and not in confrontation. This is no surrender or sellout to Quebec, but the simple realization of the need for change."[12] Paul Hellyer surprised delegates by claiming that constitutional reform was a simple matter of redistributing powers. "It is easy to have a new constitution that recognizes the legitimate aspirations of French-speaking Canadians but which leaves Ottawa enough powers to ensure full employment and a dynamic economy," he said.[13] Trudeau maintained a straight face and countered with a soft-spoken defence of his well-known position on the Constitution. "When we talk of constitutional matters, when we talk of federal-provincial relations, I like to think of the individual," he said. "I believe that it is the individual human being which is the backbone of a country. This is something we got away from when we began to deal with these various problems of national unity."[14]

The evening of April 4 was reserved for Prime Minister Lester Pearson, who appeared on the convention main stage at 8 p.m. to say farewell to roughly nine thousand party faithful. Pearson's remarks were warm, spontaneous, and surprisingly sentimental, bringing tears to the eyes of many present, including his normally stoic wife Maryon and Trudeau himself. As he had done so often in recent months, Pearson referred to 1968 as "one of the most difficult periods of political development in our history." He appealed to his audience to save the Canadian dream. "We face this problem of unity at a time when there is an organized movement to destroy it," said Pearson. "A destiny that takes Quebec outside Canada means, simply and starkly, the end of Canada."[15]

The prime minister's words had a special meaning for members of the Quebec caucus, where Trudeau and Winters supporters had very nearly carried their clandestine squabbling into open revolt on the convention floor earlier in the day. Meanwhile, in Quebec, Pearson was venerated much as he had been in English Canada, *"un grand promoteur de l'unité nationale."*[16]

While Pearson was delivering his remarks, word reached Ottawa that Martin Luther King, Jr., had been gunned down in Memphis at 6 p.m. local time. The African-American pastor and civil-rights leader had gone to the Tennessee city to show solidarity with striking city workers and to strategize with other activists about protest marches planned for later in the month. Relaxing on the balcony of his room at the Lorraine Motel before heading off to dinner at the home of a local clergyman, King was shot once in the neck by a lone white gunman, James Earl Ray. He was rushed to hospital, unconscious, where he died at 7:05 p.m.

Canadians were shocked by King's murder. The twin tragedies of his killing and the riots that devoured American cities in its aftermath dominated Canadian news coverage over the weekend of the Liberal convention and beyond.[17] Everywhere in Canada, King's singular contribution to the struggle for equality in the United States was commemorated and the man himself eulogized. Editorialists wrote in superlatives about his faith, his exemplary commitment to non-violence, and, above all, his extraordinary courage.[18] Human-interest stories proliferated—about the grievous loss to the King family and to the movement he personified, the condolences of American and world leaders, and the preparations being laid for his funeral and the hundreds of memorials planned in the United States, Canada, and elsewhere. It was an American tragedy, of course, but one that elicited Canadians' deepest sympathies.

In truth, the murder of Martin Luther King, Jr., was but one terrible flashpoint in a downward spiral that had darkened American public life since the mid-1960s. While many Canadians were out celebrating Canada's centennial over the hot and muggy summer of love, 1967, so-called race riots were laying waste to Detroit, Newark, and other American cities. University of Southern California historian Joseph Boskin described the carnage from his contemporary vantage point, in 1969. "The toll of the rioting over the four-year period was devastating," he lamented. "Between 1964 and 1967, approximately 130 civilians, mainly Negroes, and 12 civil personnel, mainly Caucasian, were killed. Approximately 4,700 Negroes and civil personnel were injured. Over 20,000 persons were arrested during the melees; property damages mounted into the hundreds of millions of dollars; many cities resembled the hollowed remnants of war-torn cities."[19]

A second crisis had also cast its long shadow over American life by the spring of 1968: Vietnam. U.S. military "advisers" had been active in Indochina since the early 1950s, but not until 1965 did President Lyndon Johnson commit regular U.S. troops to the defence of South Vietnam. The conflict was contentious in the United States practically from the outset, but in early 1968 public dissent burst into full flame. The Tet Offensive, which began on January 31, 1968, and included the short-term occupation of the U.S. embassy in Saigon, appeared to contradict official statements that the American-backed regime in South Vietnam was winning the war. President Johnson was forced to fight a rearguard action to contain the "credibility gap." But he could not prevent discord about the war from dominating the 1968 primary race and virtually all North American media. Among American students, progressives, and left-leaning Democrats like Senator J. William Fulbright, anti-war sentiment soared, as did anti-colonialism and anti-Americanism in the many parts of the world where they had already taken root.

In Canada, the U.S. war in Vietnam had become a permanent fixture on the nation's front pages and television sets well before Pierre Trudeau set his sights on the Liberal leadership. Like their American friends, Canadians became all too familiar with Vietnamese place names like Hue and Khe Sanh, and also with American military euphemisms like "strategic hamlets" and "rolling thunder." And like their U.S. counterparts, Canadian newspaper editors put the searing images of guerrilla warfare on their front pages, including, for example, Eddie Adams's Pulitzer Prize–winning photograph of South Vietnamese general Nguyen Ngoc Loan executing a Viet Cong prisoner.[20] Efforts by Washington to open peace talks were dutifully reported, alongside the mounting brutality of the war itself and the increasing incomprehensibility of American war aims (especially after General William C. Westmoreland announced that since he could not wage a war of annihilation, he would fight a war of attrition). The U.S. bombing of

North Vietnam, which the normally diffident Lester Pearson had criticized publicly in Philadelphia in 1965, remained so objectionable to Canadians that in March 1968 the government seriously considered a multi-party House of Commons resolution calling for a halt.[21]

To Canadians on the sidelines, it was not only Vietnam that was burning but the United States as well. "Only in rare circumstances, such as a civil war, has a nation been so divided as is the United States over the Vietnam war," stated the *Globe and Mail* on the eve of the 1968 New Hampshire primary. "Conflict between hawks and doves is rife at dinner parties, on campuses and at every political level; and the President's public appearances are made mostly at military bases and his itinerary is kept secret, for fear of embarrassing—or even dangerous—mob scenes."[22] The prevailing Canadian attitude towards this U.S. crisis was a mix of pity and revulsion. Less than a decade earlier, Canadians had pilloried John Diefenbaker for his presumed anti-Americanism. In 1968, by contrast, when Pierre Trudeau casually stated that he opposed the U.S. bombing of North Vietnam, or when John Turner suggested that he had no objection to American draft-dodgers taking refuge in Canada, they were saying nothing particularly controversial.

As the murder of Martin Luther King, Jr., came to symbolize so poignantly, civil strife, urban violence, and Vietnam appeared to many Canadians to be turning the United States inside out. More than this, the crisis atmosphere seemed to be distorting the political process in the United States at the highest levels. It undermined any chance Lyndon Johnson might have had at re-election, and it brought powerful dissenting voices into the Democratic primaries, including Bobby Kennedy, the brother of Johnson's slain predecessor, JFK. It also gave Republican presidential contender Richard Nixon a second lease on political life.

An *Ottawa Citizen* editorial published in the midst of the Liberal leadership campaign captured the American zeitgeist and its meaning for Canadian politics.

> Canada's new prime minister is chosen today at a perilous moment in history: a crossroads of hope and terror. After years of inconclusive warfare, the gleam of hope shines through at last for Vietnam. But almost at the same time, the United States is pushed across the borderline of anarchy by the vicious murder of a great, good man. In the midst of these world-shaking events, about which Canada can at present do very little, the Liberal party must choose its new leader, the man who will become prime minister later in the month. It is a time for courage, coolness and the application of intelligence to those problems that are within our power to solve.[23] Maxwell Cohen, dean of law at McGill University, agreed. "There will be little use in building a new Canada if at the same time we do not bear our full share of the continental, regional and international tasks besetting us and all of mankind."[24]

It would later be said of Trudeaumania that it represented the advent of a new Canadian nationalism that had been gestating in the Pearson years and born during the 1967 centennial. But this was certainly not how Pierre Trudeau understood his own place in Canadian politics. Over the turbulent winter of 1968, nationalism had no more claim on Trudeau than ever. Nor was he sympathetic in the least to the undercurrent of anti-Americanism that was taking root among left-nationalist cultural and political elites in Canada.

For the Harvard-educated Trudeau, who understood better than most Canadians the fragility of federalism and of democracy more generally, the American tragedy was no occasion for Canadian gloating.

On the evening of April 5, the final battle for the Liberal leadership took shape. Each candidate gave a thirty-minute speech after drawing straws to determine the speaking order. Most staged their passage from the convention floor onto the main stage with the traditional accoutrements of populist politics—marching bands, colour-coordinated hats and scarves, and parades of placard-waving loyalists. But even among the traditionalists, there was a sense that such quaint theatrics belonged to a bygone era. To many of the young people in the crowd, the idea that the "Colonel Bogey March" could inspire a new politics for the tumultuous sixties and beyond was simply embarrassing.

Paul Martin led off with a speech centred on national unity, which he identified as "the definitive crisis" in Canadian history. "I believe that I am the man to deal with our current crisis over the next few years when this problem will be resolved," he said. "I have lived this crisis all my life long—in my family, during my studies, in Quebec and Ontario and during my political career. I understand the frustrations and I am sensible of the aspirations of our principal cultural groups."[25] Paul Hellyer followed Martin with a speech emphasizing his achievements as a Pearson Liberal, including the unification of the Canadian Forces. On national unity, Hellyer took a thinly veiled swipe at Trudeau, as Martin had done and others would also do. "There is only one thing that would put the future of this country into jeopardy," said Hellyer, "the taking of hard positions before discussions begin."[26]

Neither Martin nor Hellyer got much of a rise out of the crowd. Only when they paid tribute to Pearson did they draw ovations beyond their own blocks of supporters. Not so Joe Greene, who took the stage after Hellyer. Greene delivered a showstopper of a stump speech, full of humour and plain talk, perking up nearly everyone in the vast arena. He tore into the Tories for deposing Diefenbaker and played to his rural Canadian base by promising a program of farm subsidies. After Greene, the earlier pall descended once again. Eric Kierans opened his speech with the wry admission that he lacked charisma. "I've had a lot more trouble selling my image than selling my ideas," he said. "Pierre Berton said if he had a magic wand, he would make me prime minister. Unfortunately, Pierre is not a delegate."[27] Kierans then gave a dusty speech on his acknowledged niche, fiscal and trade policy. Robert Winters followed with an address that emphasized sound economic and education policies as the prerequisites to national unity. Allan MacEachen positioned himself as one of the forward-looking young Liberals in the race, and cautioned delegates against voting for old-guard conservatives in the party.

By the time Trudeau took his turn as the eighth speaker, there had already been five hours of speeches. To reinforce the perception that Trudeau was in a class by himself, his young aides sent him to the podium alone, like a prizefighter, without the fanfare of pipe bands or throngs of supporters. Their instincts proved impeccable. There was chaos in the arena as Trudeau tried to make his way through the sea of delegates towards the stage. When he finally took the podium, the entire arena seemed to erupt in shouts of "Tru-deau, Tru-deau!" and "*On veut Trudeau! On veut Trudeau!*" (We want Trudeau!)

Trudeau gave a characteristically stern, professorial speech to the hushed and expectant crowd. "I am convinced that when the people of Canada are next called upon to judge the Liberal Party, they will be asking not only for achievement and experience, which we can show them. They will also be asking for a renewed expression of imagination, for a sense of national pride and purpose, and for proof of the party's ability to adapt to rapid change." He spoke about reform of Canadian federalism and the Constitution. "I have always maintained that our present constitution could be improved. In fact I have recommended many revisions, such as a charter of human rights, and changes in the Senate and the Supreme Court. I would agree to any transfer of jurisdiction which would allow us to be better and more efficiently governed." Speaking in French, he added, "Masters in our own house we must be, but our house is all of Canada."[28] At one point in his remarks, Trudeau referenced the King assassination and its tragic aftermath in the United States—reminders, he said, of the harsh realities facing the citizens of modern democracies.

By all accounts, the speech struck exactly the right tone. A *Globe and Mail* editorial praised the solemnity with which Trudeau spoke of the challenges ahead. "There was no lofty oratory in the address Pierre Trudeau gave to the Liberal convention last night. The candidate scarcely raised his voice. He spoke of the looting and the arson and the lawlessness that have followed in the wake of the assassination of Martin Luther King, and he spoke, too, of the troubles that bedevil Canada. It was not the wild ovation that greeted his arrival at the platform as much as the silence that hung over the vast arena while he spoke that measured what the crowd thought of this unconventional man."[29] Barney Danson later recalled the impact that Trudeau's speech had on convention delegates, him among them. "Trudeau stole the show. He talked about the riots at the Democratic convention in Chicago, the turmoil in modern society, the need for Canada to become a 'just society.' The sense one had was that if you agreed with him that was fine but if you didn't that was fine too. Personally, I was deeply moved, even overwhelmed. While I was intensely loyal to Hellyer, I knew that if he were forced off the ballot, my support would go to Trudeau."[30]

John Turner had drawn the short straw and got stuck with the unenviable task of following Trudeau at the podium. Undaunted, he gave a strong and earnest speech, warning delegates repeatedly that he perceived in Canada "an element of rashness, of let's give it a go, of playing with our future."[31] But Turner could no more inspire the electric atmosphere that Trudeau had brought to the convention floor than the speakers before him.

For the Liberal Party, the evening was a triumph. According to an internal party bulletin, the television broadcast of the candidates' speeches had drawn 14.5 million viewers, the largest single audience in Canadian broadcasting history.[32] If the night had been Pierre Trudeau's, as his aides believed, all of Canada knew it.

The morning of Saturday, April 6, Trudeau donned a grey suit with light shirt and blue tie, and headed out by limo to have breakfast with a group of Quebec delegates at the Château Laurier. A young woman gave him an orange carnation, which he would wear on his lapel for the rest of the day. At 10 a.m., he was driven to the Ottawa Civic Centre to take his place at the centre of what everyone expected would be a day for the history books—the day Liberal delegates would vote to choose a new leader.

The morning was taken up with a plenary session, which allowed delegates who had been revelling the night before to sleep in. With the first-ballot vote scheduled for 1 p.m., the arena filled in over the lunch hour. Trudeau arrived in his box at 12:50, accompanied by his top supporters—Goyer, Benson, Chrétien, Pépin, Gordon, and Sharp among them. Trudeau's brother, Charles, was also present, waving a placard and plainly enjoying himself. The outdoor temperature was unusually warm for Ottawa in April. Steadily rising temperatures exacerbated the hothouse political atmosphere of the convention floor. Unforgiving cameras would immortalize the event by beaming real-time images of sweating, anxious Liberals into the living rooms of the nation.

Vote-counting was expected to go quickly, courtesy of a bulky new IBM computer set up on the main stage of the hall. No such luck. Because there was so much riding on the vote and, according to the polls, no likely first-ballot victor, scrutineers ended up supervising the vote counts meticulously and slowing the process down to a very human crawl.

The results of the first ballot were announced at 2:30 p.m., an hour and a half later than scheduled. A total of 2,388 delegates cast ballots. Trudeau came out on top, as expected, with 752 votes, or just under one-third of the total. Hellyer ran a distant second with 330 votes, Winters third with 293. Turner and Martin tied for fourth place, with

277 votes each. Greene took 169 votes and MacEachen 163. Kierans trailed with 103 votes. The long-shot candidate, Presbyterian minister Lloyd Henderson, got no votes.

Until the first-ballot results were announced, Trudeau had maintained a pose of almost total detachment—like a monk at a Mardi Gras, as one observer put it.[33] Cameras were trained on him constantly, but he never acknowledged them. After the first-ballot results were announced, Trudeau broke his aloof stance momentarily to rise, smile, and bow to the crowd. Some of his aides had speculated that his support on the first ballot might run as high as 966 votes. A journalist asked him if his 752 votes had met his expectations. "Not too bad," he answered coolly. "I have no expectations."[34] He then tossed a grape in the air and caught it in his mouth.

Paul Martin knew the game was up. He withdrew without malice and urged his loyal supporters to do the same. "Over the years, I have learned how important it is to be gracious in victory, and generous and serene in defeat," Martin told his people. "The country is still going to go on. The party is going to go on, and I am going to go on—stronger than ever."[35] A well-placed camera caught Jean Marchand speaking to Trudeau. "I was sure Martin would receive more," he said. "With about forty more votes I think he would have stayed in."[36] Trudeau and Marchand made their way over to Martin's box to show their solidarity, which Martin appeared to appreciate. But he would not commit his delegates to Trudeau or to any other candidate. Barney Danson would later reveal that Martin was "furious" with him for moving, ultimately, to Trudeau.[37] But Lester Pearson called Martin's magnanimity "truly magnificent," knowing full well that after three shots at the Liberal leadership, the sixty-four-year-old would not get another.[38] Trudeau would later appoint Martin high commissioner to Britain, for which both he and his son, Paul Martin, Jr., a future prime minister of Canada, were immensely grateful.[39]

MacEachen and Kierans dropped out after the first ballot as well, MacEachen moving immediately to Trudeau's box, embracing Trudeau and donning a Trudeau button.[40] Other high-profile Liberals to move to Trudeau's box after the first ballot included Maurice Sauvé, Herb Gray, and Hugh Faulkner. Kierans announced that he would not be supporting anyone officially.

The scene was set for the second ballot, which for delegates meant a flurry of voting activity followed by hours of anxious waiting. Just before the announcement of the second ballot results, a young woman in the crowd threw a red carnation up to Trudeau. He held it in his mouth, tango-style. A hundred flashbulbs burst.

The second ballot was announced at 5:10 p.m. Of 2,379 ballots cast, Trudeau came first with 964 votes or roughly 40 per cent. Winters moved up to second place with 473 votes, and Hellyer fell to a close third with 465. Turner came fourth with 347 votes, and Greene fifth with 104. MacEachen's name had appeared in error on the second ballot because of a delay in communicating his withdrawal to party officials. The eleven meagre votes he got on the second ballot confirmed that he had made the right choice in dropping out. But the fact that MacEachen came last on the second ballot allowed Greene, the second-to-last candidate, to remain in the running.

Trudeau did not react to the announcement of the second ballot numbers but maintained his air of indifference. Winters and Hellyer discussed the possibility of a united front on the third ballot but could come to no agreement. Hellyer agonized. He asked loyalist Judy LaMarsh—MP for Niagara Falls and a prominent minister in the Pearson cabinet—whether he should throw his votes to Turner, the only candidate apart from Trudeau whose youth appeared to give him a chance of winning. On camera, LaMarsh could be heard coaching Hellyer to move to Robert Winters's camp, her voice cracking with emotion. "Go now, Paul," she yelled. "If you don't go now you're only making a Trudeau. Winters is all right. You know him and he knows you. You're all right with him. And if you don't get together, you'll both go down and let that bastard in."[41] (The bastard in question was Trudeau.) Hellyer rejected LaMarsh's advice and stayed in.

The third ballot was announced at 6:40 p.m. Of the 2,376 ballots cast, Trudeau took 1,051 votes, or just over 44 per cent. Winters came second with 621 votes, followed by Hellyer with 377, Turner with 279, and Greene with a meagre 29. Greene was now forced to drop out. He went directly to Trudeau's box. Hellyer conceded that he had taken his leadership bid as far as he could and moved to Winters's box. Turner, who had said all along that there would be no deals, announced that he would stay in the race.[42]

The results of the fourth ballot were announced at 7:50 p.m.—seven long hours after voting had begun. Exhausted delegates waited for the announcement from the stage. The tension in the air was agonizing. Finally, it came.

"Pierre—E.—Trudeau, one—two—oh—three."

Even before the words had finished reverberating through the hall, there was pandemonium, accompanied by raucous cheering and thunderous applause. "Tru-deau, Ca-na-da! Tru-deau, Ca-na-da!" cheered the crowd. Trudeau had prevailed, taking 1,203 votes to Winters's 954 and Turner's 195. He was now the Liberal leader and Canada's fifteenth prime minister.

For the first time all day, Trudeau showed genuine emotion, jumping out of his seat with a broad smile to accept the hugs and handshakes of his supporters. It had been a wild and woolly day. Lester Pearson later captured the intensity of the moment. "I have been through some fairly dramatic and exciting moments in my seventy-five years," he wrote,

> but I do not believe that I have ever experienced a more heart-tightening occasion than on that afternoon. I was fairly certain that Mr. Trudeau was going to win, though not on the

> first ballot. But there were so many other emotional aspects: Mr Sharp joining the Trudeau camp; Mr Martin getting relatively few votes, and his gallant way of taking this defeat. Then there were the adjectives thrown back and forth by Miss LaMarsh and others. There was the getting together of the candidates in full view of the spectators, and in front of the cameras. However, it all made good theatre, and a splendid show.[43]

Ramsay Cook was so excited about Trudeau's fourth-ballot victory that he "cried with joy."[44]

Trudeau gave a short victory speech to the tired but exhilarated crowd, his orange carnation now bedraggled. "This is an extremely great honour that I have received from this great assembly of Liberals," he told the delegates, "an honour and a very heavy responsibility. And the only way in which I can show my appreciation for this honour will be to bear this responsibility with all my strength, and with all my energy. Canada must be unified, Canada must be one, Canada must be progressive, and Canada must be a just society."[45]

At the end of his acceptance speech, Trudeau invited everyone to join him at the Skyline Hotel for a victory celebration. In light of his popularity, this invitation proved to be a bad idea. A crowd of roughly twenty thousand showed up at the hotel, clogging the lobby and the streets outside. The Ottawa police were called in, ostensibly to restore order. But they may have had ulterior motives. Unbeknownst to convention delegates, a bomb threat had been called in to Ottawa police at roughly 6 p.m., which Liberal officials up to and including party president John Nichol had taken extremely seriously.[46] Luckily, nothing came of it.

The morning after his fourth-ballot triumph, Trudeau gave a press conference. The CBC's Norman DePoe, whose earlier interviews with Trudeau had done so much to establish the justice minister's credibility, joked with the new leader, starting with his reputation as a contrarian.

"When does Pierre Elliott Trudeau get so popular that you begin opposing him?" asked DePoe.

"Well, I think probably this morning," Trudeau said with a laugh.

Another journalist asked Trudeau if he was still a radical.

"I'm concerned with new solutions to new problems and many conservative-minded people would call that radical," said Trudeau. "I don't care whether the label is radical, or left, or in some cases some solutions might be deemed conservative by some people. You can't, by laws, make this country greater; you can't, by laws, make it more beautiful or stronger or richer. We have to do that ourselves and this means freeing every potentiality in the individual. We are going to be living in a tough world. I'm saying the future is not for the weak and for the timid. The future of the world will belong to those who build it."

Trudeau was then asked about his relationship with Quebec premier Daniel Johnson.

"I don't think there's been any tension or animosity between Mr. Johnson and myself," he observed.

How long did he intend to be prime minister?

"My plans really don't go that far," said Trudeau. "I think I will try to get my party elected as often as I can. I'm in this game for keeps, if that is what you mean."[47]

After the press conference, Trudeau went directly to 24 Sussex Drive and from there accompanied Lester and Maryon Pearson to Ottawa's Christ Church Cathedral for a memorial service for Martin Luther King, Jr. The next day, before Trudeau discussed the transfer of power with Pearson, reporters were invited to accompany the two men as they walked the grounds of the prime minister's residence. At one point, gesturing towards the French embassy next door, Trudeau asked, "Do you think we could expropriate that?"[48] (It had been eight months since Charles de Gaulle's "*Vive le Québec libre*" remark, but the French president continued to meddle in Canadian politics.) Trudeau and Pearson then met in private for several hours. When he re-emerged, Trudeau was carrying some file folders. Reporters asked him how the meeting went. "He gave me some stuff to read" was his only answer.[49]

In the aftermath of the leadership campaign, Trudeau disappeared from public view. This was not an accident but a deliberate dodge. Over the long Easter weekend, for example, Trudeau's aides told the press that he was relaxing in the Laurentians when, in truth, he was in Fort Lauderdale, Florida. On April 9, Trudeau met in private with most of the cabinet ministers he had defeated in the Liberal leadership contest. He had made it clear from the moment he had become a leadership hopeful—and again during his acceptance speech—that healing any wounds that might have opened during the campaign would be his top priority. He then plunged into the solitary task of reading volumes of Privy Council documents and briefing himself on all the activities of the government's various departments.

The press response to Trudeau's victory was surprisingly muted—undoubtedly because the saturation coverage of the convention had generated so much hype. "The Old Guard is being swept aside and a new generation is moving into the seats of power," observed a *Toronto Star* editorial, "a cooler, more pragmatic, less partisan generation, unencumbered by old myths, more attuned to the social and economic needs of a new age."[50] Some editorialists worried that Trudeau might have trouble accommodating "the new and the old" within the party.[51] Others, including the *Calgary Herald*, asserted that he was precisely the right person for the job. "At a time when revision of the constitution is under study and the status of the French-Canadian minority within Confederation is an issue coming to the time of decision, it may be most advantageous to have a French Canadian at the leadership helm in Ottawa," said the *Herald*. "Mr. Trudeau is perfectly bilingual. He puts Canadianism above provincialism and racial nationalism. He is no demagogue. He presents himself as a cool, rational, intelligent man of modest demeanor but in no way lacking in assured self-confidence."[52]

In Quebec, Premier Daniel Johnson and Liberal leader Jean Lesage responded to Trudeau's triumph with prudent silence.[53] René Lévesque, on the other hand, called the Liberal convention an *"orgie"* and Trudeau a *"vierge de la politique"* (political virgin) who was already beginning to spin his policies.[54] Quebec editorialists were more generous. "The federal Liberals in Ottawa have turned over a new leaf," said *La Presse*. "By his behaviour, by his style and ideas, Pierre Elliott Trudeau appears as the herald of a new political era, very different from the past. If the April 6 election holds the promises that are indicated, he will be able to accomplish great things for his party and for the country, providing that he knows how to surround himself with a team combining the ability to move ahead and experiment."[55] At *Le Devoir*, Claude Ryan also tried to be magnanimous and forward-looking. The decision of the Liberal delegates must be respected, he wrote. Theirs was not a choice "without risk, but the delegates, acting with great freedom, have judged what was required." There remained, however, the reality of Quebec nationalism, which had over the last ten years taken "an affirmative and dynamic twist." If Trudeau were to grant Quebec nationalism as much moral legitimacy as he appeared to grant Canadian nationalism, Ryan affirmed, "he would eliminate at once the main barrier preventing up to now a 'civil dialogue' between himself and important elements of the Quebec community."[56]

In the United States, despite the national preoccupation with the King murder, Trudeau got a good deal of press. In a series of stories about Canada's new prime minister, the *New York Times* emphasized his youthful appeal and his promise "to strive for a just society with all possible freedom for individuals and equal sharing of the country's wealth."[57] Some American coverage proved ill-informed. The *Los Angeles Times* erroneously attributed to Trudeau a "resentment" of Canada's economic dependence on the United States, admonishing him along with "the anti-U.S. sentiments which are fashionable among many pro-Trudeau intellectuals."[58] The predominant theme in the U.S. press, however, was that Trudeau was an enigma—an unsurprising response, perhaps, given that Americans were only too familiar with the pedestrian politics of the Diefenbaker/Pearson era. "Neither Canada nor any other nation in the world has had a leader quite like Pierre Elliott Trudeau," said a *Chicago Daily News* editorial. "Skilled lawyer, blunt-talking political philosopher, playboy bachelor, blonde fancier—all this and much, much more make up the human paradox who has been named to succeed retiring Lester B. Pearson."[59]

It was all too much for Keith Spicer, the broadcaster whom Trudeau would later appoint as Canada's first commissioner of official languages. In a feature article for the *Globe and Mail*, Spicer took direct aim at the myth-making that had already attended to Trudeau—in the United States but also in Canada.

> The 'enigmatic' Trudeau is mainly a nostalgic fiction, deepened to an illusion of secrecy by the public's own astonishment and shallowness. The significant Trudeau—the thinker, activist and leader—has fought among us openly, and in widening arenas, for a generation. The people of Canada know more about their new leader at the outset of his mandate than they knew about any predecessor after years in office. We know his policies on everything from federalism to foreign ownership to fiscal integrity. We know his style, his tastes, his pastimes and his schoolboy pranks. Since his youth, the combative extrovert who leads us has revealed himself, his hopes, ideas and ideals, with a compelling clarity.[60]

Spicer was dead right, of course. The only thing Canadians did not yet know about their unconventional leader was how he would handle the reins of power. Fortunately, as the *Globe and Mail* noted, there would be plenty of time to find out. "The 'new boy,' thank goodness, has no intention now of cashing in on his leadership popularity with an early election."[61]

CHAPTER EIGHT
TELLING IT LIKE IT IS

It did not work out that way, of course. The new boy had his own ideas.

The morning of April 19, Pierre Trudeau called Lester Pearson at 24 Sussex Drive to say that he was likely to dissolve Parliament on its first day back in session. "He wished to use the excitement and momentum of the leadership convention to ask for a vote of confidence from the country while his image was still unsullied," Pearson later noted. "He considered that this was the best time to get his majority."[1] Trudeau met with his new cabinet later the same day. Of the leadership hopefuls he had defeated two weeks earlier, only Robert Winters had declined Trudeau's invitation to stay on. Mitchell Sharp took over external affairs from Paul Martin, who became minister without portfolio. John Turner was named minister of consumer and corporate affairs as well as solicitor general. Joe Greene became minister of agriculture, Eric Kierans took the communications portfolio, Paul Hellyer moved to transport, and Allan MacEachen to health and welfare. Trudeau acknowledged that his cabinet might not have a long shelf life. "This is a pretty stand-pat Cabinet," he told the press. "It is a Cabinet I could go to dissolution with or to a short session with."[2]

There were good reasons not to go to dissolution. Rank-and-file Liberals were not only recovering from the leadership race but still patching up the rivalries it had occasioned. Party leaders worried that it was too soon to tap their donors again. So-called election hawks in Trudeau's inner circle, however—Marc Lalonde, Jean Marchand, Jean Chrétien, and Donald Macdonald among them—pressed the new prime minister to act quickly. Internal polling showed that 52 per cent of decided voters intended to vote Liberal, versus 28 per cent support for the Tories and 14 per cent NDP—a vote distribution that would give the "natural-governing party" upwards of 150 seats in the 264-seat House.[3] Trudeau's rapport with young people was also likely to give him a huge lift but perhaps not indefinitely. There were one million more Canadians eligible to vote in 1968 than there had been in 1965 (for a total of 11.2 million voters).

As Pearson had anticipated, Trudeau needed little convincing. At the morning caucus meeting of April 23, he told his MPs that he would dissolve the House that very afternoon and call an election for June 25. "Gasps," Lester Pearson later remarked. "Then he very forcefully made his case for this action, and won over the doubters. It was a great performance. There was no doubt in my mind that he wanted to force a confrontation with Quebec on the national unity issue, to meet it head on."[4]

Following the caucus meeting, Trudeau walked the short distance to Rideau Hall to request a dissolution order from Governor General Roland Michener. When the afternoon session of Parliament opened, Trudeau made quick work of it. "In view of the announcement I am about to make," he told the House, "I feel any further comment by me on any other subjects would be improper. This afternoon I called on the Governor General to request him to dissolve parliament and to have writs issued for a general election on June 25. Mr. Speaker, by proclamation under the Great Seal of Canada, dated April 23, 1968, the present parliament is dissolved and members and senators are discharged from attendance. I thank you, Mr. Speaker."[5] MPs from all parties were nonplussed—none more so than Lester Pearson, who had fully expected parliamentarians to fete his "incomparable services to Canada, to the world, to the interplanetary system," as he later joked.[6] But Trudeau left no time for homage to Pearson or anything else. The House simply adjourned. Pearson's one-word diary entry for his last day as a Canadian parliamentarian: "Tough."[7]

Trudeau moved immediately to convene a press conference, which was televised. "Many changes have occurred in Canada since the last general election," he told Canadians. "Many areas of our national life are in a period of rapid evolution and will require new direction."[8] Trudeau would later tell reporters that Lester Pearson's accident-prone minority government had outlived its usefulness. "It has not been a happy Parliament," he affirmed. "I'm not underestimating the importance of representative democracy. I'm just saying this particular session, this particular Parliament, this particular time of our representative democracy to me had worn itself out."[9]

With Parliament dissolved and Canadians informed of the election call, Trudeau headed out onto the parliamentary lawns. There he was met by a crowd of "Trudeau-boppers," teenaged girls who squealed in his presence and tried to touch him as he climbed into his waiting limo. One girl, sixteen-year-old Linda Cooper, leaned into the open window of the car, and Trudeau planted a kiss right on her mouth. "I'll never wash my lips," said Cooper dreamily as the car drove off.[10]

Not to be outdone, Tory leader Robert Stanfield, who had turned fifty-four the previous week, allowed himself to be photographed being kissed—on the cheek—by fifteen-year-old Kathleen Hopper. "Stanfield Starts Pecking Away," ran the headlines the next day, cementing the contrast between the sexy Trudeau and the fatherly Stanfield.

The following day, Stanfield held his own televised press conference. "This campaign will be fought on the issues," he said, reading from a prepared statement. "After seven months as leader of the party, I welcome the opportunity to put our case before the Canadian people.

We have proven our dedication to national unity. In that spirit, we can confidently ask the people of Canada for the highest trust of all."[11] During the Q & A that followed, the normally serene Stanfield was uncharacteristically feisty. He was asked where he thought the Liberals were vulnerable. Everywhere, Stanfield replied. Pierre Trudeau had "no record, no policy, and no proof of his ability to govern the country," while his cabinet represented the "stale leftovers of five years of incompetence and mismanagement." Had the Tories been caught out by the election call? "We are ready for an election," said Stanfield, "I suspect a good deal more ready than the Liberals are in some parts of the country."

Asked about his own prospects, Stanfield was typically self-effacing. "I think I have one great advantage," he joked. "I'm such a plain-looking guy, I think people will say, 'He's not trying to be charming, so maybe he's telling the truth.'"[12]

Already Stanfield had a problem: special status for Quebec. And more than any other issue in the 1968 campaign, it would prove to be his party's undoing.

In mid-summer 1967, during Charles de Gaulle's visit to Quebec, then-premier Robert Stanfield had been campaigning to replace John Diefenbaker as the leader of the federal Tories. With the debate about special status raging all around him, Stanfield sought out a safe middle ground. "This is something that will have to be carefully explored and considered," he said. "It depends on what special status means. It is essential that we live together and recognize the desire of each group to live their own lives in their own way. This is of great importance to both Quebec and Canada. In terms of working out specific positions, there should be a continuing dialogue on constitutional and fiscal questions."[13] What, exactly, such a dialogue might be expected to produce Stanfield left to the imagination. As a three-term premier of Nova Scotia, he acknowledged that Canadians outside Quebec were unlikely to give special powers to one province.

Stanfield endeavoured to maintain his wait-and-see position well into the election campaign. Desiring not to provoke Quebec nationalists, he argued that Trudeau's stand on the Constitution was divisive and dangerous. "I hope the constitutional matter can be discussed without heat," Stanfield said early in the campaign.

> I don't take quite as simple and uncomplicated a view of the problems of the constitution and the problems of the country as the new Prime Minister seems to take. I don't feel, for example, that it would be particularly helpful in terms of national unity to have an entrenched bill of rights on other than the language question. On the other hand, I think we must recognize that Quebec consists of something like 80 percent of French-speaking Canadians. By virtue of it being a predominantly French-speaking society in the midst of 200-million English-speaking North Americans, its interest and its outlook are going to be somewhat different from other provinces.[14]

Such nuanced thinking was a gift to Trudeau, who would argue that Stanfield was not credible on national unity and was, moreover, too timid to challenge *deux nations* in Quebec even if he were. Canadians took note. "Stanfield's style is Early Nova Scotia Fuzzy," wrote one wag.[15]

Stanfield might have had the luxury of playing to his own policy strengths—regional development, for example, or a guaranteed annual income—had the Quebec question receded during the campaign. And for a while, it looked as though it might. Daniel Johnson, who at one point said that he would back Stanfield because he recognized the *deux nations* reality of Canada, announced on April 24 that he would be neutral. (Union Nationale insiders told journalist

Dominique Clift that Johnson had changed his mind because the unilingual Stanfield would be a sitting duck for René Lévesque's sovereignty movement.)[16] The next day, Quebec Liberal leader Jean Lesage announced that he, too, would be officially neutral.

But time was not on Stanfield's side. Quebec's nationalist elites had their own agenda and their own timetable. They would not break stride for federal politicians looking for an easy rapprochement.

The issue that pushed special status into the election spotlight was Quebec's prerogative to manage its own international affairs. In February 1968, Quebec City had sent representatives to an educational conference in Gabon, a French-speaking nation in central Africa, without clearing the invitation through External Affairs.[17] Ottawa responded forcefully, suspending diplomatic relations with Gabon. Then, on April 15, Quebec education minister Jean-Guy Cardinal announced that he would personally lead a Quebec delegation to an educational conference in Paris the following week. Both Lester Pearson and Pierre Trudeau had urged Cardinal to clear his plans with External beforehand, but he refused. On April 16, under orders from Pierre Trudeau, the government of Canada recalled its ambassador to France, threatening to sever diplomatic relations altogether.

Pierre Trudeau had long been on record as saying that special status for Quebec led inexorably towards separatism and the destruction of Canada. There was no better concrete example of this principle at work than in the fight over diplomatic representation, since, as every Quebec separatist from René Lévesque to Jacques Parizeau has understood, the achievement of a sovereign Quebec would be contingent on international recognition. As far as Trudeau was concerned, Quebec's assertion of an independent foreign policy was a direct threat to Canadian sovereignty. "There is one way to keep Canada united as a federal form of government and this way is to make sure that in international matters, Canada speaks with one voice," Trudeau stated in early May. "If it were just a matter of a province slipping into some occasional attitude which would bring it on the international scene, it wouldn't perhaps be too serious. But if a province is doing this with the express purpose in mind to determine a constitutional orientation which in our view would be destructive of Canadian unity, we feel the Canadian people have a right to hear the explanation."[18] To drive home the point, the feds brought out a seventy-five-page white paper, *Federalism and International Conferences on Education*, describing Ottawa's "fruitless efforts to reach agreement with Quebec on representation at international conferences."[19]

Trudeau's tough talk on Quebec's international role made the nation's front pages, giving Robert Stanfield very little room to manoeuvre.[20] Editorialists asked, "Where Do the Tories Stand?"[21] Stanfield tried to turn this criticism on Trudeau, claiming that the new prime minister had escalated Ottawa's feud with Quebec City unnecessarily and ought to be acting in a statesmanlike manner, consulting the provinces on the Constitution.[22] NDP leader Tommy Douglas agreed. "Mr. Trudeau's attempt to make election capital of this problem does nothing to promote Canadian unity," Douglas said of the diplomatic row between Ottawa and Quebec City. "The answer lies in negotiations rather than confrontation."[23]

Complicating Stanfield's position at every turn was Marcel Faribault, the Quebec businessman who had persuaded the federal Tory policy committee to endorse the phrase *deux nations* the previous autumn. Faribault, who was still serving as an economic adviser to Premier Daniel Johnson, was an avowed federalist but also a steadfast Quebec nationalist. Like Johnson, he believed that the existing Constitution should be scrapped and replaced by one that decentralized Confederation and allocated broad new powers to the provinces. But every once in a while, Faribault seemed to lapse into the old *Québec aux Québécois* talk that Trudeau and other Quebec federalists found so loathsome. "Quebec can only proceed in constitutional talks from its own nature, and thus from its twin nationalism," Faribault told the Société Saint-Jean-Baptiste of Sherbrooke in early May 1968. "One aspect of this nationalism, almost biological and at the same time spiritual, is the historical and sociological existence of Quebec, its language, its feelings, its aspirations and its drive."[24]

Some Quebec pundits, including Claude Ryan, expressed the hope early in the election campaign that Faribault would run in Quebec as a Tory. (Robert Stanfield approached Ryan himself about running as a Conservative candidate, but he declined.) On May 8, the story leaked that Stanfield was indeed holding private talks with Faribault. Less than a week later, on May 14, Stanfield confirmed happily that Faribault had agreed to run as a Progressive Conservative. Faribault would bring the Tories prestige, money, and as many as thirty-five seats in Quebec, according to his own prognostications.[25] But he also brought his own ideas about Quebec, which Stanfield knew were incompatible with his own. The news that Faribault would run as a Tory was not a day old before Stanfield admitted publicly that he and Faribault did not see eye to eye on national unity issues and thus had agreed to sit down together to hammer out a consensus position.[26]

Tommy Douglas and the NDP were also prepared at the outset of the contest to fight Trudeau on Quebec. "It has become apparent that Mr. Trudeau wishes to avoid at all costs an issue-oriented campaign," said Douglas. "He wishes to ride the crest of publicity resulting from the Liberal leadership convention and to avoid squarely confronting the major problems besetting the nation."[27] Speaking in Toronto in late April, NDP candidate (and now party vice-president) Charles Taylor told one hundred party faithful that Trudeau's public image had been "manufactured"—but not by Trudeau himself. There would be little left of his "magic aura" once his hardline views on national unity became better known, Taylor asserted. "What he's putting forward would be terrible for the country."[28] Robert Cliche, Quebec NDP leader, would speak unabashedly throughout the campaign of *deux nations*, condemning Trudeau as "the greatest obstacle" to Canadian unity. "Mr. Trudeau refuses to admit there is a constitutional problem, and he also refuses to admit that Quebec is spokesman for French Canada," said Cliche. "Quebec will never allow an iron hand, directed by a hard head, to wring its neck. It is regrettable that the prime minister refuses to consider any compromise."[29]

Trudeau plainly relished having the likes of Stanfield, Faribault, Douglas, and Cliche as adversaries. He even tried to goad Daniel Johnson into the election fight, claiming later that he had failed because the Quebec premier was too savvy to risk "a humiliating defeat."[30] As for Faribault, his nomination brought much-needed clarity to the campaign, said Trudeau, since the Tories and the NDP were now proposing the same *deux nations* policy. It was an "acid test," he said. "In Quebec they are talking about two-nations and about special status, and in the rest of the country they are talking about one nation and no special status—and they think the Canadian people do not know about this. They think the Canadian people are going to be fooled by this type of line. You have to tell the same thing in all parts of the country, and that is what the Canadian people want."[31]

Interestingly, Réal Caouette, leader of the Ralliement créditiste, played only a minor role in the campaign's national-unity debate. Known as a staunch Quebec nationalist and a formidable stump speaker, Caouette was popular in small-c conservative, rural Quebec. Out on the campaign trail, the plain-speaking Créditiste leader would echo some of Trudeau's views on Canadian federalism. Those who wished for "special status" did not even know what it was, Caouette told a Quebec City crowd in mid-May. "It is time to get rid of our blowhard mentality, to start thinking about a strong Quebec within the framework of a Canadian constitution and to start living in the world of today."[32] On social policy, however, the Créditiste leader worked rural Quebecers against Trudeau's liberal tendencies. Many were already suspicious of his reforms on homosexuality and abortion, and even more were unhappy with his critique of Quebecers' "lousy" French.[33]

The moment Trudeau dissolved Parliament, the Liberal Party machine lurched into campaign mode. A small policy committee chaired by Jim Davey was struck to hammer out the platform on which Liberal candidates would campaign. Its leading lights were Marc Lalonde, who continued to serve as Trudeau's chief policy adviser, and Bill Lee, who was promoted to policy adviser while retaining his job as Trudeau's tour manager. Joining the team were several young intellectuals, including the Princeton-trained Ph.D. Lloyd Axworthy, who had supported Turner during the leadership race. At Lalonde's request, Ramsay Cook joined Trudeau's staff as a part-time troubleshooter and speech writer. "My special assignment," Cook later recalled, "was the constitution, watching for Robert Stanfield and Marcel Faribault or Tommy Douglas and Robert Cliche to contradict each other. The wait was not long."[34] There was never any doubt about who would be the final arbiter of Liberal policy: Pierre Trudeau himself.

In mid-May, Peter C. Newman would leak the existence of a secret Liberal document setting out eighty promises that party candidates could make while campaigning. The 160-page *Liberal Candidates' Handbook*, a copy of which is today archived among the Trudeau papers in Ottawa, left no doubt about Trudeau's or the party's priorities. The first eight pages identified national unity as the country's major challenge and celebrated Trudeau as the drafter and defender of a charter of rights guaranteeing language rights across Canada. The four official themes of the campaign—The Just Society, A Prosperous Economy, A United Canada, and Canada in the World—followed from this premise.[35] When Trudeau publicly unveiled the abridged version of the Liberal Party platform in Moncton, New Brunswick, in late May, it derived almost verbatim from the eighty-point program outlined in the secret handbook.[36]

There was never any doubt about the campaign's overarching strategy. After the dramatic leadership campaign and the adulation that the winner had inspired, the campaign would centre almost exclusively on Trudeau himself. On posters, banners, and postcards, voters would see one motif endlessly repeated: Trudeau's face in grey-scale, against a flat red background, accompanied by the text "Pierre" or "Trudeau," or sometimes just the party logo, a stylized capital *L* cradling a maple leaf. This was a tried-and-true Liberal branding strategy, as earlier campaign posters for Louis St. Laurent, Joey Smallwood, and others had demonstrated. One sixties-style variation on this motif showed a headshot of Trudeau in high-contrast black and white—an obvious nod to the iconic and by then ubiquitous Alberto Korda photograph of Argentine revolutionary Che Guevara.

Trudeau kicked off his campaign tour in Vancouver on May 10, speaking at a dinner for forestry-industry executives. As he had done during the leadership contest, he would use his public appearances to roll out individual planks of his platform. On this occasion, he told British Columbian business leaders that he was serious about recognizing China, and that he expected them to play a critical role in strengthening the trade relationships that would bring that country out of its diplomatic isolation. "The present situation in which a government which represents a quarter of the world's population is diplomatically isolated even from countries with which it is actively trading is obviously unsatisfactory," he said.[37] Trudeau also took the opportunity, as he would throughout the campaign, to drive home the idea that no province's interests were distinct from the national interest. "British Columbia must not develop in isolation from the rest of the country as a centrifugal force pulling against national unity," he said.[38] Press coverage of Trudeau followed exactly as his campaign organizers had hoped. A Canadian Press photo of Trudeau chatting with a radiant Jackie Kennedy lookalike made the nation's front pages, accompanied by the caption "Trudeaumania Hit Vancouver." Women "of all shapes and sizes" swarmed Trudeau at the banquet, according to the many stories that followed, demanding kisses and autographs.[39]

On May 13, Trudeau met United Nations secretary-general U Thant in Edmonton for extensive private talks. Thant was in the Canadian city to participate in the spring convocation of University of Alberta students, where both he and Trudeau would receive honourary degrees. The UN chief used the visit to call for an unconditional halt of the U.S. bombing of North Vietnam as a prelude to a negotiated peace (the first of the Paris peace talks having taken place just days earlier, on May 10). Trudeau's message was the same. "The bombing of the north must stop immediately," he insisted. "It must stop fully, not merely nine-tenths or three-quarters, but totally. That is a precondition to fruitful peace talks in our opinion."[40] Trudeau also laid out his views on what would later be called North–South relations. "We must recognize that, in the long run, the overwhelming threat to Canada will not come from foreign investments, or foreign ideologies or even—with good fortune—from foreign nuclear weapons," he said. "It will come instead from the two-thirds of the peoples of the world who are steadily falling further and farther behind in their search for a decent standard of living. We are faced with an overwhelming challenge. In meeting it the world must be our constituency."[41]

The Liberal campaign shifted to Quebec two days later, when Trudeau gave his signature "Just Society" speech, written by Ramsay Cook. Speaking to an audience of 1,200 at the Montreal Chamber of Commerce, Trudeau attacked Marcel Faribault's *deux nations* theory and Daniel Johnson's demand for an independent voice in international relations. If nationalists like Faribault and Johnson got their way, said Trudeau, not only would Canada likely disappear but so, too, might the United Nations and other international bodies. "When Canada's participation is sought for an international conference, there is only one address for the invitation—Ottawa," Trudeau maintained. "The Maple Leaf Flag is not a federal flag—it is the flag of Canada. French Canadians are represented at Ottawa and if you do not like their work, you can throw them out in the election. But under the two-nation concept, there will be nobody to represent you at Ottawa."[42]

Robert Stanfield responded immediately to Trudeau's attack on Faribault, accusing the prime minister of the worst kind of opportunism. "The attempt by Mr. Trudeau to gain support by dividing the country, and by trying to turn English Canada against Quebec, raises very serious questions," said the Tory leader. "This is a dangerous game Mr. Trudeau is playing. He is playing with the future of Canada."[43] In turn, appearing on Ottawa's CJOH television station on May 17, Trudeau condemned Stanfield for mistaking the views of Daniel Johnson and Marcel Faribault for those of ordinary Quebecers. "This isn't Quebec," he said. "Quebec is—we will see this in the election—Canadians of all origins, but mainly French, who believe that Canada is their land and their home, and they want their representatives in Ottawa to speak for Quebec in international affairs. Mr. Johnson is elected by Quebecers to speak for provincial affairs, not federal affairs and certainly not international affairs. You can't have it both ways."[44] To Stanfield's suggestion that Trudeau stop criticizing Daniel Johnson, with whom, presumably, he would eventually have to negotiate a new constitutional arrangement, Trudeau was equally dismissive. "What does he want us to do, lie down while Mr. Johnson says that he is establishing precedents? So what we should do to please Mr. Stanfield is not to react to this, say nothing? If the people want to have us wither away the federal government, they had better vote for somebody else. They had better not vote for me."[45]

In mid-May, three weeks into the campaign, Trudeau spoke at length with George Bain of the *Globe and Mail*. The two men met at the prime minister's official summer residence at Harrington Lake. Bain started by asking Trudeau whether he thought he was taking a risk in standing up to Quebec nationalists. "Well, politics is a gamble," Trudeau replied. "But it is really a continuation, once again, of why I entered politics—because I felt that there was a real menace to Confederation if people did not stand up and stand for a united

Canada, particularly in my province. We do not want to be [in Ottawa] to be stooges; we do not want to be straw men. If we cannot speak as fully for the people of Quebec in federal matters as other ministers can speak for their constituencies and their provinces, then the game is ended. I would rather know now, because I will get out of federal politics. I will go home and I will do something else."[46]

Bain then asked Trudeau what he meant by the phrase *Just Society*, which had emerged as the Liberals' pre-eminent campaign slogan. "It means certain things in a legal sense," said Trudeau, "freeing an individual so he will be rid of his shackles and permitted to fulfill himself in society in the way which he judges best, without being bound up by standards of morality which have nothing to do with law and order but which have to do with prejudice and religious superstition. That is one aspect of it. Another aspect of it is economic. The just society for them means permitting the province or the region as a whole to have a developing economy."

Why did Trudeau believe Quebec nationalism was incompatible with the concept of a just society? Bain asked.

> Let me just say that my approach to nationalism—Quebec nationalism or Canadian nationalism, or any other—is that, to me, it is a right-wing approach because it tends to set the standards for state action, things such as ethnic or linguistic or even religious norms. To me the modern state must smooth away such types of exclusive norms. You are born white or you are born black—all right. Or you embrace one religion or another. Or you are of one ethnic origin or another. But the state should try to govern everybody well—the greatest good of the greatest number. If we have two nations in Canada, as my opponents say, it means we are going to have two states and the values of those states will be based on the idea of one or of the other nation, and this is what I reject.[47]

The campaign had barely begun when it became obvious that—even apart from Quebec—the Tories had a PR problem. If Trudeau was, as Lester Pearson had said, a man for tomorrow, Stanfield came across as a man for yesterday. The *Canadian Annual Review* would later call the Tory campaign "indolent and sloppy."[48] Even sympathetic observers like *Globe and Mail* correspondent (and Stanfield biographer) Geoffrey Stevens conceded that virtually everything about the Tories seemed old-fashioned. "Stanfield lumbered from city to city in a decaying old DC-7C that had spent its best years lugging American tourists to Japan and Canadian Legionnaires to London," Stevens wrote. "It had a cruising speed of three hundred miles per hour—barely half the speed of Trudeau's DC-9—and Stanfield always seemed to be an hour or more behind schedule."[49]

As for Stanfield, his public image as a square could not be rehabilitated by the corny campaign slogan he poached from *Laugh-In*, "Sock it to them!" According to one of the campaign's most memorable saws, "It's impossible to imagine Trudeau as an old man, and it's impossible to imagine Stanfield as a young one." By mid-campaign, the press had taken to calling the Tory leader "Silent Bob." As one typical report remarked, "Just about everywhere he's been during the election campaign, Stanfield has been the same—withdrawn, unspontaneous and a puzzle to people meeting him for the first time." In contrast with Trudeau and his "see-and-touch" approach, Stanfield was awkward and tongue-tied around ordinary Canadians.[50] On television, his chops were even worse. Commenting on Stanfield's performance during an interview with CBC's Patrick Watson, TV critic Roy Shields said he gave the impression "of a dispirited man beginning to have regrets he ever left Nova Scotia."[51] The only thing Stanfield had working for him, added Shields, was sympathy.

Trudeau's campaign organizers took full advantage, planning shorter and more numerous campaign stops to maximize the impact of their candidate's charisma. On May 18, Trudeau blitzed Toronto, dropping by helicopter into three shopping malls (at Jane and Wilson, Jane and Bloor, and the Lakeshore) and capping off his tour with an appearance at the Royal York Hotel. At each stop, he was greeted by large crowds and mobbed by young women seeking kisses and autographs. He made short speeches, posing for photo ops with local Liberal candidates and smitten fans. Three days later, Trudeau made a similar splash in southwestern Ontario. Seated in an open convertible Cadillac, he visited six towns (Mitchell, Seaforth, Clinton, Blyth, Wingham, and Listowel) in five hours. Hundreds of people lined the streets to see him, including the usual retinue of screaming fans. In Listowel, Trudeau spoke about the need for the Canadian government to live within its means. "Governments are not Santa Claus," he said. "What Ottawa gives to the people it must take from the people. We don't intend raising taxes any more than we have to and, therefore, we aren't making many promises this election. But we do promise one thing, and that is that all the people of the country will have the right to share the wealth of this country."[52]

Speaking at a whistle stop in Brantford, Ontario, in late May, Trudeau again positioned himself as a frugal fiscal conservative. "People expect more from the country," he said. "They expect more from the government. Well, we're not going around telling the people that the government will give them more and give great public works here and build a tunnel there and increase all benefits in the next place. We are saying that the revolution of rising expectations can be a danger to Canada if the people think governments have money of their own and they can give things away that don't cost the people anything."[53] By all accounts, Trudeau's message was extremely well received by rural voters. Reporters travelling with him observed that he had impressed even the most conservative Ontario farmers as a straight shooter. "He seems to be able to make up his mind and he knows what he wants," said one. "He's a frank, stubborn, independent type of guy, like us. We've had enough of this free stuff."[54]

Throughout the campaign, Tommy Douglas tried to corner Trudeau on the issue of foreign direct investment in Canada. (Douglas stated early in the race that because of critically high levels of foreign ownership, Canada was within a decade of losing its sovereignty.)[55] "He's a continentalist," Douglas said of Trudeau. "He makes no bones about it. He talks about a continental economic entity and that eventually means one political entity, dominated by the United States."[56] Halfway through the campaign, Douglas stated publicly that federal finances were a mess and the Liberals were covering it up. Trudeau responded directly. "The government is not broke, but the government, if it wants to have a sound dollar, must sustain a balanced budget," he said. "We have a balanced budget and it's going to stay that way."[57] Speaking on a Vancouver radio show in late May, Douglas countered. "When he talks of balancing the budget, he sounds to me just like a 1930s Tory," he said of Trudeau. "Why, even R.B. Bennett got over that balanced budget stuff."[58] A few days later, Douglas compared Trudeau's economic policies to those of American conservatives. "I though Barry Goldwater and former President Eisenhower were the only two people left who thought you combat inflation by balancing the budget," Douglas told a Windsor crowd, little appreciating—or perhaps caring—that painting Trudeau as a fiscal conservative made him more appealing to centre-right voters.[59]

The Tories, too, went after Trudeau in late May, particularly on the Constitution. On May 20, Marcel Faribault held a press conference in which he stated that he thought the Canadian Constitution could be reformed "before the end of the year." After all, he observed, the Americans had written their Constitution in three months, "and they had to start from scratch." A journalist asked Faribault to comment on Trudeau's hard line on the Constitution. "I wish he had said what he says now at the time when I was his constitutional law teacher at the University of Montreal," he replied. Did he support special status for Quebec? "I don't particularly relish that term myself," Faribault said, "but in reality Quebec has had a special status since Confederation. I am deeply convinced that the other provinces will not want for themselves any other status than that wanted by the province of Quebec."[60]

The next day Faribault joined Stanfield at a rally at Winnipeg's Civic Auditorium. Speaking before a crowd of 4,500, Faribault said he had come to Winnipeg to set the record straight. "There is not one square inch of this country I shall ever renounce and there is no one I will not fight who seeks to menace or tear it apart," he cheered.[61] When Stanfield took the podium, he mused about the possibility of a moratorium on discussion of the Constitution for the rest of the campaign. "We feel we have discussed it enough, and made our point," said Stanfield. "We stand for a united Canada." Asked to elaborate on his views of Canadian federalism, Stanfield stated his position. "The Progressive Conservative Party stands for one country, one Canada with a federal system of government, one country of 'two founding peoples' who have been joined by Canadians of other cultures. Neither I, as the leader of the Progressive Conservative Party, nor the party itself, accept any suggestion of 'two countries' or 'two Canadas.'"[62]

Trudeau answered the Tory leader the next day. There would be no moratorium. On the contrary, Stanfield's offer allowed Trudeau both to restate that the election was about national unity and to accuse the Tories of playing Canadians for fools. On May 22, Trudeau spoke at his own nomination meeting in the Montreal riding of Mount Royal. A standing-room-only crowd of 700 was there to see him, and another 1,500 stood in the street to listen to him on loudspeakers. Trudeau did not disappoint them. "I've been told that in taking the problems of the country to the people, by asking them to think about the constitution and about federalism, that I am making a mistake," he said. "Are they too dumb? Are they afraid to face realities? I don't agree with that."[63]

Speaking in Timmins the same evening, Faribault retaliated. Trudeau was a "socialist in disguise and a socialist of the worst kind—a doctrinaire socialist," Faribault claimed. "I have known him for 25 years. He was a student of mine at the University of Montreal, and a good student I might say. But he is basically a socialist."[64]

Trudeau reacted to Faribault's red-baiting by playing the statesman. "Look behind labels," he told a Canadian Club luncheon in Winnipeg the next day. "Don't judge a man by the labels other men put on him or by the thickness of his pocket book or by the thinness of his hair, but by his ideas."[65]

Out on the campaign trail, Trudeau was at his best where he always had been, challenging idealistic young Canadians and being challenged in turn by them. On May 23, he gave a speech to a group of students in Winnipeg, sparring with them in his familiar Socratic manner. (At one point, he told the crowd that he was enjoying himself so much that he would be happy to arrive late to his plane.) One exchange in particular captured Trudeau's sharp-witted debating style. It opened when a student shouted, "What about Vietnam?"

"It is a dirty war and it should be stopped," Trudeau replied. "It has long been the policy of the Canadian government to stop the war. But it must be ended through negotiation, not by bombing the north."

"Then why does the Canadian government continue to sell arms to the United States?" countered the student.

"What difference would it make if we stopped selling arms to the United States?" said Trudeau. "If you really want to do something to stop this war, we can stop selling wheat to China."

The students groaned.

"Well, why not?" Trudeau continued. "China has a little something to do with this war. And at the same time we can stop selling oil to the United States. And asbestos. And nickel."

"This is precisely what the federal government should do," said the student.

"Then where's our money going to come from?" Trudeau pressed him. "Oh, you might feel better. But you're not just pouring balm on your consciences. You'd have a fine world if every time you didn't agree with the foreign policy of a foreign state you decided to blockade it. We'd have to blockade France. And, of course, the British. Nobody approves of what they're doing in South Africa. And the rest of Europe. So, what would you do? You'd have clean hands. You'd have pure hands. You wouldn't be selling anything to these awful bums, eh? You'd have empty bellies and you'd be flat on your face and you'd have a prostrate economy."

When one of the students asked an ill-informed question, Trudeau reached into his pocket, threw out a dime, and said, "Go buy a newspaper and learn something." The crowd howled with laughter.[66]

Not all of Trudeau's encounters with young people were pleasant. On May 27, he confronted a group of young separatists who showed up at Fort Chambly, south of Montreal, to heckle him. "What are you afraid of?" he said angrily. "You are afraid that the country is no longer interested in your small minds and small ideas." What really enraged Trudeau was that some of the hecklers had brought along English signs saying "Get the frogs to speak English," among other anti-French slogans. "These are *agents provocateurs*," he told the crowd, "separatists pretending they are English in order to create hate in this country."[67]

Trudeau's exchanges with young activists, pleasant or otherwise, countered the popular perception that his rapport with Canadian youth was shallow or manufactured—but never completely. Everywhere he went, journalists happily reported on the many teenagers who showed up looking for autographs. "Canadian kids have found a new kick—politics," said a typical report. "It beats LSD, glue-sniffing, Beatles and transcendental meditation."[68] The condescension in such coverage was palpable—and, of course, insulting to the many young Canadians who took Trudeau and the issues of the day seriously. Occasionally, the teenyboppers themselves fired back with op-eds of their own, bearing titles like the *Toronto Star*'s "I'm a Teenage Liberal Because I Care about the Constitution."[69] Trudeau was delighted.

By late May, the Liberal "kiss-and-run" campaign began to feel contrived—even to the candidate himself. At Kentville, Nova Scotia, Trudeau flew in by helicopter, gave a three-minute speech, allowed himself to be touched and jostled for another fifteen minutes, and then promptly flew out. For those in the crowd who had travelled for hours to see him, or might have preferred that he talk about issues, the performance was off-putting. The criticism that Trudeau was a "candy-floss candidate" began to dog him, alongside the persistent refrain from his Quebec critics that he enjoyed playing the messiah. "The Trudeau campaign is, in effect, a throwaway when you think of the man's intellectual capacities and the range of his mind as demonstrated before he committed himself to the role of the showbiz campaign, showing himself to the hero-hungry people," fumed veteran *Ottawa Citizen* correspondent Charles Lynch. "Mr. Trudeau is seeking to win the prime ministry without ever demonstrating, or needing to demonstrate, his qualifications for that office."[70]

The venerable *Globe and Mail* columnist Scott Young—father of folksinger Neil Young and a man who knew something about the counterculture—was also unimpressed with Trudeaumania.

> The most difficult thing for a born-innocent bystander to understand about the federal election campaign is what moves women and young girls especially to flock around Pierre Trudeau, throw themselves upon him, press their bosoms against him, act out in all ways a human parody of reason. Have any of them read his books or speeches? Would any of

> them act as they do if Mr. Trudeau had married and now had a wife of his own age, a settled, motherly or even grandmotherly woman whose natural progression from girlhood could be measured in the steadily rising quality required in her foundation garments? Are Canadian women so starved for romance that they will seize any opportunity to carry their yearnings into the polling booth with them? It is all a puzzle to me.[71]

Trudeau's female supporters, and the prime minister himself, recognized that Young's critique contained as much condescension as puzzlement.

The more the press covered Trudeumania, in fact, the more Trudeau fretted about being overexposed. "I hope Trudeau doesn't get in," remarked a twenty-four-year-old woman at a Tory rally in Halifax. "I don't know what I have against him but he's just not the type of person to be in such a high position. You know, this business of kissing all the girls all the time. I would have liked to see him do something before calling an election."[72] In Quebec, where Trudeau refused to conceal his views or placate his political enemies, Trudeaumania was plainly a liability. "So you think this Trudeaumania is real?" a Union Nationale organizer pressed *Toronto Star* correspondent Dominique Clift. "Well, I'll tell you that it's no more spontaneous than the reception which de Gaulle got last year on Le Chemin du Roy. And I know. De Gaulle. Trudeau. Bah! It's all newspaper and television stuff. You do it with kids out of school with no vote."[73]

In early June, Trudeau put a stop to the kiss-and-run campaign, insisting that his visits be longer and that he be allowed to speak on substantive issues with Canadians. As if to atone for his spotty appearances in Atlantic Canada, on June 3 Trudeau settled in to a major speech on national unity before an open-air crowd of eight thousand in Kamloops, B.C.—a speech that even his critics acknowledged was one of the most inspired of the campaign. His voice rising, his forefinger stabbing, Trudeau charged Marcel Faribault with opening up the question of special status for Quebec and other Tories with conveniently distancing themselves from Faribault. "They are talking about two nations in one part of the country and now they think it is time to make the rest of the country forget about it," said Trudeau. "Our policy is clear and simple—all Canada belongs to all Canadians!"[74] Before he left the podium, Trudeau apologized for getting carried away and talking too long. When he left the stage, he was mobbed on his way to get a burger. Ian MacDonald, the *Vancouver Sun*'s reporter on the campaign trail, would later claim that for Westerners Trudeaumania began at that Kamloops picnic.[75]

Despite the evidence that Trudeau benefited politically from the adulation of young women, he and his advisers understood that the slightest whiff of scandal could be disastrous. Asked by journalists about all the kissing at his campaign stops, Trudeau suggested defensively that it was a harmless expression of young people's political engagement. "I'd much rather see them do that [kiss] than see them withdraw from society," he told CBC's Patrick Watson. "Real kissing is something I don't like to do in public."[76] Ottawa bureaucrats remained as risk-averse as ever. In late May, Jennifer Rae, a pretty twenty-four-year-old (and sister of Bob Rae), was asked to leave her job in the PMO because Trudeau had been seeing her socially. (Rae had been Trudeau's date to a state dinner in early May for President Habib Bourguiba of Tunisia.) She was relocated to Liberal Party headquarters in Ottawa, reportedly under protest.[77]

Just after midnight local time on Wednesday, June 5, 1968, Senator Robert F. Kennedy, Jr., brother of the late—and in Canada revered—JFK was shot down at the Ambassador Hotel in Los Angeles.

Senator Kennedy had just finished speaking to a crowd of supporters that had gathered to celebrate his victory over Senator Eugene

McCarthy in the California presidential primary. He was hit with three bullets from a .22-calibre revolver fired by Sirhan Sirhan, a Jordanian unhappy with Kennedy's pro-Israeli stand on the Middle East. Like their American friends, Canadians awakened the next morning to the shocking news that Kennedy had undergone four hours of emergency neurosurgery to remove one of the assassin's bullets from his brain. He was clinging to life at L.A.'s Good Samaritan Hospital. Kennedy's wife, Ethel, had been with him when he was shot and remained by his side. Jackie Kennedy, JFK's widow, was said to be "terribly shaken" and making her way from New York to L.A., as was his brother Senator Edward Kennedy.

Pierre Trudeau, still touring Western Canada, was awakened in his Edmonton bed by his friend and press secretary Roméo LeBlanc the moment the U.S. TV networks began broadcasting the story. The prime minister was "deeply shocked and horrified," LeBlanc told the press, but this description turned out to be an understatement. Trudeau took an early flight to Montreal for the funeral of his friend André Laurendeau, where his already anxious mood was exacerbated by the presence of Quebec nationalists. Immediately after the funeral, he flew to Sudbury, Ontario, for a campaign stop that had been on the books for weeks. In his pocket was a speech on resource policy that Ramsay Cook had written. And in his pocket it would stay.

On that night, Trudeau spoke to the Sudbury crowd of six thousand entirely extemporaneously. The normally reserved prime minister was racked with emotion, and it showed. "I do hope that in this election we will use the weeks and days remaining ahead to us to remind each other and to remind our politicians and to remind our columnists and commentators, to remind everyone whose part it is to discuss the issues of the future of Canada, that if we can't do it with the language of reason—if they must appeal in the language of civil discord and passion—we should be ashamed to be Canadians that have no right to live in peace together." Trudeau appealed directly to

Canadians not to "tolerate those who speak with a language of hate and violence to achieve what they think is justice for their ideas," citing recent FLQ bombings in Montreal as an example. Canada was fortunate not to be experiencing the extremist violence of the United States, he said, but it was easy to imagine such incidents escalating. "Frenchman Go Home, Damn Communist, or Bloody Fascist"—these were some of the epithets he had heard on the campaign trail, he told the crowd. "This is not the kind of dialogue on which a civilization is built."[78]

Journalists travelling with Trudeau noted that there was no heckling during his Sudbury speech. Again, his words seemed to strike exactly the right note. When Trudeau left the podium, Lester Pearson called Marc Lalonde to say that it was the finest political speech he had ever heard.

Medical interventions could not save Kennedy's life. He died just before 2 a.m. Los Angeles time on June 6. Pierre Trudeau kept to his campaign itinerary and gave a speech in Rouyn, Quebec, that mournful evening. He was no longer philosophical about the violence that had taken Kennedy's life. He was angry, and bitterly so. When a group of young people in the crowd of 1,500 began heckling him, Trudeau was merciless. They shouted "*Vive le Québec libre!*" Trudeau hit back with "*Vive le Canada libre!*" When they tried to drown out his speech with chants of "*Un, deux, trois, boo!*" and "*Vive Caouette!*" Trudeau assumed his gunslinger pose, with his hands on his hips and his feet planted wide apart, and lashed out. "You can have your free Quebec but what about your freedom of speech? You are giving an example of the kind of country we would have if your party came to power. There would be no freedom of speech in your *Québec libre*. You are conducting yourselves like tramps and you want to run the affairs of this province?" Then came the *coup de grâce*. "Senator Kennedy was killed by purveyors of hate like you!"[79] Trudeau was more furious at that moment than Canadians had ever seen him. Even the young acolytes who shouted "*Vive Trudeau!*" during his speech annoyed him visibly.

Many ordinary Canadians, particularly those who could recall the terrible events in Dallas in November 1963, were distressed by the news that Bobby Kennedy was dead. This was no time for one-upmanship in the Canadian election campaign, and everyone knew it. Robert Stanfield expressed disbelief along with his condolences for the beleaguered Kennedy family. "A young man of proven ability, confidence and courage, obviously dedicated to the service of his country, and somebody shoots him down," said Stanfield. "There is something deeply disturbing to me about the spread of violence in the Western world. It is senseless. It threatens the whole basis of our society."[80]

The most immediate impact of the Kennedy murder was that protecting the life of the Canadian prime minister suddenly became a national obsession. Out on the campaign trail, Trudeau had until then been guarded by two plainclothes RCMP officers, who accompanied him on his stump speeches and slept in rooms adjoining his at night. The prime minister's obvious enjoyment of large and sometimes pushy crowds—and indeed his Kennedy-like habit of riding in open Cadillacs—made the duties of his security detail challenging. More than once in the first few weeks of the campaign, Trudeau's admirers had come close to dragging him off the back seat of his convertible limo.

After June 5, neither Trudeau's RCMP guards nor local police forces were taking any chances. At his Sudbury talk, twenty plainclothes police officers were assigned to him. Everywhere Trudeau now went, sharpshooters were placed on rooftops overlooking his speaking venues and his helicopter landing sites. The number of local security police in the prime minister's motorcades came to rival or exceed the number of VIPs riding with him. Journalists and even his own aides were now routinely frisked for guns, as security precautions reached "fever pitch."[81] Everywhere he went, the press asked whether there had been threats on his life. The answer almost invariably came back in the affirmative.

A week after the Kennedy shooting, Trudeau made a scheduled appearance in Windsor, Ontario, where he would give a major speech on national unity. The big story, however, was that police had received an anonymous death threat against the prime minister, one that they were taking extremely seriously. From the moment he stepped off his plane, Trudeau was enveloped within a sixty-man security cordon, the likes of which Canadians had never seen (thirty-five local police, fifteen Ontario Provincial Police officers, and the remainder his RCMP officers).

Asked about the threat, Trudeau remained imperturbable. "There are always crack-pots," he said.[82]

CHAPTER NINE

A MAN FOR TOMORROW

In early February 1968, before Pierre Trudeau had declared himself a candidate for the Liberal leadership, a postcard was sent anonymously to Canadian MPs. On it was a cartoon depicting Trudeau driving a "Liberal bus" down "Abortion Street."

Ottawa was abuzz with the smear, but no one seemed to know its origins. Only on February 16, the day Trudeau announced his candidacy, did it come to light that the postcard campaign had been organized by someone working for Eric Kierans's leadership campaign. Kierans immediately issued a written statement. "I must accept full responsibility for the actions of those working for me," it read. "It is all the more incomprehensible since all of my supporters are fully aware of our personal friendship. Meanness has no place in this leadership campaign."[1] Speaking to reporters, Kierans was clearly rattled. "My God, I've known Pierre for years," he said. "We're friends. I can only say I hope nothing like this happens to any other candidate."[2] Kierans promptly fired the man who had sent the postcards.

The slurs did not end there. Far from it. For the duration of the 1968 campaign and beyond, Pierre Trudeau was smeared with an intensity without precedent in Canadian history.

The main aspersion made against him was that he was a closet Red. A direct-mail campaign run by an organization calling itself the Canadian Intelligence Service claimed that Trudeau, a "Communist," was using the Liberal Party as an "instrument" to impose his radical views on Canada. The Canadian Intelligence Service was run by Ron Gostick of Flesherton, Ontario. Gostick claimed, among other things, that fluoridation, racial integration, and the United Nations were subversive, and that National Brotherhood Week was "the brainchild of organized Jewry."

A "news sheet" issued by the Canadian Intelligence Service to smear Trudeau cited *American Opinion*, a publication of the right-wing John Birch Society. The Canadian document was mailed to every delegate to the April 1968 Liberal leadership convention, apparently using a mailing list poached from the Martin campaign (the evidence for which was that misspellings and typos were reproduced exactly as they appeared in the original). Martin's organization was quick to distance itself from the smear. "We deplore this," said campaign manager Duncan Edmonds. "We have not done this. Our mailing list was not used with our authority."[3] Anecdotal reports from the convention floor suggested, however, that the anti-Trudeau literature was having the desired impact, particularly among delegates from Atlantic Canada. One party member told the press he thought the misinformation campaign was the work of the CIA.

The Montreal-based Pèlerins de Saint Michel (Pilgrims of St. Michael) added their voices, praying that their patron archangel might save Canada from "the rottenness and domination of Satan." An article by Louis Even, director-general of the organization, appeared in the special election issue of their broadsheet *Vers Demain*. In it, Even claimed not merely that Pierre Trudeau was "pro-Soviet, pro-Castro, pro-Mao" but that "the beast of Sodom" had inspired his liberal legislative reforms of the previous year. "It was with the stench of Sodom that Pierre Elliott-Trudeau presented himself for the leadership of the Liberal Party," wrote Even. "He had, in fact, introduced his 'omnibus Bill' to the House of Commons, a bill of which two points have marked Trudeau with shame and which would spread shame on Canada if they were adopted. One legalizes homosexuality. The other permits abortion in certain cases, thus legalizing the murder of innocent human beings. This is Trudeau. Trudeau marked by the sign of the Beast."[4]

Even's leaflet had been translated and published as a glossy English-language pamphlet by the Reverend Harold C. Slade, minister of Jarvis Street Baptist Church in Toronto and president of the Canadian Council of Evangelical Protestant Churches. Slade advertised the sale of the pamphlet in the council's fortnightly *Gospel Witness*—cover price ten cents—and sales appeared to be brisk. By mid-June, the pamphlet was in its third print run of ten thousand copies. Slade's church happened to be in MP Donald Macdonald's Rosedale riding, which incensed the young Trudeau devotee. "The people behind this hate literature are diseased—mentally diseased," he railed in a speech to the Toronto Liberal Businessman's Club. "And the disease is as virulent as any physical sickness. They must be isolated, quarantined and, if possible, cured before they destroy us and the society we live in."[5] When Toronto reporters asked Slade about his connection to Even, Slade said only that he had demanded evidence from the Quebecer for the charges Even was making about the prime minister and that Even had provided the evidence. He would not divulge Even's address when asked. In late June 1968, with just days to go in the election campaign, an unrepentant Reverend Slade would call for a wide-ranging government investigation into the Communist conspiracy to take over Canada.[6]

Initially, Trudeau reacted casually, recounting activities from his past that his enemies cited as incriminating. For example, at the televised press conference he held on February 17, 1968, to announce his candidacy for the Liberal leadership, Trudeau was asked whether it was true that he had once been blacklisted from entering the United States.

"Yes, I can give you facts," he replied. "I assume the reasons could have been twofold. I had been to the economic conference in Moscow in 1952 at a time when Stalin was at the height of his power and not many foreigners were going into Russia, especially at government-sponsored organizations, and needless to say I was roundly attacked when I got back for being a Communist. Another thing was probably that I'd always received periodicals and papers and I suspected then that there was some check on the mails and who was on the mailing lists, and so on. So you know, they must have arrived at the conclusion that I was interested in—what's the expression in those days, the United States used to say?—in 'Liberal' or liberal-oriented organizations or 'progressive' things."

Trudeau was then asked how he had cleared himself.

"It's a very easy proposition," he said. "You say that you think that you shouldn't be blacklisted and they look into your past and they assess you, I suppose. I must say that the consulate officers who did it were extremely able and extremely nice about it. You go to the consul and you say, 'Look. I'm not as bad as the book says I am and will you look into it?' There's no problem."[7]

What about his attempt to paddle to Cuba in 1960?

"I have canoed down most of the great rivers not only of Canada but of the world," he said. "I have canoed from Hudson Bay to Montreal. I have canoed down the Coppermine River and down the Mackenzie. I have barged up the Nile and so I tried to canoe across to Cuba. I didn't make it but friends of mine who wanted to go to Cuba took a plane the very next day, from the very same place, and flew to Cuba from Key West. I was picked up by a shrimper or fishing boat, which helped bring me back to Key West. I just drove back because my vacation was over."[8]

Several weeks later, just before the Liberal leadership convention began in Ottawa, Trudeau came clean on another potentially sensitive issue. Why had he not enlisted to fight in the Second World War?

"Like most Quebecers, I had been taught to keep away from imperialistic wars," he said. "The error was on the part of the politicians who promised in the 1930s there would be no conscription and if there was it would be over their dead bodies. Many of us in those years had been brought up to think that the Canadian role was to stay out of world affairs, and keep away from imperialistic wars. We were young men caught up in this logic."[9] Trudeau added that he had been active in the anti-conscriptionist cause in Quebec in the 1940s, and that he had been a bit of a troublemaker in the Canadian Officers Training Corps, which he was required by law to join when the war broke out in 1939.

The smears continued. In late March 1968, a ninety-six-page French-language booklet entitled *On a "fourré" la vieille garde* (*Tricking the Old Guard*) was mailed to every Liberal convention delegate in Ontario and Quebec. Among its many provocations, the publication compared Trudeau to Adolf Hitler, and accused him and Jean Marchand of McCarthyite tactics and "taking themselves for God."[10] The tract was also sent to all members of the Ontario and Quebec provincial legislatures and to every national news outlet in Canada. In total, four thousand copies of the publication were shipped. The moving force behind the booklet turned out to be René Lagarde, a disgruntled Quebec Liberal organizer who had been shunted aside when the three wise men ascended within the party. He was known to be backing Paul Hellyer in the leadership race, but Hellyer claimed no knowledge of the publication.

Another active participant in the Trudeau smear campaign was Igor Gouzenko. The world's most famous Soviet defector wrote and circulated during the Liberal leadership campaign a pamphlet entitled *Trudeau, A Potential Canadian Castro*. "Because Canadian and U.S. press, radio and television largely ignored the past activities and writings of Trudeau, the public is not aware of a real possibility that on the 6th of April, 1968, the next Prime Minister of Canada might be a self-admitted radical socialist, and Canada might with ever increasing pace turn into a second Cuba," wrote Gouzenko. "The situation is already pregnant with a multiple threat to Canadian freedom."[11] Only "lack of funds" prevented Gouzenko from distributing the pamphlet to all Liberal delegates.

Having failed to prevent Trudeau's elevation to leadership, Gouzenko wrote to U.S. presidential hopeful Richard Nixon using the alias "P. Brown." The two-page letter included Gouzenko's pamphlet coupled with a warning to "the next president of the United States" that in Canada "the left-wingers" were gaining ground. "Trudeau's methods of turning the country into a radical socialist state might be different from Castro's," Gouzenko informed Nixon, "but the result would be the same in time. The dream of the Soviet government to outflank the U.S. from the south and north is becoming a reality."[12] Although in 1961 Nixon had personally assisted Gouzenko in selling the movie rights to his novel *The Fall of a Titan*, there is no evidence that he replied to Gouzenko's pleas in 1968.

The smear campaign was so successful leading up to election day that the *New York Times* covered it. Liberal Party president John Nichol estimated that Canada had been flooded by hundreds of thousands of copies of Ron Gostick's diatribe alone. "It's an expensive operation," Nichol said. "Somebody is paying for it, but we don't know who."[13] Ottawa Liberals confirmed that Gostick's pamphlets had blanketed the capital "like a snowstorm."[14] An exasperated Peter C. Newman devoted an entire column to dispelling its claims. "Never before in a Canadian election," wrote Newman, "has a prime minister been the subject of so much hatred and innuendo as has been flung at Pierre Elliott Trudeau in the current campaign."[15] Canadian editorialists followed suit.[16] Both the Canadian Council of Churches and the Evangelical Fellowship of Canada issued statements condemning the smears.

Finally, in mid-June, Trudeau took off his gloves. "I'm told that in this part of the country it might be worthwhile talking a little bit about some hate literature which is being sent around," Trudeau told a crowd of supporters in Montague, P.E.I., where thousands of copies of Gostick's pamphlet were said to be circulating. Personally, he said, he considered the claims "pretty funny." But it was also apparent that the prime minister was tired of being badgered by the mainstream press as if the extremists' claims had merit. "All these things, really, they don't matter much," he explained. "As I say, it's the first time that I've even bothered to mention them in this campaign. But I think it might be worthwhile for some of the other parties and other politicians in other provinces if they are responsible for this—I don't accuse them of it because there are all kinds of sick people in our society who don't have respect for the intelligence of the people—but I suggest that all of us politicians of our party and any other party—I suggest it is our duty to dissociate ourselves from this type of garbage."[17]

The story of Trudeau finally hitting back at "hate literature" made headlines across the country the next day. Eddie Goodman, national campaign organizer for the Progressive Conservative Party, held a press conference to express his party's "repugnance" at the slurs directed at the prime minister. Robert Stanfield issued a statement promising that he would discipline any Tory candidate participating in the smear campaign.

Alas, Stanfield's tough talk was too little, too late. Perspicacious reporters had already exposed a Tory whispering campaign against Trudeau in Quebec, which, among other things, linked his reforms on homosexuality to his being a bachelor.[18] Marcel Faribault's charge that Trudeau was "a doctrinaire socialist" had also played into this campaign. On June 15, Trudeau spoke to a crowd of six thousand in Quebec City, his last stop in a sweep that included Chicoutimi, Jonquière, Alma, and Saint-Félicien. There, he lashed out at those in Quebec who would stoop to inciting hatred to gain political advantage.

> It doesn't disturb me if they say I am trying to destroy the traditional values of French-Canada, that I am trying to pass

> laws that are bad and are mortal sins. That doesn't disturb me, but what disturbs me is this sort of campaign which is led by we don't know who, but there are publications like *Vers Demain* which are being distributed by certain Conservative candidates. It doesn't disturb me if they attack me, but they are trying to exploit in the people the hate, the ignorance and the envy. It is serious that some people are trying in this election to prevent the people of Quebec from accepting that they live in a pluralistic world, from accepting a united Canada.[19]

There was plenty of irony in all of the smears against Trudeau, of course—as there has been ever since about his ostensibly "socialist" economic policies. As an example, while right-wing extremists were branding the prime minister a radical leftist, Tommy Douglas was accusing him of adopting the vicious economic policies of the American right. William Kashtan, general secretary of Canada's Communist Party, held a press conference in April 1968 to reassure bona fide Marxist-Leninists in Canada that "Mr. Trudeau has never been and is not a Communist."[20] Far from alienating Bay Street, Trudeau had inspired the confidence of Canadian business people. "Trudeau's election would spark a regeneration of investor confidence in what Canada has to offer," remarked Toronto stockbroker T.R. Bradbury early in the election race. "Mr. Trudeau may have the positive qualities to cut through the tangled undergrowth of restrictions hampering the development of Canada's capital markets. His election may also foreshadow a saner fiscal policy and the close links he has almost magically established with Canadians at large may enable him to persuade the public to accept financial restraint."[21]

It is impossible to gauge the impact of the smear campaign on Trudeau's popular support. The slurs against him would continue well into his prime ministerial tenure, but by then they had mostly moved offshore. "We've got a crypto-Communist premier in Canada just above us," said Alabama governor George Wallace in 1971, when he was testing the waters for a second run at the U.S. presidency. "He's got a worse background than Cuban Premier Castro himself." That same year, the John Birch Society mailed to doctors and dentists in the Toronto area a glossy publication for their waiting rooms. "Since June of 1968," it read, "Canada has had as a Prime Minister a Communist named Pierre Elliott Trudeau, with a known record more blatant than that of Castro." The following year, the Birchers published a booklet entitled *Canada: How the Communists Took Control*, in which "Red Mike" Pearson and the communist Pierre Trudeau were the main villains. A 1976 editorial in the U.S. business magazine *Barron's* accused the prime minister of "virulent collectivism" and was reprinted in its entirety in the *Globe and Mail* without comment.[22]

One person who could not abide such smears was John Diefenbaker, Canada's foremost anti-communist. Diefenbaker's terse advice to Trudeau in the spring of 1968: sue those responsible for such libel.[23]

Heading into Canada's first-ever televised leaders' debate, scheduled for June 9, the prime minister and his campaign team knew they had to make up some lost ground. A June 8 Canadian Institute of Public Opinion poll revealed that the Liberals had dropped four points since May 25. They remained the first choice of 46 per cent of decided Canadian voters, as compared with 29 per cent for the Tories and 15 per cent for the NDP.[24] But the numbers seemed to confirm that the Trudeaumania blitzkrieg strategy was not delivering the Liberal vote.

Over the early part of the campaign, media buzz about a possible televised leaders' debate in Canada had been constant—undoubtedly because Canadians recalled the first televised U.S. presidential debate between JFK and Richard Nixon in 1960 as decisive to both the Kennedy mystique and the Kennedy victory. As it turned out, Canadians who spent the evening of June 9 in front of their TV sets hoping to see Pierre Trudeau's famous telegenic charisma in action were disappointed. "Nobody really won the great television debate," groused Peter C. Newman. "The clear loser was the audience."[25] Everyone agreed that, with the exception of Réal Caouette and to a lesser extent Tommy Douglas, the party leaders had appeared wooden and cautious, utterly lacking in spontaneity. Media critics joked the next day that Canadian viewers had defected in the millions to watch *Bonanza*. Chastened television executives wondered whether they should even bother with televised debates in future. "I thought the whole thing was pretty dull," Trudeau commented after the broadcast. "I wouldn't want to impose another one on the Canadian public."[26] Ramsay Cook, who had prepped Trudeau by arming him with reams of statistics, later remarked that he should have been fired.[27]

As political theatre, the debate was indeed a washout. Wearing a conservative suit and an even more conservative haircut, Trudeau spoke in a flat monotone, citing the minutiae of this or that policy study and never so much as cracking a smile. "It is true that the consumer price index over the last five years of Liberal administration have increased by 14% or thereabouts, but during the same period the disposable revenue after taxes, the take-home pay if you like, has increased by 34% . . . ," he said of inflation. "If you compare the last five years of Liberal administration with the previous years of Conservative administration, revenues are up, productivity are up, and sales are now at an average now of some 540 billion bushels, and they were as compared to 340 . . . ," he said of wheat production. Clearly, it was not the sort of performance for which viewers would wake the kids. Asked at one point about his omnibus bill, Trudeau could not even make fornication entertaining.

Yet over the course of the debate, Trudeau managed to reference every substantive plank in the Liberal platform. On the *Watkins Report*: "Our policy is not directed to the re-purchase or the recovery of those industries dominated by foreign interests, but towards the investment of Canadian savings in industries which will dominate the world of tomorrow." On the Canadian economy: "Well, if Mr. Douglas is going to quote the report of the Economic Council, it might be worthwhile adding that they said that Canada is now going through the longest uninterrupted period of economic growth that it's had, that exists in the history of the Canadian business cycle." On the diplomatic recognition of China: "I've said, and I repeat, that the recognition of the Peking government of The People's Republic of China is a necessity." On Canada's role in NATO: "I feel that we must now reassess our military participation in the defence of the free world and I feel that this should be done by, as I say, shifting the emphasis from Canadian military presence in Europe to presence in areas of continental defence."[28] For old-school Canadian viewers who had not yet embraced their inner McLuhan and were prepared to listen patiently to the party leaders, the message was still the message. And it could not have been clearer.

Three days later, Trudeau again defied conventional wisdom about how to win elections in the televisual age. Appearing at a Toronto City Hall taping of Warner Troyer's CBC show *Public Eye*, he did the unthinkable for a front-running politician in the home stretch of an election race. Instead of dissembling or deflecting, he apologized for not knowing enough about some aspects of public policy to be able to comment intelligently on them. Troyer asked Trudeau what he was planning to do for indigenous peoples. "Here, like so many Canadian politicians, I don't know enough about the Indians," Trudeau replied. "I feel strongly the need to find solutions. I can only say it is a problem I am willing to discuss with sociologists and people who know something about it. I am sorry."[29]

Later in the same interview, Trudeau alluded to the student protests then rocking Europe and North America. (In France, a student occupation at a Paris university in March 1968 had escalated by May into a massive revolt of the nation's students and workers, paralyzing the French capital. Students in Germany, Spain, Italy, Mexico, and a host of other countries followed suit over the spring and summer of 1968. In the United States, civil-rights, free-speech, and especially anti-war demonstrations on university campuses also peaked over the summer of 1968, alongside other youth-led manifestations of New Left radicalism.)[30] Troyer asked Trudeau what he was prepared to do for Canadian students. Trudeau shrugged. "I hope they don't revolt this summer. I don't have any means of holding them back. I don't have a lot of money I can dish out. I am extremely worried about it."[31]

While Trudeau's aides fretted about death threats, red-baiting, and their man's lacklustre performance on the tube, Trudeau himself was enlivening his southern Ontario campaign with antics that would have left even the Sea-Doo–riding Stockwell Day breathless. Over lunch during a mid-June visit to Oakville, Ontario, he allowed the press to photograph him diving and swimming in the outdoor pool at the Holiday Inn. "Do a Stanfield dive," shouted one of the journalists. Hamming it up for the cameras, Trudeau produced an awkward tumble into the pool, then repeated this display for an equally ungainly "Douglas dive."

Awkward and *ungainly* were among the adjectives the press would use near the end of the campaign to describe the Tories' and the NDP's unravelling positions on national unity, which Trudeau continued to trumpet as the defining issue of the election and the reason for his own entry into Canadian politics. "Some say we have not promised enough things," the prime minister stated repeatedly, "but the issue is Canada and what we are going to do with it."[32] As Peter C. Newman correctly noted, Trudeau remained willing to "gamble all" on the concept of "one nation."[33] Never did the prime minister miss an opportunity to remind Canadian voters that he alone stood against the idea of *deux nations*. "I pity those politicians who talk about two nations," he said in a typical speech before a huge Markham, Ontario, crowd, which happened to include a large contingent of new Canadians. "In a political sense there is only one nation in Canada, and if we are to talk only about the English and the French, well, that would leave a lot of you gentlemen out. There are a hell of a lot of people who are not included in the two nations concept. In a sociological sense, there are a great many nations here."[34]

Trudeau's rivals did not seem to fully appreciate either the prime minister's resolve on the national-unity question or the extent to which—amid the crisis atmosphere of early 1968—it appealed to anxious Canadian voters. Trudeau had the enormous advantage of having brought most of his own party in behind his constitutional position well before he called the election. Both the Tories and the NDP, in contrast, found themselves improvising on the national-unity question during the campaign and navigating their internal differences under Trudeau's unforgiving gaze. The New Democrats foundered in mid-June when Quebec leader Robert Cliche casually acknowledged that he had separatists working in his organization. ("I would not refuse any separatist's vote on Tuesday," he would repeat defiantly right up to election day.)[35] As for the Tories, they had their September 1967 *deux nations* policy statement to defend, along with Robert Stanfield and Marcel Faribault's still-unresolved differences on Canadian federalism. All over the country, at their campaign stops and on radio call-in shows, Tory candidates were asked to clarify their positions. "There is no such thing as a two-nation policy," said a visibly frustrated Dalton Camp at the end of May. "The phrase used last year at the Conservative Party's Thinkers' Conference at Montmorency, Quebec, was two founding peoples with the French *deux nations* in brackets. Any Canadian who knows the position of party leader Robert Stanfield and who also knows exactly what the Montmorency resolution said would support it."[36]

Such protestations were of little use. The more Trudeau and his Liberal confrères attacked Tory policies, the more confused those policies seemed—particularly when they were defended by Marcel

Faribault. Speaking to the Alberta Chamber of Commerce in Edmonton in late May, Faribault suggested that if the constitutional ideas of Quebecers and other Canadians were similar, and if they were discussed in good faith, "we shall agree very fast. If not, we shall then have to see whether there is anything more which French Canadians feel is required and which may eventually call for some particular status—to be also discussed and agreed upon."[37] Two weeks later, speaking in Jonquière, Quebec, Faribault said flatly, "What we need is a central government that will decentralize."[38]

The Liberal sharks circled. In the last week of the campaign, they ran full-page ads in regional newspapers stating expressly that Robert Stanfield stood for a "two nations" version of Canada and "special status" for Quebec. Stanfield was beside himself. In a tough speech in St. Catharines, Ontario, he accused the Liberals of maliciously distorting his ideas. "Last week, full-page advertisements in different parts of the country—in Alberta and New Brunswick—sponsored by the Liberal Party contained deliberate lies about me," he complained. "If I had to run on the record of the Liberal administration, I would try and distract attention, too, but I would not resort, I hope, to deliberate lies and, if I was ever asked to repudiate a deliberate lie made on behalf of my party, I hope I would have the courage and the decency to repudiate it."[39] The Tory leader tried yet again to clarify that his party's concept of *deux nations* had a non-political meaning in French—a language in which, it had become embarrassingly clear over the course of the campaign, he was far from fluent.

Pierre Trudeau responded to Stanfield in a series of hard-hitting speeches in British Columbia. "Believe me, even if I wanted to, I couldn't distort his position, because I don't know what his position is," the prime minister told a crowd of fifteen thousand in Victoria. "I know it looks like a pretty awkward one. He tries to lean over backwards to please Quebec and tries to keep a foothold in the Prairies. Now this is not a position I'm trying to distort. I would like to know, and I think the Canadian people would like to know, what that position is."[40] Continuing with the same theme at a Vancouver rally, Trudeau offered examples of Faribault's speeches and insisted that even a "sociological" commitment to *deux nations* imperilled Canada since there were now many ethnic nations in the country. "Perhaps the Conservatives had better decide who is speaking for them," he said.[41] In Burnaby, Trudeau laid into the New Democrats for their attachment to *deux nations*. "You can't tell lies to the people," Trudeau admonished some NDP hecklers. "They won't believe you. People are more sophisticated now. We are learning in this election that people don't want to be conned by anybody. René Lévesque's movement is supporting Robert Cliche because they feel Robert Cliche's position is as far towards separatism as any federal party can go."[42]

The volleying continued, day after day. Speaking in Hull, Quebec, on June 18, Stanfield again demanded that Trudeau "repudiate these lies."[43] Trudeau shot back the next day from a podium in Fort William, Ontario (now part of Thunder Bay). "The distressing thing is not the two-nations policy," he joked. "It is the two-policy policy."[44]

The prime minister flew into Alberta on June 19. With less than a week left in the campaign, his aides had prepped him for speeches promoting rugged individualism, free enterprise, and "fiscal responsibility." But as journalist John Dafoe noted, "in Calgary there is only one big issue in the federal election campaign—how many nations is Canada?"[45] When Trudeau spoke in Calgary and Medicine Hat, his national-unity speeches were well received, as always. And as always, the prime minister insisted that his rejection of *deux nations* was not a rejection of Quebecers. "We're not waging this campaign against Quebec," he told Albertans for the last time in the campaign. "If anyone wants to vote for our party because they think we will put Quebec in its place, they shouldn't, because that is not my intention."[46]

On Thursday, June 20, Trudeaumania reached its crescendo—just five days before Canadians would head to the polls. Trudeau's organization could not have timed it better or staged it more adroitly.

Everywhere Trudeau had appeared over the last few weeks of the campaign, including Quebec, the crowds had numbered in the thousands. There was every reason to imagine that Torontonians would turn out in even larger numbers. Trudeau's earliest and most enduring popular support had emerged in that city, where polls continued to show Liberals with a commanding lead. Trudeau's organizers sensed that Torontonians would happily spend a few minutes on a beautiful spring day ducking out of their offices and classrooms to watch the Canadian prime minister cap off the most exciting election campaign in memory. And they knew that the national media headquartered in Toronto would be equally happy to beam the good vibrations out to Canadians elsewhere. Trudeau's team had momentum on its side. But to deliver a truly once-in-a-lifetime, winner-take-all spectacle, the Liberal organizers would have to pull out all the stops. There would have to be a motorcade, *and* a tickertape parade, *and* a throng of singing children, *and* an open-air speech.

And that is exactly how the event played out.

Starting at Queen's Quay at 11 a.m., a thirty-five-car motorcade crawled its way north on Bay Street towards Nathan Phillips Square on Queen. Trudeau, dressed in a blue suit, sat in a convertible limo, waving and smiling. He was accompanied by Toronto MP Donald Macdonald and surrounded by the heaviest security ever deployed to a Canadian campaign event. At the head of the motorcade was none other than Bobby Gimby, the bandleader who had written and recorded the jingle "Ca-na-da" for the Centennial Year. With Gimby were a marching band and over a hundred children and youth, who joyously belted out his signature song—which by then virtually all Canadians knew by heart, whether they liked it or not. As the parade passed the office towers on Bay Street, Trudeau was greeted by cheering Torontonians standing six rows deep. Prominent among them were Toronto business people. Onto the heads of the spectators fell tickertape and confetti wafting down from the windows above.

The drive to Nathan Phillips Square took the motorcade thirty minutes, landing the prime minister on the main stage, exactly as planned, right at the lunch hour. Estimates of the size of the crowd ranged upwards of fifty thousand, making this the largest political rally in Canadian history. Chirpy Trudeau volunteers were on hand to distribute ten thousand "Pierre" buttons.

When he took the podium, the prime minister delivered a speech on the importance of Canadian cities and the need for government to tackle urban problems. "The future of Canada will be determined in the cities like Toronto, Montreal and Vancouver," he told the crowd. "We know that the air we breathe is not as clear as that at the mouth of the Mackenzie River. We know that the Don and the Humber are not as pure as the Copper-Mine River."[47] It was without question the most incongruous speech of the entire campaign, given Canadians' preoccupation with the national-unity debate. To paraphrase Ramsay Cook, somebody should have been fired for that speech. "Pierre Trudeau's mammoth rally in Toronto's Nathan Phillips Square yesterday would have been an unqualified triumph if the Prime Minister hadn't opened his mouth," Peter C. Newman observed. "Unhappily what this breathtaking setting inspired from the Prime Minister—the man for whom all the fuss was made—was a speech so pedestrian that if almost any other politician had made it, he would have been booed."[48] The only interesting moment in the speech came when a group of anti-war hecklers shouted "Trudeau, assassin! Trudeau, assassin!" Trudeau responded. *"Pourquoi suis-je un assassin?"* (Why am I an assassin?) he asked them coolly—in French.

From downtown Toronto, the prime minister was driven directly up Yonge Street to the North York Centennial Centre, where he appeared on stage with Lester Pearson for the first time in the campaign. Pearson introduced Trudeau to the crowd of 6,500 with such warmth that the candidate himself was visibly choked up. "A French-speaking citizen of Quebec, but above all that, a Canadian," cheered Pearson. "A man prepared to speak out loud and clear in favor of unity. A man who doesn't make idle promises. A man who believes that the proof of the pudding is more important than pie in the sky. A man for today and a man for tomorrow. My friend, my former colleague, a man for all Canada—Pierre Elliott Trudeau!"[49] Trudeau followed with a short speech praising Canadians for their exemplary engagement in the political process. But it was Pearson who stole the show.

Trudeau finished off the headiest day of his campaign with an evening speech before a crowd of ten thousand at Scarborough's Confederation Park. In one of the most interesting twists in a campaign that had been full of them, Trudeau acknowledged that his party had overplayed the Stanfield–Faribault schism. He told the Scarborough crowd that he had read in the press that Stanfield called him "an accomplice in the smear campaign." Trudeau said he took the Tory leader at his word that he did not stand for a two-nations Canada, as some Liberal campaign ads had claimed. "I repudiate such advertisements and I understand they have been discontinued."[50] The prime minister's "repudiation" was front-page news across Canada the next day—far more prominent, in fact, than the saturation coverage of Trudeaumania hitting Toronto. Stanfield himself went on record as saying that he accepted Trudeau's apology (though, of course, that word had never been used).

The prime minister's magnanimity towards Robert Stanfield did not extend to Marcel Faribault, however, who continued to state that he would decentralize Canada in order to make Quebec's demands palatable to the other provinces. While Trudeau's motorcade had been making its way up Bay Street in Toronto, Faribault was speaking at a luncheon hosted by a Montreal Kiwanis Club. There, he called once again for a new Constitution, to stand as "a pact of good faith between two founding nations."[51] By the time Trudeau appeared in Scarborough that evening, he had been apprised of Faribault's speech. No sooner had he repudiated the slur against Stanfield than Trudeau again prodded the Tories' conflicted policy on Quebec. "In fairness to us," said Trudeau, "I would like the Tories themselves to say what they do stand for."[52]

Several days earlier, Stanfield and Faribault had been photographed touring small-town Quebec together in a pontoon helicopter. On one pontoon the name "Stanfield" appeared, and on the other, "Faribault." Trudeau knew a gift horse when he saw one. "Let's just say in this last week of the campaign that the Tories have a two-pontoon policy," he told the cheering Scarborough crowd.[53]

Surprisingly, perhaps, for a campaign in which media appeared to play a decisive role, fifty-nine of ninety-nine Canadian Press outlets surveyed by CP during the final week identified themselves as officially neutral. Of those taking a partisan stand, twenty-three endorsed Trudeau and the Liberals. Seventeen came out in favour of Stanfield and the Tories.

The *Toronto Star* endorsed Trudeau—solely, it claimed, for the tenacity with which he defended national unity.

> Apart from any other political virtues, the Prime Minister's clear-cut stand on the paramount issue of English-French relations entitles him, in the *Star*'s judgment, to the support of the Canadian people. Mr. Trudeau is determined there shall be only "one Canada" with equality for all provinces and special status for none. But he is firm, as well, in the belief that French-speaking Canadians should have the right to use their own language everywhere in the country where their numbers warrant it. This is a clear, precise policy on a matter of fundamental importance

> to the future of Canada, a policy which in our view is preferable to the fuzzy doubletalk of the Conservatives and NDP.[54]

Three days later, as if to drive home the point, the *Star* ran an editorial entitled "Where *Do* the Tories Stand on Quebec?"[55]

The *Globe and Mail* endorsed Trudeau as well, for his record on "the relationship of the individual to the state" and his "disarming candor." The paper quoted a recent statement by former prime minister Lester B. Pearson. "I feel happy leaving the country and the Government of Canada in his hands," Pearson said of Trudeau. "I think of him as a very wise, mature, intelligent patriot. He has been loyal to the language, the culture and the traditions of Quebec but he has put above all of that his loyalty to Canada. Everything's going to be all right and I can sit back and enjoy my retirement." That, said the *Globe*, was certainly good enough for Canadians.[56]

In a second, powerful editorial published on June 21, the *Globe* hammered the Tories' star Quebec candidate.

> Marcel Faribault has said he wants no special status for Quebec. He just wants broad powers to be offered to all the provinces in the conviction that only Quebec would accept them. That could produce a special status for Quebec that would go far beyond anything we could accept—or anything, we suspect, that Mr. Stanfield could accept. Mr. Faribault also believes that Ottawa should be allowed only those powers the provinces wish it to have, and that the provinces should be entitled to establish sovereign international personalities in areas of their exclusive jurisdiction. Mr. Stanfield doesn't agree and has said so (there really do seem to be two Conservative pontoons). We don't agree either: we think such measures would shatter Canada. That is why we support Prime Minister Trudeau.[57]

Many of the English-Canadian news outlets that did not endorse specific candidates expressed appreciation that the campaign had been fought over serious issues by serious candidates. "No matter who forms the next government in Ottawa, the federal position has been made firmer as a result of the national debate," stated the *Winnipeg Tribune*. "Neither Quebec nor any other province will be able to push Ottawa around as has been the case in recent years. The campaign has had another salutary by-product—the difference between linguistic rights and provincial constitutional rights has been brought out into the open. It has been made clear that no province can make a valid claim of being the 'motherland' of any language group."[58]

In Quebec, meanwhile, the pundits remained as polarized as ever. Late in the campaign, thirteen prominent provincial Liberals, including Pierre Laporte, signed a statement of support for Trudeau. "We know our positions well enough so that we could hope to meet and discuss frankly with the hope of finding grounds for agreement," Laporte said of his friend Trudeau. "Out of respect for the intelligence of Québécois, out of respect for a man who frankly states his ideas, even if I don't accept them all, I will vote Trudeau on June 25."[59]

The Quebec press, on the other hand, swung almost uniformly against the prime minister. The English-language *Montreal Gazette* and the *Sherbrooke Daily Record* came out in support of the Tories, after having endorsed the Pearson Liberals in 1965. The French-language *L'Action* and *Le Devoir* also endorsed Stanfield. "Because of his choice of Mr. Faribault, Mr. Stanfield has faced for some time a campaign of perfidious insinuation in English Canada," wrote Claude Ryan in *Le Devoir*. "The very fact that, knowing what he was doing, he still accepted such a risk, shows his good faith and the seriousness of his intentions."[60] Seen from the vantage point of English Canada, Ryan's endorsement of Stanfield revealed the depth of the national-unity crisis that Trudeau had gone to Ottawa to solve. A leading federalist tastemaker in Quebec (and a future leader of the Quebec Liberal

Party) had endorsed a unilingual Tory from Atlantic Canada over a brilliant, bilingual Quebecer. How could the *nation* invoked endlessly by Quebec nationalists not include Pierre Trudeau?

René Lévesque, now the leading spokesperson for that *nation*, urged members of his new Mouvement souveraineté-association not to vote for either of the major parties but rather to pick the candidates who would best represent their local communities. At a June 22 MSA rally, Lévesque dismissed Trudeau as *un roi nègre* (a negro king), just as Trudeau had predicted he would. The prime minister was the instrument of "the federal gang," said Lévesque, trying to persuade Canadians that bilingualism could patch up the country's constitutional impasse.[61] The outcome of the federal election did not matter much either way, Lévesque mused, since Quebec would soon be independent.

With much of English Canada in the grip of Trudeaumania, Pierre Bourgault and his separatist comrades escalated their threats against the hated *vendu* prime minister. "Trudeau has heard the voice of Toronto last Wednesday," an unidentified RIN spokesperson told the press. "Now he is going to hear the voice of Quebec. It will not be the same song. No one, including Trudeau, can put the French Canadians back in their place."[62]

On June 21, Trudeau travelled in an open-air bus from Toronto to Montreal, making several short campaign stops en route. In Kingston, NHL star Bobby Hull presented him with a hockey stick. ("You can use it to beat off all the good-looking broads," said Hull.) At a mall in suburban Pointe-Claire, seven thousand Quebecers turned out to see the prime minister, where, among other diversions, he danced in a parking lot with a young woman while his bus was refuelled. Far more dramatic was Trudeau's visit to Gérard Pelletier's Hochelaga riding in Montreal, where he was greeted by a well-organized crowd of RIN protesters chanting "*Québec aux Québécois!*" and "*Trudeau, pouilleux!"* (Trudeau, lousy!). Trudeau shot back with *"Canada aux Canadiens!"* and then spoke to the rest of the crowd. "These are the kind of people who would cause violence to prevent me from attending the St. Jean Baptiste parade," he said. Calling the protesters "small people with small ideas," Trudeau added, "You can imagine what kind of a republic you would have with these people. With these guys, we'd have a police state."[63]

Trudeau capped off his Quebec campaign on June 21 with a noon-hour rally at Montreal's Place Ville Marie. There, a crowd of 35,000 supporters listened attentively to his speech and even sang "O Canada" along with him. Oddly, there were virtually no hecklers present, so the prime minister could describe his vision of Canada without interruption. "Of course one country, one ethnic group, one language, one nation—of course it would be simpler," he told Montrealers. "When we talk of one nation, we are not talking about this kind of nation. We are talking of the Canadian people, the Canadian country, the soil that belongs to all Canadians no matter where they come from. We are in a province and a city with a French majority. We want the English-speaking minority and all the others to be welcome in our province in the same way we want French Canadians to be at home everywhere in the country."[64]

Squeezing everything he could out of the short time remaining in the campaign, Trudeau gave speeches in Winnipeg, Sault Ste. Marie, and Ottawa on June 23. The next day, he appeared in Renfrew, Ontario, and Maniwaki, Quebec, before finally circling back to his hometown.

And there, in Montreal, in defiance of René Lévesque's insults, Pierre Bourgault's threats of violence, and his own advisers' cautionary advice, he attended *la fête nationale* on rue Sherbrooke, like any other proud Quebecer.

CHAPTER TEN
THE CALM AFTER THE STORM

"It was the most remarkable ending to an election campaign in Canadian political history," the venerable *Canadian Annual Review* would later say of the June 24 Saint-Jean-Baptiste riot. "The price was a savage one, but nothing would have better dramatized the issue of Canadian unity."[1]

For the vast majority of Canadians and Quebecers—including the separatists uniting under the banner of René Lévesque's MSA—there simply was no place in their democratic inheritance for political violence. They were saddened but not surprised to discover that some impatient young firebrands, in their rage for liberation, had persuaded themselves and their even younger followers that rioting in the streets would jump-start their imagined utopia of peace and harmony. "Scenes of St. Jean Baptiste Day violence in Montreal might have shocked Canadians more had they not been conditioned by films of terrorism in the streets of New York, Paris and Belgrade," lamented the *Globe and Mail* on Canadians' behalf. "It was chilling to hear the chants of 'Trudeau to the gallows.' And it was awful to know that there were, in that crowd, men who had threatened the Prime Minister's life."[2]

Pierre Trudeau emerged from the spectacle physically unscathed and politically untouchable. In any other context, Trudeau's courage would have been notable. But in the tumultuous spring of 1968, it was extraordinary. Martin Luther King, Jr., and Bobby Kennedy lay dead. In late May, President Charles de Gaulle had fled the Élysée Palace in the face of violent street protests. Yet there sat the Canadian prime minister in an open reviewing stand, face-to-face with a violent demonstration mounted specifically to challenge his authority. Everyone, including Trudeau, knew beforehand that there would be violence. The only question was how much. One answer came the next day when, coincidentally, Quebec prison escapee Gaston Plante was sentenced for illegally possessing a .38-calibre revolver, among other crimes. Plante was asked in the courtroom what he intended to do with the firearm. "I was not keeping the gun for criminal purposes," he replied. "It was for political aims. It was to be used by a terrorist to slay that traitor, Pierre Elliott Trudeau."[3] The plan was to murder the prime minister at the Saint-Jean-Baptiste parade, Plante added.

When the headlines declared "Trudeau tient tête aux manifestants" ("Trudeau stands up to protesters") the day after the Saint-Jean-Baptiste riot, Canadians knew that the man who had made his way to Ottawa in 1965 to combat Quebec separatism was no paper tiger.

In one sense at least, election day was anticlimactic. The last of the pre-election polls showed Trudeau and the Liberals still riding high, only marginally off their pre-campaign peak of 52 per cent. A Gallup survey published on June 22 showed the Liberals leading with 47 per cent of decided voters, followed by the Tories at 29 per cent, and the NDP at 18 per cent. Political scientist Peter Regenstreif, the *Toronto Star*'s campaign number-cruncher, cautioned that behind the results lay considerable volatility, estimating that the Liberals could win as many as 145 seats or as few as 128.[4] A poll of *Globe and Mail* correspondents envisaged a Liberal landslide at 152 seats.[5]

Pierre Trudeau spent most of election day in Montreal. He visited his mother in Outremont in the morning, where his neighbours greeted him with a friendly "*Bonjour, petit Pierre!*" He then cast his own vote in the riding of Mount Royal. (Informed of a bomb threat at one of several Mount Royal polling stations he visited that morning, he replied, "Oh well, Russian roulette.")[6] In the afternoon, the prime minister was driven out to Dorval airport. He made a special point of chatting with the police officers in his motorcycle escort who had friends injured in the riot.[7] Once his chartered DC-9 had dropped him in Ottawa for the last time, Trudeau was driven directly to Liberal Party headquarters, where he settled in to watch the evening election broadcast. At about 9 p.m. he asked to be driven to the Château Laurier hotel. There, he made his way through hallways and elevators packed with expectant party members, fans, and media to a fifth-floor suite where he watched the rest of the election returns with Lester and Maryon Pearson. On this auspicious night at least, Trudeau and the Liberals had the capital to themselves. Robert Stanfield had finished out the campaign in his home riding of Halifax. Tommy Douglas remained in Vancouver.

The election results trickled in, as they always do, in a staggered east-to-west sequence as polling stations in each of Canada's six time zones closed.

The results from Atlantic Canada were uniformly bad for the Liberals. Robert Stanfield's Tories took six of Newfoundland's seven seats—a province where all of the incumbents had been Liberals. ("Mr. Trudeau was a friend of Newfoundland," Joey Smallwood admonished voters in his province. "We've slapped him in the face today.")[8] Not surprisingly, given Stanfield's pre-eminent status in Nova Scotia, the Tories took ten of that province's eleven seats, including Stanfield's own Halifax riding. Allan MacEachen was the only Liberal elected in the province, a victory that boosted his political career by making him indispensable to any Trudeau cabinet. Prince Edward Island returned four out of four Tories, as it had in 1965. In New Brunswick, the Tories and the Liberals split the ten seats evenly, a one-seat gain for the Conservatives over their 1965 showing.[9]

In Quebec, arguably the province with the biggest stake in the constitutional debate that had dominated the campaign, the Liberal sweep was breathtaking. The party won fifty-six of the province's seventy-four seats—the same number as it had won in 1965—but with an eight-point increase in the popular vote (from 45.6 per cent to 53.6). Réal Caouette's Créditistes took fourteen seats, five more than in 1965 but without increasing their share of the popular vote. The big story in Quebec was the rout of the Progressive Conservatives. Stanfield's Tories took only four seats in Quebec, compared with eight in 1965. But their share of the popular vote dropped from 21.2 per cent to a paltry 5.4 per cent. Marcel Faribault lost his Montreal seat to the rookie Liberal Arthur Portelance—and lost badly, 19,051 votes to 8,866. "The people have expressed their choice," a bitter Faribault conceded after the loss. "I think they will be sorry for having simplified the issues to the extremes. Mr. Trudeau has won after conducting a campaign in a way which I cannot approve and of which I would not be proud. His tactics were tantamount to blitzkrieg and I feel sorry that Canadian politics have reached such a stage. Now I'm asking myself, 'what have we failed to do?'"[10] Quebec NDP leader Robert Cliche also lost his Montreal seat (to Liberal Eric Kierans). Like his leader, Tommy Douglas, who lost his Burnaby–Seymour seat to Liberal Ray Perrault, Cliche blamed the loss entirely on Trudeaumania.

If the scale of the Liberal victory in Quebec was surprising, the party's sweep of Ontario was not. In that province, Liberals took sixty-three of eighty-eight seats, in effect shutting their rivals out of the cities. Prairie voters turned out to be far less enamoured of Trudeau and the Liberals than their central Canadian counterparts. In Manitoba, the Liberals took five of sixteen seats, leaving five for the Tories and three for the NDP. In Saskatchewan, the Liberals took only two of thirteen seats, the Tories five, and the NDP six. In Alberta, the Liberals took a meagre four seats out of nineteen, the Tories the remainder. In B.C., in contrast, the Liberals took sixteen of the province's twenty-three seats and the NDP took the rest, shutting the Tories out altogether. A Liberal won the only seat in the Northwest Territories, and a Tory the only seat in the Yukon.

Nationally, these results amounted to a Liberal landslide larger than anyone had predicted. The party's share of the popular vote came in at 45.5 per cent, compared to the Tories' 31.4 per cent. The NDP came third with 17.0 per cent, the Créditistes fourth with 4.4 per cent. What counted, of course, was the seat distribution. Canadians had rewarded Trudeau with the first majority government in a decade. The Liberals ended up with 155 seats of 264 in the House of Commons—23 seats more than the Pearson Liberals had won in 1965. The Tories took 72 seats, the NDP 22, and the Créditistes 14. Just under eight million Canadians had cast ballots in the election. But in contrast with Pierre Trudeau's high-flying rhetoric about citizen engagement, the voter participation rate came in at 75.7 per cent—*lower* than the rate in the 1962, 1963, and 1972 elections, and only a point higher than in the "wasteful and unnecessary" election of 1965.

Once the national election results were known, Robert Stanfield gave a sombre concession speech to an almost empty room at Halifax's Lord Nelson Hotel. Ever the gentleman, he congratulated Trudeau on winning the majority mandate he had sought and wished him success on the "serious responsibilities" that lay before him. "My duty, and that of my colleagues, is to provide an Opposition in Parliament that is informed, vigorous, effective and responsible," said Stanfield. "And we will do that. But we also recognize a larger responsibility—outside Parliament as well as within—a responsibility to encourage the achievement of a genuine and effective unity in Canada—and to encourage the government to meet certain basic problems which, if they are not met, will have serious consequences for all of us."[11] Never one for dissembling, John Diefenbaker cut straight to the heart of the matter. "The Conservative party suffered a calamitous disaster," he said, fuelling speculation that Stanfield might be forced to resign the party leadership.[12] For its part, the NDP had increased its national seat count by one over its 1965 showing. Tommy Douglas was philosophical about losing his own seat, assuring his supporters that he would never stop fighting for social justice. "I'll keep smiling," he said.[13]

Pierre Trudeau gave his acceptance speech just before midnight Ottawa time—delivered in his now-famous monotone, devoid of any of the emotion normally on display at such moments. He thanked the leaders of the other parties and Canadians themselves for participating in the democratic process and fulfilling their responsibility as citizens. "For me it was a great adventure of discovery," he said.

> For all of us I think it has been a period of self-discovery. We now know things about this country which we did not know two months ago. The election has been fought in a mood of optimism and of confidence in our future. We have seen an unexpected upsurge of interest and involvement. But it was also a mood of tolerance. There is a strong desire amongst Canadians not only to make it possible for both language groups and our many cultural communities to coexist in all parts of the country without assimilation, but to take advantage of our diversity. We must intensify the opportunities for learning about each other.[14]

It was an anodyne speech, plainly meant to heal. The prime minister may well have been impressed with some Canadians' "mood of tolerance." But the fact remains that he had been the object of the worst smear campaign in Canadian electoral history, the pretext for the worst separatist riot, the recipient of credible death threats, and a witness each day to the intolerance of hecklers, bigots, and provocateurs in every Canadian province. Trudeau knew the importance of being gracious in victory. He was not about to kick off his first majority mandate with gloating. It fell to Quebec Liberal Party executives Claude Frenette and I.G. Giguere to state what Trudeau would not. The Liberal sweep meant that Quebecers had rejected the *deux nations* theory along with separatism, they asserted.[15] "Liberal organizers also feel that by winning 55 Quebec seats as opposed to the Conservatives' four," Southam correspondent Lisa Balfour reported, "they have administered a good, solid slap in the face to Premier Daniel Johnson."[16]

No issue in the campaign had been as salient to voters as *deux nations*—not even the idea of the "Just Society" that Trudeau himself had invoked and his organization had so deftly sloganized. "The issue is Canada," Trudeau had said throughout the campaign. And Canadians had drawn precisely the right inference: Was Canada one nation or two? "In the first year of its second century Canada voted yesterday to continue to grow as one nation, indivisible, free of prejudice and stronger in inter-racial harmony than ever before," answered the *Vancouver Sun*. "It rose to the tough but inspired leadership of a French-Canadian patriot at a time of crisis which he best understood and was most competent to solve. History may say that without him, the victory for national unity could not have been won."[17] Quite right, asserted *Toronto Star* columnist Peter C. Newman in his first post-election column. "Canadians have told Trudeau to settle the national unity crisis."[18]

Across Canada, editorials and op-ed pages expressed the same mix of exultation and relief. "The overall results, it is to be hoped, will put an end to the legend of Trudeaumania," said the *Globe and Mail*. "The Prime Minister has been given the mandate he sought to build a unified Canada in which the linguistic and cultural ambitions of both French and English-speaking Canadians will be respected in a federation that is hospitable to all its citizens, regardless of their racial origin."[19] The *Toronto Star* agreed. "Canada was the winner in Quebec," said the *Star*. "This was the clearest confrontation we have ever had between the ideal of a united Canada of all Canadians and that of a largely autonomous, though not independent, Quebec state."[20] The *Halifax Chronicle Herald* asserted that the Liberal "triumph" in Quebec demonstrated that separatists were "a noisy but politically insignificant faction, and that a majority of Quebecers want to remain Canadians, in a united Canada."[21] An *Ottawa Citizen* editorial observed that "Mr. Trudeau can properly interpret the result as support for his view of federalism."[22] Syndicated Southam columnist Charles Lynch added, "The outlook on the national unity problem could scarcely be brighter in the light of the Trudeau mandate."[23]

Significantly, editorialists writing for Quebec's English-language dailies—men and women with daily exposure to the nuances of Quebec politics—understood why English Canadians had welcomed Trudeau's victory so enthusiastically, but they expressed their own reaction with more reserve. "Mr. Trudeau has been able to draw to himself the country's hopes for national unity," said the *Montreal Gazette*. "These hopes have become concentrated in him in an almost mythical sense. Mr. Trudeau has offered a united Canada, not only by hope and by dream, but almost an act of will."[24] The *Sherbrooke Daily Record* agreed. "Apparently the thought uppermost in the minds of most Canadians is the need for preserving national unity, something that the Prime Minister believes can best be nurtured by a strong central government at Ottawa," it echoed. "And judging by the outcome in the voting of Quebec province the majority of the French-speaking electors agree with him."[25]

French-language editorialists in Quebec reacted to the Liberal victory philosophically, observing that Trudeau's challenge to the nationalist idea of *deux nations* had not prevented Quebecers from voting for him overwhelmingly. Op-eds in *Le Droit* and *L'Action* expressed reservations about Trudeau but acknowledged that the return of majority government would at least bring "stability" and "freedom" to Parliament.[26] *La Presse* attributed Trudeau's coast-to-coast victory to Canadians' fascination with the man himself. "What is essential now is to use this victory for the common good and to initiate an era of uninterrupted progress, of stability in harmony," it concluded.[27] Writing in *Le Soleil*, journalist Mario Cardinal correctly noted that Trudeau's majority victory in Quebec was about to complicate Daniel Johnson's life.[28] Claude Ryan was particularly gracious in the wake of the Liberal victory. "The Quebec people did not explicitly approve of the constitutional theory of Mr. Trudeau," he wrote in *Le Devoir*. "Nevertheless, they have confidence in it after having had ample opportunity to examine his constitutional opinions."[29]

Quebec sovereignists responded predictably to Trudeau's 1968 victory. "His platform had no substantial political content," René Lévesque wrote, "a few pious generalizations about a juster society; a couple of jokes at the expense of Conservative leader, Robert Stanfield; and nothing more. Trudeau only had to present himself as an elegant receptacle into which Canada could pour all its hidden hopes, among them the sneaking wish to see French Quebec put in its place. The unspoken but fiercely evident slogan that floated in the air everywhere was 'Keep Quebec Quiet!'"[30]

Today, nearly fifty years later, Trudeaumania is commonly understood to have been the beginning of something—the country's coming of age, Canadians' embrace of political modernity (including secularism, pluralism, bilingualism, and multiculturalism), the genesis of the Trudeau epoch, of course, and of Canada's constitutional odyssey. For Canadians enamoured of Pierre Trudeau's vision of Canada, the adjectives that attach themselves to this historical flashpoint are almost all forward-looking and hopeful: *new, fresh, confident, proud, buoyant, optimistic*. For Trudeau's conservative critics, Trudeaumania also marks a historic fork in the road—the moment when, in the words of David Frum, "the peace, stability and comparative prosperity" of mid-1960s Canada was "despoiled" out of "ignorance and arrogance," requiring three subsequent prime ministers to clean up "the wreckage."[31]

But Trudeaumania was also the end of something. It was the end of one Canadian's quest to figure out what made his country tick. (No wonder Canadians imagine Pierre Trudeau as the country's iconic loner, paddling his canoe serenely on flat water.)

The project of reimagining Canada was Pierre Trudeau's intellectual obsession practically from the moment he returned to Montreal from his studies and travel abroad. In *Cité libre* in the 1950s and especially in his hard-hitting polemics of the early 1960s, Trudeau applied himself to perfecting a liberal constitutional theory of Canadian federalism that would undermine what he perceived as the separatist drift in Quebec nationalist thought. This was no mere academic enterprise—though when he imagined a life spent writing and teaching in Montreal, Trudeau might well have wished it to be. It was a practical plan to save Canada from a fate that its own history had made almost inevitable. It bears repeating: Trudeau knew that his nationalist adversaries in Quebec were right about the injustices French Canadians had suffered historically. Indeed, when he fumed in 1961 that "the French Canadians had the bad grace to decline assimilation," he was expressing his own youthful nationalist ire.

Seen in the context of a world decolonizing at breakneck speed in the sixties, when Fidel Castro and other radicals were the standard-bearers of national salvation, Trudeau's formula for saving Canada was prudent and practical. "What I am thinking of," said Trudeau, "is a bill of rights which will guarantee French rights across the country. If you say the government of Quebec alone represents French-Canadian aspirations, if you say that to start with, it is clear that my formula won't work. My formula tries to preserve Canadian unity." Trudeau's formula did not envisage a (leftist) revolution or a (rightist) *coup d'état*. It did not require hyperbole, or arm-twisting, or bait-and-switch demagoguery. *Here are my ideas,* Trudeau told Canadians. *What do you think?*

By 1968, Canadians knew that Trudeau was unyielding in his opposition to Quebec nationalists and especially to radical separatists, whom he accused of fomenting "a dictatorship of their minority." But behind these barbs lay a sharp-eyed diagnosis of both the political origins of Quebec nationalism and its likely trajectory. Political scientists may debate whether Trudeau's diagnosis was accurate, but they cannot deny that it *appeared* accurate to many Canadians. Even apart from the revolutionary dogma of *Parti pris* and the programmatic violence of groups like the FLQ, which most Canadians found abhorrent, Trudeau maintained that moderate nationalist ideas in Quebec like *statut particulier* and *deux nations* led directly to "doctrinaire separatism." When he began saying this publicly in the early 1960s, René Lévesque was a top minister in the Liberal cabinet of Jean Lesage. By 1967, Lévesque was the head of the Mouvement souveraineté-association, a political party dedicated to the principle that "Quebec should become a sovereign state." Similarly, RIN leader Pierre Bourgault had sought to achieve his separatist goals democratically during Quebec's 1966 election, but by 1968 he was openly threatening violence against those who "do not believe in our nation." Quebec nationalists spoke of *la nation* as inclusive, tolerant, and progressive. But for Pierre Trudeau and other French Canadians who thought as he did, that *nation* was unwelcoming. Even Canadians sympathetic to Quebec's national aspirations noticed the incongruity.

In his 1964 brief to the Charlottetown conference, Trudeau had stated that "cold, unemotional rationality" could save the Canadian ship. After 1965—when he, Jean Marchand, and Gérard Pelletier joined the Pearson Liberals—Trudeau personified this cold, unemotional rationality (and for many Canadians he does still). More significantly, he positioned himself as the voice of cautious incrementalism. "You already have enough powers," he said of Canada's political elites. "Do a job with them." His boss, Prime Minister Lester Pearson, agreed. Pearson was a serious student of Canadian history. He understood the pride and dignity that the Quiet Revolution had brought Quebecers. His abiding inclination after taking power in 1963 was to accommodate Quebec's demands for a new Confederation deal via the Bi and Bi Commission, the Fulton-Favreau formula, and bilateral fora for quiet consultation. But Pearson, and Trudeau with him, ran out of time. Quebec City forced their hands. The Lesage Liberals started the constitutional clock ticking in 1963 when they commissioned exhaustive studies on Quebec's constitutional options—bequeathing them, in effect, to Daniel Johnson's Union Nationale in 1966. Ontario premier John Robarts imposed a deadline on the process by calling his interprovincial constitutional conference for November 1967.

Pearson would have preferred not to provoke a "full constitutional confrontation" in 1968, as he himself put it. But push had come to shove. The federal government had to either act or forfeit constitutional leadership to the provinces. Over the course of 1967, Pearson's own constitutional steering committee adopted Trudeau's idea of a "charter of human rights"—even though Trudeau himself still hoped that constitutional "tinkering" could be deferred indefinitely. Only in late 1967, after several false starts, did Pearson and his Quebec caucus fall in behind Trudeau's idea of a charter, and only because Daniel Johnson had concluded that the *British North America Act* could not be rehabilitated. By then, Trudeau had stepped forward to spearhead the reform of Canadian laws respecting divorce, abortion, and homosexuality. He became a national figure just as the national-unity crisis was peaking. Many Canadians were pleasantly surprised by his leadership skills, his straight talk, and his "gutsiness." But more important, they understood that Trudeau's principled defence of his legislative reforms—the need to separate "the sacred and the profane" in a "pluralistic" society—had direct application to the national-unity crisis.

In late January 1968, before he declared himself a candidate for the Liberal leadership, Trudeau told members of the party's Quebec caucus to keep their minds clear and sharp. "Do not confuse the rights of French Canadians with provincial powers," he said. Trudeau plainly enjoyed playing the role of the nationalists' *bête noire* and even scrapping occasionally with Daniel Johnson, as he did during the televised constitutional conference of February 1968. He continued to pillory nationalist politicians for ghettoizing Quebecers (and for building their own "little empires") when even the avowed federalists among them, like Marcel Faribault, knew that Quebecers' birthright was the whole of Canada. But Trudeau was unerringly careful never to attack Quebecers themselves, nor to appear as a federal centralizer "nibbling" at Quebec's powers and "carrying them off to Ottawa," as he put it. Any time he suggested that power be ceded to Canadian citizens in a new constitutional arrangement, he explained that this change would require sacrifice from the feds as well as the provinces. Any time he was accused of defending the status quo—by Claude Ryan, most notably—he denied it, insisting that the conversion of Canada into the national homeland of French Canadians as well as English Canadians would require political vision and determined effort. And any time he was praised for putting Quebec in its place, his blunt rejoinder was that Quebec's place was in Canada. "If people think I would be a good choice for PM because I would be hard on Quebec," he said, "they had better not vote for me."

Above all, Trudeau knew better than anyone that his formula for national unity was the starting point for a process that was likely to be long and arduous. It was Marcel Faribault who said, rather blithely, that Canadians could write a new Constitution in six months if they put their minds to it. It was Pierre Trudeau who said that Canadians should be careful what they wished for: once the Constitution was cracked open, there were no guarantees that it could be put back together again.

At the short midnight press conference that followed his 1968 victory address, Prime Minister Trudeau put Canadians on notice once again. Do not imagine that the majority of Quebecers had voted

Liberal because they endorsed his vision of Canadian federalism, he warned. Canadians should not delude themselves. The election had not been a referendum on the Constitution. "The election has aroused high expectations among the people of Canada. It will be up to all of us in the government and in parliament to justify these expectations. Throughout this campaign I have insisted that although there are no magic solutions to our problems, we must reform and adapt in many areas—in parliament, in our constitution and in many of our laws, in the development of our economy and in our foreign policy. Much hard work lies ahead."[32]

EPILOGUE
TRUDEAUMANIA 2.0

Dynasties are rare in North American politics—in large measure because we rightly think of inherited power as the preserve of monarchies and dictatorships. Only twice in U.S. history have the children of presidents assumed the presidency themselves. John Quincy Adams was elected president in 1824 after his father, John Adams, had held the office in the years 1797 to 1801. George W. Bush became a two-term president in 2001 after his father, George H.W. Bush, held the office between 1989 and 1993. (As this book goes to press, Americans have before them the unprecedented possibility that the spouse of a former president might become the next occupant of the White House.)

In Canada, the children of politicians have occasionally followed their parents' example, as in the cases of Ernest Manning's son Preston, W.A.C. Bennett's son Bill, Paul Martin's son Paul, and Daniel Johnson's sons Pierre-Marc and Daniel. But before October 2015, no child of a Canadian prime minister had ever gone on to hold the country's highest political office. It was probably inevitable, therefore, that the term *Trudeaumania* would attach itself to Justin Trudeau's ascent in Canadian politics. The book on Justin's extraordinary rise to power has yet to be written—extraordinary not because he has nice abs and a Haida raven tattoo but because he led a moribund third-place party to a stunning majority victory. Yet even at this early stage, less than a year into Prime Minister Justin Trudeau's first mandate, his complex connection to his father's political legacy has fascinated Canadians—as well it should.

Justin Trudeau has spent much of his life in the fishbowl that is Canadian federal politics. The first of three children born to Pierre and Margaret, on Christmas Day, 1971, he spent most of his childhood at 24 Sussex Drive. The drafty—and by all accounts dilapidated—prime ministerial mansion holds few secrets for him. Given that his parents' marriage foundered in the mid-1970s when Justin and his brothers, Alexandre and Michel, were small boys, 24 Sussex is surely a place of mixed memories for its current occupant. He knows better than anyone how the public lives of his own children will unfold as they take their place under the media microscope and attend school in the company of RCMP officers, just as he did. He knows, too, the challenges of keeping his private life private and of maintaining some semblance of domestic normalcy under conditions that militate against it.

After Pierre Trudeau's retirement from politics in 1984, he and his boys moved back to Montreal and civilian life. Justin attended Collège Jean-de-Brébeuf, just as his father had, then took undergraduate degrees in English from McGill and education from UBC. As a young man, he taught snowboarding, did some barroom bouncing, and ended up teaching English and math at two B.C. private schools. He studied engineering and environmental geography at McGill but did not complete degrees in either. As Justin noted in his 2014 memoir, *Common Ground,* he was never academically gifted in the manner of Pierre. After flunking an exam in experimental psychology, he had a "serious heart-to-heart" with his father. It was an epiphany of sorts. "I realized, and announced to him, that I was not like him," Justin recalled. "All my childhood, my father had been my hero, my model, my guide, my instruction booklet to life. But when, trying to be helpful, he showed me his report cards dating from his time at Brébeuf in the 1930s, featuring a straight line of As stretching from top to bottom, I knew we were fundamentally different people, with different approaches to life."[1]

Pierre Trudeau died on September 28, 2000, less than two years after the tragic death of his youngest son, Michel, in an avalanche at B.C.'s Kokanee Glacier Park. Justin's dramatic reappearance on the national stage was one of the many unanticipated by-products of his father's state funeral that October. Against the backdrop of a massive outpouring of popular affection for Pierre, and in front of millions of Canadians watching the funeral on television, Justin gave an extraordinary eulogy. It concluded with a haunting farewell that many Canadians will remember: "*Je t'aime, Papa*."[2]

Following the eulogy, Justin became a celebrity. Wherever he appeared, Canadians sought autographs and pictures with him. "It makes me a bit uncomfortable, but who am I to argue?" he said of all the fuss. "My dad always taught me to be polite, get their name, write a little message if that's what they're looking for. People want the personal connection."[3] Rumours persisted that Justin might enter Canadian politics. He was flattered but genuinely noncommittal—attracting criticisms that, like his father before him, he was playing hard-to-get. "I'm far from a finished product," he joked. "I'm a moderately engaging, reasonably intelligent 30-year-old, who's had an interesting life—like someone who was raised by wolves, or the person that cultivated an extremely large pumpkin."[4] Yet when he was challenged to define his core conception of Canada in twenty-five words or less, his answer was pure, undiluted Pierre. "The nation is no longer a legitimate basis for the state," he said, "and the rights of the individual are never secondary to the rights of the collective."[5] When Justin criticized Michael Ignatieff's willingness to recognize Quebec as a nation, he invoked his father's idea of nationalism as retrograde. And when he lauded the *Canadian Charter of Rights and Freedoms*, which was often, he would say that he was the child of Pierre but that all Canadians were "children of that *Charter*."

Justin was active within the Liberal Party on and off for most of his adult life, lending his name to this or that candidate but restricting his appearances to cameos. In November 2006, however, he had a road-to-Damascus conversion experience when he attended the Liberal leadership convention and threw himself headlong into Gerard Kennedy's campaign. Until then, Trudeau had never been able to come to grips with his father's larger-than-life legacy. "The association with my father was never a reason for me to get into politics," he later wrote. "It was, rather, a reason for me to *avoid* entering the political arena."[6] Asked in 2012 whether it had been difficult entering federal politics as Pierre Trudeau's son, Justin was forthright. "Listen," he replied, "it was difficult showing up in Grade One as Pierre Elliott Trudeau's son, it was difficult becoming a high-school teacher as Pierre Elliott Trudeau's son. That's something that I've lived with all my life."[7]

But at that 2006 convention, held at Montreal's Palais des congrès, Justin got the political bug. More important, he discovered gifts and aptitudes that were uniquely his own. "From the beginning of his political career, my father assumed an intellectual approach to all his political activities, including campaigning," he later recalled. "Busying myself on the convention floor revealed to me that where political campaigning was involved, I wasn't at all my father's son—I was Jimmy Sinclair's grandson. Grandpa Jimmy had perhaps been the ultimate retail politician, a man who loved mixing with people, shaking hands, listening, and, yes, when the opportunity arose, kissing babies. The contrast between the two men is dramatic, and the more it became clear to me, the more it eased my concern about being compared with my father."[8] (Grandpa Jimmy was prominent B.C. Liberal James Sinclair, Margaret's father.)

Gerard Kennedy lost his leadership bid to Stéphane Dion. But the fight was fair, allowing the Liberals to put the acrimony of the Chrétien–Martin years behind them. Trudeau threw his support to Dion on the second ballot. He was rewarded with Dion's blessing to contest the party nomination in the Montreal riding of Papineau—for decades a Liberal stronghold but, after 2006, a Bloc Québécois seat. In April 2007, Trudeau won the Liberal nomination easily. He campaigned full out in the months leading up to the October 2008 federal election, only narrowly defeating Bloc incumbent Vivian Barbot. When he arrived in Ottawa for his first parliamentary session in the fall of 2008, he was one of the seventy-seven Liberal MPs who formed the Official Opposition. Dion named him "associate critic for human resources and skills development (youth)" and promptly assigned him a seat in the back row of the Opposition benches. In stark contrast with his father's expedited ascent in federal politics, Justin's rise to power was proving to be anything but meteoric.

Once he entered Parliament, comparisons with his father became incessant. Justin was far more gracious about them than ever Pierre would have been. "I am aware that there's an image that goes with me," he said. "And I'm satisfied that that image, every day that goes by, it becomes a little more me and a little less my father. The proportion can be debated, but I know that I'm taking the givens that my father's legacy gave me and I'm building onto it my own identity."[9] Like Pierre, Justin was dogged by the suggestion that he was a dilettante. "I'm willing to work extremely hard," he insisted. "The idea that my father raised sons that expected anything to be handed to them, to not roll up their sleeves and work harder than anyone around them, is to not know my dad."[10] Above all, Justin had to deal with Canadian conservatives' ad hominem attacks on his late father and with the now-familiar charge that Pierre had inherited a perfectly idyllic Canada in 1968 and proceeded to destroy it out of arrogance and spite.[11]

One of those critics was Stephen Harper, who, as president of the National Citizens Coalition (NCC), penned a screed against Pierre just a week after his death that included the line "only a liberal intellectual could believe the assignment of benefits and 'rights' would not become an arbitrary, politicized game."[12] Gerry Nicholls, Harper's colleague at the NCC, would later state what all Canadians could see plainly. "To lose to Justin Trudeau would be devastating to Stephen Harper on a real personal level," he said. "Harper wanted to undo all of the things that Pierre Trudeau did and now he's facing his son who wants to bring back all of those Trudeau values and traditions to Canada."[13] Justin has tried to be philosophical about being a scapegoat for his father's enemies, but it cannot be easy. "I've really thought about this, about how it's going to be harder for me to dismiss all the haters from now on," he said when he entered politics. "Up until now, it's been about how they hated my father, and therefore hated the son, for superficial, silly reasons. Now I'm going to start bringing forward ideas and positions and representing a level of threat to certain people. It's going to lead to people disliking me. But at least it will be for real, substantial reasons, not because of my hair."[14]

Revenge, of course, is best served cold. Justin Trudeau answered conservatives' critique of his ostensibly effete liberal style by beating the daylights out of tough-guy Senator Patrick Brazeau in a March 2011 charity boxing match. It was Pierre Trudeau who had taught Justin to box—and also to leave nothing to chance when the opportunity to best an opponent presented itself. "Patrick never stood a chance against me," Justin said after the bout. "He wasn't in very good shape. I had trained against bruisers like him for the previous three months and I learned, thank God, that I could take whatever they dished out and still punch back." For Canadians who remembered Pierre's pugilistic spirit fondly, it was a sweet moment—the more so because conservative commentator Ezra Levant had camped out ringside to savour Trudeau's humiliation. More than any other flashpoint in Justin's political ascent, the boxing match cemented his claim to his father's toughness and marked his own coming of age in the era of the brawling Harper Conservatives.

In May 2011, Trudeau was re-elected in his Papineau riding. He was one of the few Quebec Liberals to survive the "orange wave" that put Jack Layton's NDP on the Opposition benches for the first time in history and nearly obliterated the Bloc Québécois. The Harper Conservatives won their first (and only) majority government, winning 166 seats of 308, with 39.6 per cent of the popular vote. The Liberals' seat count fell from 77 to a dismal 34, and their share of the popular vote dropped to just under 19 per cent. It became more obvious than ever that the Liberals' leadership woes had become chronic.

One week after the election, a *Toronto Star* poll revealed that if Justin Trudeau were Liberal leader, the party would attract 42 per cent of decided voters. In August 2012, after testing the waters among Liberals everywhere in Canada, Trudeau took the bait. He instructed Gerry Butts, his old McGill friend and one-time principal secretary to Ontario premier Dalton McGuinty, to put together an organization. "My father's values and vision of this country obviously form everything I have as values and ideals," he said in his announcement speech. "But this is not the ghost of my father running for the leadership of the Liberal party. This is me."[15] By then he had put his misgivings about living up to Pierre's legacy behind him. "My father was incredibly focused, incredibly linear," he said.

> All his life, he basically wrote and thought and read and prepared on a very intellectual level. He was a complete package, to a large degree, before he stepped up as minister of justice. I'm not at all the same way. I am very strong in my core values, my ideology, my beliefs, my sense of what is right and wrong and what is good and just in the world and in Canada. But I'm open to discussion. I'm a high school

> teacher. I'm someone who stumbles my way through, leads with my chin in some cases, leads with my heart in all cases. It leaves me way open for all sorts of criticisms left, right and centre. You know what? I was raised with pretty thick skin. And I think people are hungry for politicians who aren't afraid to say what they think and mean it.[16]

The Canadian press knew how to sex up the story of Justin's Liberal leadership bid. "Will the 40-year-old with the fantastic hair, piercing eyes and same crooked smile as Pierre replicate the Trudeaumania that carried his dad to 24 Sussex Dr. back in 1968, three years before he was born?" asked *Maclean's* correspondent Jonathon Gatehouse sardonically. "Should anyone even bother to run against such a media darling?"[17]

On April 14, 2013, to no one's surprise, Justin Trudeau won the Liberal leadership on the first ballot.

By the time the October 19, 2015, federal election rolled around, Canadians had enjoyed (or endured) nearly a decade of Conservative rule, most of it under minority government, all of it under a mandate that had never exceeded 40 per cent of the popular vote. Superficially at least, Canada's fifteenth decade thus appeared much like its tenth, 1957 to 1967, which meant that Justin Trudeau entered the election contest with some of the advantages that had accrued to his father in 1968: a tired Parliament, a Canadian electorate ready for change, the advent of a new generation of politically active young Canadians.

The Liberal campaign in 2015 made the most of the party's youthful, telegenic, and fluently bilingual leader, of course. But Trudeau and his advisers perceived, correctly, that they could defeat Stephen Harper only by playing the game his way—that is, by promising competent managerial-style government. The Liberal platform focused on reviving the beleaguered middle-class Canadian family, with promises of tax cuts, child tax credits, flexible parental benefits, and new spending on youth. There would be massive new infrastructure spending requiring deficits in the first three years of a Liberal mandate. Government scientists, diplomats, and other experts would be unmuzzled, and the long-form census restored. Climate change would be confronted, the green economy nurtured. The government's relationship with First Nations would be renewed, starting with a public inquiry into missing and murdered indigenous women. Marijuana would be legalized. The purchase of the F-35 stealth fighter-bomber would be cancelled, and Canada's combat mission in Iraq terminated. Twenty-five thousand Syrian refugees would be given safe haven in Canada.

Liberal campaign advertising focused largely on Trudeau, positioning him as the country's first Gen-X leader—an environmentally and socially conscious consensus-builder who could connect on a personal level with Canadians. Trudeau's natural charm and affability took material form in the thousands of selfies for which he happily posed. "There's a puppy-like quality to him and that's not Pierre," observed Robert Bothwell, a Canadian historian who had been around for Trudeaumania in 1968. "His father was just not at ease with dealing with crowds or pressing the flesh, but looking at Justin, it comes really natural to him and that's a big difference. Pierre had magnetism and was fascinating and beautiful to watch, but he didn't want them to get close."[18] The Conservatives tried to paint Justin as immature and inexperienced, using the tag line "He's Just Not Ready." It proved to be a strategic blunder, allowing Trudeau to adopt the time-honoured strategy of being underestimated. In the home stretch of the campaign, polls showed that Conservative attack ads had actually increased voter sympathy for him.

In marked contrast to Pierre Trudeau's massive lead throughout the 1968 campaign, the distinguishing feature of the 2015 contest was the virtual dead heat among the three major parties. Until Justin's dark-horse sprint in the final weeks of the campaign, none of the party leaders were able to punch through the pollsters' margin of error. Five public debates—two in French, one devoted entirely to foreign affairs, all of them posted online—meant abundant opportunities for Canadians to acquaint themselves with the leaders and their ideas. The long campaign also allowed voters to observe the candidates reacting to current events in real time—the Syrian refugee crisis, most notably, and the apparent slide of the Canadian economy into recession. Trudeau (and NDP leader Tom Mulcair) took every opportunity to stake out vastly divergent positions on such hot-button issues as the Conservatives' Bill C-24, the *Strengthening Canadian Citizenship Act*, which allowed dual nationals to be stripped of citizenship if they were convicted of treason or terrorism. In one of the campaign's oddest twists, the wearing of niqabs during citizenship ceremonies became a national preoccupation. Although the courts had struck down his niqab legislation, Prime Minister Stephen Harper defended it with the blithe serenity of an old-school majoritarian. "I think the legislation is broadly reflective of the large, large majority of Canadians," he said. This issue was one of many gifts to Trudeau, whose politics is multicultural, inclusive, and keenly attentive to minority rights.

There were very few explicit references in the 2015 election campaign to Pierre Trudeau—evidence of Justin's determination to chart his own course. But when Justin invoked his father's memory during the September 28 Munk Debate on Canadian foreign policy, the effect was powerful. Reacting to a barb from Tom Mulcair, Justin looked straight into the camera and reminded Canadians that it was the fifteenth anniversary of his father's death. "Let me say very clearly, I am incredibly proud to be Pierre Elliott Trudeau's son," Justin affirmed. "I know he wouldn't want us to be fighting the battles of the past. He'd want us squarely focused on the future and how we're going to respond to Canadians' needs, and that's what we're doing tonight."[19]

By the end of the campaign, Justin Trudeau had emerged as his own man, very different indeed from his father but also very different from his recent Liberal predecessors. Canadians rewarded him and his party with their first majority government in fifteen years. The Liberals won 184 seats in the newly expanded Parliament of 338, with 39.5 per cent of the popular vote. Stephen Harper's Conservatives won 99 seats, with 31.9 per cent of the popular vote, becoming the Official Opposition. Tom Mulcair's NDP won 44 seats, with 19.7 per cent of the popular vote.

In 1968, the mass adulation that was Trudeaumania peaked for the first time during the Liberal leadership race and again towards the end of the election campaign. Pierre Trudeau's popularity among decided voters never fell below 45 per cent, which meant that, barring something utterly unforeseen, his triumph was practically a *fait accompli.* Even his opponents sensed this.

Not so Justin Trudeau in 2015, for whom victory was far from certain. There was no evidence of Trudeaumania when, early in the campaign, the Liberal leader was gamely pressing the flesh among indifferent shoppers in the suburban big-box stores of southern Ontario. Whenever the term *Trudeaumania* appeared in the media, it was tentative and self-referential, a nod to his father's 1968 sweep rather than an affirmation that the phenomenon would, or could, be repeated.

Even on election night, Canadians were hard-pressed to make sense of what, exactly, had happened. *Vancouver Sun* columnist Shelley Fralic captured the mood brilliantly the next morning. "Pierre Elliott Trudeau had the royal jelly," she wrote.

> His boy Justin does not. Instead, Justin's new-age version of Trudeaumania, and surely that is the red tide that swept across our country Monday night, is something quite different, quite unlike the heady alchemic mix of confidence, arrogance and *joie de vivre* that so defined his father's reign. Because while

> dad was a maverick who traded on intellect and controversy, the son is a reined-in populist who represents hope and change, a difference never more clear than the sudden realization, upon waking up Tuesday morning, that Canada has suddenly emerged from a prolonged fog, a shroud of staleness erased by a brisk wind and a fresh coat of paint.[20]

Trudeaumania 2.0 crashed in upon Canadians over the next few days as national media scrambled to provide new narratives for the Liberal victory. Even more important, it took scant hours for international media and wired citizens everywhere to render "viral" their discovery that Canada's new prime minister was a warm and sexy Gen-Xer. "Canada's new Prime Minister is a Smoking-Hot Syrupy Fox," said one of "a zillion" Twitter feeds.[21] Trudeau himself lost no time stoking this international media frenzy. The morning after his electoral triumph, he was filmed greeting commuters in a Montreal Metro station and posing for the "Justin and me" selfies that had become the symbol of his populist appeal. It was the most un-Stephen-Harper way the new prime minister could have ushered in his majority mandate, proof that a new political day had dawned in Canada. One week after this election victory, Trudeau's national approval rating rose to an astounding 60 per cent.

As in 1968, analogies were made to JFK, and not merely because the new Canadian prime minister and his picture-perfect family were the stuff of Canadian royalty. Even before he was sworn in, Trudeau made it clear that he would move immediately on the key planks of the Liberal platform (tax cuts and the admission of Syrian refugees), giving his government a "one hundred days" urgency reminiscent of Kennedy's 1960 inaugural. Ordinary Canadians were invited to Rideau Hall on November 4, 2015, and 3,500 of them showed up—transforming a stodgy parliamentary ritual into one of the most memorable swearing-in ceremonies in Canadian history. When

Trudeau unveiled his diverse-by-design cabinet, he told Canadians that it was an "incredible pleasure to present a cabinet that looks like Canada." Asked why he had named an equal number of men and women to cabinet, he replied with a terse one-liner that would have made his late father smile: "Because it's 2015."[22]

New York Times columnist Roger Cohen gave voice to many Canadians'—and Americans'—quiet pleasure at witnessing the Trudeau succession. "Camelot has come to Canada," he wrote. "For a moment at least, the duller part of North America looks sexier than its overweening cousin to the south. The incoming prime minister is very much his father's son, a natural charmer. There's no point denying it. The American political field looks wizened by comparison. The political tide has turned in Canada."[23]

The day he was sworn in, November 4, 2015, Prime Minister Justin Trudeau took his two eldest children, Xavier and Ella-Grace, to the Centre Block of the Canadian Parliament Buildings, which then stood empty and silent. At one point, they walked along the south corridor of the Commons foyer, which is lined with the official portraits of Canadian prime ministers. Stopping at the portrait of Pierre Elliott Trudeau, Justin asked, "Who is that?"

"Grandpapa," said Ella-Grace with a smile.[24]

NOTES

ABBREVIATIONS USED IN NOTES

AP—Associated Press
CAR—Canadian Annual Review
CBC—Canadian Broadcasting Corporation
CBCDA—CBC Digital Archives
CH—*Calgary Herald*
CP—Canadian Press
CWM—CanWest Media
CL—*Cité libre*
GM—*Globe and Mail*
HCH—*Halifax Chronicle Herald*
JM—*Le Journal de Montréal*
LA—*L'Action*
LAC—*Library and Archives Canada*
LD—*Le Devoir*
LDR—*Le Droit*
LP—*La Presse*
LS—*Le Soleil*
M—*Maclean's*
MG—*Montreal Gazette*
NP—*National Post*
NYT—*New York Times*
OC—*Ottawa Citizen*
SDR—*Sherbrooke Daily Record*
TS—*Toronto Star*
VS—*Vancouver Sun*
WT—*Winnipeg Tribune*

PROLOGUE: TRUDEAU TO THE GALLOWS!

1. Pierre Trudeau, cited in "Trudeau Flirted with Socialism," *TS* (April 8, 1968), 10.
2. Cited in Andrew Salwyn, "We'll Kill Trudeau Monday," *TS* (June 24, 1968), 9.
3. See Jean-Claude Leclerc, "Au congrès des sociétés Saint-Jean-Baptiste: Une attaque contre le fédéralisme de Trudeau," *LD* (June 6, 1968), 2.
4. Pierre Bourgault, cited in Ronald Lebel, "PM Asked to Review SJB Parade," *GM* (May 31, 1968), 8; and "Trudeau assistera au défilé de la St-Jean," *LD* (June 19, 1968), 2.
5. Ramsay Cook, *The Teeth of Time: Remembering Pierre Elliott Trudeau* (Montreal: McGill-Queen's University Press, 2006), 76.

6. Pierre Trudeau, cited in Frank Jones, "Trudeau Defies Separatists," *TS* (June 25, 1968), 1, 4.
7. Cook, *The Teeth of Time*, 76.
8. Graham Fraser, *René Lévesque and the Parti Québécois in Power* (Montreal: McGill-Queen's University Press, 1984), 44–45.
9. Pierre Trudeau, cited in Peter C. Newman, "Separatism? It's Dying Says Quebec Thinker," *TS* (January 30, 1965), 7.
10. Pierre Elliott Trudeau, *Federalism and the French Canadians* (Toronto: Macmillan, 1968), 204–12.
11. Fraser, *René Lévesque and the Parti Québécois in Power*, 38.
12. Pierre Bourgault, cited in Robert McKenzie, "Quebec's 'International Role' Theme of St. Jean Baptiste Day," *TS* (June 26, 1967), 3.
13. "Lévesque Suspends Negotiations with Bourgault Separatists," *CH* (June 28, 1968), 7.
14. "The FLQ Manifesto," in *Quebec States Her Case*, ed. Frank Scott and Michael Oliver (Toronto: Macmillan, 1964), 83–87.
15. Gérard Pelletier, "Stage Two on the Road to Disaster," in Scott and Oliver, *Quebec States Her Case*, 88–90.
16. David A. Charters, "The (Un)Peaceable Kingdom? Terrorism and Canada before 9/11," *IRPP Policy Matters* 9, 4 (October 2008): 16.
17. René Lévesque, "For an Independent Quebec," in *Quebec since 1945*, ed. Michael D. Behiels (Toronto: Copp Clark Pitman, 1987), 272.
18. See John Saywell, ed., *CAR 1964* (Toronto: University of Toronto Press, 1965), 45.
19. Louis Fournier, *FLQ: The Anatomy of an Underground Movement* (Toronto: NC Press, 1984), 28.
20. Pierre Trudeau, cited in Peter C. Newman, "Trudeau: I Have a Feeling for Canada," *TS* (April 29, 1968), 1, 4.
21. Pierre Bourgault, cited in "Rhinoceros Party Is All-Out for Trudeau," *TS* (March 13, 1968), 3.
22. Pierre Bourgault, cited in "Separatists Want Trudeau as Next PM," *GM* (February 19, 1968), 1.
23. Pierre Bourgault, cited in Andrew Salwyn, "Police in Montreal Fear Anti-PM Riot," *TS* (June 21, 1968), 58; Ronald Lebel, "Separatists Assail PM," *GM* (June 22, 1968), 10; and editorial, "Separatist Hatred Would Push Quebec into Past," *GM* (June 22, 1968), 6.

24. Claude Ryan, cited in Robert Miller, "The Flying Bottle, the Ugly Infamy, Horrified Drapeau," *TS* (June 25, 1968), 1, 4. See also Claude Ryan, "Les événements de lundi soir," *LD* (June 26, 1968), 4; and Stan McDowell, "Editor Criticizes Trudeau for Braving Parade Threat," *VS* (June 26, 1968), 22A.
25. Marcel Faribault, cited in "Trudeau, Faribault Meet at Party," CP (June 25, 1968); and "PM Provoked Trouble—Faribault," *OC* (June 25, 1968), 4A.
26. Pierre Trudeau, cited in "Trudeau, Faribault Meet at Party."
27. Editorial, "Hate's Bitter Contagion," *GM* (June 25, 1968), 6. See also Vincent Prince, "M. Bourgault et son appel à la violence," *LD* (June 25, 1968), 4; and editorial, "Separatist Riots," *CH* (June 26, 1968), 6.
28. Jean-Paul Gilbert, cited in Andrew Salwyn, "Police Ask: Who Trained the Terrorists?" *TS* (June 25, 1968), 1.
29. Jones, "Trudeau Defies Separatists," 1, 4; Ian MacDonald, "Pierre Confronts Rioters," *VS* (June 25, 1968), 7; "Trudeau tient tête aux manifestants," *LD* (June 25, 1968), 1; and "Réactions diverses à la soirée de violence," *LD* (June 26, 1968), 3.
30. Pierre Trudeau, cited in Jones, "Trudeau Defies Separatists," 1, 4.
31. Ibid.
32. John Saywell, ed., *CAR 1968* (Toronto: University of Toronto Press, 1969), 50–52.
33. Gerd-Rainer Horn, *The Spirit of '68: Rebellion in Western Europe and North America, 1956–1976* (Oxford: Oxford University Press, 2007), 1. See also Carole Fink, Philipp Gassert, and Detlef Junker, *1968: The World Transformed* (Washington, D.C.: German Historical Institute, 1998), introduction.
34. See, for example, Bob Plamondon, *The Truth about Trudeau* (Ottawa: Great River Media, 2013), ch. 9.
35. See, for example, James Laxer and Robert Laxer, *The Liberal Idea of Canada: Pierre Trudeau and the Question of Canada's Survival* (Toronto: Lorimer, 1977).
36. Guy Laforest, *Trudeau et la fin d'un rêve canadien* (Montréal: Septentrion, 1992).
37. For example, Kenneth McRoberts wrote: "Needless to say, such an intense rejection of nationalism and of ethnically or culturally defined collectivities came naturally to someone who himself did not feel a clear membership in any such collectivity. Clearly, the vision of Canada that Trudeau had so carefully and eloquently constructed differed radically from the way in which most Canadians saw their country. This was true even of French Canadians. Despite some superficial similarities, the Trudeau vision was in fact quite removed from mainstream French-Canadian thought. But most English Canadians did not know that." See

McRoberts, *Misconceiving Canada: The Struggle for National Unity* (Toronto: Oxford University Press, 1997), 59–64. See also Michel Vastel, *The Outsider: The Life of Pierre Elliott Trudeau* (Toronto: Macmillan, 1992).

38. See Richard Gwyn, *The Northern Magus: Pierre Trudeau and Canadians* (Toronto: PaperJacks, 1981), 295; and Richard Gwyn, "Trudeau: The Idea of Canadianism," in *Trudeau's Shadow: The Life and Legacy of Pierre Elliott Trudeau*, eds. Andrew Cohen and J.L. Granatstein (Toronto: Vintage Canada, 1998), 26.
39. Larry Zolf, *Dance of the Dialectic* (Toronto: James, Lewis & Samuel, 1973), 25.
40. Pierre Berton, *1967: The Last Good Year* (Toronto: Doubleday, 1997), 108.
41. Bryan D. Palmer, *Canada's 1960s: The Ironies of Identity in a Rebellious Era* (Toronto: University of Toronto Press, 2009), 169.
42. Peter C. Newman, *Here Be Dragons: Telling Tales of People, Passion and Power* (Toronto: McClelland & Stewart, 2004), 322.
43. Peter C. Newman, *The Distemper of Our Times* (Toronto: McClelland & Stewart, 1968), 435.
44. Peter C. Newman, *A Nation Divided: Canada and the Coming of Pierre Trudeau* (New York: Knopf, 1969), xiii.
45. Lester B. Pearson, *Mike: The Memoirs of the Right Honourable Lester B. Pearson*, vol. 3, *1957–1968*, ed. John A. Munro and Alex I. Inglis (Toronto: University of Toronto Press, 1975), 304.
46. W.A.C. Bennett, cited in "Bennett Calls Trudeau a 'Playboy,'" CP (March 20, 1968).
47. Michael Oliver, "Introduction," in Scott and Oliver, *Quebec States Her Case*, 5.
48. Maxwell Cohen, "The Five Steps to a United Canada," *GM* (October 3, 1967), 7.
49. Walter Stewart, *Shrug: Trudeau in Power* (Toronto: New Press, 1971), 12.
50. Christina McCall and Stephen Clarkson, *Trudeau and Our Times*, vol. 1, *The Magnificent Obsession* (Toronto: McClelland & Stewart, 1990), 113.
51. Pierre Trudeau, cited in "Trudeau Doesn't Want Parliament Televised," *TS* (March 21, 1968), 40.
52. Frank Jones, "How Does Trudeau Rate in the Commons?" *TS* (April 20, 1968), 8.
53. Larry Zolf, "Humble Arrogance: A Cautionary Tale of Trudeau and the Media,"in Cohen and Granatstein, *Trudeau's Shadow*, 39.
54. Turner had his own problems, according to one unnamed supporter: "His problem is he's too good-looking. People see him and they think there must be something phony. If he were just a little uglier, he'd be a lot better off." Cited in Jack

Cahill, *John Turner: The Long Run* (Toronto: McClelland & Stewart, 1984), 121.

55. Christina McCall-Newman, *Grits: An Intimate Portrait of the Liberal Party* (Toronto: Macmillan, 1982), 60–61.
56. Ibid., 120.
57. Pierre Trudeau wrote, "I never claimed to speak 'on behalf' of anyone. If the [Liberal] Party does not agree with my opinions, it can repudiate me; if my constituents do not, they can elect someone else." See Trudeau, *Federalism and the French Canadians*, xxvi.
58. Gérard Pelletier, "Preface to the French Edition," in Trudeau, *Federalism and the French Canadians*, xvi. See also Pelletier, "Trudeau Travelled the World with a Knapsack on His Back," *TS* (January 6, 1968), 8.
59. John Porter, cited in Frank Jones, "Trudeau Would be Legalistic Quibbler Sociologist Warns," *TS* (June 13, 1968), 8.
60. Trudeau, *Federalism and the French Canadians*, 53.

CHAPTER ONE: THE STUBBORN ECCENTRIC

1. In his 1986 memoir, René Lévesque identified himself as one of four "musketeers" contemplating entering provincial politics in 1960 as a Lesage Liberal. The others were Marchand, Pelletier, and Trudeau. See Lévesque, *Memoirs*, trans. Philip Stratford (Toronto: McClelland & Stewart, 1986), 150.
2. See Max Nemni and Monique Nemni, *Young Trudeau: Son of Quebec, Father of Canada, 1919–1944*, trans. William Johnson (Toronto: McClelland & Stewart, 2006); and Max Nemni and Monique Nemni, *Trudeau Transformed: The Shaping of a Statesman*, trans. George Tombs (Toronto: McClelland & Stewart, 2011).
3. Pierre Trudeau, cited in Nemni and Nemni, *Young Trudeau*, 51.
4. Pierre Trudeau, cited ibid., 95.
5. Pierre Elliott Trudeau, *Memoirs* (Toronto: McClelland & Stewart, 1993), 38, 61.
6. See Michael Gauvreau, *Catholic Origins of Quebec's Quiet Revolution, 1931–1970* (Montreal: McGill-Queen's University Press, 2005), 117–19.
7. Pierre Elliott Trudeau, *Federalism and the French Canadians* (Toronto: Macmillan, 1968), xxiii.
8. Trudeau, *Memoirs*, 40.
9. See Benedict Anderson, *Imagined Communities: Reflections on the Origin and Spread of Nationalism* (London: Verso, 1983). See also George Orwell, *Notes on Nationalism* (London: Secker and Warburg, 1953; first published in 1945).

10. Pierre Elliott Trudeau, "The Conflicts of Nationalisms in Canada," in *Quebec States Her Case*, ed. Frank Scott and Michael Oliver (Toronto: Macmillan, 1964), 63. Ramsay Cook noted that "Trudeau knew that the distinction often drawn by nationalists between 'good' nationalism (mine) and 'bad' nationalism (yours) did not stand up to serious analysis." See Cook, *The Teeth of Time: Remembering Pierre Elliott Trudeau* (Montreal: McGill-Queen's University Press, 2006), 32–33.
11. Michel Brunet, "The French Canadians' Search for a Fatherland," in *Nationalism in Canada*, ed. Peter Russell (Toronto: McGraw-Hill, 1966), 56.
12. Ibid., 60.
13. Pierre Trudeau, cited in Jocelyn Maclure, *Quebec Identity: The Challenge of Pluralism* (Montreal: McGill-Queen's University Press 2003), 91. See also Michel Brunet, *L'Historien Michel Brunet Juge Pierre Elliott Trudeau* (Montréal: Guérin, 2000), ch. 1.
14. Trudeau, *Memoirs*, 48.
15. Ibid., 52.
16. Ibid., 53.
17. See Robert Wright, *Three Nights in Havana: Pierre Trudeau, Fidel Castro and the Cold War World* (Toronto: HarperCollins, 2007).
18. Trudeau once called Joe Clark "head waiter to the provinces," for example, and Brian Mulroney "our Great Oarsman." See Thomas S. Axworthy and Pierre Elliott Trudeau, *Towards a Just Society: The Trudeau Years* (Toronto: Penguin Canada, 1992), 429.
19. Trudeau, *Memoirs*, 62–63.
20. Pierre Elliott Trudeau, "The Asbestos Strike," in *Against the Current: Selected Writings 1939–1996* (Toronto: McClelland & Stewart, 1996), 43. See also Pierre Elliott Trudeau, *La grève de l'amiante* (Montréal: Éditions Cité libre, 1956); Trudeau, *Memoirs*, 62–63; Christo Aivalis, "In the Name of Liberalism: Pierre Trudeau, Organized Labour, and the Canadian Social Democratic Left, 1949–1959," *Canadian Historical Review* 94, 2 (June 2013): 263–88; and Kristy A. Holmes, "Negotiating Citizenship: Joyce Wieland's *Reason over Passion*," in *The Sixties: Passion, Politics, and Style*, ed. Dimitry Anastakis (Montreal: McGill-Queen's University Press, 2008), 45.
21. John English, "War and the Canadian Liberal Conscience," in *Australia, Canada and Iraq: Perspectives on an Invasion*, ed. Ramesh Thakur and Jack Cunningham (Toronto: Dundurn, 2015), 115.
22. Trudeau, *Memoirs*, 65.

23. Gérard Pelletier, cited in Michael D. Behiels, *Prelude to Quebec's Quiet Revolution: Liberalism versus Neo-Nationalism, 1945–1960* (Montreal: McGill-Queen's University Press, 1985), 64.
24. Pierre Trudeau, "Politique fonctionnelle I," *CL* 1 (June 1950): 21.
25. Gretta Chambers, "The Sixties in Print: Remembering Quebec's Quiet Revolution," in Anastakis, *The Sixties*, 19.
26. Trudeau, *Memoirs*, 71–75.
27. Frank Howard, "Will Ottawa Lure Back Quebec Talent?" *GM* (September 25, 1965), A2.
28. See Kenneth McRoberts, *Quebec: Social Change and Political Crisis*, 3rd ed. (Toronto: Oxford University Press, 1993), ch. 5.
29. Trudeau, *Memoirs*, 71–75.
30. Marcel Chaput, *Pourquoi je suis séparatiste* (Montréal: Les Éditions du Jour, 1961).
31. Trudeau, "The Conflicts of Nationalisms in Canada," 57. This article was excerpted from Trudeau's 1962 article "The New Treason of the Intellectuals."
32. Pierre Trudeau, cited in Ramsay Cook, *Watching Quebec: Selected Essays* (Montreal: McGill-Queen's University Press, 2005), 50.
33. Trudeau, "The Conflicts of Nationalisms in Canada," 66–68.
34. Trudeau, *Federalism and the French Canadians*, xi.
35. Trudeau, "The Conflicts of Nationalisms in Canada," 68–69.
36. This conviction helps to explain the apparent paradox, one among many, that Trudeau was an outspoken critic of federal meddling in Quebec education policy in the 1950s, a position that put him on Premier Duplessis's side of the issue. See Trudeau, "Federal Grants to Universities," in *Federalism and the French Canadians*, 79.
37. Trudeau, *Federalism and the French Canadians*, xix.
38. Trudeau, *Memoirs*, 71–75.
39. See John English, *Citizen of the World: The Life of Pierre Elliott Trudeau*, vol. 1, *1919–1968* (Toronto: Vintage Canada, 2006), 222; Nemni and Nemni, *Trudeau Transformed*, 318; and Christina McCall-Newman, *Grits: An Intimate Portrait of the Liberal Party* (Toronto: Macmillan, 1982), 92–93. Trudeau's "La nouvelle trahison des clercs" was itself a play on Julien Benda's influential *La trahison des clercs*, originally published in 1927. See Benda, *The Treason of the Intellectuals*, trans. Richard Aldington (New Brunswick: Transaction, 2009).
40. Chaput, *Pourquoi je suis séparatiste*, 1.

41. Trudeau, *Federalism and the French Canadians*, 153–54.
42. Ibid., 166.
43. Ibid., 167–68.
44. "7 Quebec Moderates Offer Anti-Separatism Blueprint," *TS* (May 15, 1964), 7; and Thomas Sloan, "Anti-Nationalists Counterattack," *GM* (June 6, 1964), SM4.
45. Cited in "7 Quebec Moderates," 7.
46. "René Lévesque Speaks of Quebec, National State of the French Canadians," in Scott and Oliver, *Quebec States Her Case*, 132–45.
47. Daniel Johnson, cited in Kenneth McRoberts, *Misconceiving Canada: The Struggle for National Unity* (Toronto: Oxford University Press, 1997), 34–35. See also Donald Smiley, "Federalism, Nationalism and the Scope of Public Activity in Canada," in Russell, *Nationalism in Canada*, 104–5.
48. Pierre Trudeau, cited in Frank Howard, "Special Status or Separatism?" *GM* (December 18, 1965), 8.
49. Trudeau, *Federalism and the French Canadians*, 3–43.
50. Norman DePoe, interview with Pierre Trudeau, CBC-TV (Available online as "The Many Lives of Pierre Elliott Trudeau," CBCDA, http:www.cbc.ca / player / play / 1797435890.
51. Trudeau, *Memoirs*, 69.
52. Gérard Pelletier, "Trudeau Travelled the World with a Knapsack on His Back," *TS* (January 6, 1968), 8.
53. Pierre Trudeau, cited in Robert McKenzie, "Quebec Students Tell Trudeau He's 'Isolated,'" *TS* (March 27, 1968), 8.
54. See Howard, "Special Status or Separatism?" 8.
55. René Lévesque said in 1963: "I am a Quebecer first, a French Canadian second . . . and I really have . . . well, no sense at all of being a Canadian." Cited in Ramsay Cook, *Canada, Quebec and the Uses of Nationalism*, 2nd ed. (Toronto: McClelland & Stewart, 1995), 140.
56. Pierre Trudeau, cited in Peter C. Newman, "Canada at the Crossroads," *TS* (February 2, 1968), 1, 4. Charles Taylor wrote of Trudeau as the guarantor of the status quo: "The Trudeau image offered all the excitement of change, the 'spirit of Expo' and all that, while offering the reassurance—which the average man could read in the benign reactions of power and privilege—that no serious challenge would be offered to the way things are." See Taylor, *Reconciling the Solitudes: Essays on Canadian Federalism and Nationalism* (Montreal: McGill-Queen's University Press, 1993), 30.

57. Pierre Trudeau, cited in Peter C. Newman, "Trudeau Tells the Star: This Particular Parliament Has Worn Itself Out," *TS* (April 27, 1968), 1; and Peter C. Newman, "Trudeau: I Have a Feeling for Canada," *TS* (April 29, 1968), 1, 4.

CHAPTER TWO: THE THREE MUSKETEERS

1. Mason Wade, ed., *Canadian Dualism: Studies of French-English Relations* (Toronto: University of Toronto Press, 1960). The article is also reprinted in *Against the Current: Selected Writings 1939–1996* (Toronto: McClelland & Stewart, 1996), 79–101.
2. Robert Fulford, "Manifesto for Separatists," *TS* (January 24, 1962), 35.
3. Robert Fulford, "'Seven Days': If You Can't Lick 'Em, Go Low-Brow," *TS* (December 12, 1964), 21, 28. Reviews of other edited collections adopted the same tone. *Globe and Mail* reviewer Ronald Bates identified "Pierre-Elliott Trudeau" as fighting the good fight against "leftist separatists," for example, in his review of Frank Scott and Michael Oliver, eds., *Quebec States Her Case* (Toronto: Macmillan, 1964). See Bates, "An Education for the Xenophobes," *GM* (November 28, 1964), A15.
4. "Four-Part Series Evaluates Confederation," *GM* (January 4, 1963), T1.
5. "Alcock Will Head Peace Institute," *GM* (March 31, 1962), 5; and Harold Morrison, "Norman Alcock's Peace Dream Is Dying for Lack of Money," *TS* (January 26, 1966), 7.
6. See "A Matter of Basic Justice," *GM* (June 11, 1963), 6; and "After Coroner's Act, Quebec Group Urges," *GM* (June 28, 1963), 2.
7. Editorial, "The Problem: Stifle Hate While Preserving Freedom," *GM* (January 12, 1965), 6.
8. See Robert Wright, "From Liberalism to Nationalism: Peter C. Newman's Discovery of Canada," in *Creating Postwar Canada: Community, Diversity, and Dissent, 1945–1975*, ed. Robert Rutherdale and Magda Fahrni (Vancouver: UBC Press, 2007), 111–36.
9. Peter C. Newman, "Separatism? It's Dying Says Quebec Thinker," *TS* (January 30, 1965), 7.
10. Pierre Trudeau, cited in George Radwanski, *Trudeau* (Toronto: Macmillan, 1978), 89.
11. See George Grant, *Lament for a Nation: The Defeat of Canadian Nationalism* (Toronto: McClelland & Stewart, 1965).

12. Trudeau was never a card-carrying member of the NDP. A scribbled memo in the Trudeau papers circa 1965 reads, "If I ever had been in the NDP-CCF I would have left it in 1961 founding convention [*sic*] when it adopted the 2 nation theory. What is the use in belonging to an ideological party if it is going to be opportunist?" See LAC Trudeau Fonds (MG26-020, Volume 28, File 1).
13. Lester B. Pearson, *Mike: The Memoirs of the Right Honourable Lester B. Pearson*, vol. 3, *1957–1968*, ed. John A. Munro and Alex I. Inglis (Toronto: University of Toronto Press, 1975), 217.
14. Trudeau, "Some Obstacles to Democracy in Quebec," *Against the Current*, 97–98.
15. Pierre Trudeau wrote, "Pelletier and I had on numerous occasions written scathing criticisms of the Liberals. I seem to recall one of my articles using the word 'donkeys:' not in a complimentary way." See Trudeau, *Memoirs* (Toronto: McClelland & Stewart, 1993), 76–77.
16. See "Cowan Out to Block Trudeau as Leader," *TS* (February 15, 1968), 1; and Geoffrey Stevens, "Smear Tactics Against Trudeau Start in Ottawa," *GM* (February 15, 1968), 1.
17. Pierre Trudeau to Ramsay Cook, cited in Cook, *The Teeth of Time: Remembering Pierre Elliott Trudeau* (Montreal: McGill-Queen's University Press, 2006), 29.
18. Marc Lalonde, cited in Radwanski, *Trudeau*, 88.
19. Pearson, *Mike*, 219.
20. Jean Marchand, cited in Langevin Coté, "Political Party End, Not Means, New Look Quebec Liberals Say," *GM* (October 25, 1965), 8.
21. Pearson, *Mike*, 218. René Lévesque's recollection was that it was Trudeau and not Pelletier whose entry into the ranks of the federal Liberals made things difficult for Pearson. Lévesque was with Maurice Sauvé when Marchand called. "I've just come from seeing Pearson," Marchand told Sauvé, "and things aren't going too well. As for myself, there's no problem, they're dying to get me. They're ready to take Pelletier, too. But as far as Trudeau is concerned, it's no soap. In their eyes he's nothing but a little drawing-room socialist who had the nerve not so long ago to call them a bunch of idiots." See Lévesque, *Memoirs*, trans. Philip Stratford (Toronto: McClelland & Stewart, 1986), 194.
22. See Andrew Webster, "Marchand, Pelletier, Trudeau Plan to Run," *GM* (September 11, 1965), 4.
23. Pierre Trudeau, cited in Peter C. Newman, "PM Stabbed in the Back from Quebec

He Tried to Reconcile," *TS* (November 25, 1964), 1; and Robert Rice, "Trudeau Battles Three at Mount Royal Meeting Tonight," *GM* (October 7, 1965), 9.

24. Andrew Cohen, *Lester B. Pearson* (Toronto: Penguin, 2008), 70.
25. Lester Pearson, cited in Kenneth McRoberts, *Misconceiving Canada: The Struggle for National Unity* (Toronto: Oxford University Press, 1997), 39–43.
26. André Laurendeau and Arnold Davidson Dunton, *A Preliminary Report of the Royal Commission on Bilingualism and Biculturalism* (Ottawa: Royal Commission on Bilingualism and Biculturalism, 1965), 13.
27. See Matthew Hayday, *Bilingual Today, United Tomorrow: Official Languages in Education and Canadian Federalism* (Montreal: McGill-Queen's University Press, 2005), ch. 2; and Lucie Lecomte, *Official Languages or National Languages? Canada's Decision* (Ottawa: Parliamentary Information and Research Service, 2015), ch. 1.
28. Pearson, *Mike*, 241.
29. Bora Laskin, cited in Philip Girard, *Bora Laskin: Bringing Law to Life* (Toronto: University of Toronto Press, 2005), 214. See also Bora Laskin, "Amendment of the Constitution: Applying the Fulton-Favreau Formula," *McGill Law Journal* 11, 1 (1965): 2–18.
30. Pearson, *Mike*, 245.
31. See Donald Smiley, "Federalism, Nationalism and the Scope of Public Activity in Canada," in *Nationalism in Canada*, ed. Peter Russell (Toronto: McGraw-Hill, 1966), 106.
32. See McRoberts, *Misconceiving Canada*, 39–43.
33. Historian John English uses this term to describe Pearson's approach to Quebec, likening it to his approach to Nazi Germany in the 1930s. See English, *The Life of Lester Pearson*, vol. 2, *The Worldly Years* (Toronto: Vintage, 1992), 181–82.
34. Smiley, "Federalism, Nationalism and the Scope of Public Activity," 107–8. Peter C. Newman would later write perceptively that bringing Trudeau, Pelletier, and Marchand into the federal Liberal Party "flies directly in the face of Prime Minister Lester Pearson's policy of non-confrontation. By dealing on all important issues directly with Jean Lesage instead of through the Quebec ministers in his own Cabinet, Pearson has sacrificed much of the remaining respect for Ottawa among thinking French-Canadians." See "Quebec's 'Three Musketeers' Carry the Gospel to Ottawa," *TS* (September 14, 1965), 7.
35. Pierre Elliott Trudeau, "Concepts of Federalism" (June 11, 1964), LAC Trudeau Fonds (MG26-020, Volume 28, File 1), 1–30.

36. Ibid.
37. Cook, *The Teeth of Time*, 30.
38. Lester B. Pearson, cited in "Text of Prime Minister's Speech," *GM* (September 8, 1965), 8. See also editorial, "An Unnecessary Election," *OC* (September 8, 1965), 6; and Don McGillivray, "Election Battle Lines Drawn," *OC* (September 8, 1965), 7.
39. Jean Marchand, cited in "Liberals Press 3," *VS* (September 10, 1965), 10.
40. See Struan Matheson, "Three 'New' Liberals Win Seats," *MG* (November 9, 1965), 3.
41. Dominique Clift, "Splash! It's Quebec's 'New Wave,'" *TS* (September 11, 1965), 18. See also Frank Howard, "Election Word Expected from Unionist today," *GM* (September 10, 1965), 4; and Robert McKenzie, "Liberals Launch Quebec 'New Look,'" *TS* (September 11, 1965), 1, 18.
42. Pierre Trudeau, cited in Webster, "Marchand, Pelletier, Trudeau Plan to Run," 4.
43. Dominique Clift, "Marchand May Face Opposition, County Liberals Lure Candidate," *TS* (September 25, 1965), 4.
44. Editorial, "Power for Power's Sake," *GM* (November 2, 1965), 6.
45. See Frank Howard, "Three Quebec Moderates Begin an Election Odyssey," *GM* (September 14, 1965), 7.
46. Cited in editorial, "Trading Pulpits for Power," *GM* (September 16, 1965), 6.
47. "Quebeckers to be Gobbled Up—Cliche," *TS* (September 17, 1965), 32.
48. John Diefenbaker, cited in "Quebec Trio Called Three Wise Men," *GM* (September 29, 1965), 42.
49. Jacques Bouchard, cited in "Quebec Farmers Will Back PCs, Party Chief Says after Parley," *GM* (September 20, 1963), 8.
50. Cited in Langevin Coté, "Political Party End, Not Means, New Look Quebec Liberals Say," *GM* (October 25, 1965), 8.
51. "Separatism Could Be Fatal," CP (September 9, 1965).
52. Keith Cronshaw, "Trudeau Tops Taylor in Mt. Royal," *MG* (November 9, 1965), 3.
53. Editorial, "A New Guard from Quebec?" *GM* (September 14, 1965), 6. See also editorial, "A Gain for the Country" *OC* (September 13, 1965), 6.
54. Editorial, "A New Guard?" 6.
55. Editorial, "Quebec's 'New Wave' Good News for Canada," *TS* (September 13, 1965), 6.
56. Peter C. Newman, "Quebec's 'Three Musketeers' Carry the Gospel to Ottawa," *TS* (September 14, 1965), 7.

57. Howard, "Three Quebec Moderates," 7.
58. Editorial, "The Voice of Moderation Has an Inflamed Throat," *GM* (January 31, 1966), 6.
59. Pierre Trudeau, cited in Robert Rice, "Mount Royal Riding Chosen by Trudeau, Only Pelletier Left," *GM* (September 27, 1965), 8.
60. Taylor was two years younger than Trudeau but the product of a similar bilingual upbringing and Ivy League education. Never did Trudeau and Taylor see eye to eye on Quebec. "We disagreed at the beginning and we disagreed at the end on a very fundamental issue that I still think he was terribly wrong about—that you can treat Quebec exactly like any other province," Taylor recalled in 2007. "I think he had a very different reading of Quebec nationalism. He overreacted against it." Cited in "Canadian Philosopher Taylor Wins $1.5M Religion Prize," CWM (March 14, 2007).
61. Rice, "Trudeau Battles Three," 9.
62. Ibid., 9; and Jean Marchand, cited in Dominique Clift, "Diefenbaker Out to Crush Quebec Says Firebrand Marchand," *TS* (September 28, 1965), 1, 2.
63. Pierre Trudeau, cited in Robert Rice, "Mount Royal Liberals Nominate Trudeau," *GM* (October 8, 1965), 8.
64. Pierre Trudeau, "Open Letter to the Delegates to the Mount Royal Nominating Committee" (October 1965), LAC Trudeau Fonds (MG26-020, Volume 28, File 1), 1. Writing in the local *Town of Mount Royal Weekly Post* on October 28, 1965, Trudeau would appeal to constituents to return a majority government: "There are challenges that must be met squarely and realistically, for the time has come to claim our heritage. . . . To build a great Canada, there is no better base than constitutionalism and the rule of law. But the present conflicts over the constitution, although urgent, are not as overwhelming as some claim. Now, without ignoring the possibility of constitutional amendment in the future, we should devote our energies to more constructive and rewarding endeavours. This calls for strengthened cooperation between a strong central government and strong provincial governments." See clipping, "The Liberal Point of View," 2, LAC Trudeau Fonds (MG26-020, Volume 28, File 1).
65. Arthur Blakely, "Liberals Still on Top but Not Much Change," *MG* (November 9, 1965), 1.
66. W.A.C. Bennett, cited in Ian MacAlpine, "PM Must Resign, Bennett Insists," *VS* (November 9, 1965), 13.

67. Editorial, "Get Back to Work," *GM* (November 9, 1965), 6. See also editorial "Pearson Wins But Loses," *MG* (November 9, 1965), 6; editorial, "Not the Same as They Were," *MG* (November 10, 1965), 6; and editorial, "Time for Party Leaders to Bow Out," *SDR* (November 9, 1965), 4.
68. Frank Rutter, "As you Were, Says British Columbia," *VS* (November 9, 1965), 12. See also editorial, "Rebuff to Mr. Pearson," *WT* (November 9, 1965), 2.
69. "Les Canadiens ont voté exactement pour rien," *JM* (November 9, 1965), 3.
70. Editorial, "Du pareil au même," *LS* (November 9, 1965), 4. See also Benoit Houle, "Gouvernement minoritaire: Libéraux reportés au pouvoir," *AC* (November 9, 1965), 1; editorial, "Où trouver la lumière?" *LP* (November 9, 1965), 4; Lorenzo Paré, "Les jeux sont finis!" *AC* (November 9, 1965), 4; "Les Canadiens en étaient à leur cinquième scrutin général depuis 1957," *AC* (November 9, 1965), 8; "Ce qu'a déclaré Pearson en déclenchant l'élection," *LP* (November 9, 1965), 2; Vincent Prince, "Le gouvernement reste libéral et minoritaire," *LP* (November 9, 1965), 1; editorial, "Rien n'a changé," *LD* (November 9, 1965), 1; and "Pearson accepte le verdict du peuple," *LD* (November 9, 1965), 2.
71. See "Les trois intellectuels de la nouvelle garde libérale élus," *AC* (November 9, 1965), 8; "Jean Marchand a connu une soirée angoissante," *LP* (November 9, 1965), 31; and "New Liberal Hopeful Pushed Quebec Bid Right to Wire!" *CH* (November 8, 1965), 3.
72. The NDP managed to improve its standing in the popular vote in Quebec from 7.2 per cent in 1963 to 12 per cent in 1965, though without winning any seats in the province (it had never won a Quebec seat).
73. Cited in Cronshaw, "Trudeau Tops Taylor," 3. See also Michèle Juneau, "Pierre-Elliott Trudeau: majorité de 12,966 voix," *LP* (November 9, 1965), 3.
74. Charles Taylor, cited in "Charles Taylor a été défait par un vieil ami," *AC* (November 9, 1965), 8. See also "Elliott-Trudeau regrettera sa nouvelle adhésion," *LS* (November 9, 1965), 9.
75. Gretta Chambers, cited in "Canadian Philosopher Taylor Wins $1.5M.
76. Pierre Trudeau, cited in Cronshaw, "Trudeau Tops Taylor," 3.
77. Alec Bollini, interview with Pierre Trudeau, CBC Radio News (November 8, 1965). Available online as "Pierre Trudeau: A Triple March Toward Ottawa," CBCDA, http:www.cbc.ca/archives/entry/pierre-trudeau-a-triple-march-toward-ottawa.

78. Pierre Trudeau, cited in Robert Rice, "Liberals Hold Montreal Bastion," *GM* (November 9, 1965), 11. See also "Lester Pearson doit un gros merci à la province de Québec," *LS* (November 9, 1965), 9.
79. See André Béliveau, "Les trois 'colombes' prennent leur envol dans un ciel incertain," *LP* (November 9, 1965), 5.
80. Stan McDowell, "Lazy Liberal Swing Halted by Tories' Quebec Strength," *VS* (November 9, 1965), 12. See also "Three Intellectuals Win Seats in Quebec," *WT* (November 9, 1965), 7.
81. Frank Howard, "Another Minority Government Could Ease Quebec's Exit from Confederation," *GM* (November 10, 1965), 9.
82. Robert Rice, "Quebec's New-Look Trio to Play Powerful Role for Liberals," *GM* (November 10, 1965), 9.
83. Jean Bouchard, cited in "Bomb Scare, Goon Squads at Montreal Polls," *GM* (November 9, 1965), 1.
84. "'Bomb' Slows Montreal Voting," *VS* (November 8, 1965), 1; "1 bombe fantôme, 21 arrestations et l'incendie d'un poll, seuls incidents d'une journée généralement tranquille," *JM* (November 9, 1965), 3; and "Québec a connu une élection sans incident," *LP* (November 9, 1965), 2.
85. See Newman, "Quebec's 'Three Musketeers' Carry the Gospel," 7.
86. Peter C. Newman, "The Left Wing Takes a Beating in Cabinet Shuffle," *TS* (December 18, 1965), 7.
87. Bernard Dufresne, "Liberal Caucus Probes Election and Votes Confidence in Pearson," *GM* (January 4, 1966), 3.
88. Trudeau, *Memoirs*, 78–79.
89. Editorial, "The Convert," *GM* (January 13, 1966), 6.
90. McRoberts, *Misconceiving Canada*, 44.
91. Patricia Smart, ed., *The Diary of André Laurendeau* (Toronto: Lorimer, 1991), 154.
92. John Diefenbaker, cited in Robert McKenzie, "Quebec PCs Want Confederation Talks," *TS* (January 17, 1966), 8; and Geoffrey Stevens, "PC Chief Quotes Auditor, Leaves Them in the Aisles," *GM* (February 3, 1966), 8.
93. John Diefenbaker, *Hansard* (January 20, 1966), 54.
94. Dominique Clift, "Trudeau—A Voice in the PM's Ear," *TS* (January 22, 1966), 7.
95. Pierre Trudeau, cited in "Quebec Doesn't Need Special Status: MPs," *GM* (February 24, 1966), 23.
96. Ibid.

97. Pierre Trudeau, cited in "Human Rights Declaration Soon in Quebec, Says Lesage," *TS* (May 18, 1966), 71.
98. Pierre Trudeau, cited in "Quebec Special Status Bid Seen Threat to Bilingualism" [*sic*], *GM* (March 14, 1967), 31.
99. Pierre Trudeau, cited in "Separatist Warning," *TS* (March 9, 1967), 42.
100. See Geoffrey Stevens, "New-Old Faces Making a Mark in Commons," *GM* (March 19, 1966), A3.
101. Pierre Trudeau, *Hansard* (June 21, 1966), 6742.
102. Ibid., 6743.
103. Pierre Trudeau, *Hansard* (June 28, 1966), 6999–7000.
104. *Hansard* (July 7, 1966), 7370.
105. Frank Howard, "Favreau Remains on Top of Liberals' Quebec Wing," *GM* (March 28, 1966), 8.
106. Pierre Trudeau, "Le Réalisme Constitutionnel" (March 26, 1966), LAC Trudeau Fonds (MG26-020, Volume 29, File 4), 13–14; and Pierre Trudeau, cited in "Quebec Liberals Define Roles," *GM* (March 28, 1966), 9.
107. See "Quebec Wants Bilingual Ontario," *TS* (March 28, 1966), 2.
108. Pierre Trudeau, cited in "Quebec Liberals Define Roles," 9.
109. "Liberal Extremists Take a Beating," *TS* (March 28, 1966), 2; Normand Gérard, "P.E.-Trudeau condamne ceux qui sabordent le fédéralisme," *LS* (March 28, 1966), 3; and Lewis Seale, "Trudeau Wins Point on Constitution," *SDR* (March 28, 1966), 4.
110. Editorial, "Quebec's New Federal Voice," *GM* (March 29, 1966), 6.
111. Peter C. Newman, "Now There's a Third Viewpoint in the French-English Dialogue," *TS* (April 2, 1966), 7. See also Newman, "Dans la course à la succession de Pearson," *LP* (March 26, 1966), 4; "Les successeurs éventuels de Pearson ne sont pas à Québec," *LP* (March 26, 1966), 6; Tim Creery, "3-Pronged Pearson Talk Wins Quebec Support," *CH* (March 28, 1966), 1; Tim Creery, "Most Liberals Expect Pearson to Stay into 1967," *CH* (March 28, 1966), 1; editorial, "What Quebec Liberals Want," *OC* (March 29, 1966), 6; and Victor Mackie, "Top Liberals Give Quebec Wide Berth," *VS* (March 25, 1966), 14.
112. Pierre Trudeau, cited in Newman, "Now There's a Third Viewpoint," 7.
113. Pierre Trudeau, cited ibid.

CHAPTER THREE: FORKS IN THE ROAD

1. Dennis Braithwaite, "Different Views," *GM* (April 6, 1967), 23.
2. Anthony Westell, "Old Quebec Guard Leaves Cabinet for Trudeau, Chrétien," *GM* (April 5, 1967), 3.
3. Lester Pearson, cited in "Cabinet Shuffle Gives Quebec Younger, More Radical Voice," *TS* (April 5, 1967), 1, 11.
4. Pierre Elliott Trudeau, *Memoirs* (Toronto: McClelland & Stewart, 1993), 82–84.
5. See Martin O'Malley, "RC Bishops Preparing Fight on Abortion," *GM* (April 7, 1967), 1.
6. Editorial, "New Generation Up Front," *TS* (April 5, 1967), 6.
7. Editorial, "The Cabinet Changes," *CH* (April 5, 1967), 6. See also editorial, "Strength for the Cabinet and for the New Quebec," *GM* (April 6, 1967), 6.
8. Peter C. Newman, "Federalism Will Be the Big Winner in Cabinet Shuffle," *TS* (April 5, 1967), 7. See also John Walker, "Swinging Quebec Up Front," *WT* (April 5, 1967), 1.
9. Editorial, "The Cabinet Changes," *MG* (April 4, 1967), 6. See also "Trudeau Named Justice Minister as Cabinet Changes Stress Youth," *MG* (April 4, 1967), 1, 37; Greg Connolley, "4 New Cabinet Choices Bring Stamp of Youth," *OC* (April 5, 1967), 2; Charles King, "Big Doings on a Dull Day in Parliament," *OC* (April 5, 1967), 6; Ken Kelly, "Quebec Talent Enlisted by PM," *HCH* (April 5, 1967), 1; J.R. Walker, "Quebec 'Swingers' in Cabinet," *CH* (April 5, 1967), 11; Ian MacDonald, "Pearson Tries Young Look," *VS* (April 5, 1967), 3; editorial, "Mr. Pearson Draws Two Aces," *VS* (April 5, 1967), 4; and John Walker, "Trudeau Heads a Bright Young Team," *OC* (April 6, 1967), 6.
10. Braithwaite, "Different Views," 23.
11. John Diefenbaker, cited in "Cabinet Shuffle Gives Quebec," 11.
12. *Hansard* (April 5, 1967), 14546–47. See also "Dief trouve une âme soeur en Pierre Elliott-Trudeau," *AC* (April 5, 1967), 1; "Pour Diefenbaker, Trudeau est une âme soeur," *LDR* (April 5, 1967), 3; George Bain, "Mr. Trudeau Speaks Up," *GM* (April 6, 1967), 6; "Trudeau Fields First Commons Question," CP (April 6, 1967); and Arthur Blakely, "Dief Went to Dine and Found Pierre a Tough Stone," *MG* (April 6, 1967), 1.
13. "Pour Diefenbaker, Trudeau est une 'âme soeur,'" 3; and "Dief trouve une âme soeur en Pierre Elliott-Trudeau," 1.
14. Claude Ryan, cited in "Two Views of Who Should Be Quebec's Voice in Ottawa," *GM* (April 21, 1967), 7.

15. Editorial, "Please Allow Us to Be Pleased," *GM* (April 21, 1967), 6.
16. Bain, "Mr. Trudeau Speaks Up," 6.
17. Sylvio St.-Amant, cited in Frank Howard, "A Bouquet of Barbs from the Boys Back Home," *GM* (June 24, 1967), A16. See also "Trudeau 'dans le vent' Cowan dans l'eau chaude," *LS* (April 4, 1967), 3; "Pierre-E. Trudeau et Jean Chrétien font désormais partie du Cabinet," *LP* (April 4, 1965), 1; "M. Pearson remplace MM. Cardin et Favreau par 2 québécois, MM. Eliot [*sic*] Trudeau et Chrétien," *JM* (April 4, 1967), 4; "Un Cabinet Pearson rajeuni," *LS* (April 4, 1965), 1; and "An Unlikely Alliance Which Cherishes an Inward Gaze," *GM* (April 22, 1967), 8.
18. Edward McWhinney, "Confederation: Is the Time Ripe for Talks?" *GM* (February 18, 1967), 9.
19. Ibid.
20. The NDP motion was actually a sub-amendment to an amendment proposed during the Throne Speech debate by John Diefenbaker, who demanded that the government repatriate and reform the Canadian Constitution. See *Hansard* (May 11, 1967), 69–70.
21. Tommy Douglas, cited in Michael Gillan, "156–17 Vote Defeats Non-Confidence Motion Introduced by Douglas," *GM* (May 12, 1967), 4. See also editorial, "What the NDP Really Wants," *GM* (May 15, 1967), 6.
22. Pierre Trudeau, cited in Norman Webster, "Go Slow on Changes, Trudeau Tells Quebec," *GM* (October 26, 1965), 10.
23. Pierre Trudeau, cited in Irwin Block, "Provincial Pacts 'Could Destroy Canada,'" *TS* (May 30, 1967), 1; and "Provinces Have Power to Bust Nation," *GM* (May 31, 1967), 4.
24. One month later, the advisers to the Steering Committee on Constitutional Questions were named: G.E. Le Dain, dean of Osgoode Hall law school; Mark MacGuigan, dean of law at the University of Windsor; Gérard La Forest of the University of New Brunswick; and Barry Strayer of the University of Saskatchewan.
25. Pierre Trudeau, *Hansard* (May 31, 1967), 790.
26. Editorial, "Let's Confess: It's Great to Be Canadians," *TS* (July 1, 1967), 6.
27. Cited in John Dafoe, "Premiers Meet and Save Face for Ottawa," *GM* (July 6, 1967), 9.
28. John Diefenbaker, *Hansard* (July 5, 1967), 2275.

29. Paul Martin, *Hansard* (July 5, 1967), 2275.
30. John Diefenbaker, *Hansard* (July 5, 1967), 2275.
31. Pierre Trudeau, cited in Dominique Clift, "Quebec Convention Triumph for Trudeau," *TS* (January 29, 1968), 1.
32. Cited in Michael Gillan, "Gad, Trudeau!" *GM* (July 6, 1967), 1.
33. George Bain, "Away Convention," *GM* (July 6, 1967), 6.
34. Tom Hazlitt, "Trudeau's Ascot Isn't So Dandy," *TS* (July 6, 1967), 10.
35. Pierre Trudeau, cited in Mary Jukes, "'It's Very Fetching' Woman MP Comments," *GM* (July 7, 1967), 9.
36. Lester Pearson, cited in "Trudeau Wears a Tie—and Sandals in House," *GM* (July 7, 1967), 9.
37. Margaret Rideout, cited in Jukes, "'It's Very Fetching,'" 9.
38. Grace MacInnis, cited ibid.
39. Jean Wadds, cited ibid.
40. Charles de Gaulle, cited in Robert McKenzie, "De Gaulle Boosts 'Quebec-First' Mood," *TS* (July 24, 1967), 1.
41. Editorial, "De Gaulle Brinksmanship Has Canada on Edge," *TS* (July 24, 1967), 6. See also "Le 'Vive la Nouvelle-France' a choqué les fédéralistes," *LD* (July 24, 1967), 1.
42. See "Des pancartes à slogans séparatistes," *LS* (July 25, 1967), 3.
43. Cited in "'Long Live Free Quebec' de Gaulle Tells Montrealers," *GM* (July 25, 1967), 1. See also Tim Creery, "Separatist Cry Rouses Quebecers," *OC* (July 25, 1967), 1; and Fernande Lemieux, "De Gaulle: Vive le Québec libre," *LS* (July 25, 1967), 1.
44. Lester B. Pearson, *Mike: The Memoirs of the Right Honourable Lester B. Pearson*, vol. 3, *1957–1968*, ed. John A. Munro and Alex I. Inglis (Toronto: University of Toronto Press, 1975), 267–68.
45. Ibid., 268.
46. Lester Pearson, cited in "De Gaulle Rebuked by Pearson," *GM* (July 26, 1967), 1. See also "Les beaux discours de de Gaulle ne changeront rien au Québec," *LS* (July 25, 1967), 19; and "La patience des autorités fédérales mise à l'épreuve," *LD* (July 25, 1967), 1.
47. John Diefenbaker, cited in "PM Didn't Scare de Gaulle," *TS* (July 26, 1967), 2. See also "'Une intrusion inexcusable' (Diefenbaker)," *LS* (July 25, 1967), 1.
48. Editorial, "This Meddlesome Old Man Abuses Our Courtesy," *TS* (July 25, 1967), 6.

49. *Edmonton Journal* editorial, cited in "Just What Was Said about de Gaulle," *GM* (July 26, 1967), 7; editorial ,"A Deplorable Note of Discord," *MG* (July 25, 1967), 6; and editorial, "Go Home, de Gaulle," *CH* (July 25, 1967), 4. See also Ian MacDonald, "De Gaulle Fans Fires of Pride," *VS* (July 24, 1967), 1; Ian MacDonald, "De Gaulle Sounds Battle Cry," *VS* (July 25, 1967), 1; "B.C. Leaders Roused to Fury," *VS* (July 25, 1967), 1; "World Press Hits de Gaulle's Stand," *VS* (July 25, 1967), 10; Victor Mackie, "Pearson Scolds de Gaulle," *VS* (July 25, 1967), 1; John Walker, "To Snub, or Not to Snub, de Gaulle?" *OC* (July 25, 1967), 1; editorial, "De Gaulle Rubs the Sore Spot," *OC* (July 25, 1967), 6; and Tim Creery, "Long Live Free Quebec," *CH* (July 25, 1967), 1.
50. Editorial, "Vive le Québec libre," *LS* (July 25, 1967), 4. See also Fernande Lemieux, "Le Général a parlé avec courage et franchise," *LS* (July 25, 1967), 3.
51. Claude Ryan, cited in "De Gaulle Is 'Intruding' Montreal Newspaper Says," *TS* (July 25, 1967), 1.
52. Daniel Johnson, cited in "New Era Predicted by Premier Johnson," *MG* (July 26, 1967), 2.
53. Charles de Gaulle, cited in "De Gaulle Going Home," *TS* (July 26, 1967), 1.
54. Editorial, "Go Home, de Gaulle," *CH* (July 25, 1967), 6; editorial, "Good Riddance," *CH* (July 26, 1967), 6; Clive Cocking, "B.C. Woman Says de Gaulle Uses Separatists as Pawns," *VS* (July 26, 1967), 11; Norman Campbell, "De Gaulle Calls Off Visit," *OC* (July 26, 1967), 1; editorial, "A Sad Moment for de Gaulle," *OC* (July 26, 1967), 6; Charles King, "Was de Gaulle's '*Vive*' Just a Bad Joke?" *OC* (July 26, 1967), 6; editorial, "Drapeau Talks for All Canada," *OC* (July 27, 1967), 6; and "De Gaulle Snubs Pearson, Drapeau Rebukes General," *CH* (July 27, 1967), 1.
55. Lester Pearson, cited in Michael Gillan, "Pearson Absolves Ottawa," *GM* (July 27, 1967), 10.
56. Cited in "De Gaulle Did Not Interfere," CP (August 14, 1967).
57. See John Saywell, ed., *CAR 1967* (Toronto: University of Toronto Press, 1968), 54.
58. Pierre Bourgault, cited in "Hypocrisy Assailed by Separatist Chief," *GM* (July 26, 1967), 4.
59. See "De Gaulle Pledges Aid to Quebec," *GM* (August 1, 1967), 1.
60. Ibid.; and Michael Gillan, "PM Again Rejects de Gaulle's Stand," *GM* (August 2, 1967), 1.
61. Lester Pearson, cited in Gillan, "PM Again Rejects de Gaulle's Stand," 1.

62. Pierre Trudeau, cited ibid.
63. See Christopher MacLennan, *Toward the Charter: Canadians and the Demand for a National Bill of Rights, 1929–1960* (Montreal: McGill-Queen's University Press, 2004).
64. Pierre Elliott Trudeau, "A Constitutional Declaration of Rights," in *Federalism and the French Canadians* (Toronto: Macmillan, 1968), 52–60.
65. W.R. Lederman, cited in Ralph Hyman, "Law Experts Find Flaws in Proposal for Constitutional Bill of Rights," *GM* (September 6, 1967), 3.
66. Jacques-Yvan Morin, cited in "Trudeau: Autonomy Calls Cut Quebec's Influence," *TS* (September 6, 1967), 1, 4.
67. Pierre Trudeau, cited ibid.
68. Pierre Trudeau, cited ibid.
69. Pierre Trudeau, cited in Rae Corelli, "Quebec Must Back Down on Autonomy, Trudeau's Warning," *TS* (September 6, 1967), 5.
70. Edward McWhinney, "Why Pearson Should Lead the Robarts Conference," *GM* (October 31, 1967), 7.
71. Editorial, "All Canada Is French Homeland," *TS* (September 6, 1967), 6.
72. Editorial, "No Conflict in Principle," *GM* (September 7, 1967), 6.
73. Daniel Johnson, cited in "Johnson Claims Talks Only Hope for Canada," *GM* (September 7, 1967), 9.
74. Jean-Noël Tremblay, cited in "Robarts' Constitution Talks Could Save Nation—Johnson," CP (September 7, 1967).
75. Jean-Noël Tremblay, cited in "National State Is Goal, Quebec Minister Says," *GM* (September 12, 1967), 1.
76. See Frank Howard, "An Underground Policy Fades in the Light of Scrutiny," *GM* (September 30, 1967), 8.
77. See editorial, "Meanwhile, Back in Quebec," *GM* (September 13, 1967), 6.
78. Jean Lesage, cited in Frank Howard, "Trudeau out of Touch with Quebec Goals, Jean Lesage Tells Liberals," *GM* (September 15, 1967), 1.
79. Jean Lesage, cited in "Lesage Hoists Flag of Truce on French-Canada Question," CP (September 18, 1967).
80. Jean Lesage, cited in Dominique Clift, "Lesage Attacks Ottawa over '2 Nations,'" *TS* (September 15, 1967), 1, 9.
81. Pierre Trudeau, cited in Frank Howard, "Jean Lesage Has No Special Right to Speak for Quebec, Trudeau Says," *GM* (September 16, 1967), 3.

82. Dominique Clift, "Lesage Attacks Ottawa over '2 Nations,'" *TS* (September 15, 1967), 1, 9.
83. Pierre Trudeau, cited in Dominique Clift, "Liberal Ready to Change Direction on Quebec," *TS* (September 18, 1967), 7.
84. Jean Marchand, cited in "Minister's Views at Variance," *GM* (September 14, 1967), 2.
85. Tom Hazlitt, "Liberal Caucus Cheers as Pearson Says He'll Stay as Their Leader," *TS* (September 26, 1967), 1, 3; and "Pearson Forecasts Government Statement," *GM* (September 25, 1967), 10.
86. Lester Pearson, cited in Alastair Dow, "Full Commons Debate Likely, Says Pearson," *TS* (September 25, 1967), 1.
87. Maxwell Cohen, "The Five Steps to a United Canada," *GM* (October 3, 1967), 7.
88. Marcel Faribault, cited in Kenneth McRoberts, *Misconceiving Canada: The Struggle for National Unity* (Toronto: Oxford University Press, 1997), 47–48.
89. Cited ibid., 48. The italics and parentheses appeared in the original text.
90. See Robert McKenzie, "'Deux Nations' Plan Wins Despite Dief," *GM* (September 7, 1967), 57.
91. See Lewis Seale, "The Two-Language Problem of Nation," *GM* (September 8, 1967), 7.
92. John Diefenbaker, cited in George C. Perlin, *The Tory Syndrome: Leadership Politics in the Progressive Conservative Party* (Montreal: McGill-Queen's University Press, 1980), 94.
93. René Lévesque, cited in Saywell, *CAR 1967*, 64–65.
94. Editorial, "The Task Belongs to Quebec," *GM* (September 21, 1967), 6.
95. See Walter Gray, "Constitutional Changes Sped by Separatists?" *TS* (September 21, 1967), 1.
96. A "senior government source," cited ibid.
97. Jean Lesage, cited in Dominique Clift, "Lesage: I'll Fight for Quebec's Stake in Wealth of Canada," *TS* (September 25, 1967), 1.
98. Eric Kierans, cited in Frank Howard, "Liberals Reject 'Free Quebec,'" *GM* (September 20, 1967), 9.
99. Saywell, *CAR 1967*, 67.
100. See René Lévesque, *Memoirs*, trans. Philip Stratford (Toronto: McClelland & Stewart, 1986), ch. 30.
101. Meanwhile, on October 16, Jacques Parizeau, future Parti Québécois premier and instigator of the second (1995) Quebec referendum on sovereignty, was in Banff, Alberta, explaining to "disturbed and even shocked" delegates to a

conference on the economics of national unity that there would be no limit to how much Quebec would ask for from the rest of Canada and thus how much it would get. "When a society has been for so long in search of fulfillment and has found it within itself, it is very unlikely it can be distracted from this purpose," said Parizeau. "This historical process is quite inevitable. The fact is that the so-called quiet revolution has had deep roots in all of French-Canadian society and is now quite irreversible. It can be slowed down but one does not really see how it can be stopped. [Quebec] might even become independent." See "Quebecker Says Province Can Never Be Appeased," *TS* (October 17, 1967), 2.

102. Cited in "Johnson: Only Want Our Rights," CP (October 4, 1967).
103. Pierre Trudeau, *Hansard* (October 5, 1967), 2827.
104. Pierre Trudeau, cited in Lewis Seale, "Trudeau Delighted by Johnson's 'Realistic' Statement," *GM* (October 6, 1967), 10.
105. Alan C. Cairns, "Why Is It So Difficult to Talk to Each Other?" *McGill Law Journal* 42 (1997): 71.
106. Government of Québec, "Preliminary Statement" (November 27–30, 1967), LAC Trudeau Fonds (MG26-020, Volume 22, File 17), 14–22. See also "Twenty Million Questions" (December 13, 1967), LAC Trudeau Fonds (MG26-020, Volume 22, File 17), 1–7; and Saywell, *CAR 1967*, 88.
107. Pierre Trudeau, cited in Lewis Seale, "Trudeau More Worried about Issue of French after Manning Speech," *GM* (November 23, 1967), 56.
108. Pierre Trudeau, cited in Dominique Clift, "Trudeau Tells Robarts Avoid 'Demolition Job,'" *TS* (September 18, 1967), 1.
109. Pierre Trudeau, *Hansard* (November 21, 1967), 4504.
110. Pearson, 255. See also Tom Hazlitt, "Trudeau Backs Premiers on Federalism," *TS* (December 14, 1967), 12.
111. Lester B. Pearson, "Draft Memorandum to Cabinet: Preparations for Constitutional Discussions" (November 13, 1967), LAC Trudeau Fonds (MG26-020, Volume 22, File 18), 4.
112. "How does this sort of doc come to be made without consultation of the committee?" a visibly irritated Trudeau scribbled in the margins of an accompanying note from his adviser Jean Beetz, demonstrating that Trudeau and his steering committee really were working in isolation. See Jean Beetz to Pierre Trudeau (November 16, 1967), LAC Trudeau Fonds (MG26-020, Volume 22, File 18), 1.
113. Pearson, "Draft Memorandum to Cabinet,"4–7.

CHAPTER FOUR: FROM CELEBRATION TO SURVIVAL

1. Having followed the trail of Trudeau's romantic life as far as it led, Trudeau biographer John English accepts Margaret Trudeau's account of her failed marriage: Pierre could have granted her a divorce after three years' separation, but he forced her to wait five, at which time she was free to file for divorce unilaterally. See English, *Just Watch Me: The Life of Pierre Elliott Trudeau, 1968–2000* (Toronto: Knopf, 2009), 334.
2. Pierre Trudeau, *Hansard* (December 4, 1967), 5014.
3. Ibid, 5014–15.
4. Andrew Brewin, *Hansard* (December 4, 1967), 5017.
5. Ibid., 5018.
6. Pierre Trudeau, *Hansard* (December 5, 1967), 5083–84.
7. Ibid., 5085.
8. Ibid., 5087.
9. Ibid., 5088.
10. Pierre Trudeau, *Hansard* (December 18, 1967), 5548.
11. Geoffrey Stevens, "MPs Unanimous in Approving Divorce Reform," *GM* (December 20, 1967), 27.
12. Pierre Trudeau, cited in "Divorce Bill May Be Passed Tonight," *TS* (December 19, 1967), 4. See also F.J.E. Jordan, "The Federal Divorce Act (1968) and the Constitution," *McGill Law Journal* 14, 2 (1968): 209–71.
13. "Johnson Wants to Take Over Divorce Laws," *GM* (December 22, 1967), 5.
14. See, for example, Marc Lalonde, "Mémoire à l'hon. Pierre Trudeau" (December 4, 1967), LAC Trudeau Fonds (MG26-020, Volume 22, File 18), 1.
15. "Unlocking the Locked Step of Law and Morality," *GM* (December 12, 1967), 6. See also editorial, "The Beginning of Reform," *GM* (December 6, 1967), 6.
16. See *Hansard* (December 21, 1967), 5722–28.
17. See *Hansard* (February 24, 1967), 13431–32.
18. See Angus McLaren and Arlene Tigar McLaren, *The Bedroom and the State: The Changing Practices and Politics of Contraception and Abortion in Canada, 1880–1997* (Toronto: Oxford University Press, 1997); and Mollie Dunsmuir, "Abortion: Constitutional and Legal Developments" (Ottawa: Parliament of Canada, Law and Government Division, 1998), http://www.publications.gc.ca/Collection-R/LoPBdP/CIR/8910-e.htm.
19. Michael Gillan, "Trudeau Gets Green Light to Ease Law on Abortions," *GM* (December 20, 1967), 1.

20. Pierre Trudeau, cited in Geoffrey Stevens, "Draft Bill Makes Breath Test Compulsory," *GM* (June 28, 1967), 1.
21. Editorial, "This Would Be Heartless Legalism," *TS* (June 30, 1967), 6.
22. Pierre Trudeau, cited in "Doctors Would Make Decisions on Abortions," *TS* (December 22, 1967), 3.
23. Pierre Trudeau, cited ibid.; "Life, Health of Woman Would Be Abortion Ground," *GM* (December 22, 1967), 5; and "Trudeau Abortion Stand Angers Priest," CP (December 26, 1967).
24. See Stuart Chambers, "Pierre Elliott Trudeau and Bill C-150: A Rational Approach to Homosexual Acts, 1968–69," *Journal of Homosexuality* 57, 2 (December 2009): 249–66.
25. Klippert v. The Queen (November 7, 1967), Canada Law Reports: Supreme Court of Canada, 832.
26. Ibid., 831.
27. Editorial, "A Return to the Middle Ages," *TS* (November 10, 1967), 6.
28. Editorial, "Not Parliament's Intention," *GM* (November 11, 1967), 6.
29. Stephen Neiger, cited in Sidney Katz, "Homosexuals Shocked by Life Term Ruling," *TS* (November 11, 1967), 5.
30. See Tom Hazlitt, "Trudeau Backs Change in Homosexual Law," *TS* (November 9, 1967), 56.
31. Pierre Trudeau, cited ibid.
32. Pierre Trudeau, interview CBC-TV (December 21, 1967). Available online as "Omnibus Bill: 'There's no place for the state in the bedrooms of the nation," CBCDA, http://www.cbc.ca/player/play/1811727781.
33. Pierre Trudeau, cited in Don Peacock, *Journey to Power* (Toronto: Ryerson, 1968), 262.
34. Pierre Trudeau, cited in Christina McCall and Stephen Clarkson, *Trudeau and Our Times*, vol. 1, *The Magnificent Obsession* (Toronto: McClelland & Stewart, 1990), 73.
35. R.E. Turner, cited in "Authorities Favor Change in Sex Laws," *GM* (December 22, 1967), 5.
36. Cited ibid.
37. Cited in Katz, "Homosexuals Shocked,"5.
38. Editorial, "Trudeau: The Boldest Reformer of Them All," *TS* (December 22, 1967), 4.
39. Cited in Peacock, *Journey to Power*, 178.
40. George Bain, "Leg-Up for a Long-Shot," *GM* (December 28, 1967), 6.
41. Robert Stanbury, cited in Douglas Stuebing, with John Marshall and Gary Oakes, *Trudeau: A Man for Tomorrow* (Toronto: Clark-Irwin, 1978), 43.

42. Gérard Pelletier, "Trudeau Travelled the World with a Knapsack on His Back," *TS* (January 6, 1968), 8. Again in early January 1968, an unnamed Ottawa insider commented on Trudeau's softening style: "Mr. Trudeau has suddenly gained new credibility in the Quebec wing. An important factor in the change appears to have been a private meeting he had with Quebec MPs late last month to outline the Government's constitutional policy. Conditioned to think of him as an arrogant, ivory-tower intellectual, many of the MPs were reported to be favorably surprised by his manner and his thinking." Cited in Lewis Seale, "Trudeau Gaining Quebec Backing for Leadership," *GM* (January 4, 1968), 3.
43. See Doug Owram, *Born at the Right Time: A History of the Baby Boom Generation* (Toronto: University of Toronto Press, 1996), 218; and Myrna Kostash, *Long Way from Home: The Story of the Sixties Generation in Canada* (Toronto: Lorimer, 1980).
44. Lester B. Pearson, *Mike: The Memoirs of the Right Honourable Lester B. Pearson*, vol. 3, *1957–1968*, ed. John A. Munro and Alex I. Inglis (Toronto: University of Toronto Press, 1975), 310.
45. See Peter J. Nicholson, "The Growth Story: Canada's Long-run Economic Performance and Prospects," *International Productivity Monitor* 7 (Fall 2003): 1–23.
46. See, for example, Peter C. Newman, "The Quiet Race to Become Pearson's Heir," *TS* (December 16, 1965), 7.
47. Anthony Westell, "Pearson's Greatest Challenge Lies Ahead," *GM* (December 15, 1967), 7.
48. Daniel Johnson, cited in "PM's Resignation Leaves Question Mark over Bill of Rights Conference," *GM* (December 15, 1967), 9.
49. Pearson, *Mike*, 314.
50. "The Big Day," CP (December 15, 1967).
51. Pierre Elliott Trudeau, *Memoirs* (Toronto: McClelland & Stewart, 1993), 84–85.
52. Jean Marchand, cited in George Radwanski, *Trudeau* (Toronto: Macmillan, 1978), 98.
53. Ibid.
54. Pierre Trudeau, cited ibid., 99.
55. Ramsay Cook, "What's Special about the NDP's Status for Quebec?" *GM* (August 3, 1967), 7.
56. See Roger Newman, "Special Status Plans Lack Logic, Trudeau Says," *GM* (October 13, 1967), 1–2; and "Trudeau Says Special Status Bad," *TS* (October 13, 1967), 2.
57. Editorial, "Quebec Can't Play in Both Leagues," *TS* (October 13, 1967), 6.

58. Pierre Trudeau, cited in "Trudeau Urges Guarantee for French Culture Rights," CP (October 17, 1967). Towards the end of the Liberal leadership campaign, Trudeau's backers brought out a second book of his writings, this one aimed at ordinary Quebec voters and eschewing the erudite tone of *Federalism and the French Canadians.* Entitled *Réponses* (*Answers*) and introduced by Gérard Pelletier, the 143-page work comprised statements Trudeau had made on various issues—much like the better-known *Conversations with Canadians* published in 1972. See Pierre Elliott Trudeau, *Réponses* (Montréal: Éditions du Jour, 1968).
59. Cited in George Bain, "A Prospective Candidate," *GM* (December 27, 1967), 6.
60. Peter C. Newman, *A Nation Divided: Canada and the Coming of Pierre Trudeau* (New York: Knopf, 1969), 446–48.
61. Michael Bliss, *Writing History: A Professor's Life* (Toronto: Dundurn, 2011), 70–72.
62. Frank Jones, "They're Boosters (er) of Pierre (cough) Elliott (ahem) Trudeau," *TS* (January 23, 1968), 7.
63. Ramsay Cook, cited ibid.
64. Bain, "A Prospective Candidate," 6.
65. Bain, "Leg-Up for a Long Shot," 6.
66. Peter C. Newman, "Opinion-makers Pick Their Man: Pierre Trudeau," *TS* (January 12, 1968), 7.
67. Peter C. Newman, "Trudeau," *TS* (December 30, 1967), 2.
68. Pierre Berton, cited in Newman, "Opinion-makers Pick Their Man," 7.
69. Alastair Dow, "Trudeau: Trend to Tomorrow's Society," *TS* (December 23, 1967), 7.
70. See John Saywell, ed., *CAR 1968* (Toronto: University of Toronto Press, 1969), 17; and Newman, *A Nation Divided*, 446–48.
71. Marc Lalonde, cited in Radwanski, *Trudeau*, 98–99.
72. "8 Prospective Leadership Candidates," *TS* (January 3, 1968), 2.
73. Cited in Peacock, *Journey to Power*, 186.
74. See George Bain, "How Quebec Rates Them," *GM* (January 13, 1968), 6.
75. See "Le bill Trudeau et l'ivresse au volant," *LD* (January 10, 1968), 5; Vincent Prince, "Devant la légalisation des tests d'haleine," *LD* (January 10, 1968), 4; Vincent Harvey and Hélène Pelletier-Baillargeon, "De Salomon à Pierre Elliott Trudeau," *LD* (January 12, 1968), 4; and Claude Ryan, "M. Marchand ou M. Trudeau," *LD* (January 17, 1968), 4.
76. See "Quebeckers Map Leadership Plans," *TS* (January 16, 1968), 29.
77. "2 Discuss Candidates for Quebec," *GM* (January 16, 1968), 9.

78. John Turner, cited in Geoffrey Stevens, "Turner Enters Liberal Leadership Race," *GM* (January 19, 1968), 4.
79. Ibid. See also editorial, "La candidature de John Turner," *LD* (January 19, 1968), 4; and the twin editorials "Mr. Sharp Brings Experience" and "Mr. Turner Brings Youth," *GM* (January 19, 1968), 6.
80. Frank McGee, "Sharp as PM?" *TS* (January 19, 1968), 7.
81. Editorial, "Mr. Martin Tries Again," *GM* (January 20, 1968), 6.
82. Geoffrey Stevens, "PM Lectures Leadership Hopefuls on Need for Cabinet Solidarity," *GM* (January 18, 1968), 1. See also "La campagne des aspirants se déplace vers les Maritimes," *LD* (January 13, 1968), 1; "Le débat de Halifax accentue les rumeurs de dissension au sein du gouvernement libéral," *LD* (January 15, 1968), 1; and "Pearson rappelle aux candidats les exigences de la solidarité," *LD* (January 18, 1968), 1.
83. "Turner Joins the Liberal Race," *TS* (January 18, 1968), 3. Trudeau was opposed to the feds' introduction of medicare at this stage of the debate, but only on constitutional grounds.
84. "M. Winters annonce sa décision de quitter la politique fédérale," *LD* (January 13, 1968), 1.
85. Zündel, a German immigrant to Canada, announced March 8, 1968, that he was entering the Liberal leadership race to represent what he called "Canada's third element," its immigrant population. See "New Canadian Tries for PM's Job," *TS* (March 13, 1968), 3.
86. Lester Pearson, cited in "Pearson Says Unity Make-or-Break Issue," *TS* (January 22, 1968), 1.
87. Lester Pearson, cited in George Bain, "Mr. Trudeau's Mission," *GM* (January 20, 1968), 6.
88. "Trudeau Visits Premiers in Arranging Conference," *GM* (January 20, 1968), 2. See also Bain, "Mr. Trudeau's Mission," 6; "Trudeau Still Hedges on Leadership Plans," *TS* (January 24, 1968), 1; and Pierre-C. O'Neill, "Trudeau a entrepris en grand secret une tournée des capitales de l'Ouest," *LD* (January 19, 1968), 1.
89. Bain, "Mr. Trudeau's Mission," 6.
90. "Trudeau Visits Premiers," 2.
91. H. Carl Goldenberg, "Notes on Meetings with Provincial Premiers on Constitutional Conference" (January 19–31, 1968), LAC Trudeau Fonds (MG26-020, Volume 22, File 18), 11–19.

92. Pierre Trudeau, cited in "Trudeau Visits Premiers," 2.
93. W.A.C. Bennett, cited ibid.
94. W.A.C. Bennett, cited in "The Old Constitution Good Enough: Bennett," CP (January 26, 1968).
95. "Quebec's Johnson Renews Call for New Constitution," CP (January 27, 1968), 4.
96. Pierre Trudeau, cited in Jack Cahill, "Ontario, Ottawa Reach Accord on Confederation Meeting," *TS* (January 22, 1968), 1, 3.
97. John Robarts, cited ibid.
98. Jean Marchand, cited ibid.
99. Ibid.
100. Pierre Trudeau, cited in Robert Miller, "'Showdown' with Provinces Is Hinted," *TS* (January 24, 1968), 3; and "Trudeau croit encore que la réforme constitutionnelle n'est pas une priorité," *LD* (January 25, 1968), 16.
101. Roy Shields, "All at Once, Canadian Politics Is the Hottest Programming on TV," *TS* (January 31, 1968), 7.
102. Editorial, "Trudeau Won't Be Visiting Munich," *TS* (January 24, 1968), 6.
103. Joey Smallwood, cited in "Smallwood Accepts Ottawa Constitutional Plan," CP (January 26, 1968).
104. Pierre Trudeau, cited in "Trudeau Mum on Leadership as He Meets with Premiers," *TS* (January 26, 1968), 8.
105. Peter C. Newman, "Trudeau Is the Man Who's Got Liberals Excited," *TS* (January 27, 1968), 1–2.
106. "He Still Likes Those Cool Clothes," *TS* (January 29, 1968), 1.
107. Lewis Seale, "Quebec Liberals Wait for a Sign from Trudeau," *GM* (January 19, 1968), 7.
108. Jean Marchand, cited in "Marchand 'Cool-It' Paves Way for Trudeau," *TS* (January 28, 1968), 4.
109. See Walter Gray, "Marchand Not Likely to Run for Leadership," *TS* (January 25, 1968), 4.
110. Jean Marchand, cited in Lewis Seale, "Marchand Tells Quebec Liberals to Avoid Sidetracking," *GM* (January 27, 1968), 11.
111. See Ronald Lebel, "Trudeau to Be the Star of the Show," *TS* (January 25, 1968), 9; and Dominique Clift, "Quebec Liberal Meeting Is Tailored to Launch Trudeau," *TS* (January 26, 1968), 7.
112. "Pour l'abolition de la monarchie," *LD* (January 29, 1968), 1.

113. Pierre Trudeau, cited in Peter C. Newman, "Canada at the Crossroads," *TS* (February 2, 1968), 1, 4.
114. Pierre Trudeau, cited in Peacock, *Journey to Power*, 197.
115. Michel Roy, "Trudeau se déclare prêt à une alliance avec Johnson," *LD* (January 29, 1968), 1, 14. See also Claude Ryan, "Les deux 'événements' du congrès libéral," *LD* (January 29, 1968), 4.
116. Pierre Trudeau, cited in Ronald Lebel, "Strong Ottawa Backed by Quebec Liberal Wing," *GM* (January 29, 1968), 1.
117. Dominique Clift, "Quebec Convention Triumph for Trudeau," *TS* (January 29, 1968), 1, 4.
118. Lewis Seale, "Quebec Liberals Wait for a Sign from Trudeau," *GM* (January 19, 1968), 7.
119. Cited in Peacock, *Journey to Power*, 202.
120. Editorial, "Quebec Liberals Choose Canadianism," *TS* (January 29, 1968), 6.
121. Claude Ryan, "La vieille tentation du Canada anglais," *LD* (February 1, 1968), 4.
122. Daniel Johnson, cited in "Johnson Rejects Separatism," CP (January 30, 1968); "Johnson accuse Trudeau de partisanerie," *LD* (January 30, 1968), 1; editorial, "À propos du 'petit empire' québécois," *LD* (January 31, 1968), 4; and "M. Johnson voit un acte d'agression contre Québec," *LD* (February 1, 1968), 1.
123. See "Sauvé signale le danger d'une candidature du Québec," *LD* (January 6, 1968), 1.
124. Claude Ryan, cited in Val Sears, "How Trudeau Dazzled the Quebec Liberals," *TS* (January 29, 1968), 7.
125. See Newman, "Trudeau Is the Man," 2.
126. Yves Paré, a fifty-two-year-old Montreal businessman with connections to the party's old guard, openly challenged Jean Marchand's hand-picked successor in the race for the presidency of the Quebec Liberal Federation, thirty-two-year-old Claude Frenette. Frenette ended up winning handily, 521 votes to 181, but Paré's stated intention to bring Quebec Liberals in behind Paul Hellyer's leadership bid lingered. See Clift, "Marchand's 'Cool It' Plea," 1, 4.
127. Cited in Seale, "Quebec Liberals Wait," 7. See also Michel Roy, "Trudeau, candidat malgré lui?" *LD* (January 31, 1968), 1.

CHAPTER FIVE: THE SACRED AND THE PROFANE

1. Roy Shields, "All at Once, Canadian Politics Is the Hottest Programming on TV," *TS* (January 31, 1968), 7.
2. Hugh Thomson, "Trudeau et al.," *GM* (February 2, 1968), n.p.
3. Editorial, "All Canada Belongs at This Conference," *GM* (February 1, 1968), 6.
4. Peter C. Newman, "At Stake Next Monday Morning: National Survival," *TS* (February 3, 1968), 1.
5. Lester Pearson, cited in Tom Hazlitt, "Disunited Canada Could Die, PM Warns," *TS* (January 29, 1968), 4. See also Pierre-C. O'Neill, "La conférence de février amorcera le processus de réforme de la constitution," *LD* (January 29, 1968), 1; and Pierre-C. O'Neill, "Que faut-il attendre au juste de cette conférence de la 'dernière chance'?" *LD* (February 2, 1968), 1.
6. Lester Pearson recalled, "I did most of the talking for the federal government but there was one notable occasion when Mr. Trudeau had to intervene in reply to some previous interjections by Daniel Johnson. The forceful impression he made as a strong man and a quick debater, as an agile intellect with firm views, was not limited to the conference hall; his intervention was remarked throughout the country. Until then Mr. Trudeau had little occasion to reveal himself to the public mind except in connection with criminal law reform. As I have noted, we wanted to focus the conference on our proposal for a Bill of Rights entrenched in our constitution (Trudeau was very keen about this and made an admirable case for it)." See Lester B. Pearson, *Mike: The Memoirs of the Right Honourable Lester B. Pearson*, vol. 3, *1957–1968*, ed. John A. Munro and Alex I. Inglis (Toronto: University of Toronto Press, 1975), 257.
7. *Federalism for the Future/Le fédéralisme et l'avenir* (Ottawa: Queen's Printer, 1968), 36.
8. Lester Pearson, cited in "Pearson Affirms Charter of Rights Start of Overhaul of Constitution," *GM* (February 2, 1968), 8.
9. See "Premiers to Study 'Package' on Human Rights," *TS* (February 2, 1968), 3. See also Peter C. Newman, "Canada at the Crossroads," *TS* (February 2, 1968), 1.
10. Pierre Trudeau, cited in Newman, "Canada at the Crossroads," 1, 4.
11. "Draft Bill/Charter of Rights for Canadians" (December 1967), LAC Trudeau Fonds (MG26-020, Volume 22, File 18), 1. See also, from the same collection, "DRAFT Bill of Rights" (December 4, 1967), 1–4.
12. Pierre Trudeau, cited in Newman, "Canada at the Crossroads," 1, 4.
13. Ivan Head, cited in "The Rights of a Canadian," *TS* (February 3, 1968), 7.

14. Cited in "Two-Nation Constitution Is Demanded by Johnson," *TS* (February 5, 1968), 9. See also Michel Roy, "Une constitution entièrement nouvelle associant dans l'égalité les deux peuples fondateurs," *LD* (February 5, 1968), 1; and Frank Howard, "Call for Decentralized Canada," *GM* (January 20, 1968), 1.
15. Daniel Johnson, cited in Dominique Clift, "Johnson Says 'No' to Trudeau Charter of Human Rights," *TS* (February 2, 1968), 1; Michel Roy, "La plus grande discrétion entoure les derniers préparatifs du Québec," *LD* (February 3, 1968), 1; and Claude Ryan, "Les défis de la conférence Ottawa" *LD* (February 3, 1968), 4.
16. Jean-Claude Leclerc, "Abandonner le 'chimère' d'un Canada entièrement bilingue," *LD* (February 2, 1968), 1.
17. Pierre Trudeau, cited in Peter C. Newman, "Trudeau Tells the Star: This Particular Parliament Has Worn Itself Out," *TS* (April 27, 1968), 1.
18. Pearson, *Mike*, 245.
19. Peter C. Newman, "In TV's Goldfish Bowl They're All Good Guys," *TS* (February 7, 1968), 10.
20. Editorial, "Ideal and Realization and the Battle Between," *GM* (February 3, 1968), 6. See also Paul Sauriol, "Comment insérer une charte des droits dans la constitution?" *LD* (February 5, 1968), 4.
21. Lester Pearson, cited in "Reform or Die," *TS* (February 5, 1968), 4.
22. John Robarts, cited in "Robarts: A Hope That Canada Will Be Home for All," *GM* (February 6, 1968), 7.
23. Joey Smallwood, cited in Robert Miller, "Put 'Special Status' to Voters, Joey Dares Johnson," *TS* (February 6, 1968), 11.
24. Daniel Johnson, cited in Jack Cahill, "Monarchy's No Problem, Says Daniel Johnson," *TS* (February 6, 1968), 2.
25. Daniel Johnson, cited in John Saywell, ed., *CAR 1968* (Toronto: University of Toronto Press, 1969), 74. See also "10 propositions du Québec," *LD* (February 6, 1968), 2; and "Le Québec et l'avenir constitutionnel du Canada," *LD* (February 6, 1968), 5.
26. Ross Thatcher, cited in Jack Cahill, "Johnson, Trudeau Clash," *TS* (February 6, 1968), 1, 4. See also Claude Ryan, "Ottawa et Québec: deux mondes," *LD* (February 6, 1968), 4.
27. Ernest Manning, cited in Anthony Westell, "Eight Provinces Back Changes," *GM* (February 6, 1968), 1.

28. Ernest Manning, cited in "Manning: Quebec Should Tell All Now," *GM* (February 6, 1968), 7.
29. Lester Pearson, cited in Cahill, "Johnson, Trudeau Clash," 1, 4. See also "Les autres provinces sympathie, prudence, voire même hostilité," *LD* (February 6, 1968), 1.
30. Pierre Trudeau, cited in Robert Miller, "Trudeau—His Future Tied to Nation's," *TS* (February 6, 1968), 11.
31. Daniel Johnson, cited in Cahill, "Johnson, Trudeau Clash," 1, 4.
32. Daniel Johnson, cited in Westell, "Eight Provinces Back Changes," 1, 4.
33. Pierre Trudeau, cited in Cahill, "Johnson, Trudeau Clash," 1, 4.
34. Daniel Johnson, cited ibid.
35. Pierre Trudeau, cited ibid.; and "Johnson, Trudeau Duel over Powers," *GM* (February 7, 1968), 1, 8.
36. Daniel Johnson, cited in Frank Jones, "Trudeau, Johnson Clash over Special Status for Quebec," *TS* (February 7, 1968), 1.
37. Pierre Trudeau, cited ibid.
38. Daniel Johnson, cited in Cahill,"Johnson, Trudeau Clash," 1, 4. See also Pierre-C. O'Neill, "Journée décisive pour la cause du bilinguisme," *LD* (February 6, 1968), 1; and Michel Roy, "Inévitable, le débat Trudeau-Johnson a éclate hier sur le fond de la crise," *LD* (February 7, 1968), 1.
39. Daniel Johnson, cited in Cahill, "Johnson, Trudeau Clash," 1, 4.
40. Pierre Trudeau, cited ibid.
41. G.I. Smith, cited in "Ringside Says Row 'Good Thing,'" *TS* (February 6, 1968), 10.
42. Ross Thatcher, cited ibid.
43. Pierre Trudeau, cited in "Johnson, Trudeau Duel over Powers," 1, 8.
44. "Statement by the Honourable Pierre Elliott Trudeau, Minister of Justice and Attorney General of Canada, on a Constitutional Charter of Human Rights" (February 6, 1968), LAC Trudeau Fonds (MG26-020, Volume 29, File 14), 1–14. Emphasis in the original, as underscoring. See also "The Constitution," *GM* (February 7, 1968), 7.
45. Saywell, *CAR 1968*, 80. See also Pierre-C. O'Neil, "La déclaration des droits de l'homme se heurte à de vigoureuses oppositions," *LD* (February 7, 1968), 1.
46. Editorial, "Mr. Trudeau's Case Stood," *GM* (February 7, 1968), 6.
47. Anthony Westell, "A Breakthrough to a New Canada?" *GM* (February 8, 1968), 7.
48. Editorial, "Why Did Mr. Trudeau Lose His Nerve?" *TS* (February 7, 1968), 6.

49. Claude Ryan, "Le duel Johnson-Trudeau," *LD* (February 7, 1968), 4.
50. Frank Jones, "Confederation Show Ends," *TS* (February 8, 1968), 12. Political cartoons for the day showed Trudeau and Johnson arm-wrestling and duelling with pistols.
51. Daniel Johnson, cited in "Johnson, Trudeau Duel over Powers," 1, 8.
52. Vincent Prince, "Les provinces sont unanimes sur les droits des minorités," *LD* (February 8, 1968), 1.
53. Cited in Saywell, *CAR 1968*, 78–82. For earlier "secret" drafts from the federal government delegation, see "Communiqué of the Constitutional Conference 1968, February 7, 1968," LAC Trudeau Fonds (MG26-020, Volume 22, File 17), 1–8.
54. Anthony Westell and Lewis Seale, "11 Leaders Agree on Means to Reshape Confederation," *GM* (February 8, 1968), 1, 8. See also Michel Roy, "Pearson et Johnson sont d'accord: Très bon départ et grand déblocage," *LD* (February 8, 1968), 1.
55. Editorial, "A Constitutional Design Lies in Pieces," *TS* (February 8, 1968), 6.
56. Editorial, "A Long Second Step," *GM* (February 8, 1968), 6.
57. Daniel Johnson, cited in Michael Best, "How Lester Pearson Met His Greatest Challenge," *TS* (February 8, 1968), 7.
58. Lester Pearson, cited in Westell and Seale, "11 Leaders Agree," 1, 8. "I remember the February 1968 conference with a good deal of satisfaction," Pearson later recalled. "I think that this was a good meeting and that the main paper on the federal approach to constitutional change was a fine presentation. The process has, of course, continued, although in the years since I retired it has lost much of its impetus. I regret that very much. Constitutional change can be the means to a stronger unity." See Pearson, *Mike,* 258.
59. Daniel Johnson, cited in Westell and Seale, "11 Leaders Agree," 1, 8; and Dominique Clift, "Johnson Hails Victory for 'French Homeland Quebec,'" *TS* (February 8, 1968), 12.
60. Daniel Johnson, cited in Clift, "Johnson Hails Victory," 12. See also Claude Ryan, "Bilan de la conférence d'Ottawa," *LD* (February 8, 1968), 4; and Vincent Prince, "Le rôle de M. Johnson à la conférence d'Ottawa," *LD* (February 12, 1968), 4.
61. "René Lévesque: La conférence constitutionnel, l'amorce d'une vaste supercherie où les vrais intérêts du Québec n'étaient pas représentés," *LD* (February 12, 1968), 6.
62. Roy Shields, "Networks Covered in Glory," *TS* (February 6, 1968), 20. The Trudeau–Lévesque epic would be immortalized in Donald Brittain's 1978 NFB series *The Champions*.

63. Daniel Johnson, cited in "Johnson Opposes Forcing Provinces to Turn Bilingual," *TS* (February 8, 1968), 12.
64. Pierre Trudeau, cited in Frank Jones, "Trudeau Still Wavering on Seeking Leadership," *TS* (February 8, 1968), 13.
65. Bruce West, "A Winner?" *GM* (February 8, 1968), 5.
66. Paul Fox, "Quebec: From Colony to Nation," *TS* (February 10, 1968), 35.
67. Abraham Rotstein, cited in Saywell, *CAR 1968, 78*–82. Tory president Dalton Camp made the same point, making the front pages of the Quebec press. See, for example, "Camp: Trudeau ne veut pas admettre l'existence d'une crise québécoise," *LD* (February 15, 1968), 2.
68. J.L. Granatstein and Peter Oliver, "Will History Repeat Itself?" *GM* (February 14, 1968), 7. See also Ramsay Cook, "Case for Trudeau," *GM* (February 16, 1968), 6; and Michel Roy, "À Ottawa, on n'est pas mécontent de l'attitude prise par M. Trudeau," *LD* (February 9, 1968), 1.
69. Pierre Trudeau, cited in "Debate Defines Gap," *GM* (February 7, 1968), 8.
70. Pierre Trudeau, "1968: Trudeau Says He's Ready to Write a 'New' Contituition," interview, CBC (February 8, 1968), https://www.youtube.com/watch?v=A2mRv_6T9YQ.

CHAPTER SIX: NOW YOU'RE STUCK WITH ME

1. Lester Pearson, cited in "Marchand Not in Running for Leadership: Pearson," *TS* (February 8, 1968), 12.
2. Donald S. Macdonald, cited in "Trudeau Comes Here for 3-Hour Blitz," *TS* (February 9, 1968), 1. See also Donald Newman, "Metro Liberals Start Draft-Trudeau Drive," *GM* (February 1, 1968), 1.
3. Pierre Trudeau, cited in Geoffrey Stevens, "Still Hedging, But Trudeau Steals Show," *GM* (February 10, 1968), 1.
4. Claude Ryan, "Une pétition canadienne-français en faveur de M. Trudeau," *LD* (February 15, 1968), 4. See also "Une pétition du Québec invite Trudeau à poser sa candidature," *LD* (February 15, 1968), 7.
5. Andrew Szende, "The Political Science Experts Agree Almost to a Man 'Trudeau Is for Us,'" *TS* (February 12, 1968), 7.
6. See Judith McKenzie, *Pauline Jewett: A Passion for Canada* (Montreal: McGill-Queen's University Press, 1999), 75–76.
7. Pauline Jewett, cited in Lotta Dempsey, "What Dr. Pauline Jewett Thinks of Pierre Elliott Trudeau," *TS* (April 5, 1968), 57.

8. Ramsay Cook, *The Teeth of Time: Remembering Pierre Elliott Trudeau* (Montreal: McGill-Queen's University Press, 2006), 45–51. See also "Les Libéraux de l'Ontario font une réception enthousiaste à Trudeau," *LD* (February 10, 1968), 1.
9. Cited in Peter Regenstreif, "Trudeau Candidacy Would Further Split Ontario Delegates," *TS* (February 12, 1968), 1, 13.
10. Pierre Trudeau, cited in Val Sears, "Trudeau Wows 'Em," *TS* (February 10, 1968), 11; and "M. Trudeau fera connaître sa décision cette semaine," *LD* (February 14, 1968), 1.
11. Cook, *The Teeth of Time*, 54–55.
12. Jack Cahill, "Liberals Make It a 'Love-in' for Pierre Trudeau," *TS* (February 10, 1968), 1, 11. See also Stevens, "Still Hedging," 1.
13. Editorial, "Not Sudden, Not a Messiah," *GM* (February 9, 1968), 6.
14. Claude Ryan, "M. Trudeau suivra-t-il le courant?" *LD* (February 10, 1968), 4.
15. Cited in Irwin Block, "Wine, Punch, Coffee—All Upstaged by Suite That Didn't Exist," *TS* (February 10, 1968), 3; and Stevens, "Still Hedging," 1.
16. Cited in Val Sears, "The Exasperating Non-Runner Trudeau," *TS* (February 12, 1968), 7.
17. Anthony Westell, "Is Charisma the Key to Solving the Trudeau Mystery?" *GM* (February 12, 1968), 7. See also G. J. Szablowski, "Les raisons d'une certaine opposition à la candidature de M. Trudeau," *LD* (February 15, 1968), 5.
18. Pierre Trudeau, cited in Lewis Seale, "Trudeau Wavers over Bidding for Leadership," *GM* (February 16, 1968), 1.
19. Cited in George Radwanski, *Trudeau* (Toronto: Macmillan, 1978), 101.
20. Marc Lalonde, cited ibid.
21. Pierre Trudeau, cited in "Trudeau to Quebec: Quit Worrying about Rights, Improve Lousy French," *TS* (February 14, 1968), 68.
22. Pierre Trudeau, cited ibid.; Robert McKenzie, "Trudeau in Hot Water," *TS* (February 17, 1968), 11; "Trudeau: À Québec d'améliorer d'abord son 'mauvais français,'" *LD* (February 15, 1968), 2; and "Le français pouilleux: Trudeau s'explique," *LD* (February 16, 1968), 1.
23. Pierre Trudeau, cited in Radwanski, *Trudeau*, 40.
24. René Lévesque, cited in McKenzie, "Trudeau in Hot Water," 11; and "Lévesque: Trudeau continue à mépriser un peuple qu'il n'a jamais représenté," *LD* (February 16, 1968), 9.

25. Daniel Johnson, cited in McKenzie, "Trudeau in Hot Water," 11.
26. Jean-Noël Tremblay, cited in "Tremblay Fires Verbal Salvo at Trudeau," CP (February 16, 1968).
27. Pierre Trudeau, cited in Seale, "Trudeau Wavers over Bidding," 1; Robert Miller, "Now Trudeau Makes It Official," *TS* (February 16, 1968), 1; and Pierre-C. O'Neill, "Trudeau connaîtra aujourd'hui ses appuis réels au sien du caucus de députés du Québec," *LD* (February 15, 1968), 1.
28. Lewis Seale, "23 Quebec Liberals Sign Trudeau Pact," *GM* (March 20, 1968), 8.
29. Pierre Trudeau, cited in Anthony Westell and Geoffrey Stevens, "What Made Trudeau Decide to Run," *GM* (February 17, 1968), 7; and Pierre-C. O'Neill, "Trudeau se présente comme antinationaliste et homme de gauche," *LD* (February 17, 1968), 1.
30. Pierre Elliott Trudeau, *Memoirs* (Toronto: McClelland & Stewart, 1993), 87–88.
31. Claude Ryan, "Les ambiguïtés de la candidature de M. Trudeau," *LD* (February 17, 1968), 4. See also Albert Lévesque, "Les sophismes de M. Trudeau," *LD* (February 20, 1968), 5.
32. Editorial, "Is Canada Ready for Pierre Trudeau?" *TS* (February 17, 1968), 6.
33. Editorial, "And Now, the Real Trudeau?" *GM* (February 17, 1968), 6.
34. Patricia Jolivet, cited in Jack Cahill, "Time for Gamble on Trudeau," *TS* (February 23, 1968), 3.
35. Szablowski, "Les raisons d'une certaine opposition," 5.
36. Cited in Michael Best, "Hellyer Is Prairies' Favourite," *TS* (February 26, 1968), 7.
37. For a taste of this voluminous literature, see George Grant, *Lament for a Nation: The Defeat of Canadian Nationalism* (Toronto: McClelland & Stewart, 1965); Phillip Resnick, *The Land of Cain: Class and Nationalism in English Canada, 1945–1975* (Vancouver: New Star Books, 1977); James Laxer and Robert Laxer, *The Liberal Idea of Canada: Pierre Trudeau and the Question of Canada's Survival* (Toronto: Lorimer, 1977); Sylvia Bashevkin, *True Patriot Love: The Politics of Canadian Nationalism* (Toronto: Oxford University Press, 1991); and Stephen Clarkson, *Uncle Sam and Us: Globalization, Neoconservatism and the Canadian State* (Toronto: University of Toronto Press, 2002).
38. Pierre Trudeau, cited in "Trudeau Says Gordon Nationalism Is Not the Answer," *TS* (February 16, 1968), 1.
39. Walter Gordon, cited in Geoffrey Stevens, "Liberals Kick Fringe Candidates," *TS* (March 26, 1968), 8.

40. Pierre Trudeau, cited in Jack Cahill, "Trudeau No Gordon Disciple," *TS* (March 28, 1968), 8.
41. Pierre Trudeau, cited in "Opposed 1939 War, Trudeau Admits," *GM* (March 30, 1968), 4.
42. See Lewis Seale, "Five Key Men," *GM* (February 17, 1968), 1; and editorial "Liberals Pick Their Man," *VS* (April 8, 1968), 4.
43. Lester B. Pearson. *Mike: The Memoirs of the Right Honourable Lester B. Pearson*, vol. 3, *1957–1968*, ed. John A. Munro and Alex I. Inglis (Toronto: University of Toronto Press, 1975), 316.
44. Ibid., 317.
45. Peter C. Newman, *A Nation Divided: Canada and the Coming of Pierre Trudeau* (New York: Knopf, 1969), 451–53.
46. Editorial, "All Present and Incorrect," *GM* (February 29, 1968), 6.
47. Peter C. Newman, "Leadership and the Crisis," *TS* (February 24, 1968), 1.
48. Mitchell Sharp was the biggest loser in the non-confidence episode, since the defeat of the tax bill had occurred on his watch. See editorial, "Now, Alas, a New Blunder," *GM* (March 30, 1968), 7.
49. "Most Canadians Still Want Martin—But Trudeau Is Gaining," *TS* (February 28, 1968), 1.
50. "Trudeau, Winters Top Star's Poll," *TS* (March 2, 1968), 1.
51. Pierre Trudeau, cited in "Trudeau Continues Feud with Johnson," *GM* (March 7, 1968), 9.
52. See John Saywell, ed., *CAR 1968* (Toronto: University of Toronto Press, 1969), 24; and Stephen Clarkson, *The Big Red Machine: How the Liberal Party Dominates Canadian Politics* (Vancouver: UBC Press, 2005), 21.
53. Eric Kierans, cited in Lewis Seale, "One Nation or Two?" *GM* (March 30, 1968), 7.
54. John Turner, cited in Donald Newman, "Quebec Different, Turner Says," *GM* (February 20, 1968), 5.
55. Pierre Trudeau, cited in Don Peacock, *Journey to Power* (Toronto: Ryerson, 1968), 254–56.
56. Robert McKenzie, "Trudeau Hits Gimmicks in Quebec Power Pitch," *TS* (March 2, 1968), 1.
57. Pierre Trudeau, cited ibid.
58. Pierre Trudeau, cited in Robert McKenzie, "Coolest Figure in the Blinding TV Lights," *TS* (March 2, 1968), 37; "Trudeau: En m'attaquant Johnson

m'aide à gagner," *LD* (March 4, 1968), 1; and Vincent Prince, "Lutte à la direction du parti libéral ou guérilla entre MM. Johnson et Trudeau," *LD* (March 7, 1968), 4.

59. Pierre Trudeau, cited in McKenzie, "Trudeau Hits Gimmicks," 1.
60. Pierre Trudeau, cited in McKenzie, "Coolest Figure," 37.
61. Pierre Trudeau, cited in Donald Newman, "Trudeau Wants Government Powers Divided on Basis of Efficiency," *GM* (March 4, 1968), 11.
62. Pierre Trudeau, cited in "Trudeau Promises Sandal Sacrifice," CP (March 9, 1968).
63. Pierre Trudeau, cited in Frank Jones, "Timmins Gives Trudeau Biggest-Ever Turnout," *TS* (March 25, 1968), 8.
64. "Trudeau Would Cut NATO Role," *GM* (March 14, 1968), 1.
65. Pierre Trudeau, cited in "Resolve Often Lacking, Trudeau Says," *TS* (March 26, 1968), 8.
66. David Croll, "Trudeau Is a Winner and the Best Man for Canada," *TS* (March 9, 1968), 6.
67. Paul Fox, "Trudeau: The Eternal Way Is Not Enough," *TS* (March 9, 1968), 27.
68. See, for example, Tom Buston, "Unity Is THE Issue in the Leadership Race," *TS* (March 29, 1968), 7.
69. Seale, "One Nation or Two?" 7.
70. Paul Hellyer, cited ibid.
71. Paul Martin, cited in Tom Hazlitt, "Martin Takes Step toward Special Status for Quebec," *TS* (April 1, 1968), 8.
72. Mitchell Sharp, cited in Seale, "One Nation or Two?" 7; and "Sharp: Les droits linguistiques ne suffisent plus au Québec," *LD* (March 26, 1968), 1. See also "Kierans: Les propos de Trudeau sur les langues officielles sont une 'perversion' de la réalité," *LD* (March 27, 1968), 1; and Mitchell Sharp, "La crise canadienne, ses deux dimensions essentielles," *LD* (March 27, 1968), 5.
73. Editorial, "The Course That Takes Guts," *GM* (March 28, 1968), 6. See also "Les libéraux restent divises sur la façon de mener à bien la reforme constitutionnelle," *LD* (April 5, 1968), 1.
74. John Turner, "Turner Tackles Trudeau's Quebec Policies—By Innuendo," *TS* (March 29, 1968), 8; and Pierre-C. O'Neill, "Turner: On pourrait prévoir une positon spéciale pour le Québec," *LD* (March 16, 1968), 1.
75. Cited in Robert McKenzie, "Quebec Students Tell Trudeau He's 'Isolated,'" *TS* (March 27, 1968), 8.

76. See Dominique Clift, "To the French-Canadian Press Trudeau Is as Objectionable as Diefenbaker," *TS* (March 21, 1968), 10.
77. Gilles Lesage, "Johnson reproche à Trudeau d'empoisonner l'atmosphère en ressuscitant de vieux mythes," *LD* (February 26, 1968), 1, 14.
78. Pierre Trudeau, cited in Max Nemni and Monique Nemni, *Trudeau Transformed: The Shaping of a Statesman*, trans. George Tombs (Toronto: McClelland & Stewart, 2011), 340. See also "Most Excitement Is in Federalism, Not in Separatism, Trudeau Says," *GM* (April 3, 1968), 8; and "Le sénateur Lamontagne appuie Trudeau dont il dit partager 'en gros' les positions constitutionnelles," *LD* (March 29, 1968), 1.
79. Laurier LaPierre, "M. Trudeau reste un politicien traditionaliste, donc dangereux," *LD* (April 5, 1968), 4.
80. Elmer Sopha, cited in Frank Jones, "Timmins Gives Trudeau Biggest-Ever Turnout," *TS* (March 25, 1968), 8.
81. Elmer Sopha, cited in "Sopha Disenchanted by Trudeau Policy," *TS* (March 29, 1968), 4.
82. Peter Regenstreif, "The Delegates Say It's Trudeau to Win," *TS* (March 23, 1968), 1.
83. Michael Best, "Winters' Pal Joey Leaves Him Stunned," *TS* (April 4, 1968), 4.
84. Clyde Batten, cited in Earl McRae, "MacEachen Scoffs at 'Trudeau Deal,'" *TS* (March 26, 1968), 9.
85. Pierre Trudeau, cited in Jack Cahill, "Voters Who Elected Trudeau Jump on Leadership Wagon," *TS* (March 29, 1968), 8.
86. Pierre Trudeau, cited ibid.
87. Huguette Marleau, cited in William Johnson, "Trudeau No Charmer to Woman Opponent," *GM* (June 6, 1968), 11.
88. Suzanne Morrison, "Businessmen, Teeny-Boppers—They All Love Pierre," *TS* (March 30, 1968), 39.
89. See Radwanski, *Trudeau*, 104.
90. Editorial, "Mr. Trudeau's Charm Is Elusive," *TS* (March 5, 1968), 6.
91. Peter C. Newman, "Everybody Wants to Know: What IS It about Trudeau?" *TS* (April 5, 1968), 11; and Newman, "The Trudeau Magic," *TS Evening Edition* (April 5, 1968), 11.
92. Cited in "Trudeau: They All Like Him," *TS* (March 18, 1968), 3.
93. Editorial, "Three Candidates of Special Merit," *GM* (April 3, 1968), 6.
94. Claude Ryan, "Les trois candidats les plus marquants," *LD* (April 3, 1968), 4; and Claude Ryan, "Qui doit être l'élu?" *LD* (April 4, 1968), 4.

95. Editorial, "Trudeau: The Best Choice for Canada," *TS* (March 28, 1968), 6. See also editorial, "Trudeau Is a Risky Choice—But Who Isn't?" *TS* (April 3, 1968), 6.
96. Dalton Camp, cited in Geoffrey Stevens, *Stanfield* (Toronto: McClelland & Stewart, 1973), 213.
97. "CBC Poll Gives Trudeau a Big Lead," CP (April 1, 1968), 8; and Pierre-C. O'Neill and Michel Roy, "Trudeau domine toujours, et de loin, le peloton des aspirants," *LD* (April 6, 1968), 1.
98. CIPO poll, "Most Canadians Want a Young English PM," *TS* (March 20, 1968), 7.

CHAPTER SEVEN: WE WANT TRUDEAU!

1. Mitchell Sharp, cited in "Sharp Withdraws and Supports Trudeau," *TS* (April 3, 1968), 1.
2. Pierre-C. O'Neill and Michel Roy, "Trudeau paraît maintenant invincible," *LD* (April 4, 1968), 1.
3. Lawrence Martin, *Chrétien*, vol. 1, *The Will to Win* (Toronto: Lester, 1995), 185.
4. Cited in Lewis Seale, "First-Ballot Victory a Happy Thought for Trudeau," *GM* (April 4, 1968), 37.
5. Pierre Trudeau, cited in "Convention Win for Trudeau Expected," *GM* (April 4, 1968), 8.
6. Pierre Trudeau, cited in George Radwanski, *Trudeau* (Toronto: Macmillan, 1978), 113.
7. Cited in Don Peacock, *Journey to Power* (Toronto: Ryerson, 1968), 278.
8. Peter C. Newman, "Sharp Puts the Establishment behind Trudeau," *TS* (April 4, 1968), 1. See also "Hellyer Camp Claims 60 Votes of Former Sharp Supporters," CP (April 4, 1968).
9. Editorial, "A Man Who Can Lead," *GM* (April 4, 1968), 6.
10. Pierre Trudeau, cited in Frank Jones, "Trudeau on Social Welfare: 'Enough of This Free Stuff,'" *TS* (April 4, 1968), 1.
11. Jack McArthur, "Into the Future with Trudeau and the Means Test," *TS* (April 8, 1968), 30.
12. John Turner, cited in Dominique Clift, "Trudeau Stands Apart from the Pack," *TS* (April 5, 1968), 11; and John Turner, "Pour un fédéralisme adapté aux besoin et conditions actuelles," *LD* (April 6, 1968), 4.
13. Paul Hellyer, cited in Clift, "Trudeau Stands Apart," 11.
14. Pierre Trudeau, cited ibid.

15. Lester Pearson, cited in Val Sears, "Separate Quebec Means End of Canada: Pearson," *TS* (April 5, 1968), 1, 12.
16. Vincent Prince, "M. Pearson aura été l'un des grands promoteurs de l'unité nationale," *LD* (April 4, 1968), 4.
17. On the 124 riots that erupted in the wake of King's murder, see Alyssa Ribeiro, "'A Period of Turmoil': Pittsburgh's April 1968 Riots and Their Aftermath," *Journal of Urban History* 39, 2 (2012): 147.
18. Editorial, "The Greatest Moral Leader of Our time," *TS* (April 5, 1968), 6; and Paul Sauriol, "Devant la mort tragique du pasteur Luther King," *LD* (April 6, 1968), 4.
19. Joseph Boskin, "The Revolt of the Urban Ghettos, 1964–1967," *Annals of the American Academy of Political and Social Science* 382 (March 1969): 1–14. See also Marvin E. Wolfgang, "Violence U.S.A.: Riots and Crime," *Crime and Delinquency* 14, 4 (October 1968): 289–305; and Terry Ann Knopf, "Race, Riots and Reporting," *Journal of Black Studies* 4, 3 (March 1975): 303–327.
20. See, for example, the front page of the *Toronto Star* (February 1, 1968).
21. Geoffrey Stevens, "Vote on Vietnam Bombs to Be Considered by PM," *GM* (March 9, 1968), 4.
22. Editorial, "A Country Divided," *GM* (March 12, 1968), 6. See also "La guerre de Sécession américaine pourrait ne pas être la dernière," *LS* (April 8, 1968), 16.
23. Editorial, "A Time of Danger: The Right Man to Lead Canada," *OC* (April 6, 1968), 6. See also Austin C. Clarke, "Two Nations the End Result of Black Power," *TS* (May 14, 1968), 7.
24. Maxwell Cohen, "How Canada Can Export 'Just Society,'" *TS* (May 17, 1968), 7.
25. Paul Martin, cited in "Martin Says He's the Man in Unity Crisis," *TS* (April 6, 1968), 10.
26. Paul Hellyer, cited in "Hellyer Gets His Biggest Cheer When He Mentions Unification," *GM* (April 6, 1968), 10.
27. Eric Kierans, cited in Irwin Block, "Kierans Wants New Role for Canada," *TS* (April 6, 1968), 10.
28. Pierre Trudeau, cited in "Trudeau Meets Critics of His Swinger Image," *GM* (April 6, 1968), 10.
29. Editorial, "A Declaration of Faith," *GM* (April 6, 1968), 6. See also "Trudeau Ignites Delegate Spark," *VS* (April 6, 1968), 1–2; Allan Fotheringham, "Trudeau, Turner, Big Joe Put On a Really Big Show," *VS* (April 6, 1968), 3; "Trudeau Took

Ovation Title," *CH* (April 6, 1968), 1; and "Strongest Applause Crests Trudeau's Bid for Top Job," *CH* (April 6, 1968), 6.

30. Barney Danson, *Not Bad for a Sergeant* (Toronto: Dundurn, 2006), 83.
31. John Turner, cited in Sally Barnes, "Turner Warns of Rashness," *TS* (April 6, 1968), 10.
32. *Election Bulletin* (May 27, 1968), LAC Trudeau Fonds (MG26-020, Volume 20, File 13), 1.
33. Frank Jones, "From 8 to 8," *TS* (April 8, 1968), 11.
34. Pierre Trudeau, cited in Lewis Seale, "Humorous, Challenging in Victory, Trudeau Calls for Just Society," *GM* (April 8, 1968), 8.
35. Paul Martin, cited in Peacock, *Journey to Power*, 293. See also Mario Cardinal, "Dès le premier tour, Martin sut que c'était la fin . . ." *LS* (April 8, 1968), 16.
36. Jean Marchand, cited in Jones, "From 8 to 8," 11.
37. Danson, *Not Bad for a Sergeant*, 84.
38. Lester B. Pearson, *Mike: The Memoirs of the Right Honourable Lester B. Pearson*, vol. 3, *1957–1968*, ed. John A. Munro and Alex I. Inglis (Toronto: University of Toronto Press, 1975), 329.
39. Paul Martin, *Hell or High Water: My Life in and out of Politics* (Toronto: McClelland & Stewart, 2008), 53–54.
40. Ron MacDonald, "Nova Scotians Will Try to Stop Trudeau," *HCH* (April 6, 1968), 1.
41. Judy LaMarsh, cited in Jack Cahill, "Go Now Paul—Don't Make a Trudeau," *TS* (April 18, 1968), 12.
42. Bob Cohen, "Turner Determined to the End That There Would Be No Deals," *WT* (April 8, 1968), 3.
43. Pearson, *Mike*, 329.
44. Ramsay Cook, *The Teeth of Time: Remembering Pierre Elliott Trudeau* (Montreal: McGill-Queen's University Press, 2006), 66.
45. "PET 1968," (April 6, 1968), https://www.youtube.com/watch?v=s0VhEOXrpmE; Tim Creery, "Along the Way, Oranges, Grapes and an Unfailing Wit," *WT* (April 8, 1968), 5.
46. "Nichol Ignored Bomb Scare," *HCH* (April 8, 1968), 4.
47. Cited in Eric Dennis, "Trudeau to Remodel Image before Fighting Election," *HCH* (April 8, 1968), 1; and John Brehl, "Trudeau's Aim: A Just Society," *TS* (April 8, 1968), 1.
48. Pierre Trudeau, cited in Geoffrey Stevens, "PM Shows Trudeau the Ropes," *GM* (April 9, 1968), 1.

49. Pierre Trudeau, cited in "Domain Shown Trudeau," *TS* (April 9, 1968), 4.
50. Editorial, "Pierre Trudeau: A Promise of Excellence," *TS* (April 8, 1968), 6. See also Frank Howard, "Trudeau's Win Gives New Hope to Quebec's Federalists," *TS* (April 9, 1968), 7.
51. Editorial, "The New Liberal Leader," *HCH* (April 8, 1968), 3; "Who Is He?" *WT* (April 8, 1968), 1; editorial, "The Promise of Trudeau," *WT* (April 8, 1968), 3; editorial, "A 'Just' Distribution," *HCH* (April 18, 1968), 4; editorial, "On to Trudeau's 'Just Society,'" *OC* (April 8, 1968), 6; Charles Lynch, "New Foreign Policy Certain," *CH* (April 8, 1968), 1; Ian MacDonald, "Trudeau, Pearson Discuss Handover of PM's Post," *VS* (April 8, 1968), 1; and Allan Fotheringham, "Liberal Right Wingers Pushed into Exile," *VS* (April 8, 1968), 1.
52. Editorial, "New Prime Minister," *CH* (April 8, 1968), 6. See also John Walker, "Trudeau's Triumph: How He Achieved It," *OC* (April 8, 1968), 7; Ian MacDonald, "No Labels, No Radicalism: Trudeau's a Pragmatist," *VS* (April 8, 1968), 13; J.R. Walker, "Trudeau: Unsightly Problems, Glorious Chance," *CH* (April 9, 1968), 8; George Radwanski, "Enter a Political Phenomenon," *MG* (April 8, 1968), 7; and editorial, "Freedom of Choice Is Restored to Canadians," *SDR* (April 8, 1968), 4.
53. Lucien Bouchard, "Lesage et Johnson attendront que Trudeau pose des actes avant de porter un jugement," *AC* (April 9, 1968), 18.
54. René Lévesque, "Trudeau commence déjà à patiner," *LP* (April 8, 1968), 17; and Gilles Lesage, "Selon René Lévesque: Trudeau offre aux Québécois une 'joyeuse noyade' minoritaire," *LD* (April 11, 1968), 3.
55. Editorial, "Héraut d'une nouvelle ère," *LP* (April 8, 1968), 4. See also Marcel Desjardins, "Trudeau n'a pas balayé le congrès, il a bien mérité sa victoire," *LD* (April 8, 1968), 3; and "Le Canada doit devenir une société de justice (Trudeau)," *AC* (April 8, 1968), 3.
56. Claude Ryan, "Le nouveau chef libéral," *LD* (April 8, 1968), 4. See also editorial, "La victoire de Trudeau," *LS* (April 8, 1968), 4; Michel Roy, "Y a-t-il nouveau Pierre Elliott Trudeau?" *LD* (April 8, 1968), 8; Gilles Lesage, "Lesage croit Trudeau capable de 'souplesse,'" *LD* (April 9, 1968), 1; "Ce que pense la presse de l'élection de M. Trudeau," *LA* (April 9, 1968), 5.
57. "Trudeau to Seek a 'Just Society'; Next Leader of Canada Also Pledges Work for Unity," *NYT* (April 8, 1968), 9. See also Jay Walz, "Trudeau Elected to Pearson Post; French-Canadian, Minister of Justice, Is Chosen by Liberals to Head Party,"

NYT (April 7, 1968), 1; and "Canada's Next Prime Minister Pierre Elliott Trudeau," *NYT* (April 8, 1968), 8.

58. Cited in Bruce MacDonald, "Pierre the Paradox Grabs the Headlines," *GM* (April 20, 1968), 9.
59. Cited ibid.
60. Keith Spicer, "Strange He Is, but He Is Not a Stranger," *GM* (April 23, 1968), 7.
61. Editorial, "The Enigma That Survived a Campaign," *GM* (April 8, 1968), 6. See also Marcel Pépin, "Pas d'élections hâtives," *LD* (April 8, 1968), 1; "Trudeau Begins New Era, Won't Call Early Election," *WT* (April 8, 1968), 1; and "M. Trudeau est salué comme l'homme qui annonce des changements profonds," *LD* (April 9, 1968), 2.

CHAPTER EIGHT: TELLING IT LIKE IT IS

1. Lester B. Pearson, *Mike: The Memoirs of the Right Honourable Lester B. Pearson*, vol. 3, *1957–1968*, ed. John A. Munro and Alex I. Inglis (Toronto: University of Toronto Press, 1975), 331.
2. Pierre Trudeau, cited in Ian MacDonald, "Trudeau Picks Caretaker Government," *VS* (April 20, 1968), 1; Greg Connolley, "PM Trudeau Ponders Snap June 17 Vote," *OC* (April 20, 1968), 1; and Arthur Blakely, "Trudeau Cabinet Leans Heavily towards Quebec," *MG* (April 22, 1968), 1.
3. Cited in Peter C. Newman, "Trudeau Plans Early Reshuffle of Cabinet," *TS* (April 24, 1968), 7.
4. Pearson, *Mike*, 331–32.
5. Pierre Trudeau, *Hansard* (April 23, 1968), 8145.
6. Pearson, *Mike*, 332.
7. Ibid.
8. Pierre Trudeau, cited in "Trudeau's Opening Gun," *TS* (April 24, 1968), 7.
9. Pierre Trudeau, cited in Peter C. Newman, "Trudeau Tells the Star: This Particular Parliament Has Worn Itself Out," *TS* (April 27, 1968), 1; Peter C. Newman, "Trudeau: I Have a Feeling for Canada," *TS* (April 29, 1968), 1, 4; and "Pourquoi des élections? M. Trudeau s'explique," *LD* (April 24, 1968), 1.
10. Linda Cooper, cited in Robert Miller, "Kissing Pierre," *TS* (April 24, 1968), 8.
11. Robert Stanfield, cited in "Statement by Stanfield," CP (April 24, 1968), 8
12. Robert Stanfield, cited in Alastair Dow, "Stanfield on PM: No Record, No Policy, No Proof of Ability," *TS* (April 24, 1968), 1; and "Stanfield Would 'Dearly Love' to Fight PM," *HCH* (April 23, 1968), 1.

13. Robert Stanfield, cited in Roger Newman, "No Stand on Quebec by Stanfield," *GM* (August 2, 1967), 25.
14. Robert Stanfield, cited in Peter C. Newman, "Stanfield: I Want a Canada with a Sense of Purpose," *TS* (May 6, 1968), 7; and "Stanfield Steers Cautious Course over Special Status for Quebec," *GM* (May 9, 1968), 8.
15. Jack McArthur, "Trudeau's Still the Talented Amateur, Stanfield Still Fuzzy," *TS* (May 8, 1968), 15.
16. Dominique Clift, "Fear of Lévesque Sidelines Premier," *TS* (April 24, 1968), 1.
17. "Le Canada accuse le Gabon d'avoir agi contre le droit international," *LD* (March 5, 1968), 1.
18. Pierre Trudeau, cited in John Saywell, ed., *CAR 1968* (Toronto: University of Toronto Press, 1969), 45–47.
19. Anthony Westell, "Book Details Ottawa Position on Quebec International Role," *GM* (May 9, 1968), 9; and "Le Canada ne peut avoir qu'un seul porte-parole à l'étranger," *LD* (May 9, 1968), 1.
20. "PM Makes Quebec Aims an Issue," *GM* (May 9, 1968), 1; and Alastair Dow, "Trudeau Challenges Quebec's Aims in Foreign Affairs," *TS* (May 9, 1968), 1.
21. Editorial, "Where Do the Tories Stand?" *GM* (May 10, 1968), 6; and editorial, "Can't Have It Both Ways," *GM* (May 14, 1968), 6.
22. See Anthony Westell, "Stanfield Says Prime Minister Escalating Quebec Conflict," *GM* (May 10, 1968), 11.
23. Tommy Douglas, cited in "Douglas Assails PM's Tactics in Quebec," *GM* (May 11, 1968), 12.
24. Marcel Faribault, cited in Claude Ryan, "M. Marcel Faribault ou l'autre volet de la pensée fédérale canadienne-française," *LD* (May 7, 1968), 4, published in English as "Two French-Canadian Views of Federalism," *GM* (May 10, 1968), 7.
25. "M. Faribault prédit 35 sièges aux conservateurs au Québec," *LD* (May 21, 1968), 1; Pierre-C. O'Neill, "Le Canada menacé doit revenir à ses valeurs essentielles: Faribault," *LD* (May 22, 1968), 1; and "Faribault est le symbole d'une réconciliation qui seule préservera l'unité," *LD* (May 22, 1968), 1.
26. See Tom Hazlitt, "Faribault Brings New Strength to Stanfield in Quebec," *TS* (May 15, 1968), 25.
27. Tommy Douglas, cited in Saywell, *CAR 1968*, 33. See also "Douglas: Trudeau a divisé le pays comme il ne l'a jamais été avant!" *LD* (June 21, 1968), 1.

28. Charles Taylor, cited in "Trudeau 'Aura' Won't Last, Says a Pal," *TS* (April 24, 1968), 8. See also "Le NDP et le statut particulier pour le Québec," *LD* (April 25, 1968), 1; and editorial, "Le NDP et le statut particulier," *LD* (April 26, 1968), 4.
29. "Cliche Demands Special Status for Quebec," *GM* (May 14, 1968), 8; and "Trudeau 'Obstacle to Unity': Cliche," *TS* (June 13, 1968), 8.
30. Pierre Trudeau, cited in "Johnson ne prendra pas le risque d'une humiliante défaite: Trudeau," *LD* (May 16, 1968), 1.
31. Pierre Trudeau, cited in Don Peacock, *Journey to Power* (Toronto: Ryerson, 1968), 358.
32. Réal Caouette, cited in "Caouette: Cessons donc de blâmer les autres et prenons nos responsabilités," *LD* (May 14, 1968), 7.
33. See Peter Regenstreif, "Rural Quebec Voters Wary of Trudeau," *TS* (May 28, 1968), 7.
34. Ramsay Cook, *The Teeth of Time: Remembering Pierre Elliott Trudeau* (Montreal: McGill-Queen's University Press, 2006), 70.
35. *Liberal Candidates' Handbook 1968 General Election*, LAC Trudeau Fonds (MG26-020, Volume 30, File 13).
36. See "Liberals, PCs Unveil Major Policy Stands," *GM* (June 1, 1968), 1; and Geoffrey Stevens, "Liberal Candidates Get Little Red Book on Instant Policy," *GM* (June 1, 1968), 10.
37. Pierre Trudeau, cited in "Trudeau in Favor of Intensified Contacts with China," *GM* (May 11, 1968), 11.
38. Pierre Trudeau, cited in "Trudeau Hints He'll Recognize Red China," CP (May 11, 1968); and "Trudeau met la C.-B. en garde contre l'isolement," *LD* (May 11, 1968), 1.
39. Lotta Dempsey, "Now B.C. Gets in on Pierre's Kissing Game," *TS* (May 11, 1968), 72.
40. Pierre Trudeau, cited in "PM Says End to Raiding Key to Paris Conference," *GM* (May 14, 1968), 1.
41. Pierre Trudeau, cited in "PM Favours Revisions in Foreign Aid Plans," *GM* (May 14, 1968), 2.
42. Pierre Trudeau, cited in "Ottawa Only Address for International Invitations, PM Tells Quebec," *GM* (May 15, 1968), 1; and Roger Newman, "Trudeau Insists Canada Must Have a Single Voice," *GM* (May 15, 1968), 8.
43. Robert Stanfield, cited in "Trudeau Turning English upon Quebec Just to Win Votes, Stanfield Charges," *GM* (May 16, 1968), 8; and "Stanfield accuse Trudeau de chercher à dresser le Canada anglais contre Québec," *LD* (May 16, 1968), 8.
44. Pierre Trudeau, cited in Anthony Westell, "PM Warns against Mistaking Views of Johnson for Quebec's," *GM* (May 18, 1968), 4.

45. Pierre Trudeau, cited ibid.
46. Pierre Trudeau, cited in George Bain, "A Conversation with the Prime Minister I," *GM* (May 21, 1968), 6.
47. Pierre Trudeau, cited in George Bain, "A Conversation with the Prime Minister II," *GM* (May 22, 1968), 6.
48. Saywell, *CAR 1968*, 56.
49. Geoffrey Stevens, *Stanfield* (Toronto: McClelland & Stewart, 1973), 214–15.
50. Frank Jones, "Silent Bob Stanfield Talks West," *TS* (May 23, 1968), 1.
51. Roy Shields, "TV for Two," *TS* (May 27, 1968), 20.
52. Pierre Trudeau, cited in Robert Miller, "Trudeau Tells Prosperous: You'll Have to Share Wealth," *TS* (May 22, 1968), 1; and Geoffrey Stevens, "Trudeau Sounds Like a Conservative," *GM* (May 22, 1968), 8.
53. Pierre Trudeau, cited in Lewis Seale, "PM Has Small-C Conservative Message for Ontario," *GM* (May 27, 1968), 8.
54. Cited in Jack Cahill, "Trudeau Fever Jars Tories' Rural Ontario Bastions," *TS* (May 27, 1968), 7.
55. See Alastair Dow, "Douglas: Buy Canada Back or Lose Sovereignty," *TS* (June 24, 1968), 9.
56. Tommy Douglas, cited in "U.S. Domination of Canada Likely under Trudeau, Douglas Predicts," *GM* (May 14, 1968), 8.
57. Pierre Trudeau, cited in "PM Promises Balanced Budget," *GM* (May 21, 1968), 9; and "Trudeau Hides Deficit Charge: We Hide Nothing," *GM* (May 21, 1968), 50.
58. Tommy Douglas, cited in George McFarlane, "Douglas Says PM a 1930s Tory," *GM* (May 25, 1968), 10.
59. Tommy Douglas, cited in Wilfred List, "Trudeau Economic Policy Likened to Goldwater's," *GM* (May 29, 1968), 8.
60. Marcel Faribault, cited in "Constitutional Reform Possible before 1969, Faribault Declares," *GM* (May 21, 1968), 9.
61. Marcel Faribault, cited in "Stanfield's Quebec Man Steals Show," *TS* (May 22, 1968), 1.
62. Robert Stanfield, cited in Anthony Westell, "Willing to Drop Quebec Issue: Stanfield," *GM* (May 22, 1968), 9.
63. Pierre Trudeau, cited in Robert Miller, "Trudeau Ridicules Critics of His One-Canada Stand," *TS* (May 23, 1968), 1, 16.
64. Marcel Faribault, cited in "Faribault Calls PM Socialist in Disguise," CP (May 23, 1968); and Pierre-C. O'Neill, "Faribault: Je combats le socialisme 'déguise' et

'doctrinaire' de Trudeau," *LD* (May 23, 1968), 6. When Gérard Pelletier got wind of Faribault's comments, he stepped immediately into the fray, accusing Faribault of being one of the professors who had refused to give Trudeau a teaching job at Université de Montréal in the 1950s because Trudeau had studied under the socialist Harold Laski at the London School of Economics. Faribault denied the charge.

65. Pierre Trudeau, cited in Robert Miller, "Charming and Tough—PM Tackles Prairies," *TS* (May 24, 1968), 1, 5.
66. Cited ibid.
67. Pierre Trudeau, cited in Lewis Seale, "PM Takes Off Gloves, Rips into Separatists," *GM* (May 28, 1968), 8.
68. Earl McRae, "'Pied Piper' Trudeau Puts Youth Power in Politics," *TS* (May 11, 1968), 11.
69. Ann Cuthbert, "I'm a Teenage Liberal Because I Care about the Constitution," *TS* (May 15, 1968), 6.
70. Charles Lynch, cited in Saywell, *CAR 1968*, 50.
71. Scott Young, "Does Only Bachelorhood Lie behind the Admiration of Trudeau?" *GM* (May 21, 1968), 7.
72. Cited in Peter Regenstreif, "Solid 'Silent Bob' Rules the Roost in the Maritimes," *TS* (May 22, 1968), 7.
73. Cited in Dominique Clift, "Trudeaumania? Bah! It's All Done with Kids," *TS* (May 30, 1968), 7.
74. Pierre Trudeau, cited in Anthony Westell, "PM Assails Tories over Quebec," *GM* (June 4, 1968), 9.
75. Ian MacDonald, "Trudeaumania Turned On One Sunny June Evening," *VS* (June 26, 1968), 17.
76. Pierre Trudeau, cited in "Kiss Power," *GM* (May 27, 1968), 9.
77. See "Trudeau's Date Will Leave Her Job in Prime Minister's Office Today," *GM* (May 27, 1968), 13.
78. Pierre Trudeau, cited in Anthony Westell, "Trudeau Stills Crowd," *GM* (June 6, 1968), 13; and Frank Jones, "Heavy Guard for PM in Sober Sudbury Talk," *TS* (June 6, 1968), 51. See also Robert C. Vipond, "Citizenship and the Charter of Rights: The Two Sides of Pierre Trudeau," *International Journal of Canadian Studies* 14 (Fall 1996): 179–92.
79. Pierre Trudeau, cited in Frank Jones, "PM Shouts at Separatists," *TS* (June 7, 1968), 1; and Vincent Prince, "M. Trudeau et les chahuteurs," *LD* (June 10, 1968), 4.

80. Robert Stanfield, cited in "Stanfield Disturbed by Spread of Violence," *TS* (June 5, 1968), 8. See also Claude Ryan, "La tragédie de Los Angeles," *LD* (June 6, 1968), 4.
81. Frank Jones, "Even the Newsmen Were Frisked for Guns," *TS* (June 15, 1968), 1.
82. Pierre Trudeau, cited in Robert Miller, "Trudeau Rips into 'Two-Faced' NDP," *TS* (June 12, 1968), 1.

CHAPTER NINE: A MAN FOR TOMORROW

1. Eric Kierans, cited in "Kierans Apologizes for Aide's Cartoon Ridiculing Trudeau," *TS* (February 16, 1968), 1.
2. Eric Kierans, cited in "Kierans Fires Man," *TS* (February 17, 1968), 3.
3. Duncan Edmonds, cited in Ron Haggart, "Martin Mailing List Used for Smear: Trudeau Aides," *TS* (April 3, 1968), 9.
4. Cited in Frank Howard, "Right-Wing Quebec Group Identifies PM with Communism, Perversion, Subversion," *GM* (June 8, 1968), 13.
5. Donald C. Macdonald, cited in "Baptist Minister Publishes 24-Page Attack on Trudeau," *TS* (June 12, 1968), 36.
6. See "Minister Advocates McCarthy-like Probe," *TS* (June 19, 1968), 46.
7. Pierre Trudeau, cited in "Trudeau Once on Blacklist," *GM* (February 17, 1968), 10.
8. Pierre Trudeau, cited in Frank Jones, "Trudeau Hits Back at 'Hate Literature' Linking Him to Reds," *TS* (June 14, 1968), 1, 4.
9. Pierre Trudeau, cited in "Trudeau Tells Us Why He Wasn't in the War," *TS* (March 30, 1968), 2; and "Opposed 1939 War, Trudeau Admits," *GM* (March 30, 1968), 4.
10. René Lagarde, *On a "fourré" la vieille garde: Congrès Libéral Fédéral des 26, 27 et 28 janvier 1968 et la course à la chefferie* (Quebec: self-published, 1968). See also Robert McKenzie, "Quebec Pamphlet Hits Trudeau," *TS* (March 21, 1968), 9.
11. Igor Gouzenko, *Trudeau, A Potential Canadian Castro* (April 1968), Richard Nixon Presidential Library, White House Special Files Collection (Box 1, File 7), 1.
12. Igor Gouzenko to Richard M. Nixon (April 16, 1968), Richard Nixon Presidential Library, White House Special Files Collection (Box 1, File 7), 1–2.
13. John Nichol, cited in "Smear Campaign Sickens Tories," *GM* (June 14, 1968), 4. See also "Macdonald Says Big Money behind the Smear-the-PM Plot," *TS* (June 15, 1968), 3.
14. Cited in Michael Gillan, "Tories, NDP Condemn Leaflet," *GM* (June 14, 1968), 12.
15. Peter C. Newman, "The Facts and Fictions of the Trudeau Smears," *TS* (June 15, 1968), 7.

16. See, for example, editorial, "Let Hate Have No Home," *TS* (June 15, 1968), 6.
17. Pierre Trudeau, cited in Lewis Seale, "PM Assails Pamphlets Linking Him with Reds," *GM* (June 14, 1968), 1; "Trudeau s'élève contre les imprimes tendancieux qu'on fait circuler à son sujet," *LD* (June 14, 1968), 1; and Frank Jones, "Trudeau Hits Back at 'Hate Literature' Linking Him to Reds," *TS* (June 14, 1968), 1.
18. See Dominique Clift, "Quebec Tories Use Crude Whispers about Homosexuality," *TS* (June 14, 1968), 8.
19. Pierre Trudeau, cited in Dominique Clift, "Trudeau: Quebec Cheers as He Calls for One Canada," *TS* (June 17, 1968), 5.
20. William Kashtan, cited in Marian Bruce, "Trudeau No Communist," *CH* (April 6, 1968), 7.
21. T.R. Bradbury, cited in "Trudeau: A Rosy View from Bay Street," *TS* (April 15, 1968), 22; and Robertson Cochrane, "Cautious Bay Street Is Torn between Solid Stanfield, Swinger Trudeau," *TS* (May 25, 1968), 19.
22. See Robert Wright, *Three Nights in Havana: Pierre Trudeau, Fidel Castro and the Cold War World* (Toronto: HarperCollins, 2007), ch. 3.
23. "Trudeau Urged to Sue Hate Literature Authors," CP (June 20, 1968).
24. "Poll Shows Liberals Down 4 Points," *TS* (June 8, 1968), 1.
25. Peter C. Newman, "The 'Great Debate': Nobody Won It," *TS* (June 10, 1968), 1.
26. Pierre Trudeau, cited in Anthony Westell, "Canada's First National Debate," *GM* (June 10, 1968), 1.
27. Ramsay Cook, *The Teeth of Time: Remembering Pierre Elliott Trudeau* (Montreal: McGill-Queen's University Press, 2006), 75.
28. See "Le débat télévisé de dimanche soir: Douglas, Stanfield, Trudeau et la question constitutionnelle," *LD* (June 11, 1968), 5; "Trudeau Sees Exchange of Views and Debate as Essential in Public Life," *GM* (June 10, 1968), 8; and "Election 68: Partial Transcript of Great TV Debate," *TS* (June 10, 1968), 10.
29. Pierre Trudeau, cited in Frank Jones, "Trudeau: PM Can't Aid Students," *TS* (June 13, 1968), 8.
30. See Gerd-Rainer Horn, *The Spirit of '68: Rebellion in Western Europe and North America, 1956–1976* (Oxford: Oxford University Press, 2007); and Carole Fink, Philipp Gassert, and Detlef Junker, *1968: The World Transformed* (Washington, D.C.: German Historical Institute, 1998).
31. Pierre Trudeau, cited in Jones, "Trudeau: PM Can't Aid Students," 8.

32. Pierre Trudeau, cited in "Trudeau: I'll Invite the Best Brains to Ottawa," *TS* (June 24, 1968), 1.
33. Peter C. Newman, "One Nation: Trudeau Gambles All," *TS* (June 8, 1968), 7.
34. Pierre Trudeau, cited in "Trudeau Hints He'd Lower Voting Age," *TS* (May 27, 1968), 27.
35. Robert Cliche, cited in Mark Starowicz, "Quebec NDP Split over Accepting Separatist Support," *TS* (June 24, 1968), 9.
36. Dalton Camp, cited in "Camp Denies Tories Have 2-Nation Policy," CP (May 27, 1968), 9.
37. Marcel Faribault, cited in "Special Status Only Solution for Quebec in Sight: Faribault," CP (May 29, 1968).
38. Marcel Faribault, cited in "Faribault's Status Left to Tory Caucus," *GM* (June 19, 1968), 9.
39. Robert Stanfield, cited in Geoffrey Stevens, "Liberals Basing Campaign on Lies and Distortions," *GM* (June 18, 1968), 8; and "Trudeau déforme les positions du parti conservateur," *LD* (June 17, 1968), 1.
40. Pierre Trudeau, cited in Frank Jones, "Trudeau: He Attacks Opponents," *TS* (June 18, 1968), 9.
41. Pierre Trudeau, cited in Anthony Westell, "'Particular Status' Quote Attributed to Faribault," *GM* (June 18, 1968), 8.
42. Pierre Trudeau, cited in Jones, "Trudeau: He Attacks Opponents," 9; and "Violente sortie de Trudeau contre le parti néo-démocrate," *LD* (June 12, 1968), 1.
43. Robert Stanfield, cited in "Goodwill Evaporating, Canadian Unity Is in Danger, Stanfield Warns," *GM* (June 19, 1968), 9; and "Le statut particulier: Trudeau somme Stanfield de clarifier ses positions," *LD* (June 19, 1968), 1.
44. Pierre Trudeau, cited in Frank Jones, "Opposition Tries to Buy Power with Promises, Trudeau Says," *TS* (June 19, 1968), 9.
45. John Dafoe, "Calgary PCs in Defense over Two-Nation Issue," *GM* (June 20, 1968), 99.
46. Pierre Trudeau, cited in Anthony Westell, "Wearing Stetson, Trudeau Urges Calgary to Individualism, Free Enterprise," *GM* (June 19, 1968), 8.
47. Pierre Trudeau, cited in "40,000 Make Trudeau Rally Metro's Biggest," *GM* (June 20, 1968), 1.
48. Peter C. Newman, "Trudeau's Toronto Rally a Great One—If He Hadn't Opened His Mouth," *TS* (June 20, 1968), 7.

49. Lester B. Pearson, cited in Don Peacock, *Journey to Power* (Toronto: Ryerson, 1968), 368.
50. Pierre Trudeau, cited in David Gorrell, "Trudeau Repudiates Ads," *GM* (June 20, 1968), 1.
51. Marcel Faribault, cited in "Conservatives Do Not Differ on Constitution, Faribault Says," *GM* (June 20, 1968), 1.
52. Pierre Trudeau, cited in Gorrell, "Trudeau Repudiates Ads," 1.
53. Pierre Trudeau, cited in ibid.
54. Editorial, "Pierre Trudeau: A Modern Man for Canada," *TS* (June 18, 1968), 6.
55. Editorial, "Where *Do* the Tories Stand on Quebec? *TS* (June 21, 1968), 6.
56. Editorial, "The Man for the Future," *GM* (June 20, 1968), 6.
57. Editorial, "No Change of Mind," *GM* (June 21, 1968), 6.
58. Editorial, "Election Day," *WT* (June 25, 1968), 8.
59. Pierre Laporte, cited in Peacock, *Journey to Power*, 371.
60. Claude Ryan, "Le choix du 25 juin," *LD* (June 19, 1968), 4.
61. "La consigne du leader du MSA: 'Ne votez ni rouge ni bleu,'" *LD* (June 25, 1968), 2; and "English Too Weak to Hold Quebec, Lévesque Says," CP (June 24, 1968).
62. Cited in Andrew Salwyn, "Police in Montreal Fear Anti-PM Riot," *TS* (June 21, 1968), 58.
63. Pierre Trudeau, cited in Frank Jones, "PM Leads 35,000 Singing O Canada," *TS* (June 22, 1968), 1, 4.
64. Pierre Trudeau, cited in Lewis Seale, "PM Says Stake Extends beyond Quebec," *GM* (June 22, 1968), 10; "Trudeau à Montréal et à Joliette: Le Canada est à nous; prenons-en possession!" *LD* (June 22, 1968), 1; and Jones, "PM Leads 35,000," 1.

CHAPTER TEN: THE CALM AFTER THE STORM

1. John Saywell, ed., *CAR 1968* (Toronto: University of Toronto Press, 1969), 50–52.
2. Editorial, "Hate's Bitter Contagion," *GM* (June 25, 1968), 6. See also Vincent Prince, "M. Bourgault et son appel à la violence," *LD* (June 25, 1968), 4; Raymond Daoust, "Ce sinistre lundi de Fête Nationale," *JM* (June 26, 1968), 8; and editorial, "Separatist Riots," *CH* (June 26, 1968), 6.
3. Gaston Plante, cited in "Quebec Convict Says His Gun Was to Assassinate Trudeau," CP (June 26, 1968).
4. Peter Regenstreif, "All Signs Say It's a Victory for Trudeau," *TS* (June 22, 1968), 8.
5. "The Forecast," *GM* (June 22, 1968), 8.

6. Pierre Trudeau, cited in "To PM, It's Russian Roulette," CP (June 26, 1968).
7. "Trudeau remercie la police pour sa façon d'agir à la Saint-Jean," *LP* (June 26, 1968), 44.
8. Joey Smallwood, cited in "Just What Was Said," *GM* (June 26, 1968), 1.
9. See "Liberal Majority: PCs Capture 25 of 32 Atlantic Seats," *HCH* (June 26, 1968), 1.
10. Marcel Faribault, cited in F.T. Collier and George Radwanski, "Marcel Faribault Bows to 'Blitzkrieg,'" *MG* (June 26, 1968), 1; Gilles Racine, "Acceptant avec réalisme sa défaite dans Gamelin, Faribault attribue la victoire libérale à Trudeau," *LP* (June 26, 1968), 42; and Andrew Salwyn, "Tory Faribault Blames Defeat on 'Blitzkrieg,'" *TS* (June 26, 1968), 16.
11. Robert Stanfield, cited in Tom Hazlitt, "Stanfield Wonders: Where Do We Go Now?" *TS* (June 26, 1968), 8; and "Stanfield: Très déçu des résultats dans le Québec," *LA* (June 26, 1968), 9.
12. John Diefenbaker, cited in "Disaster for PCs—DIEF," CP (June 26, 1968).
13. Tommy Douglas, cited in "Douglas: I'll Keep Smiling," CP (June 26, 1968).
14. Pierre Trudeau, cited in Frank Jones, "Campaign 'Great Adventure': Trudeau," *TS* (June 26, 1968), 1; J.R. Walker, "Stunning Liberal Win Rips Opposition Ranks," *CH* (June 26, 1968), 1; Ian MacDonald, "Trudeau Leads Liberals to Strong Majority Government," *VS* (June 26, 1968), 1; Ian MacDonald, "Trudeau Still Played It Cool until B.C. Was in the Bag," *VS* (June 26, 1968), 1; and Stan McDowell, "Trudeau Keeps Firm Hold on Quebec Power Base," *VS* (June 26, 1968), 15.
15. See Lisa Balfour, "Quebec Voted Anti-Separatist, Liberals Claim," *WT* (June 26, 1968), 6.
16. Lisa Balfour, "Quebec Says 'No' to Separation," *OC* (June 26, 1968), 20.
17. Editorial, "One Nation, Indivisible," *VS* (June 26, 1968), 4.
18. Peter C. Newman, "Canadians Have Told Trudeau to Settle National Unity Crisis," *TS* (June 26, 1968), 1.
19. Editorial, "A Balance Restored, A Threat Averted," *GM* (June 16, 1968), 6.
20. Editorial, "Canada Was the Winner in Quebec," *TS* (June 26, 1968), 6.
21. Editorial, "A Clear Mandate," *HCH* (June 26, 1968), 4. See also editorial, "Down to Work," *HCH* (June 27, 1968), 4.
22. Editorial, "Quebec Opts for Federalism," *OC* (June 27, 1968), 3. See also editorial, "Future Rides with Trudeau," *OC* (June 26, 1968), 3; editorial, "The Election," *CH* (June 26, 1968), 6; and editorial, "The Nation," *CH* (June 27, 1968), 6.

23. Charles Lynch, "Now It's Up to Trudeau," *WT* (June 26, 1968), special election supplement.
24. Editorial, "Canada Votes Confidence in Trudeau," *MG* (June 26, 1968), 6.
25. Editorial, "Majority Government," *SDR* (June 26, 1968), 4.
26. Editorial, "Le retour au bon sens," *LDR* (June 26, 1968), 4. See also editorial, "Un verdict clair," *AC* (June 27, 1968), 1; "La thèse de Trudeau est bien accueillie par les Québécois," *AC* (June 26, 1968), 1; and editorial, "Le peuple s'est prononcé," *AC* (June 26, 1968), 4.
27. Editorial "Un parti, un chef, une équipe," *LP* (June 26, 1968), 4. See also editorial "Le Québec a parlé clair," *LP* (June 26, 1968), 4.
28. Mario Cardinal, "Avec Trudeau, le Québec consent à un gouvernement majoritaire et complique la vie à Daniel Johnson," *LS* (June 26, 1968), 14. See also editorial, "La victoire libérale," *LS* (June 26, 1968), 4.
29. Claude Ryan, "Le scrutin de mardi et la tension entre les deux nationalismes," *LD* (June 27, 1968), 4.
30. Lévesque, *Memoirs*, trans. Philip Stratford (Toronto: McClelland & Stewart, 1986), 228–29. See also André Fortin, "L'élection du gouvernement Trudeau signifie la séparation du Québec d'ici cinq ans (Martial Asselin)," *LS* (June 26, 1968), 32. Quebec sociologist Marcel Rioux recalled, "In June of 1968 the English Canadians realized that Trudeau was the man to bring Quebec to heel and voted overwhelmingly in his favour. The French Canadians went along with the trend, giving in to their old mania for self-flagellation, and elected a great majority of Liberals to represent them in Ottawa." See Rioux, *Quebec in Question* (Toronto: Lorimer, 1978), 82.
31. David Frum, "The Disastrous Legacy of Pierre Elliott Trudeau," *NP* (March 24, 2001).
32. Pierre Trudeau, cited in Bruce Phillips, "Trudeau Cool and Unflappable in Victory," *CH* (June 26, 1968), 10.

EPILOGUE: TRUDEAUMANIA 2.0

1. Justin Trudeau, *Common Ground* (Toronto: HarperCollins, 2014), 80.
2. See Robert Wright, *Three Nights in Havana: Pierre Trudeau, Fidel Castro and the Cold War World* (Toronto: HarperCollins, 2007), prologue.
3. Justin Trudeau, cited in Jonathon Gatehouse, "When I Run: Justin Trudeau Considers Politics," *M* (December 23, 2002).
4. Justin Trudeau, cited ibid.
5. Justin Trudeau, cited ibid.

6. Trudeau, *Common Ground*, 165, emphasis in original.
7. Justin Trudeau, cited in John Geddes, "In Conversation: Justin Trudeau," *M* (February 27, 2012).
8. Trudeau, *Common Ground*, 166.
9. Justin Trudeau, cited in Aaron Wherry, "A Star Rookie's Shot," *M* (January 12, 2009).
10. Justin Trudeau, cited in Jonathon Gatehouse, "On His Own Terms: Justin Runs for the Liberal Leadership," *M* (October 11, 2012).
11. See David Frum, "The Disastrous Legacy of Pierre Elliott Trudeau," *NP* (March 24, 2011).
12. Stephen Harper, "Looking Back at Trudeau," *NP* (October 5, 1999).
13. Gerry Nicholls, cited in Rob Gillies, "'Trudeaumania' Heir Could Become Canada's Next PM," AP (October 18, 2015).
14. Justin Trudeau, cited in Gatehouse, "On His Own Terms."
15. Justin Trudeau, cited ibid.
16. Justin Trudeau, cited in Geddes, "In Conversation: Justin Trudeau."
17. Gatehouse, "On His Own Terms."
18. Robert Bothwell, cited in Gillies, "'Trudeaumania' Heir."
19. Justin Trudeau, cited in Bruce Cheadle, "Justin Trudeau, Born into Political Spotlight, Seeks to Fulfil Nixon Prophecy," CP (October 19, 2015).
20. Shelley Fralic, "Welcome to the New Trudeaumania," *VS* (October 20, 2015).
21. Emma Teitel, "What America's Lust for Trudeau Says about Canada: Teitel," *TS* (October 22, 2015).
22. Justin Trudeau, cited in Tonda MacCharles, "Prime Minister Justin Trudeau Unveils Diverse Cabinet in Touching Ceremony," CBC (November 4, 2015).
23. Roger Cohen, "Camelot Comes to Canada," *NYT* (October 22, 2015).
24. Cited in Peter Mansbridge, "Behind the Scenes with Justin Trudeau on His First Day as PM," CBC News, www.cbc.ca (November 4, 2015).

INDEX

A

Adams, Eddie, 207
Adams, John, 287
Adams, John Quincy, 287
Alcock, Norman, 54
Allard, Maurice, 78
Axworthy, Lloyd, 231

B

Bain, George, 85, 90, 125, 133, 140, 234–235
Balfour, Lisa, 278
Barbot, Vivian, 291
Batten, Clyde, 197
Batten, Herman, 185
Beetz, Jean, 86, 111, 153
Beloff, Max, 68
Bennett, Bill, 287
Bennett, R.B., 238
Bennett, W.A.C., 22, 287
  1965 federal election, 71
  1968 constitutional conference, 140–143, 156, 159, 166
Benson, Edgar, 129, 202, 213
Berger, Monty, 69
Berton, Pierre, 20, 28, 77, 88, 134, 210
Bibliothèque de la Ville de Montréal, 4, 13
Bibliothèque et Archives nationales du Québec, 4
Bill C-24 *Strengthening Canadian Citizenship Act*, 296
Bliss, Michael, 132
Bloc Québécois, 291, 293
Boskin, Joseph, 206
Bouchard, Jacques, 67, 73
Boucher, Marie-Claire, 14
Bourgault, Pierre, 3, 12–13, 16, 22, 46, 51, 68, 172, 270–271, 282
  English Canadians, 96
  and monarchy, 146
  and Mouvement souveraineté-association, 108
  and Rassemblement pour l'indépendance nationale, 7–11, 39
Bowker, Wilbur, 99
Bradbury, T.R., 256
Braithwaite, Dennis, 84
Brazeau, Patrick, 292
Breton, Albert, 46

Breton, Raymond, 46
Brewin, Andrew, 111, 116–118
British North America Act (BNA Act), 27, 41, 63, 70, 108, 110, 142, 194, 283
Brouillard, Robert, 184
Brunet, Michel, 33, 54
Brüning, Heinrich, 32
Bush, George H.W., 287
Bush, George W., 287
Butts, Gerry, 293

C

Cairns, Alan C., 110
Camp, Dalton, 18, 199, 261
Campbell, Alexander, 143, 158, 197
Canadian Bar Association (CBA), 97–98, 100–103, 111, 136
Canadian Charter of Rights and Freedoms, 152–159, 163–164, 168–169, 193, 211, 231, 283, 290
  Bill of Rights, 63, 152, 153
Charter rights, 26
Charter values, 28
  "Trudeau's charter," 27, 110, 152–155, 163, 167
Canadian Council of Churches, 254
Canadian Forum, 47, 169
Caouette, Réal, 246, 258, 275
  and Ralliement créditiste, 230
Cardin, Lucien, 82
Cardinal, Jean-Guy, 227
Cardinal, Mario, 280
Cartwright, John R., 122
Castro, Fidel, 43, 45, 250, 253–254, 257, 281
Centre des Recherches Sociales, 46–47
Chambers, Gretta, 38, 72
Chaput, Marcel, 39, 44, 53
Charters, David A., 12
Chayka, Freda, 198
Chrétien, Jean, 74, 82, 83, 85, 148, 202, 213, 223, 291
Cité libre, 9, 12, 24, 36–56, 67, 102, 130–132, 183, 191, 281
civil rights, 41, 155, 205, 260
Clarkson, Stephen, 23, 28
Cliche, Robert, 66–67
  deux nations, 229–231
  and separatists, 261, 263
  and Trudeaumania, 275
Clift, Dominique, 65, 76–77, 147, 227, 243
Cohen, Andrew, 59
Cohen, Maxwell, 22, 104, 209
Cohen, Roger, 299
Cold War, 19, 34, 253–254
Collège Jean-de-Brébeuf, 7, 31, 288, 289
Cook, Ramsay, 3, 4, 184, 217
  "draft-Trudeau" movement, 130–134, 172–175
  and Lester Pearson, 63
  and NDP, 28, 57
  as speech writer, 231–233, 245, 258, 265
Cooper, Linda, 224
Cresthol, Leon, 69
Cresthol, Sophie, 69
Croll, David, 192

D

Danson, Barney, 212, 214
Davey, Jim, 135, 174, 184, 231

de Gaulle, Charles, 101, 147, 218, 225, 243, 273
"Vive le Québec libre!" 10, 92–96, 218
DePoe, Norman, 49, 217, 218
Diefenbaker, John, xiv, 22, 55, 56, 59, 61, 64, 101, 175, 194, 208, 210, 221, 225, 257, 276
1965 election, 67, 70
Canadian Bill of Rights, 98, 152
and Charles de Gaulle, 94
"One Canada" policy, 76, 87, 105–106
and Pierre Trudeau, 84, 90
Dion, Léon, 31
Dion, Stéphane, 291
Douglas, Tommy, 1, 26, 127, 258, 274, 275, 277
and foreign ownership, 238, 256
and homosexuality, 123
Quebec special status, 86–88, 228–231
Dow, Alastair, 134
Drapeau, Jean, 5, 14–17, 31
Duplessis, Maurice, 8, 9, 36, 155–156, 162
Dupuis, Yvon, 59
Durham, Lord, 194–195

E

Edmonds, Duncan, 250
Eisenhower, Dwight D., 238
English, John, 36
Evangelical Fellowship of Canada, 254
Expo 67, xiv, 19, 21, 88, 112

F

Faribault, Marcel, 17, 230, 231, 244, 255, 263, 266–269, 275
constitutional reform, 238–239, 261–262, 284
deux nations, 104–105, 233–234
red-baiting, 240
and Robert Stanfield, 228–229
Vers une nouvelle constitution, 24
Faulkner, Hugh, 215
Favreau, Guy, 54, 59, 65, 73, 82
Federalism and International Conferences on Education, 228
FLQ. *See* Front de libération du Québec
Fox, Paul, 169, 192
Fralic, Shelley, 297
Fraser, Graham, 9
Frenette, Claude, 278
Front de libération du Québec (FLQ), xiv, 2–3, 11, 12, 22, 46, 51, 54, 108, 246, 282
Front de libération populaire, 11
Frum, David, 280
Fulbright, J. William, 207
Fulford, Robert, 28, 53
Fulton-Favreau formula, 61, 283

G

Gatehouse, Jonathon, 294
Gibson, Gordon, 135, 174, 184
Giguere, I.G., 278
Gilbert, Jean-Paul, 5, 18
Gillan, Michael, 120
Gimby, Bobby, 21, 264
Gingras, Marcel, 85
Goldbloom, Victor, 69
Goldenberg, H. Carl, 87, 111, 140, 157
Goldwater, Barry, 238
Goodman, Eddie, 255

Gordon, Walter, 129, 182, 183, 190, 197
Gostick, Ron, 250, 254, 255
Gouzenko, Igor, 253, 254
Goyer, Jean-Pierre, 135, 174, 180, 184, 213
    Liberal policy committee, 145–148
Granatstein, J.L., 170
Gray, Herb, 215
Gray, John, 130
Greene, Joe, 139, 185, 196, 210, 214–216, 222
Grégoire, Gilles, 78
Grégoire, Paul, 14, 16
Gwyn, Richard, 20

H

Hall, Emmett, 122
Harper, Stephen, 292, 294
    2015 federal election, 296–298
Harvard University, 31, 32, 132, 134, 172, 209
Head, Ivan, 87, 154
Hellyer, Paul, 127, 134, 136, 138, 144, 173, 177, 182, 188, 192, 197, 199, 203, 212–213, 215–216, 222, 253
    constitutional reform, 204, 210
    Quebec, 192–193
Henderson, Lloyd, 214
Honey, Russell, 173
Hopper, Kathleen, 224
Howard, Frank, 73
Hull, Bobby, 270

I

Ignatieff, Michael, 28, 289

J

Jewett, Pauline, 28, 172, 173
John Birch Society, 250, 257
Johnson, Daniel, 14–17, 31, 51, 85, 101, 106, 112, 144, 147–148, 158, 165, 168, 172, 179, 184, 187, 188, 189, 194–195, 218, 220, 226–228, 230, 233, 234, 278, 280, 284, 287
    1966 Quebec election, 86
    1967 Confederation of Tomorrow conference, 109–111
    1968 constitutional conference, 160–163, 166–167
    and Charles de Gaulle, 95
    constitutional reform, 48, 108–109, 127, 141, 155, 283
    deux nations, 159
    on divorce, 119
    Égalité ou indépendance, 24
    and Lester Pearson, 156
    and monarchy, 102, 146
    and Pierre Bourgault, 9
Johnson, Daniel, Jr., 287
Johnson, Lyndon, 22, 207, 208
Johnson, Pierre-Marc, 287
Jolivet, Larry, 182
Jolivet, Patricia, 182
Jones, Frank, 24, 133
Just Society, 20, 212, 217, 220, 231, 233, 235, 278
Jutras, René, 10

K

Kashtan, William, 256
Kennedy, Edward, 245

Kennedy, Gerard, 290, 291
Kennedy, Jackie, 232, 245
Kennedy, John F. (JFK), xiii, 2, 19, 24, 84, 142, 175, 208, 244, 245, 247, 257, 298
Kennedy, Robert F., xiv, 22, 208, 244–245, 246, 247, 248, 273
Kierans, Eric, 138, 144, 173, 186–188, 199, 203, 210–211, 214, 215, 222, 275
  separatism, 107, 136
  smear campaign, 249
King, Mackenzie, 31
King, Martin Luther, Jr., xiv, 3, 22, 205, 206, 208, 212, 218, 273
Kinsey, Alfred, 122
Klippert, Everett George, 122–123
Korean War, 36

L

Lalonde, Marc, 46, 57, 94, 99, 111, 119, 131, 135, 139–140, 143, 148, 157, 177, 183, 223, 231, 246
LaMarsh, Judy, 215, 216, 217
Lamontagne, Maurice, 59, 65, 66, 102, 107
language rights, 26, 27, 89, 100, 110, 146, 152, 157, 161, 166, 167, 231
LaPierre, Laurier, 196
Laporte, Pierre, 12, 31, 269
Laskin, Bora, 61
Laurendeau, André, 30, 60, 61, 75, 245
Layton, Jack, 293
LeBlanc, Roméo, 245
Lederman, William, 99
Lee, Bill, 14, 184, 231
Lefebvre, T.H., 104
Lagarde, René, 253
Legault, Laurent, 10
Léger, Jean-Marc, 47, 85
Leja, Walter, 11
Lesage, Jean, 7, 8, 9, 31, 38, 51, 55, 56, 67, 85, 86, 106, 146, 220, 227, 282, 283
  1962 Quebec election, 43
  constitutional reform, 101–102
  and Lester Pearson, 61–63
  separatism, 107
  statut particulier, 48
Levant, Ezra, 292
Levasseur, Pierre, 15, 135, 184
Lévesque, René, 7, 22, 51, 52, 53, 127, 144, 146, 150, 156, 159, 168, 172, 176, 178, 220, 227, 263, 271, 272, 282
  1968 federal election, 270, 280
  deux nations, 47
  and FLQ, 12
  Hydro Québec, 43
  and Mouvement souveraineté-association, 10–11, 106–108
  Option Québec, 24
  and Pierre Bourgault, 9
  and Pierre Trudeau, 30, 43
Liberal Candidates' Handbook, 231
Lynch, Charles, 242, 279

M

Macdonald, Donald, 135, 173–174, 223, 251, 264
MacDonald, Ian, 244
MacEachen, Allan, 136, 138, 197, 211, 214–215, 222, 274
MacGuigan, Mark, 54, 55
MacInnis, Grace, 91

Mackasey, Bryce, 127, 200, 202
Macnaughton, Alan, 56, 69, 72
Manning, Ernest, 110, 112, 159, 164, 287
 and Pierre Trudeau, 140
Manning, Preston, 287
Marchand, Jean, 10, 30, 49, 56, 59, 63, 65, 66, 68–71, 85, 92, 138–139, 141, 144–145, 148, 149, 171, 184, 189, 194, 202, 223, 253, 282
 and André Laurendeau, 75–76
 constitutional reform, 103
 and Lester Pearson, 58, 128–130
 and Pierre Trudeau, 74–75, 135–137, 177, 179–180, 214
Marcotte, Gilles, 172
marijuana, 295
Marleau, Huguette, 198
Martin, Paul, 90, 92, 94, 127, 128, 134, 136, 138, 144, 148, 184, 185, 186, 187, 188, 197, 199, 203, 213, 214, 217, 222, 250, 287
 national unity, 210
 Quebec, 193
Martin, Paul, Jr., 214, 287, 291
Martineau, Jean, 172
Mathieu, Dollard, 14, 15
McArthur, Jack, 204
McCall-Newman, Christina, 23, 25
McCarthy, Eugene, 244–245
McDowell, Stan, 73
McGee, Frank, 138
McGill University, xvi, 22, 38, 54, 86, 100, 104, 209, 288, 293
McGuinty, Dalton, 293
McLuhan, Marshall, 23, 259
McRoberts, Kenneth, 75
McWhinney, Edward, 86, 100
McWilliam, G.R., 104
Meech Lake Accord, 150, 282
Michener, Roland, 84, 223
Monaghan, Barry, 139
Morin, Jacques-Yvan, 99
Morin, Thérèse, 12
Mouvement souveraineté-association (MSA), 10, 11, 108, 127, 168, 270, 272, 282
Mulcair, Tom, 296
multiculturalism, 28

N

National Citizens Coalition (NCC), 292
National Liberal Federation of Canada, 79
NATO, 128, 191, 192, 203, 259
NDP. *See* New Democratic Party
Neiger, Stephen, 123
Nemni, Max, 31
Nemni, Monique, 31
New Democratic Party (NDP), 1, 28, 50, 56, 57, 66, 68, 69, 71, 73, 86, 87, 91, 111, 116, 123, 131, 133, 185, 223, 228, 229, 230, 257, 260, 261, 263, 268, 273, 275, 276, 277, 293, 296, 297
Newman, Peter C., 9, 16, 21, 28, 55, 56, 64, 68, 74, 80, 81, 83, 132, 134, 143, 148, 154, 156, 168, 186, 198, 202, 203, 231, 254, 258, 260, 265, 278
Nichol, John, xvi, 217, 254
Nicholls, Gerry, 292
niqab, 296
Nixon, Richard, 13, 208, 254, 257

O

Oliver, Michael, 22
Oliver, Peter, 170
Ouellet, André, 135

P

Parc La Fontaine, 5, 7, 13, 17
Parizeau, Jacques, 8, 54, 227
Parti pris, 11, 282
Parti Québécois, 10, 108
Peacock, Don, 184
Pearson, Lester B., xiv, 1, 10, 21, 22, 23, 48, 49, 74, 75, 90, 102, 120, 126–127, 131, 134, 135, 136, 139, 140, 171, 185–186, 208, 210, 214, 216–217, 218, 219, 221, 222, 223, 224, 227, 236, 246, 266, 282
  1965 federal election, 64–68, 71
  1968 constitutional conference, 151–152, 156–162, 166–170
  and Charles de Gaulle, 92–96
  constitutional reform, 89, 103–104, 112–113
  farewell speech, 205
  and Jean Marchand, 58
  Liberal succession, 128–130, 138
  and Pierre Trudeau, 56–57, 63, 80–84, 91
  Quebec, 59–63, 75–76
Pearson, Maryon, 205, 218, 274
Pelletier, Gérard, 12, 49, 54, 56, 63, 65–69, 72, 73, 74, 78, 129, 135–137, 179, 184, 270, 282
  and FLQ, 11
  and Lester Pearson, 58–59
  and Pierre Trudeau, 26, 30, 35–37, 50, 125
Pennell, Larry, 129
Pépin, Jean-Luc, 148, 213
Perrault, Ray, 275
Pinard, Maurice, 46
Pitfield, Michael, 135
Plante, Gaston, 273
Plourde, Lucien, 72
Portelance, Arthur, 275
Porteous, Tim, 184
Porter, John, 26
Pronovost, Martin, 108

Q

Queen Elizabeth II, 8, 89
Queen's University, 36, 99
Quiet Revolution (Quebec), 4, 7, 8, 31, 37, 39, 43, 51, 53, 59, 283

R

Rae, Bob, 28, 244
Rae, Jennifer, 244
Ralliement créditiste, 72, 78, 185, 186, 230, 275, 276
Rassemblement pour l'indépendance nationale (RIN), 3, 7, 8, 9, 10, 11, 12, 13, 39, 44, 68, 92, 93, 96, 108, 270, 282
RCMP. *See* Royal Canadian Mounted Police
Regenstreif, Peter, 273
Rice, Robert, 73
Richards, Maurice, 67
Rideout, Margaret, 91
Robarts, John, 89, 101, 104, 111, 112, 141, 142, 143, 157, 158, 283
Robert, Michel, 79

Robertson, Gordon, 36, 157
Robichaud, Louis, 143, 158
Rose, Paul, 12
Rotstein, Abraham, 169
Roux, Jean-Louis, 172
Royal Canadian Mounted Police (RCMP), 1, 5, 11, 14, 15, 247, 248, 288
Royal Commission on Bilingualism and Biculturalism, 60, 62, 64, 68, 75, 111, 145, 157, 163, 168, 169, 283
  Blue Pages, 60–61, 111
Rubin, Eddie, 135
Ryan, Claude, 14, 17, 26, 31, 84, 85, 95, 147, 148, 165, 172, 176, 181, 188, 220, 229, 269, 280, 284

S

Saint-Jean-Baptiste Day, 3, 4, 7, 13, 14, 17, 18, 19, 155, 229, 271, 272, 273
  1968 riot, 6, 8, 13–19, 272–273, 274
Sauvé, Maurice, 65, 148, 215
Saywell, John T., 28, 130
Scott, Frank, 54
Seale, Lewis, 144, 147, 192
Sharp, Mitchell, 82, 127, 134, 136, 138, 144, 148, 185, 188, 193, 201, 202, 213, 217, 222
Shields, Roy, 142, 236
Sinclair, James ("Jimmy"), 290
Sinclair, Margaret, 134
Sirhan, Sirhan, 245
Slade, Harold C., 251
Smallwood, Joey, 143, 158, 163, 197, 203, 232, 274
Smiley, Donald, 62
Smith, G.I., 143, 158, 162
Sopha, Elmer, 196, 197
Spicer, Keith, 221
St.-Amant, Sylvio, 85
Stanbury, Robert, 125, 135
Stanfield, Robert, 1, 26, 89, 230, 231, 234, 239, 247, 255
  1968 election campaign, 235–236, 260–263, 266–269, 274–280
  deux nations, 105
  and Marcel Faribault, 228–229
  smear campaign, 255
  special status, 225–228
Steering Committee on Constitutional Questions, 86, 151, 153, 283
Stevens, Geoffrey, 118, 138, 236
Stewart, Walter, 23
Syrian refugees, 295, 296, 298
Szablowski, G.J., 182
Szende, Andrew, 172

T

Tarnopolsky, Walter, 99
Taylor, Charles, 56, 69, 70, 72, 229
Teitelbaum, Ethel, 131
Teitelbaum, Mashel, 131
terrorism, 11, 12, 17, 19, 22, 272–273, 296
Thant, U, 233
Thatcher, Ross, 141, 158, 159, 162
Tremblay, Jean-Noël, 101, 179
Tremblay, René, 59
Troyer, Warner, 259, 260
Trudeau, Alexandre, 288
Trudeau, Justin, xiii, 20, 34, 287–299
  2011 federal election, 293

2015 federal election, 294–299
Brazeau boxing match, 292–293
childhood, 288–289
comparisons with Pierre, 291–292
eulogy for Pierre, 289
Liberal leadership, 293–294
Trudeau, Michel, 288
Trudeau, Pierre Elliott, xiii, xiv, 20–28
abortion rights, 27, 35, 83, 120, 121, 125, 173, 230, 249, 251, 283
Asbestos (Quebec), 35
death of, xiii, 289
divorce, 27, 35, 83, 114–115, 116, 117, 119, 120, 125, 126, 129, 137, 169, 173, 283
education, 31–34
eulogy, 34–35
and homosexuality, 9, 27, 35, 83, 115, 120, 122, 123, 124, 173, 197, 204, 230, 251, 255, 283
justice minister, 10, 27, 35, 82–86, 88–89, 91, 96, 97, 100, 109, 114, 119, 124, 126, 130, 131, 133, 134, 137, 139, 140, 142, 143, 149, 154–156, 165, 167, 169, 172, 175, 176, 180, 185, 186, 197, 217
Liberal leadership, 35, 130, 136, 137, 140, 148, 172, 174, 180, 182, 201
Privy Council, 29, 36
Robert Kennedy assassination, 246–248
world travels, 31–32, 34
World War II, 18, 31, 32, 252–253
Turner, John, 24, 82, 137, 138, 144, 185–188, 193, 197, 204, 208, 212, 213, 215, 216, 222, 231
Turner, R.E., 124

U

Union Nationale, 9, 86, 101, 108, 146, 155, 161, 194, 226, 243, 283
Université de Montréal, 33, 37, 38, 99
University of British Columbia, 62, 288
University of Toronto, 28, 54, 61, 99, 132, 169, 182

V

Vallières, Pierre, 12
Vietnam War, xiv, 22, 190–191, 196, 207–209, 233, 240

W

Wadds, Jean Casselman, 91
Waite, Peter, 54
Walker, James, 135
Wallace, George, 257
Watkins, Mel, 182–183, 190
Watson, Patrick, 196, 236, 244
Weir, Walter, 141, 158
West, Bruce, 169
Westell, Anthony, 127, 165, 167, 176
Westmoreland, William C., 207
Winters, Robert, 134, 139, 177, 187, 188, 197, 205, 211, 213, 215, 216, 222
Wolfenden Report, 122

Z

Zolf, Larry, 20, 24
Zündel, Ernst, 139